Mastering Professional Responsibility

Carolina Academic Press Mastering Series

Russell Weaver, Series Editor

Mastering Administrative Law
William R. Andersen

Mastering Alternative Dispute Resolution
Kelly M. Feeley & James A. Sheehan

Mastering American Indian Law
Angelique Townsend EagleWoman & Stacy L. Leeds

Mastering Appellate Advocacy and Process
Donna C. Looper & George W. Kuney

Mastering Art Law
Herbert Lazerow

Mastering Bankruptcy
George W. Kuney

Mastering Civil Procedure, 2d e
David Charles Hricik

Mastering Constitutional Law, 2d e
John C. Knechtle & Christopher J. Roederer

Mastering Contract Law
Irma S. Russell & Barbara K. Bucholtz

Mastering Corporate Tax
Reginald Mombrun, Gail Levin Richmond & Felicia Branch

Mastering Corporations and Other Business Entities, 2d e
Lee Harris

Mastering Criminal Law, 2d e
Ellen S. Podgor, Peter J. Henning & Neil P. Cohen

Mastering Criminal Procedure, Volume 1: The Investigative Stage, 2d e
Peter J. Henning, Andrew Taslitz, Margaret L. Paris,
Cynthia E. Jones & Ellen S. Podgor

Mastering Criminal Procedure, Volume 2: The Adjudicatory Stage, 2d e
Peter J. Henning, Andrew Taslitz, Margaret L. Paris,
Cynthia E. Jones & Ellen S. Podgor

Mastering Elder Law, 2d e
Ralph C. Brashier

Mastering Employment Discrimination Law
Paul M. Secunda & Jeffrey M. Hirsch

Mastering Evidence
Ronald W. Eades

Mastering Family Law
Janet Leach Richards

Mastering Income Tax
Christopher M. Pietruszkiewicz & Gail Levin Richmond

Mastering Intellectual Property
George W. Kuney & Donna C. Looper

Mastering Labor Law
Paul M. Secunda, Anne Marie Lofaso,
Joseph E. Slater & Jeffrey M. Hirsch

Mastering Legal Analysis and Communication
David T. Ritchie

Mastering Legal Analysis and Drafting
George W. Kuney & Donna C. Looper

Mastering Negotiable Instruments (UCC Articles 3 and 4) and Other Payment Systems
Michael D. Floyd

Mastering Partnership Taxation
Stuart Lazar

Mastering Products Liability
Ronald W. Eades

Mastering Professional Responsibility, 2d e
Grace M. Giesel

Mastering Property Law, Revised Printing
Darryl C. Wilson & Cynthia H. DeBose

Mastering Secured Transactions (UCC Article 9), 2d e
Richard H. Nowka

Mastering Statutory Interpretation, 2d e
Linda D. Jellum

Mastering Tort Law
Russell L. Weaver, Edward C. Martin, Andrew R. Klein,
Paul J. Zwier II, Ronald W. Eades & John H. Bauman

Mastering Trademark and Unfair Competition Law
Lars S. Smith & Llewellyn Joseph Gibbons

Mastering Professional Responsibility

SECOND EDITION

Grace M. Giesel
Bernard Flexner Professor
and
Distinguished Teaching Professor
University of Louisville, Louis D. Brandeis School of Law

Carolina Academic Press
Durham, North Carolina

Library of Congress Cataloging in Publication Data

Giesel, Grace M., author.
Mastering professional responsibility / Grace M. Giesel. -- Second edition.
pages cm -- (Carolina Academic Press mastering series)
Includes bibliographical references and index.
ISBN 978-1-61163-620-8 (alk. paper)
1. Legal ethics--United States. 2. Attorney and client--United States. 3. Practice of law--United States. I. Title.

KF306.G547 2015
174'.30973--dc23

2014042079

Carolina Academic Press
700 Kent Street
Durham, NC 27701
Telephone (919) 489-7486
Fax (919) 493-5668
www.cap-press.com

Printed in the United States of America

Contents

Section VI
When a Lawyer Is Not in an Advocate Role

Section VII
The Lawyer as an Advocate

Section VIII
Dealing with Nonclients

Section XII
General Duties

Series Editor's Foreword

The Carolina Academic Press Mastering Series is designed to provide you with a tool that will enable you to easily and efficiently "master" the substance and content of law school courses. Throughout the series, the focus is on quality writing that makes legal concepts understandable. As a result, the series is designed to be easy to read and is not unduly cluttered with footnotes or cites to secondary sources.

In order to facilitate student mastery of topics, the Mastering Series includes a number of pedagogical features designed to improve learning and retention. At the beginning of each chapter, you will find a "Roadmap" that tells you about the chapter and provides you with a sense of the material that you will cover. A "Checkpoint" at the end of each chapter encourages you to stop and review the key concepts, reiterating what you have learned. Throughout the book, key terms are explained and emphasized. Finally, a "Master Checklist" at the end of each book reinforces what you have learned and helps you identify any areas that need review or further study.

We hope that you will enjoy studying with, and learning from, the Mastering Series.

Russell L. Weaver
Professor of Law & Distinguished University Scholar
University of Louisville, Louis D. Brandeis School of Law

Acknowledgments

I would like to thank all the people who helped me make this book and its revision happen. In particular, I would like to thank the members of the faculty and staff at the Louis D. Brandeis School of Law at the University of Louisville for the overall support and day-to-day assistance my work colleagues have given me. I would also like to thank Russ Weaver, the Series Editor, and the folks at Carolina Academic Press for sharing their expertise and providing help when needed. Finally, I would like to thank James, Austin, Margaret, and David for all the small acts of support and encouragement.

Preface

Any law student should have three goals in the study of professional responsibility. The short-term goal, and the one law students usually have no trouble identifying, is mastering the subject so that the students will do well in the law school professional responsibility course. Second, most law students have, as a long-term goal, the practice of law. To accomplish this goal, generally one must be admitted to practice in a jurisdiction. Most jurisdictions require applicants to the bar to have achieved a certain score on the Multistate Professional Responsibility Exam (MPRE). Thus, a second goal of law students is mastering the subject matter so as to obtain the requisite score on the MPRE. Finally, all law students should have the goal of mastering the subject of professional responsibility in an effort to be ethical and competent lawyers for the duration of their professional lives.

My goal with this book is to assist law students in these endeavors. This book is not a replacement for professional responsibility textbooks and classroom experience; it is a supplement to those vital elements of the study of professional responsibility. I attempt to discuss the rules and concepts clearly and concisely with reference to relevant case law and other authorities.

In addition to a thorough discussion of the American Bar Association's Model Rules of Professional Conduct, any course in professional responsibility must also explore the related constitutional requirements, evidentiary rules, rules of procedure, and case law dealing with matters that touch upon lawyer conduct. All of these matters are covered by the MPRE as well. This book discusses them, too.

A Note about the Rules Quoted or Discussed in This Book

Forty-nine states (all but California) and the District of Columbia follow some version of the American Bar Association's Model Rules of Professional Conduct as the standards governing lawyer conduct. Law school professional responsibility courses focus on these rules as well. Also, the Multistate Professional Responsibility Exam (MPRE) tests, among other things, the most recent version the Model Rules. The ABA holds the copyright on the Model Rules.

State rules are in the public domain. Thus, the rules of professional responsibility can be studied by focusing on the rules of states that have made the Model Rules the applicable rules of the state. This book often refers to the Delaware Lawyers' Rules of Professional Conduct because Delaware has adopted many of the Model Rules and comments verbatim, or virtually so. If the relevant Delaware rule varies significantly from the Model Rule, this book discusses another state's rule that is the same, or almost the same, as the Model Rule. Whenever the book refers to a rule, the accompanying state abbreviation indicates the state rule being discussed. For example, the discussion of "Rule 1.1(DE)" indicates that Delaware's version of Rule 1.1, which is substantially the same as Model Rule 1.1, is being discussed.

Section I
Regulation of the Legal Profession

Chapter 1

Sources of Professional Responsibility Law

Roadmap

- The ABA Model Rules of Professional Conduct
- Prior formulations of lawyer conduct standards
- Ethics opinions
- The *Restatement (Third) of the Law Governing Lawyers*
- The ABA Model Code of Judicial Conduct

A. The Many Sources of Standards for Lawyer and Judge Conduct

The study of professional responsibility is the study of the rules and standards governing the conduct of lawyers and judges. In the United States, the individual states, not the federal government or local agencies, regulate the legal profession. Each state has developed its own bar admission requirements, discipline procedures, rules applicable to the conduct of lawyers, and rules applicable to the conduct of judges. *See Chapter 2 Admission to the Bar* and *Chapter 3 The Discipline Process and Jurisdiction for Discipline.* Fortunately, there are many similarities of procedures and standards among the states. The similarities are the result of the American Bar Association (ABA) taking a leading role in the area of lawyer and judge regulation. Over the years, the ABA has drafted model standards of lawyer and judge conduct and the states have adopted these standards with only slight variation.

There are other sources of standards governing lawyer and judge conduct, however. Constitutional law provides standards for ineffective assistance of counsel, and evidence rules and case law provide standards for the application of the attorney-client privilege, for example. *See Chapter 7 Ineffective Assis-*

tance of Counsel and *Chapter 16 The Attorney-Client Privilege and the Work-Product Doctrine.*

B. Standards for Lawyers

1. The Current ABA Model Rules of Professional Conduct

The most important source of the law for *lawyer* conduct is the ABA Model Rules of Professional Conduct. Law school courses in professional responsibility are centered on the Model Rules. The Multistate Professional Responsibility Examination (MPRE) covers the Model Rules. The District of Columbia and all states except California have as their state standards for lawyer conduct a version of the Model Rules. Even if a state has significant differences between its standards and the Model Rules, the District of Columbia and all states except Maryland and Wisconsin require applicants to the bar to take the MPRE. Thus, mastery of the Model Rules is necessary regardless of the state's rules. It is important to be aware of revisions to the Model Rules because the MPRE incorporates revisions to the Model Rules one year after ABA approval.

2. A Brief History of Lawyer Conduct Standards

a. 1908–1969: The Canons

Until 1969, the most influential source of standards for the conduct of lawyers was the ABA's Canons of Professional Ethics. The Canons were largely aspirational, meaning they stated no definite conduct that must be taken or avoided; they simply stated what a lawyer should do. The Canons were taken in part from the Code of Ethics of the Alabama Bar Association and were derived in part from Judge George Sharswood's work in the 1800s.

By the early 1960s, the Canons did not fit well with the modern practice of law. Many lawyers believed that the Canons fell well short of providing adequate guidance.

b. 1969–1983: The ABA Model Code of Professional Responsibility

Lewis Powell, the ABA President and later a United States Supreme Court Justice, in 1964 initiated a study of lawyer standards. The ABA created a special committee, known as the Wright Committee, to evaluate the Canons in light of the needs of lawyers of the time. The result of the study was the ABA Model Code of Professional Responsibility. The ABA adopted the Model Code in 1969. A majority of United States jurisdictions adopted the Model Code or a substantially similar body of ethical principles.

The Model Code contained Canons, Ethical Considerations (ECs), and Disciplinary Rules (DRs). The Canons in the Model Code were statements of norms for lawyer conduct. Under each Canon, the Model Code contained Ethical Considerations. These were aspirational statements. Also, under each Canon and following the Ethical Considerations were the Disciplinary Rules. The Disciplinary Rules were concrete statements of required lawyer conduct. A violation of a Disciplinary Rule could result in lawyer discipline. Lawyers soon found the Model Code, while an improvement on the Canons, hard to deal with and ill-suited for the rapidly changing practice of law.

c. 1983–2002: The Initial ABA Model Rules of Professional Conduct

In 1977, the ABA created a commission to study professional standards for lawyers. This commission, known as the Kutak Commission, developed the ABA Model Rules of Professional Conduct. This set of standards takes the form of rules with commentary. The ABA adopted the Model Rules in 1983 and the District of Columbia and all states except California have adopted state standards substantially similar to the Model Rules.

d. 2002–Present: Substantial Revision of the Model Rules

In 1997, the ABA created a commission to evaluate the Model Rules in light of the constantly changing landscape of law practice. The work of this group, known as the Ethics 2000 Commission, resulted in many modifications to the Model Rules in 2002. In addition, another ABA commission, one appointed to study the multijurisdictional practice of law, recommended several significant modifications which the ABA adopted. Finally, as a result of lawyer involvement in the corporate scandals such as Enron, an ABA commission on corporate responsibility recommended several modifications. By August of 2003, the ABA had adopted these changes, many of which were significant. Many states adopted all or most of these changes.

Since 2003, several of the Model Rules have been revised. Most of the revisions occurred in 2012 and were the result of recommendations of the ABA Commission on Ethics 20/20 which was created to study the rules in light of technological developments affecting law practice and also the globalization of the practice of law.

3. Ethics Opinions

The ABA Standing Committee on Ethics and Professional Responsibility publishes ethics opinions as do some state ethics entities. The ABA opinions clarify application of the Model Rules to particular facts. They are not binding on any state. Opinions of a state ethics entity apply that state's rules to particular facts. Obviously, one state's opinion is not binding on another state. Generally, ethics opinions have an educational and advisory purpose only. A few local bar entities, such as the Los Angeles County Bar Association, also issue ethics opinions.

4. The *Restatement (Third) of the Law Governing Lawyers*

The American Law Institute in 2000 published the *Restatement (Third) of the Law Governing Lawyers*. Despite the title, there was no first or second treatment of the topic. While the *Restatement* is not controlling in any jurisdiction, it generally states norms of professional conduct for lawyers. It is helpful in filling in gaps left by the Model Rules and sometimes in explaining some of the principles at issue.

5. Other Sources

A full picture of standards governing lawyer conduct cannot be obtained without looking at other sources. Sometimes one must consider other law to determine standards of lawyer conduct. For example, the Model Rules deal with many issues regarding lawyer conduct but do not deal with admission requirements and the discipline process. These matters are usually dealt with in state rules. In the study of professional responsibility, admission and discipline standards are best studied by identifying commonalities in various state rules and case law. The attorney-client privilege is relevant to lawyer conduct and yet it is often a creature of evidentiary statute or judge-made rule. To study the work-product doctrine, one must consider a rule of civil procedure. To understand the standards governing the issue of ineffective assistance of counsel, one must study constitutional principles. To decipher disqualification standards, one must evaluate case law involving disqualification motions. *See Chapter 2 Admission to the Bar, Chapter 3 The Discipline Process and Jurisdiction for Discipline, Chapter 7 Ineffective Assistance of Counsel, Chapter 16 The*

Attorney-Client Privilege and the Work-Product Doctrine, and *Chapter 17 Introduction to Conflicts of Interest Concepts.*

C. Standards for Judges

The ABA adopted the Canons of Judicial Ethics in 1924. In 1972 the ABA replaced the Canons with the first Code of Judicial Conduct. The ABA substantially revised the Code in 1990. The 1990 ABA Model Code of Judicial Conduct is the basis for many state judicial codes today. The ABA substantially revised the Model Code in 2007 with slight revisions in 2010.

The MPRE tests the Model Code of Judicial Conduct. Thus, an applicant for admission to the bar of a state must know the Model Code of Judicial Conduct even if the standards of judicial conduct for that particular state are somewhat different.

Checkpoints

- A mastery of professional responsibility law regarding lawyers requires knowledge and understanding of
  1. the ABA Model Rules of Professional Conduct,
  2. constitutional requirements touching upon lawyer conduct, and
  3. principles of lawyer conduct found in case law, statutes, and procedural and evidentiary rules.
- A mastery of professional responsibility law regarding judges requires knowledge and understanding of the ABA Model Code of Judicial Conduct and accepted principles of conduct for judges found in statutes and case law.

Chapter 2

Admission to the Bar

Roadmap

- Rule 8.1(DE)
- Requirements for admission to practice law in a jurisdiction
- The duty of honesty regarding the bar application

A. Each State's Highest Court Regulates the Practice of Law

The highest court in each state regulates the legal profession within each state. So, for example, the South Carolina Supreme Court has the authority to regulate lawyers in South Carolina. Each state's highest court ultimately is responsible for deciding who may practice law in the jurisdiction, creating the standards of conduct for those practicing law in the jurisdiction, and disciplining lawyers who fall afoul of those rules of conduct. *See Chapter 3 The Discipline Process and Jurisdiction for Discipline.*

In most jurisdictions, the highest court does not actually handle the day-to-day admissions activities. The courts delegate these tasks to a subordinate entity such as an office of bar examiners. A jurisdiction's highest court may continue supervisory involvement on policy matters.

B. Admission Requirements

1. The Novice Lawyer: The Person Not Admitted in Any Jurisdiction

Traditionally, to practice law in a jurisdiction, a person has to be admitted to the bar of that jurisdiction. In recent years Rule 5.5(KS) has provided that a lawyer admitted in one jurisdiction may practice, in certain limited situations, in another jurisdiction. A person not yet admitted in any jurisdiction cannot benefit from this rule. *See Chapter 40 The Unauthorized Practice of Law.* Some states have created other narrow exceptions to the general rule of bar admission. These exceptions allow nonlawyers to practice law in very specific settings. For example, some states allow law students who have completed the equivalent of two years of legal education to practice law under supervision. In general, there is no escape from the rule requiring bar admission.

Most states have four basic requirements for admission for the novice lawyer. First, a person must graduate from a law school. Usually, the law school must be accredited by the ABA. Some states also may require that the person have taken certain specific courses in law school, such as a course in professional responsibility.

The second and third requirements involve tests. The person must pass a national exam dealing specifically with the topic of professional responsibility, called the Multistate Professional Responsibility Examination (MPRE). In addition, the person must pass a bar examination that tests various law subjects. Usually, this exam is composed of a multiple-choice national exam portion as well as an essay portion that may include state-specific questions. Each state has its own list of subjects covered by this exam. Some states' exams cover many subjects while other states' exams cover very few.

The last typical admission requirement is that the person be of appropriate character and fitness for the practice of law. A candidate for admission has the burden of proving that he or she has this character and fitness. Often, the requirement is stated as a mandate of "good moral character." To determine present character, the admissions committees often look to past acts.

An admissions entity may not find a candidate for admission to have the appropriate character and fitness if the candidate has exhibited significant acts of dishonesty. After all, lawyers must be honest. *See Chapter 28 Honesty and Candor* and *Chapter 48 General Misconduct.* The problematic dishonesty can occur in any setting: financial dishonesty, plagiarism or other forms of academic dishonesty, or even a failure to disclose information on the law school application or bar application.

A candidate sometimes is found to be lacking the appropriate character and fitness because the candidate has exhibited a lack of respect for law. For example, a candidate who has repeatedly violated the law with regard to small matters may not be deemed to have the appropriate character and fitness to practice law. A candidate with a single violent offense may have the same problem. Some states are particularly suspect of anyone with a past that includes a felony crime, even if the felony did not involve violence.

2. The Experienced Lawyer: The Lawyer Admitted in One Jurisdiction Seeking to Practice or be Admitted in Another Jurisdiction

Many states have different requirements if the person seeking admission is not a novice lawyer but rather is admitted to practice in another jurisdiction. States often have a rule of admission that recognizes the validity of a lawyer's admission and practice in another jurisdiction. For example, a state may have a provision that allows a person admitted to the bar in another jurisdiction and who has practiced law for five recent years to be admitted in the new jurisdiction without taking the usual exams. Such a person might be required to undergo the character and fitness evaluation only.

In addition, Rule 5.5(KS) provides exceptions for temporary practice in a jurisdiction if the person is an admitted lawyer in another jurisdiction. Also, Rule 5.5(KS) allows a person admitted in another jurisdiction to practice in a jurisdiction in which the lawyer is not admitted if the lawyer works as an in-house lawyer. Finally, Rule 5.5(KS) notes that a lawyer may be permitted to practice law in a jurisdiction in which the lawyer is not admitted by operation of federal law or other state law. *See Chapter 40 The Unauthorized Practice of Law.*

C. The Bar Application Process

1. The Applicant Who Ultimately is Admitted

A person who desires to be admitted to a bar must complete a long and detailed application. The person must be forthcoming with requested information, subject, of course, to constitutional protections and protections provided by other law. If a person wishes to rely on a right of nondisclosure such as the Fifth Amendment, the person should disclose this as the basis of the nondisclosure. The person must submit to any required investigation by the admitting entity. Practicing law in a particular jurisdiction is viewed as a privilege, not an entitlement, so one would expect a candidate who wants to be admitted to be honest and forthright in the application process.

Such honesty and forthrightness is also an ethical requirement. While a candidate for admission is not yet an admitted lawyer and thus is not technically within the bounds of the rules of professional conduct for lawyers, the rules perform a sleight of hand on this issue. Rule 8.1(DE) states that an applicant for admission must not "knowingly make a false statement of material fact." In addition, the candidate must not fail to disclose a fact necessary to correct a known misapprehension. Finally, an applicant must not "knowingly fail to respond" to demands for information unless the duty of confidentiality of Rule 1.6(DE) protects such information. *See Chapter 15 The Duty of Confidentiality.* If an applicant is admitted to the bar of a jurisdiction and then the discipline authorities discover that the applicant was dishonest or not forthcoming with regard to the bar admission application, the admitted lawyer can be disciplined for a violation of Rule 8.1(DE).

Lori, a bar applicant, may not want to disclose that she was terminated from a job in college because she took money from the cash register wrongfully. If the bar application contains a query about past employment terminations and Lori does not disclose the employment history, her nondisclosure, if discovered during the admission process, can block her admission. If the nondisclosure is not discovered until after Lori is admitted, Lori can be disciplined for violating Rule 8.1(DE).

2. A Lawyer Involved in an Application for Admission

Lawyers often are called upon to provide information to admitting entities in connection with applicants to the bar. Law students work for lawyers during law school and the lawyers often have significant contact with these students. Rule 8.1(DE) applies with equal force to these lawyers. Such lawyers must not "make a false statement of material fact" and must not fail to disclose a fact necessary to correct a known misapprehension. A lawyer must not knowingly fail to respond to a demand for information unless the duty of confidentiality of Rule 1.6(DE) protects such information. *See Chapter 15 The Duty of Confidentiality.*

Related Sections of the *Restatement (Third) of the Law Governing Lawyers*

Sections 1, 2, 3, and 4

Checkpoints

- The highest court in each jurisdiction regulates all aspects of the practice of law in the jurisdiction.
- Generally, to practice law in a jurisdiction, a person must be admitted to the bar of that jurisdiction.
- For admission, states typically require
  1. graduation from an accredited law school,
  2. a passing score on the Multistate Professional Responsibility Exam (MPRE),
  3. a passing score on a general bar exam, and
  4. a determination that the applicant is of "good moral character."
- Some jurisdictions have lighter requirements for lawyers who have been admitted in another jurisdiction and have practiced for a certain number of years.
- Rule 5.5(KS) allows a lawyer admitted in another jurisdiction to practice in a non-admitted jurisdiction as in-house counsel, or temporarily as long as the temporary practice satisfies certain conditions, or if other law permits the activity.
- A bar applicant or lawyer in connection with a bar admission application
  1. must not "knowingly make a false statement of material fact,"
  2. must correct known misapprehensions with regard to the bar application and process, and
  3. must respond to lawful demands for information.

Chapter 3

The Discipline Process and Jurisdiction for Discipline

Roadmap

- Rule 8.1(DE)
- Rule 8.5(ID)
- The discipline process
- The duty to disclose information in the process
- The authority of admitting jurisdictions to discipline lawyers
- The authority of other jurisdictions to discipline lawyers
- Reciprocal discipline
- Choice of law for discipline

A. The Discipline Process

Because the highest court in a state is the ultimate regulator of the practice of law in that state, that court is also the arbiter of discipline within the state. Typically, the highest court in the state delegates the operation of the day-to-day discipline system to a lesser entity. The disciplinary authority may, or may not, be a part of the state bar association. The disciplinary authority investigates complaints filed against lawyers. If this entity concludes that a complaint has merit, it may present the matter to a board or tribunal of some sort for a determination of whether probable cause exists to charge the lawyer with professional misconduct. If the lawyer is charged, the lawyer has the opportunity to oppose the charge. A hearing body made up of lawyers and, sometimes, a few nonlawyers, hears the matter and reaches a decision on guilt and the appropriate discipline. The state's highest court may have the right to review the findings and conclusions of the hearing body. The court can decline to adopt the hearing body's decision on guilt and the hearing body's decision on the appropriate punishment.

The following is a typical scenario. Perhaps a disgruntled client files a complaint with the state Office of Bar Counsel against Larry Lawyer, claiming that Larry stole from the client. Theft is a criminal act and a violation of the applicable rules of professional conduct. In Larry's state, Bar Counsel is a part of the state bar association. Bar Counsel investigates and determines that there is sufficient evidence to present the matter to an inquiry tribunal. The inquiry tribunal, a small group of lawyers, determines that there is probable cause that Larry violated the rules of professional conduct. After a time for discovery and the filing of briefs, Bar Counsel presents the matter to the bar association's Board of Governors and Larry has an opportunity to defend himself. In Larry's state, the Board of Governors has been charged by the Supreme Court, the highest court in the state, with the job of hearing disciplinary matters. Perhaps the Board of Governors finds that Larry has violated the rules of professional conduct and should be disbarred. The Supreme Court then might decide that the Board of Governors is incorrect in concluding that Larry violated the rules. The Court could decide that Larry violated the rules but that he should not be disbarred but rather he should be suspended from the practice of law for two years. Or the Supreme Court could affirm the Board of Governors in all respects.

B. A Lawyer's Responsibility to Disclose Information

As is true in the admissions context, a lawyer may not "knowingly make a false statement of material fact" in the context of disciplinary matter. Rule 8.1(DE) prohibits such conduct with equal force for the admission setting and the discipline setting. Likewise, a lawyer may not "knowingly fail to respond to a lawful demand for information" regarding a disciplinary matter unless the duty of confidentiality of Rule 1.6(DE) protects the information. Also, a lawyer may not fail to disclose a fact in connection with a discipline matter if disclosure of the fact is necessary to avoid a known misapprehension. Again, however, the duty of confidentiality of Rule 1.6(DE) limits the duty to disclose. The lawyer need not disclose information protected by the duty of confidentiality of Rule 1.6(DE). *See Chapter 15 The Duty of Confidentiality.*

If a lawyer is a target of a disciplinary matter, the lawyer's constitutional rights, such as the Fifth Amendment right not to self-incriminate, overrides the lawyer's Rule 8.1(DE) disclosure obligation. The lawyer, if relying on constitutional rights, should clearly so state.

C. Authority to Discipline

1. The Lawyer's State of Admission

Lawyers can be admitted to practice in more than one jurisdiction. A lawyer who has clients in several states may be admitted to the bar of each state by satisfying the admission requirements of each state. So, for example, Larry Lawyer, a lawyer with clients in Virginia and Maryland, might desire to be licensed to practice law in both states. *See Chapter 2 Admission to the Bar.* As a Virginia lawyer, Larry must abide by all the rules and requirements of Virginia. As a Maryland lawyer, Larry must abide by all the rules and requirements of Maryland. Larry must pay dues to each state and must fulfill the continuing legal education requirements for each state.

Rule 8.5(a)(ID) states the long-recognized principle that a state that has admitted a lawyer to practice in that jurisdiction has the authority to discipline that lawyer regardless of where the problematic conduct occurs. Thus, Larry, a lawyer admitted in Maryland and Virginia, is subject to discipline by both Maryland and Virginia if his conduct violates the rules of those jurisdictions. Since each state has granted Larry a license to practice within that state, each state can take that entitlement away on the basis of Larry's failure to abide by the standards of lawyer conduct in effect in that jurisdiction. If Larry commits an act of deceit in California, Virginia and Maryland have the authority to discipline Larry.

2. The State in Which the Lawyer Offers or Provides Legal Services

Rule 5.5(KS) provides that, in certain situations, lawyers may practice in jurisdictions other than those in which they are admitted. For example, a lawyer may practice law in a state in which the lawyer is not admitted if the activity is on a temporary basis and relates to a proceeding in an admitted jurisdiction. Likewise, a court may admit a lawyer *pro hac vice* in a case in a state in which the lawyer is not otherwise admitted. *See Chapter 40 The Unauthorized Practice of Law.*

Rule 8.5(a)(ID) states that any jurisdiction in which a lawyer provides legal services or offers to provide legal services may discipline the lawyer for a violation of its rules. So if Larry is admitted to the bars of Virginia and Maryland and commits an act of deceit in California, all three states have the authority to discipline Larry if Larry provides legal services or offers to provide legal services in California.

Because Rule 8.5(a)(ID) grants a state authority to discipline on the basis of offers of service, all lawyers must take special note of where their advertisements can be viewed because if an advertisement can be viewed in California, for example, then a reasonable person would believe the advertisement offers legal services in California. If Larry advertises on television and people in California can view the ad, California may discipline Larry if he violates California standards of conduct for lawyers such as the California rules on lawyer advertising. *See Chapter 45 Communications about Lawyer Services.*

3. Reciprocal Discipline

If one state disciplines a lawyer, other states may issue reciprocal discipline. If Virginia disciplines Larry, a lawyer admitted in Virginia and Maryland, Maryland may give effect to the Virginia disciplinary action and discipline Larry as well. So disbarment by Virginia can result in disbarment in Maryland too, although Maryland is not required to impose the same discipline or any discipline at all. Some states require admitted lawyers to notify the state discipline authority of any discipline imposed by another state.

D. Choice of Law

1. One State Involved

In the vast majority of situations, a lawyer who engages in improper conduct does so in a state in which the lawyer is admitted and the effect of that conduct is in that state. Then there is no question of which law to apply. The ethics rules of the state of admission clearly apply.

2. More Than One State Involved

When more than one state is involved, the question of the standards to apply is more complex. In this situation, a state choosing to exercise authority to discipline a lawyer for improper conduct must determine which jurisdiction's rules to apply. In an effort to create a situation in which only one set of rules can apply to particular conduct, Rule 8.5(b)(ID) provides the following guides.

First, if the problematic conduct relates to a matter before a tribunal, the professional responsibility rules of the jurisdiction in which the tribunal sits apply unless that set of rules says otherwise. If Larry, a Virginia lawyer, appears *pro hac vice* in a court in Oregon and engages in improper conduct, any discipline should be measured against the rules in effect in Oregon. Virginia may be the state disciplining Larry, but his conduct is measured by Oregon standards.

Second, in any other situation, the disciplining jurisdiction should apply the law of the jurisdiction in which the problematic conduct occurred unless the "predominant effect" of the conduct is in another jurisdiction. Assume that Larry, a lawyer admitted in Virginia and Maryland, commits an act of deceit in relation to the provision of legal services in California. Regardless of which state seeks to discipline him, the rules of California should apply unless the "predominant effect" of Larry's deceit is in a jurisdiction other than California.

3. Safe Harbor

Rule 8.5(b)(ID) provides a bit of a safe harbor for a lawyer. Choice of law decisions are made in hindsight. A discipline authority makes a choice of law decision long after the problematic conduct occurs. A lawyer, at the time of taking action and providing legal services, may not know definitively which set of rules apply to that conduct. Occasionally, the rules of the various jurisdictions conflict starkly. For example, one state may allow disclosure of confidential information in a particular circumstance while another state may not allow that disclosure. *See Chapter 15 The Duty of Confidentiality.* The lawyer must then decide which jurisdiction's standards to follow.

The safe harbor provides a circumstance in which the lawyer cannot be disciplined even if the lawyer's conduct violates the standards of the jurisdiction whose law ultimately applies. If the lawyer's actions are in accord with standards of the jurisdiction in which the lawyer "reasonably believes" the conduct will have "predominant effect," the lawyer is free from discipline. This provision means that if Larry provides legal services in California and "reasonably believes" that his conduct will have "predominant effect" in California, Larry cannot be disciplined for violating Virginia's standards if a discipline authority later determines that Virginia law applies. This is true, however, only if Larry acts in accord with California standards.

A comment to the rule contemplates that a lawyer and the client can specify the jurisdiction reasonably believed to be the jurisdiction that the lawyer's conduct will have "predominant effect." While the agreement is not completely determinative, if the agreement is the product of and confirms the client's "informed consent," the discipline authority may consider it as evidence of the lawyer's reasonable belief. "Informed consent," as defined in Rule 1.0(e)(DE), is agreement after the client has been informed by the lawyer of the "material risks" of the proposed course of conduct and the "reasonably available alternatives" to the proposed course of conduct.

Related Sections of the *Restatement (Third) of the Law Governing Lawyers*

Section 5

Checkpoints

- A lawyer has a duty to be truthful in the context of a discipline matter and to disclose information not protected by the duty of confidentiality when necessary to avoid a known misapprehension or when such is lawfully demanded.
- Any jurisdiction that has admitted a lawyer to the practice of law has authority to discipline that lawyer regardless of where the conduct occurs.
- Any jurisdiction in which a lawyer renders legal services or offers to render legal services has authority to discipline that lawyer.
- If one state disciplines a lawyer, other states in which the lawyer is admitted may impose reciprocal discipline.
- If a lawyer is being disciplined for conduct relating to a matter before a tribunal, the standards of the jurisdiction of the tribunal apply to the lawyer's conduct unless the law of that jurisdiction directs otherwise.
- If a lawyer is being disciplined for conduct not related to a matter before a tribunal, the standards of the jurisdiction in which the conduct occurred apply unless the "predominant effect" of the conduct is elsewhere. If the "predominant effect" is elsewhere, the rules of the jurisdiction of "predominant effect" apply.
- If a lawyer "reasonably believes" that the lawyer's conduct will have "predominant effect" in one jurisdiction and the lawyer's conduct conforms to the standards of that jurisdiction, the lawyer is not subject to discipline if a discipline authority later determines that another jurisdiction's rules apply and have been violated.

Section II
Basics of the Lawyer-Client Relationship

Chapter 4

Basis of Duty: The Lawyer-Client Relationship

Roadmap

- Creation of the lawyer-client relationship and lawyer-prospective client relationship

A. General Rule

A lawyer owes duties to the lawyer's clients and, to a lesser extent, to the lawyer's prospective clients. Anyone with whom the lawyer has entered into an engagement agreement is, without doubt, a client and the lawyer owes that person or entity a duty of care as a matter of tort law. The lawyer also owes that person or entity other duties stated in the professional responsibility rules such as confidentiality and loyalty and duties recognized as a part of a fiduciary relationship.

Regardless of the existence of an engagement agreement, courts often find that a lawyer owes a tort duty of care and duties under the rules of professional conduct to anyone who has the reasonable belief that the lawyer represents him or her even if the lawyer does not believe that a lawyer-client relationship has formed. The existence of the relationship often depends on the reasonable belief of the person in the client's position.

Rule 1.18(a)(DE) provides that a lawyer owes prospective clients duties as well. Rule 1.18(a)(DE) defines a prospective client as "a person who consults with a lawyer about the possibility of forming a client-lawyer relationship with respect to a matter." The comments to the rule clarify that the prospective client must reasonably believe that the lawyer is willing to discuss the possibility of forming a lawyer-client relationship. This reasonable belief can be based on written, oral, or electronic communications and can occur if the lawyer, without cautionary warnings, generally requests the submission of information about a possible representation on a website or otherwise.

B. Applying the Rule

A good example of the reasonable belief test for the existence of a lawyer-client relationship or a prospective client-lawyer relationship is *Togstad v. Vesely, Otto, Miller & Keefe*, 291 N.W.2d 686 (Minn. 1980). Joan Togstad met with a lawyer, Miller, for approximately one hour. The meeting occurred fourteen months after Togstad's husband was hospitalized for a carotid artery aneurysm. As a result of the treatment for the aneurysm, Togstad's husband was paralyzed. Togstad told Miller the story of her husband's treatment. Togstad later testified that Miller told her that he did not think there was a case but that he would discuss the matter with a partner. Togstad believed that Miller would call her if he decided that there was a case. Lawyer Miller did not discuss a fee with Togstad and Togstad completed no medical records release authorizations.

A year later, Togstad consulted with another lawyer. This second lawyer told Togstad that she and her husband had a possible medical malpractice claim but that the statute of limitations had run. The statute had run in the time between Togstad's conversation with Miller and her conversation with the second lawyer.

Togstad sued Miller and his firm for malpractice. Deciding the matter before formal recognition in the Model Rules of the prospective client category, the court recognized the existence of a lawyer-client relationship for purposes of malpractice liability. The court stated that a lawyer-client relationship forms whenever a party seeks and receives legal advice in circumstances that would lead a reasonable person to rely on the advice.

While the Togstad case involved the tort duty of care, other duties a lawyer customarily owes a client can be implicated. For example, if the lawyer in *Togstad* had later sought to represent the treating physician in Ms. Togstad's medical malpractice action, assuming the statute of limitations had not run on such an action, Ms. Togstad's reasonable belief that Miller was her lawyer would perhaps bar Miller's representation of the physician under conflict of interest principles. *See Chapter 19 Conflicts and Former Clients* and *Chapter 20 Conflicts and Prospective Clients.*

Related Sections of the *Restatement (Third) of the Law Governing Lawyers*

Sections 14, 15, 50, and 51(1)

Checkpoints

- A lawyer owes a tort duty of care and professional responsibility duties to anyone who the lawyer agrees to represent.
- Often a lawyer owes these same duties to a person even absent an agreement to represent that person if the person has a reasonable belief that the lawyer represents him or her.
- A lawyer owes professional responsibility duties to prospective clients and may owe a tort duty of care as well.

Chapter 5

Competence and Diligence

Roadmap

- Rule 1.1(DE)
- Rule 1.3(DE)
- The duty of competence
- The duty of diligence

A. Competence

1. Threshold Competence for Admission

The admission process is designed to ensure that members of the bar have a minimum competence for the practice of law. Requiring candidates to have taken certain courses, to have attended law school, and to pass the MPRE and the bar examination ensures knowledge of topics and jurisdictions deemed necessary for the competent practice of law. But the admissions process can only address competence in a very general manner—that is, that the admission candidate has a threshold level of understanding about certain substantive areas of the law. *See Chapter 2 Admission to the Bar.*

2. Continuing Competence in Each Representation

The rules continue this theme by requiring lawyers to exercise competence in every client representation. A comment to Rule 1.18(DE) notes that Rule 1.1(DE) also states the duty owed to prospective clients with regard to any assistance given on the "merits of a matter." Rule 1.1(DE) states that competence "requires the legal knowledge, skill, thoroughness and preparation reasonably necessary for the representation." A failure to render competent representation can result in discipline. Conduct that evidences a lack of competence also may evidence a failure to provide representation in accord with the tort duty of care and thus can be a basis for malpractice liability. Such conduct might also be the basis of an ineffective assistance of counsel claim. *See Chapter 6 Malpractice and Other Civil Liability* and *Chapter 7 Ineffective Assistance of Counsel.*

a. Basic Skills

Competence in any legal matter requires certain basic legal skills such as the ability to identify the types of legal problems a matter might involve, the ability to draft required documents or pleadings, the ability to analyze precedent, and the ability to analyze evidence. Presumably, one cannot be admitted to the profession without these basic skills.

A lawyer cannot allow his or her skills to stagnate, however. A lawyer, to maintain competence, must stay up-to-date with regard to both the substantive law and also practice issues such as relevant technology. States require lawyers to complete a minimum number of continuing legal education hours each year. In this way states attempt to assist lawyers maintain competence.

b. Knowledge of Law and Procedure

A competent lawyer knows the law and procedure relevant to a particular matter and the rules of the court or setting in which the matter appears. A competent lawyer has this knowledge because of prior experience or because of research and other preparation.

If Larry Lawyer does not know the statute of limitations applicable to the subject matter of the representation of Clint Client, Larry does not render competent representation. If Larry Lawyer files an appellate brief in a form not allowed by the court rules, he has not rendered competent representation.

c. Preparation

In addition, competence requires analysis and preparation reasonable given the subject matter and the customary standards of lawyer conduct. Competence requires investigation of the factual basis of the matter. Competence is judged by measuring lawyer conduct against a standard of reasonableness with consideration of all the surrounding circumstances. Thus, a competent representation of a complex matter may require more effort in investigation and other preparation than a simple matter.

Perhaps Larry Lawyer is defending Clint Client in a criminal matter. Clint faces a possible death penalty. Because Larry is over-extended, he does not review a file regarding a prior conviction and fails to investigate Clint's past. Larry does not exercise judgment and decide not to review the file because such a review would be tactically injurious to Clint, nor does Larry decide that investigating Clint's past would be a bad move strategically. Rather, Larry simply does not get around to those tasks because he does not have the time. If a reasonable lawyer in these circumstances would have reviewed the file or investigated the client's past, there is a good argument that Larry Lawyer has not rendered competent legal representation. Also, Larry may have committed malpractice and may have rendered ineffective assistance of counsel.

d. The New Lawyer

Even a new lawyer handling a type of matter the lawyer has never handled before can render competent representation. If Larry Lawyer is new to the practice of law and has been asked to handle a medical malpractice action, a matter with which he has no experience, he can act competently by doing the research, investigation, and other work necessary to represent the client. If Larry Lawyer believes that he cannot do all the work necessary, he can associate with counsel who has experience in this kind of representation.

e. The Emergency Situation

In an emergency situation a lesser level of research and investigation may be required to reach a threshold level of competence. There may not be sufficient time for a reasonable lawyer to research the matter or consult with others with more expertise. In the interest of the client receiving some guidance, though not perhaps perfect guidance, there is recognition that the lawyer's conduct must be judged by a standard of reasonableness considering all circumstances including the emergency nature of the client consultation. Thus, competence in an emergency may differ from competence in other settings.

f. Outsourcing

In representing a client, a lawyer may decide that certain aspects of the representation are best handled by a lawyer who is not a part of the original lawyer's firm. The duty of competence requires that the attorney reasonably believe that the use of the outside attorney will be consistent with competent and ethical representation. To make such a determination, a lawyer might consider factors such as the education and experience of the outside lawyer. In addition, the client ordinarily must give informed consent to such an outsourcing arrangement.

B. Diligence

Closely tied to the concept of competence is that of diligence. Rule 1.3(DE) requires "reasonable diligence and promptness in representing a client." The client entrusts a legal matter to a lawyer. The lawyer is a fiduciary with regard to the legal matter and thus must act reasonably to advance the client's interest even to the disadvantage of the lawyer. A lawyer must actively pursue the client's goals within the bounds of the lawyer's good judgment and proper respect for the rights of parties, third parties, and the courts. A lawyer should not allow a client's matter to languish unreasonably, and ultimately, should pursue the matter to its conclusion.

Rule 3.2(DE) contains a related duty. It instructs lawyers to act reasonably to expedite litigation "consistent with the interests of the client." *See Chapter 27 The Duty to Expedite Litigation.*

C. Caseload Management

In every state every year there are many, many lawyers who are disciplined for agreeing to represent clients on matters and then failing to follow through with the representation. Clearly, these lawyers have not acted diligently and, usually, not competently as well. In many of these discipline cases, the lawyer breaches the duties of competence and diligence because the lawyer agrees to represent too many clients in too many matters. Lawyers must maintain control of their workload so as to avoid competence and diligence problems. Caseload management is a part of every lawyer's duty of competence.

ABA Formal Opinion 06-443 (2006) recognizes the effect an excessive caseload may have on a lawyer's competence and diligence in the context of lawyers representing indigent defendants. The *Opinion* cautions that a lawyer whose workload prevents competent and diligent representation must refuse new clients and should withdraw from some of the representations so that competent and diligent representation is possible for other matters entrusted to the lawyer. The same advice applies to lawyers in other practice settings.

Related Sections of the *Restatement (Third) of the Law Governing Lawyers*

Section 16

Checkpoints

- A lawyer must handle every representation with competence.
- If a lawyer gives assistance to a prospective client on the "merits of a matter," the duty of competence applies to that assistance.
- Competence is "the legal knowledge, skill, thoroughness and preparation reasonably necessary for the representation."
- Competence includes basic legal skills such as the identification and classification of legal problems as well as knowledge of the relevant law and procedure.
- Competence involves reasonable preparation.
- A new lawyer can obtain competence by research and preparation or by associating more experienced counsel.
- A lawyer must constantly work to maintain currency regarding the law and also issues relating to the practice of law, such as technology.
- In an emergency situation, what is reasonable knowledge, skill, or preparation may differ from what would be reasonable outside of the emergency context.
- The duty of competence allows a lawyer to outsource legal work only if the outsourcing is consistent with competent and ethical representation.
- A lawyer must handle every representation with diligence. This requires pursuing every matter to its conclusion in a timely manner.
- A lawyer must avoid an excessive caseload that prevents competent and diligent representation.

Chapter 6

Malpractice and Other Civil Liability

Roadmap

- Rule 1.8(h)(DE)
- Elements of a malpractice claim
- The duty of care
- Breach of fiduciary duty
- Breach of contract
- Liability to nonclients
- Agreements prospectively limiting a lawyer's liability to a client
- Agreements settling claims of clients against lawyers

A. Bases of Civil Liability

While avoiding bar discipline is a consideration for lawyers, avoiding the fiscal bite of civil liability to clients is also a significant concern of practicing lawyers. Clients can pursue several different types of claims against lawyers if these clients feel their lawyers have behaved wrongly toward them.

Without a doubt, the greatest threat is a tort action for malpractice. In such an action, the client claims that the lawyer has been professionally negligent. A second possibility is a breach of fiduciary duty claim. Because a lawyer is a fiduciary of the client, the lawyer owes the client all the duties that accompany fiduciary status. Thirdly, the lawyer-client relationship usually is the product of a contract. A lawyer can be responsible to the client for a breach of that contract. A lawyer is responsible on these bases regardless of whether the lawyer works for a fee, works on a pro bono basis, is a public defender, or is otherwise appointed.

B. Malpractice

A malpractice claim is basically a tort claim of negligence in the context of legal representation. The client making a claim for malpractice must prove that the lawyer owed the client a duty of care, that the lawyer failed to meet that duty, and that the lawyer's breach of the duty of care caused injury to the client in the form of damages.

1. Duty: The Lawyer-Client Relationship

A lawyer owes a duty of care to anyone the courts of the jurisdiction are willing to recognize as being in a lawyer-client relationship with the lawyer. Courts recognize that lawyers owe a duty of care to only a few other narrow categories of persons such as those people that the lawyer knows will be relying on his or her work. Courts sometimes state that an express or implied representation agreement is required though courts often find a relationship if the client has a reasonable belief that the lawyer represents him or her. Clearly, if Lisa Lawyer has entered into an engagement agreement with Cindy Client, Lisa owes Cindy a duty of care. Even without such an agreement, however, Lisa may owe a duty of care to Cindy if Cindy has the reasonable belief that Lisa represents her. Lisa's opinion on the relationship is not relevant. *See Chapter 4 Basis of Duty: The Lawyer-Client Relationship.*

2. Standard of Care

A lawyer must act with a level of competence and diligence of a reasonable lawyer in similar circumstances. The standard does not make the lawyer responsible for an unpleasant outcome in the client's matter unless the lawyer rendered services below the standard of a reasonable lawyer—unless the lawyer was negligent.

Lawyers generally are not responsible in malpractice for exercises of judgment. If Lisa Lawyer interviews all the witnesses in a matter and decides to forego presenting one of the witnesses because she thinks the witness would not be well-perceived by the jury, Lisa has exercised judgment. Cindy Client may later disagree on this tactic and claim that Lisa was negligent in making that decision. Judgments, if based on the proper level of preparation, are not examples of negligence even when the result is not as the lawyer intended.

This reasonable lawyer standard takes into account the peculiar situation in which the lawyer labors. The relevant location usually is defined by the locality, though there are certain subject practice areas, such as securities law, that might have a national scope. The standard of the reasonable lawyer also takes into consideration time pressures under which the lawyer may have been laboring. Lawyers presenting themselves as specialists in areas of law may be held to a higher standard than generalists in that area of specialty.

A ready-made source of standards for lawyer conduct is the relevant rules of professional conduct. It is logical to assume that if Lisa Lawyer has acted contrary to a rule of professional conduct, she also may have violated the standard of care owed to clients for purposes of malpractice. Yet, paragraph 20 of the "Scope" section of the *Delaware Lawyers' Rules of Professional Conduct,* which is the same as paragraph 20 of the "Scope" section of most states' rules and the Model Rules, warns that violation of a rule should not "itself give rise to a cause of action against a lawyer nor should it create any presumption in such a case that a legal duty has been breached." Paragraph 20 continues that the rules are not crafted to be the basis of civil liability. Violation of the rules can be evidence of breach of the standard of care, though not conclusive evidence.

3. Causation

a. General Rule

To recover in a malpractice action, the client must prove that but for the lawyer's negligence, the client would have enjoyed a more favorable result. In effect, this client must prove that the original matter would have ended more favorably and also that the lawyer's negligence caused the less favorable result. The client must win the case within the case. For example, assume that Cindy Client sues Lisa Lawyer claiming that Lisa missed the relevant statute of limitations for Cindy's medical malpractice claim. Cindy and Lisa had agreed that Lisa would represent Cindy in this matter. Without doubt Lisa owed Cindy a duty of care and missed the statute of limitations. Cindy must prove that Lisa was negligent by missing the statute of limitations. Cindy would do this by proving that a reasonable lawyer in the same circumstances would not miss the statute of limitations. Cindy also must prove that if the medical malpractice complaint had been filed in a timely manner, she likely would have recovered.

b. Settlement Setting

Clients can recover for lawyer negligence in cases in which the clients settle the underlying claim. For example, in Cindy Client's medical malpractice action, perhaps Cindy's lawyer, Lisa, recommended that Cindy settle because the proof of medical impropriety was lacking. Cindy settled. Cindy later has second thoughts. Cindy might successfully sue Lisa for malpractice claiming that

Lisa was negligent in not doing a proper investigation that would have uncovered much more substantial evidence of medical negligence. Cindy can claim that she would not have settled for so little if she (and Lisa) had access to the additional evidence.

c. Criminal Setting

A criminal defendant can claim malpractice just as a client in a civil matter can claim malpractice. As in the civil context, a criminal defendant must prove that his or her lawyer was negligent and that the negligence caused a less favorable outcome. In requiring that the client prove that the result would have been more favorable absent the lawyer's breach of duty, many courts require the criminal defendant to prove actual innocence. Proof of actual innocence requires having the conviction set aside.

Some courts take the position that the criminal defendant satisfies the proof requirement by showing that the result in the criminal matter would have been different absent the lawyer's negligence. These courts do not require the criminal defendant to prove actual innocence.

4. Damages

The client who successfully proves malpractice can recover the difference between the position the client would be in absent the lawyer's malfeasance and the position the client is in with the malfeasance. A client who was a plaintiff may recover the difference between the result of the actual proceeding and the result that would have occurred without the lawyer's negligence.

In addition, the client can recover the lawyer's fees paid in the original proceeding—fees paid for substandard representation. The client also can recover the amount paid to a replacement lawyer to remedy the situation.

Damages for emotional distress are not generally recoverable in legal malpractice actions because such damages are not foreseeable. Foreseeability is the general test for recovery of emotional distress damages in any setting. Some courts, such as the Supreme Court of Iowa in *Miranda v. Said,* 836 N.W.2d 8 (Iowa 2013), have allowed recovery of emotional distress damages if the setting of the legal malpractice is such that emotional distress damages are foreseeable as a very likely result of the lawyer's professional negligence. In *Miranda,* the lawyer's negligence in the immigration context resulted in long-term separation of family members.

A wronged client may be able to recover punitive damages if the lawyer's conduct constituting the malpractice was intentional or reckless. Punitive damages are not generally awarded in any context unless the wrongdoer acted intentionally or at least recklessly.

C. Breach of Fiduciary Duty

A lawyer is a fiduciary of the client. This status exists because the client places some matter of great importance to the client in the hands of the lawyer and, in effect, gives the lawyer the ability to affect the client's rights and act on behalf of the client regarding that matter. As a result of this fiduciary status, a lawyer owes the client certain duties that all fiduciaries owe. For example, a lawyer must always be honest with the client and must communicate with the client about the matter in the lawyer's charge. A lawyer must follow the client's direction regarding the matter within the bounds of the law and ethical conduct and must safeguard the client's property and confidences. A lawyer must avoid conflicts of interest and must not use the position as lawyer for the client to the disadvantage of the client. A client can make a claim against a lawyer for the breach of these duties.

D. Breach of Contract

A lawyer often provides the client with an engagement letter very near the beginning of the relationship. In this engagement letter, the lawyer spells out the lawyer's responsibilities in handling the matter and the client's responsibilities as well. The lawyer explains the terms of the arrangement to the client and obtains the client's agreement to those terms. This engagement letter can be the basis of a breach of contract action against the lawyer if the lawyer does not perform as the lawyer has promised.

E. Liability to Nonclients on the Basis of Professional Negligence

A lawyer can be responsible to a nonclient for professional negligence but only in rare circumstances. If the lawyer or the client, with the lawyer's knowledge, invites a third party to rely on the lawyer's opinion in a particular matter, the lawyer can be responsible to that third party. A court's recognition of such a claim cannot interfere with or conflict with the duties the lawyer owes to the client.

For example, Cindy Client may desire Lisa Lawyer's assistance in the sale of property. The sale may require Lisa to issue an opinion stating that Cindy's property is unencumbered. Cindy benefits from the issuance of the opinion letter because the sale can now occur—the buyer will now feel comfortable in agreeing to buy the property. It is also reasonable for the nonclient buyer to rely on Lisa's opinion letter. If Lisa's opinion letter is flawed as the result of professional negligence, Lisa may be responsible to the nonclient buyer for damages the buyer suffers.

Another typical setting in which lawyers may be responsible to nonclients is the situation in which the lawyer knows that the client intends for a third party to benefit from the lawyer's services. Perhaps Clint, an elderly client, seeks to have Lisa, his lawyer, draft a will leaving Clint's bounty to his daughter, Denise. If Lisa is professionally negligent in the drafting of the will, Lisa can be responsible to Denise for that negligence. As a practical matter, Clint, at that point, is no longer around to pursue a malpractice claim.

F. Agreements to Limit Liability to Clients

1. Prospective Agreements

a. General Rule

A lawyer might conclude that the risk of clients claiming malpractice is significant. A lawyer might seek to limit that malpractice liability potential. Such a lawyer might have a client agree to a statement like "Cindy Client will not pursue an action based on legal services rendered against Lisa Lawyer." Or perhaps the lawyer desires to limit the amount of liability for a mistake. The lawyer might make these liability-limiting provisions part of the initial engagement agreement.

While such provisions might be a good idea from the perspective of the lawyer, they are not such a great idea for the client. Unless the client or potential client has independent counsel for purposes of the agreement, any such prospective liability limitation violates Rule 1.8(h)(1)(DE) and thus is not permitted. Independent counsel is a lawyer not in the same firm with the lawyer seeking the agreement and not otherwise linked to the lawyer seeking the agreement.

Lawyers at the beginning of a lawyer-client relationship usually are not comfortable telling a new client that the lawyer wants the client to sign an agreement that requires the advice of yet another lawyer. The client may properly question the nature and quality of the representation the lawyer will provide.

There is also the possibility that the client may decide that the second lawyer should handle the original matter. This is especially true since that second lawyer will likely tell the client not to sign the liability-limiting agreement. Rule 1.8(h)(1)(DE), therefore, greatly limits the possibility of prospectively limiting liability.

The rationale for this rule is that a lawyer subject to no civil liability or limited civil liability may not represent the client competently and diligently. Clients also may not have the ability without assistance to understand all the potential issues that might arise in the future. These clients may not understand what they are agreeing to forego by agreeing to such a limitation. *See Chapter 21 Conflict of Interest Rules for Particular Situations.*

b. Arbitration Provisions

A lawyer may obtain a client's agreement to submit claims to arbitration if the jurisdiction has no prohibition of such agreements. A comment to Rule 1.8(DE) specifically states that the rule does not prohibit such agreements. The client must, of course, understand the implication of such an agreement for it to be proper and contractually enforceable. When the question of enforceability has come before the courts, the courts decide whether the provision is unconscionable, and thus unenforceable, by evaluating the understanding of the client and thus the disclosures made by the lawyer. *See, e.g., Hodges v. Reasonover*, 103 So. 3d 1069 (La. 2012) (court refused to enforce arbitration clause because lawyer did not explain and client did not understand that the clause was to apply to malpractice claims as well as fee disputes).

c. Limited Liability Forms of Practice

Lawyers often practice in limited liability entities. Lisa Lawyer may practice as Lisa Lawyer and Associates, LLC. "LLC" is an abbreviation for "limited liability company." Doing so does not violate any rule if the lawyer is personally responsible for his or her own conduct. This is true with a limited liability company.

The entity must, of course, follow the rules of the particular jurisdiction regarding notice of the liability limitation inherent in the practice form. Rule 7.5(d)(DE) forbids lawyers from implying that they are practicing as partners when that is not true. *See Chapter 45 Communications about Lawyer Services.* Lawyers practicing in limited liability entities must always indicate the form, as Lisa does with her firm name carrying the "LLC" designation. The entities and lawyers involved must maintain the proper levels of malpractice insurance as required by the particular state as well.

2. Settling a Claim

If a client already has a claim against a lawyer or has not yet made a claim but the lawyer perceives the possibility of a claim, the lawyer may want to settle the matter quickly to avoid the cost and unpleasantness sure to come. For example, Lisa Lawyer may know that she missed the statute of limitations but that Cindy does not yet know.

Rule 1.8(h)(2)(DE) provides that a lawyer may not settle such a matter with a client or former client unless the lawyer explains in writing the "desirability" of the client or former client obtaining the advice of independent counsel. In addition, the lawyer seeking the settlement agreement must give the client or former client reasonable time to consult with independent counsel. The requirement of informing the client of the "desirability" of independent counsel minimizes the possibility that the lawyer will exercise undue influence over the client in obtaining the agreement. Independent counsel is a lawyer not in the same firm with the lawyer seeking the agreement and not otherwise linked to the lawyer seeking the agreement. *See Chapter 21 Conflict of Interest Rules for Particular Situations.*

Related Sections of the *Restatement (Third) of the Law Governing Lawyers*

Sections 48–57

Checkpoints

- The primary basis for civil liability to clients is malpractice—an action based on professional negligence of the lawyer.
- To succeed on a malpractice claim, a person must prove that
    1. the lawyer owed a duty of care to the person,
    2. the lawyer breached that duty of care, and
    3. the breach caused damage to the party.

- A lawyer owes all persons with whom the lawyer is in a lawyer-client relationship a duty of care. That duty is to act with regard to the representation with a level of competence and diligence that would be exercised by a reasonable lawyer in similar circumstances.
- Because the lawyer-client relationship is a fiduciary one, clients may pursue breach of fiduciary duty claims against lawyers.
- A client may pursue a breach of contract action against a lawyer if the lawyer has failed to perform as promised in the engagement contract or other contract with the client.
- Lawyers are not liable for malpractice to persons with whom the lawyer is not in a lawyer-client relationship except in rare circumstances. Two primary settings for such liability are the following:
    1. the lawyer renders services to the client knowing that the client or the lawyer has invited a third party to rely on those services; and
    2. the lawyer renders services to the client knowing that the client intends for a third party to benefit from those services.
- A lawyer may not enter into an agreement with a client or potential client that prospectively limits the lawyer's liability to the client unless the client has independent counsel advising him or her on the merits and demerits of agreeing to the liability limitation.
- An agreement to arbitrate future malpractice claims is not a limitation on liability and is allowed with proper explanation of its effect.
- A lawyer may not enter into an agreement with a client or former client that settles an existing claim that the client may have against the lawyer unless the lawyer explains in writing that the client should seek the advice of independent counsel. The lawyer must give the client a reasonable opportunity to consult with independent counsel but such counsel need not actually be consulted.

Chapter 7

Ineffective Assistance of Counsel

Roadmap

- The Sixth Amendment right to assistance of counsel
- Requirements for proving ineffective assistance of counsel

A. The Sixth Amendment Basis

In addition to competence being an issue for lawyer discipline and malpractice liability, the constitutional standard of ineffective assistance of counsel also speaks to lawyer competence in the area of criminal defense representation. A defendant who suffers ineffective assistance of counsel may have the conviction or sentence set aside. A lawyer whose conduct amounts to ineffective assistance also almost certainly has violated the professional responsibility duty to represent the client competently. *See Chapter 5 Competence and Diligence.*

The Sixth Amendment to the United States Constitution provides that in a criminal prosecution, an accused person has the right to "have the Assistance of Counsel for his defence." The assistance of a lawyer is necessary to ensure that the broader promise of the Sixth Amendment, the right to a fair trial, can occur. The rationale is that, without the assistance of a lawyer, the adversarial testing process necessary for a fair trial is not likely to occur.

B. The Ineffective Assistance of Counsel Analysis

In 1984 in the case of *Strickland v. Washington,* 466 U.S. 668 (1984), the United States Supreme Court set out the proper analysis to use with a claim of ineffective assistance of counsel. The Court identified two separate elements of the claim that a defendant must prove in order to succeed on an ineffective assistance of counsel argument. First, the defendant must prove that the lawyer's conduct was not "reasonably effective assistance." *Id.* at 680. Second, the defendant must prove that "there is a reasonable probability that, but for counsel's unprofessional errors, the result of the proceeding would have been different." *Id.* at 688.

1. Lack of "Reasonably Effective Assistance"

In explaining the kind of lawyer conduct that would be ineffective, the Supreme Court in *Strickland* noted that a lawyer's conduct must be "outside the wide range of professionally competent assistance," *id.* at 692, and "below an objective standard of reasonableness." *Id.* at 688. A court must evaluate the lawyer's conduct using a standard of "reasonableness under prevailing professional norms." *Id.*

a. Strategic Judgments

Ineffective assistance claims based on tactical or strategic judgments of a lawyer made after proper investigation are generally unsuccessful unless the exercise of judgment is outside the range of reasonable lawyer conduct. For example, Larry Lawyer might decide not to obtain and use a presentence report because it would reveal Cindy Client's past criminal conduct and contradict Cindy's own statements to the court that she had no significant criminal history. Larry's decision does not constitute ineffective assistance of counsel unless it is unreasonable lawyer conduct. In determining reasonableness, Larry's exercise of judgment must be evaluated in view of the time he made that judgment and not with the benefit of hindsight.

b. Failure to Investigate

A failure to research the applicable law or a failure to investigate the facts of the situation can be a basis for a successful ineffective assistance claim if a reasonable lawyer would have done the research or conducted the investigation. Often a court concludes that a reasonable lawyer would have done the research or would have investigated the facts. This is especially true when the stakes are high. In *Hinton v. Alabama,* 134 S. Ct. 1081 (2014), the Supreme Court found a lawyer's representation deficient. The lawyer knew he needed additional funding to hire a qualified expert yet he did not investigate and find a statute that provided for funding.

A court is more likely to conclude that a lawyer has not acted reasonably if the lawyer fails to investigate mitigation evidence in a matter involving the death penalty. A court is likely to conclude that a reasonable lawyer would investigate mitigation evidence since the discovery of such evidence could help the defendant avoid the death penalty. For example, the Supreme Court, in *Rompilla v. Beard,* 545 U.S. 374 (2005), found a lawyer's conduct, in representing a defendant subject to the death penalty, to be below the standard of a reasonable lawyer. The lawyer neglected to examine a file about the defendant's prior conviction for rape and assault even though the lawyer knew that the prosecution would use the prior conviction and its violent circumstances as an aggravating factor that would justify imposition of the death penalty.

c. Plea Agreements

In recent years the Supreme Court has issued several opinions fleshing out the "reasonably effective assistance" constitutionally required in the context of plea agreements. In *Padilla v. Kentucky,* 559 U.S. 356 (2010), a lawyer advised the noncitizen defendant, a legal resident, about a plea deal but did not inform the defendant that a probable result of a guilty plea was deportation. The Court found a lack of "reasonably effective assistance." In *Lafler v. Cooper,* 132 S. Ct. 1376 (2012), the Court found a lack of "reasonably effective assistance" because the defendant followed the advice of his lawyer who urged the defendant to reject a plea deal. The lawyer's advice was based on an erroneous view of the applicable law. And in *Missouri v. Frye,* 132 S. Ct. 1399 (2012), the Court found a lack of "reasonably effective assistance" because counsel did not inform the defendant of a plea offer that might have been favorable for the defendant.

2. Prejudice to the Proceeding

a. Proving Prejudice

In addition to stating that the defendant must prove substandard conduct by a lawyer, the Supreme Court in *Strickland* clarified that the defendant also must prove prejudice to the proceeding. Prejudice, for purposes of an ineffective assistance of counsel claim, exists if the defendant can prove that "there is a reasonable probability that, but for counsel's unprofessional errors, the result of the proceeding would have been different." 466 U.S. at 694. The *Strickland* Court stated that there was sufficient prejudice if "absent the errors, the fact finder would have had a reasonable doubt." *Id.* at 695. In such a situation a court could conclude that the lawyer's error had deprived the defendant of a fair trial.

In the *Rompilla* case, the lawyer failed to examine a file about the defendant's prior conviction for rape and assault. If the lawyer had consulted the file, the lawyer would have become aware of potentially mitigating evidence about the defendant's childhood and mental health. Specifically, the lawyer would have discovered test results suggesting schizophrenia and other disorders and test results suggesting that the defendant had cognition capabilities at a third-grade level despite nine years of education. No other source available to the defendant's lawyer had pointed to these mitigation issues. With this information, post-conviction counsel unearthed evidence of an extraordinarily abusive childhood and mental illness. Because the jury in the sentencing proceeding was made aware of none of this evidence, the Supreme Court concluded that the likelihood that the jury would have reached a different conclusion regarding sentencing was enough to satisfy the prejudice prong of the ineffective assistance of counsel analysis. 545 U.S. at 390.

b. Presuming Prejudice

In certain situations, courts presume prejudice; prejudice need not be proved. This is true when the defendant suffers an actual or constructive denial of counsel's assistance for a critical stage of the proceeding. For example, a lawyer may not be present at trial. In such a situation, there is an entire failure to test the prosecution's case and so the denial of assistance calls into question the fairness of the trial and the reliability of the verdict.

A second situation of presumed prejudice is when the government interferes with counsel's assistance. Again, the fairness of the trial and the reliability of the verdict are suspect.

A third situation in which the defendant need not prove prejudice is if the lawyer labors under a conflict of interest. The *Strickland* Court noted that if the lawyer "actively represented conflicting interests," the defendant need only show that "an actual conflict of interest adversely affected his lawyer's performance." *Id.* at 692 (quoting Cuyler v. Sullivan, 446 U.S. 335, 348 (1980)).

Checkpoints

- The Sixth Amendment requires that a criminal defendant have effective assistance of counsel.
- Proof of ineffective assistance of counsel is a basis for having a conviction or sentence set aside.
- To prove ineffective assistance, one must prove
    1. lawyer conduct below the standard of reasonable professional norms and
    2. prejudice to the proceeding.
- Prejudice need not be proved if
    1. there is a complete denial of assistance at a critical stage of the proceeding,
    2. the government interferes with counsel's assistance, or
    3. the lawyer operates under a conflict of interest.
- If a lawyer operates under a conflict of interest, the defendant need not prove prejudice but must prove that the conflict "adversely affected [the] lawyer's performance."

Chapter 8

Scope of the Representation and Communication with the Client

Roadmap

- Rule 1.2(DE)
- Rule 1.4(DE)
- Defining the scope of a representation
- Decision-making within the lawyer-client relationship
- Prohibition of assisting a crime or fraud or counseling the client to commit a crime or fraud
- The duty to communicate with the client

A. Introduction

The rules of professional responsibility do not give detailed guidance about many facets of the day-to-day lawyer-client relationship. Rule 1.2(DE) contains several concepts, however, to give some general direction to lawyers about the framework of the relationship. In addition, Rule 1.4(DE) provides guidance about the necessary communication that must occur for this day-to-day relationship to accomplish successfully its goals.

B. The Scope of the Representation

Perhaps in a far-away land in a far-away time, a client engaged one lawyer or law firm to handle all of the client's legal needs. These days it is common for a client to engage different lawyers for different legal needs. For example,

Big Corporation might engage Larry Lawyer, a lawyer with expertise in employment issues, to handle employment matters. Big Corporation might engage Lisa Lawyer, a lawyer with expertise in product liability law, to defend it in product liability matters. Big Corporation might even divide its matters further. Big Corporation might ask Lisa to handle the pretrial preemption issues in product liability cases because Lisa has an exceptional record with preemption in past cases. Big Corporation might ask Lance, a lawyer with general trial experience, to handle the product liability matters once the courts rule on the preemption issues.

A client or lawyer can limit the scope of a representation in other ways as well. A client might want the lawyer to pursue only certain avenues of legal argument. The lawyer might agree to represent the client if only certain avenues of legal argument are to be used. A client might want the lawyer to conduct the representation by foregoing certain costly processes. Cindy Client might ask Lisa Lawyer to bring a breach of contract action against Fred. Because Cindy and Fred were once friends, Cindy might request that Lisa avoid certain legal arguments that might embarrass Fred. Perhaps Cindy asks that Lisa not pursue any allegation of fraud. Cindy also might ask Lisa to handle the matter without taking more than three depositions because Cindy does not want to pay for costly depositions.

Rule 1.2(c)(DE) simply provides that a lawyer may limit the scope of a representation if the limitation is reasonable and the client gives "informed consent." "Informed consent," as defined by Rule 1.0(e)(DE), requires that the client consent after being informed of the "material risks" of the conduct and the "available alternatives" to the conduct. Thus, Larry may agree to represent Big Corporation on labor matters. Lisa may agree to handle product liability preemption issues and Lance may agree to handle the product liability matters after resolution of the preemption issues. Lisa might agree to pursue the breach of contract claim for Cindy against Fred without raising fraud as an issue. Lisa could agree to the deposition limitation, however, only if the limitation was reasonable in that it allowed Lisa to render competent legal representation with the limitation.

Often the client dictates these representation limitations and so the requirement of informed client consent is not a problem. Still, the lawyer must fully explain the alternatives and risks of such a path to ensure "informed consent." If the lawyer is the source of the limitation, the lawyer must take special care to explain the limitation to the client and obtain "informed consent." Note that Rule 1.5(b)(NE) provides that generally a lawyer must communicate the scope of the representation to the client, along with fee information, at or near the beginning of a representation. *See Chapter 9 Fees.*

C. Decision-Making Authority within the Representation

A very murky area of the lawyer-client relationship is the roles the lawyer and client should play in the process of decision-making. Whereas in the past the lawyer may have been viewed as the superior decision-maker who needed to take care of and shepherd the less-able client, today there is more recognition of the client's ability to make all sorts of decisions about the representation. One reason the area of decision-making is murky is that the lawyer-client relationship is also one of agent and principal and thus agency principles overlay the professional responsibility rules. The rules of professional responsibility themselves are not very elucidating.

A basic concept in this area is that a client is in charge of the ultimate goals of the representation. Rule 1.2(a)(DE) begins by stating that a lawyer "shall abide by a client's decisions concerning the objectives of representation." The rule then specifies that the client must decide the following important matters concerning the representation:

- in a civil matter, whether to settle;
- in a criminal matter, the plea;
- in a criminal matter, whether to waive a jury trial; and
- in a criminal matter, whether to testify.

In regard to each of these specific issues and in regard to objectives in general, a lawyer must communicate with the client as required by Rule 1.4(DE) and counsel the client about the possible courses of action. While the rule clearly states that the client is the decider of these issues, the client may, as any other principal may in an agent and principal relationship, give the lawyer agent the authority to decide such matters. Comment three to Rule 1.2(DE) acknowledges that the client may give the lawyer authority to "take specific action on the client's behalf without further consultation." Of course, the client may revoke this authority just as any other principal may revoke authority earlier granted. Some courts, when the question is the validity of a settlement agreement entered into by a lawyer, seem to indicate that a client may authorize a lawyer to accept a specific offer of settlement or settlement within a certain range but that a client cannot authorize more generally. This is inconsistent with the usual power of a principal to grant authority to an agent.

In cases involving the death penalty, the application of the rule that the client is the ultimate decision-maker regarding objectives is particularly bothersome to some. Occasionally, a defendant instructs his or her lawyer to not present mitigating evidence and in effect concedes a sentence of death. If the defendant is competent, some courts give effect to the client's wishes on the theory that the decision the defendant is making is one relating to the essence of the representation, an objective, and is thus a decision very properly the defendant's. For example, in *Red Dog v. State*, 625 A.2d 245 (Del. 1993), a case involving a competent defendant who wished to accept the death penalty, the court stated, "A defendant's wish to forego further appeals and accept the death penalty, like other decisions relating to the objectives of litigation, is essentially that of the client, whose decision the attorney must respect." *Id.* at 247.

Traditionally, just as the goals or objectives of the representation were seen as the choice of the client, the means of achieving the objectives were seen as the lawyer's decision. Rule 1.2(a)(DE) does not explicitly grant that power to the lawyer. The rule states that the lawyer must "consult with the client as to the means" to be used. The rule refers to Rule 1.4(DE) with regard to the proper communication and consultation with the client. Comment two to Rule 1.2(DE) states that with regard to certain means decisions such as "technical, legal and tactical" matters, clients usually defer to their lawyers. The comment does not state that the lawyer has the right to take a path contrary to the wishes of the client on such matters. The comment states that lawyers usually listen to client wishes on matters of expenses and effects on third persons. If the client and the lawyer disagree on a resolution of a means question, the comment states, "this Rule does not prescribe how such disagreements are to be resolved." The comment directs the lawyer to seek help from other applicable law. If the lawyer and the client reach an impasse, the lawyer may withdraw under Rule 1.16(b)(4)(DE) or the client may discharge the lawyer. *See Chapter 11 Refusing to Form a Lawyer-Client Relationship or Ending a Lawyer-Client Relationship.* This approach places the client squarely in the middle of decision-making with regard to all matters of the representation.

Establishing a lawyer-client relationship for purposes of a matter does impliedly authorize the lawyer to take certain actions on behalf of the client. The nature of the authorization depends on the nature of the representation. If Cindy Client agrees that Lisa Lawyer will represent Cindy in an ongoing matter filed in United States District Court for the Southern District of New York, Cindy is impliedly authorizing Lisa to appear in court on behalf of Cindy in this matter.

D. No Lawyer Involvement in Criminal or Fraudulent Activity of the Client

A rare bright line rule is that a lawyer may not assist a client in criminal or fraudulent conduct. Likewise, a lawyer may not counsel a client to commit a crime or fraud or to engage in conduct that is criminal or fraudulent. After stating these prohibitions, Rule 1.2(d)(DE) clarifies that a lawyer may explain the consequences of possible courses of action to the client. A lawyer also may assist a client in determining whether particular conduct is criminal or fraudulent and in determining the validity, scope, and meaning of any possibly applicable laws. As defined by Rule 1.0(d)(DE), fraudulent conduct is conduct that would constitute fraud under the laws of the jurisdiction and which a person does with the "purpose to deceive." The unanswered question is whether a lawyer's conduct rises (or falls!) to the level of assisting the client in or counseling the client to commit the problematic conduct.

Cindy Client might present a possible course of action to Lisa Lawyer and ask for Lisa's advice. Lisa should explain the legal consequences of the conduct set out by Cindy. Lisa might conclude that the proposed conduct would constitute a crime. Lisa may and should explain this to Cindy but must take care not to indicate in any way that Cindy should pursue the course of action proposed.

Perhaps Lisa Lawyer has assisted Cindy in raising capital for the marketing of an invention. Lisa assisted in the preparation of documents Cindy presented to potential investors. One of the documents prepared by Lisa states that Cindy has the patent on the invention. Lisa later learns that Cindy does not have the patent and that obtaining the patent will be difficult if not impossible. Lisa learns that Cindy has intentionally misled her and the investors because she knows that she will not be able to interest investors otherwise. Several investors have already committed to investing on a continuing basis. Cindy continues to seek other potential investors. In this situation, Lisa has not acted improperly because she did not *know* that she was assisting a crime or fraud. Lisa must withdraw from the representation of Cindy, however, because her continued involvement in light of her current knowledge and the documents she prepared would be assistance in a crime or fraud in violation of Rule 1.2(d)(DE). Rule 1.16(a)(DE) demands withdrawal when a representation would result in a violation of the rules of professional conduct. *See Chapter 11 Refusing to Form a Lawyer-Client Relationship or Ending a Lawyer-Client Relationship.* Because of the continuing nature of the investments already committed on the basis of the incorrect documents prepared by Lisa, Lisa may need to disaffirm the documents and give notice of her withdrawal. In addition, Lisa may have a duty under Rule 4.1(DE) to disclose the problem to the investors. *See Chapter 35 Truthfulness to Third Parties.*

E. Representing a Client Is Not an Endorsement of the Client's Activities

A lawyer does not endorse a client's views or actions simply because the lawyer represents the client. Rule 1.2(b)(DE) states this proposition. This principle is a recognition that even people with distasteful beliefs or people who have committed distasteful acts should have legal representation. This concept is consistent with the notion inherent in Rule 6.2(DE) that a lawyer has a duty to represent certain clients when appointed to do so even though the lawyer otherwise may not have chosen that path. Rule 6.2(DE) provides that a lawyer who is appointed to represent a client may not seek to avoid the appointment except in very narrow circumstances. *See Chapter 11 Refusing to Form a Lawyer-Client Relationship or Ending the Lawyer-Client Relationship.* This demand to accept appointments is more acceptable if the lawyer is not judged by the acts or beliefs of his or her client.

Unfortunately, members of the public do not always view lawyers in light of this principle. Often, the public paints the lawyer with the same brush as the client. If Lisa Lawyer represents someone with racist beliefs, some members of the public judge Lisa as racist as well. This is a burden lawyers bear.

F. Communicating with the Client

1. Communication and Explanation

The lawyer-client relationship as envisioned in Rule 1.2(DE) cannot operate successfully without significant communication between the lawyer and the client. Rule 1.4(DE) requires that a lawyer keep the client informed about matters in general and that the lawyer explain issues to the client so that the client not only knows that a decision must be made but also understands the implications of the decision. The client then can make informed decisions and an informed contribution to any conversation about the direction of the representation.

2. When the Client Must Give "Informed Consent"

Many of the rules of professional conduct require the client's "informed consent" with regard to various issues. For example, Rule 1.8(a)(DE) requires "informed consent" of the client for any business transaction between the client and the lawyer. If Lisa Lawyer wishes to buy Cindy Client's beach bungalow, Cindy must give "informed consent." Rule 1.0(e)(DE) defines "informed consent" as agreement to a course of action "after the lawyer has communicated adequate information and explanation about the material risks of and reasonably available alternatives" to the course of action. Rule 1.4(a)(DE) requires that the lawyer "promptly inform" the client regarding matters requiring "informed consent."

3. Communication about Objectives

Since Rule 1.2(DE) provides that the client sets the objectives of a representation, a lawyer must communicate with the client in a manner that allows such. In particular, the lawyer must take care to explain issues to the client so that the client may make informed decisions. The lawyer should tailor the explanation to the client's needs. A client who is a sophisticated user of legal services may require less explanation from the lawyer than a less sophisticated client. A client whose contact with the outside lawyer is an in-house lawyer needs much less explanation.

4. Communication about Means

A lawyer must "reasonably consult" with a client about the means used to further the client's objectives. If Lisa Lawyer represents Cindy Client in a personal injury matter, Lisa should consult with Cindy about steps to take to move the matter to resolution. Once the trial begins, however, circumstances may not afford an opportunity for Lisa to discuss certain matters with Cindy before Lisa must act on those matters. Not consulting with Cindy is reasonable in that situation.

5. Communication about Status

A lawyer must keep the client "reasonably informed" about the client's matter. In the context of litigation, a lawyer must notify the client about actions taken by the lawyer, the opposition, and the court. A lawyer does not necessarily have to notify the client of every small event. The rule of reason governs this duty to inform. Generally, this duty requires a lawyer to communicate with the client about all significant developments.

6. When the Client Requests Information

A lawyer must "promptly" provide information to the client when the client requests such information if the request is "reasonable." If Lisa Lawyer keeps Cindy Client reasonably informed, Cindy is not likely to make a request for information. But if Cindy does make a request, Lisa must respond with the information or must explain when she will be able to provide the information.

Regardless of the professional responsibility duty to communicate with the client, the lawyer must be mindful that a failure to timely respond to a request for information will not please the client. If Lisa Lawyer does not keep Cindy Client informed about her matter and does not respond to Cindy's requests for information, Cindy will be displeased with the quality of Lisa's representation. Cindy might decide to discharge Lisa and engage a lawyer who is more responsive. Cindy also might consider a malpractice action or a discipline complaint against Lisa.

7. Communication about the Lawyer's Ethical Boundaries

A client may believe that his or her lawyer must do or will do whatever the client requests. Perhaps Larry Lawyer is defending Big Corporation against a claim that Big Corporation knowingly and illegally bribed officials of foreign governments. Big Corporation shows Larry several damning documents and instructs Larry to make sure that the opposition does not discover the documents. Rule 1.4(a)(DE) provides that Larry must clarify with Big Corporation that he will fight disclosure within the bounds of the law and the rules of professional conduct. Larry must tell Big Corporation that if disclosure is ultimately required, however, Larry cannot conceal, destroy, or alter the documents.

8. Not Sharing Information with the Client

The rule contains no provision specifically allowing a lawyer to withhold information from a client. Comment seven to Rule 1.4(DE) notes, however, two situations in which a lawyer could be acting properly by withholding information from a client. A lawyer would be proper in not disclosing information to the client if a court forbids the disclosure or if disclosure would harm the client.

a. A Court Forbids Disclosure to the Client

In a litigation matter a court might issue an order forbidding a lawyer from sharing certain information with a client. This might occur, for example, in a matter involving trade secrets of a competitor of the client. In such a matter, the court might allow limited disclosure to the lawyer but forbid disclosure to the client. The lawyer would then be acting properly by not disclosing the information to the client.

b. Disclosure Would Harm the Client

A lawyer might reasonably believe that immediate disclosure might harm the client. A delay in disclosure could be justified in such circumstances. For example, a lawyer might delay revealing a psychiatric report of the client to the client until the client is mentally ready to deal with it. Such a delay would not violate the rules of professional conduct.

Related Sections of the *Restatement (Third) of the Law Governing Lawyers*

Sections 19, 20, 21, 22, 23, and 94

Checkpoints

- A lawyer and a client may enter into an agreement limiting the scope of the representation but the lawyer cannot agree to an unreasonable limitation that would prevent competent representation. The client must give "informed consent" to the limitation.
- Within the lawyer-client relationship, a client has the decision-making authority with regard to goals or objectives of the representation.
- In the civil context, the decision whether to settle is the client's decision.
- In the criminal context,
    1. the decision regarding the plea,
    2. the decision regarding waiving a jury trial, and
    3. the decision to testify

    are the client's decisions.

- By engaging a lawyer for a representation, the client impliedly authorizes the lawyer to take certain actions on behalf of the client.
- A client may grant a lawyer authority beyond that implied by the engagement.
- A lawyer must communicate with the client so that the client can make decisions about objectives and must "reasonably consult" with the client about decisions about the means of achieving the objectives of the client.
- A lawyer may not assist a client in a crime or fraud and may not counsel a client to commit a crime or fraud.
- A lawyer may discuss and counsel a client about the legal consequences of possible courses of conduct.
- A lawyer does not endorse a client's beliefs or actions by virtue of the representation of that client.
- A lawyer must explain matters to the client so that the client can make informed decisions.
- A lawyer must "keep the client reasonably informed" about a matter.
- A lawyer must promptly inform the client about matters requiring "informed consent."
- A lawyer must respond "promptly" to a client's "reasonable requests for information."
- When a lawyer knows the client expects the lawyer to perform in a manner contrary to the rules of professional conduct or other law, the lawyer must explain the proper bounds of lawyer conduct to the client.

Chapter 9

Fees

Roadmap

- Rule 1.5(NE)
- Rule 1.8(a)(DE)
- Required communications relating to the fee arrangement
- Characteristics of a reasonable fee
- Contingency fees
- Limits on sharing fees
- Fee refunds
- Billing

A. Procedural Requirements for Fees

1. Generally

Most lawyers these days must charge their clients for their professional services. Yet lawyers are fiduciaries of their clients. This means that even when the fee arrangements are made at the very beginning of the relationship, the fee arrangements are generally not made in a typical bargaining setting.

Even so, the professional responsibility rules place very few restrictions on the fees lawyers charge clients and the process used to develop the fee arrangement. In most matters lawyers may charge by the hour or agree to a contingency fee. They may charge flat fees and they may be paid a flat fee with a bonus or premium for certain results. Clients may pay fees in advance of the work to be done or after the representation is complete. The possible fee frameworks abound. The issue of fees is often a source of disgruntled clients, however, perhaps because clients do not fully understand how they are being charged or perhaps because clients do not understand exactly what the lawyer does to earn the fee.

2. Specific Requirements for Fees That are Not Contingent

Not surprisingly given the fiduciary nature of the lawyer-client relationship, the professional responsibility rules require that a lawyer clearly discuss the issue of fees with the lawyer's client. Rule 1.5(b)(NE) deals with the disclosure that must occur with regard to the fee arrangement.

a. Scope of the Representation

First, the lawyer must be clear with the client about the scope of the representation for which the client incurs the fee. In other words, if Larry Lawyer agrees to handle a worker compensation matter for Cindy Client for a flat $500 fee, Larry must make clear to Cindy that the fee does not cover representation with regard to any related personal injury tort action. *See Chapter 8 Scope of the Representation and Communication with the Client.*

b. Basis of the Fee and Expenses Charged to the Client

Second, the lawyer must communicate the basis or rate of the fee to the client. Thus, Larry Lawyer must explain, for example, that Cindy Client will be required to pay on the basis of the number of hours Larry works on the matter and that Larry keeps track of his time in tenths of the hour. Larry must also state the hourly rate that he charges. If Cindy Client is to be responsible for expenses, Larry must disclose this to Cindy and explain to her the customary expenses in a matter like Cindy's.

c. A Writing is Preferred

This disclosure and explanation *should* be in writing but is not required to be in writing. Proving the existence of disclosures and explanations that are not in writing is a daunting task, so as a matter of business and ethics, a writing is best *for the lawyer.* In contrast, contingency fee agreements must be in writing and the client *must* sign the writing.

d. Communication at the Beginning of the Relationship

These fee disclosures and explanations must occur at the beginning of the representation or within a reasonable time of the beginning of the representation. The goal is to prevent a representation from being well under way before the client discovers the nature of the fee. If the representation is in progress, the client may feel that avoiding an unsatisfactory fee arrangement by moving to a different lawyer is impossible.

e. *The Regularly Represented Client*

When a lawyer agrees to handle a new matter for a current or regular client, the rules do not require the same disclosure as is the case with a new client. The lawyer need not disclose and explain the fee arrangement if the arrangement is on the same basis or rate that the parties have used in the past. Larry Lawyer may represent Big Store in all slip and fall cases. In these cases Larry charges on an hourly basis at a set hourly rate. Larry may take a new matter from Big Store and need not restate the terms of the fee if the terms are the same as the terms for earlier slip and fall cases. Larry may decide to explain the terms simply to prevent any misunderstanding.

3. Specific Requirements for Contingency Fees

a. *The Fee Agreement Must be in Writing*

Not all fee agreements must be in writing, but if the fee is contingent, the rule requires that the fee agreement be in a writing and that the client sign the writing. This formalism better ensures that the client understands the true nature of the fee.

b. *The Writing Must Explain the Details of the Fee*

The rule requires that the writing explain the details of the contingency fee. If Larry Lawyer plans to represent Cindy Client on a contingency fee basis, the writing containing the fee agreement, which Cindy must sign, must explain how Larry will calculate his fee. For example, Larry and Cindy may agree that Larry's fee will equal twenty percent of any recovery by judgment or settlement before trial, twenty-five percent of any recovery by judgment or settlement after trial begins, and thirty percent of any recovery by judgment or settlement once an appeal is filed. The writing must contain this sort of detail.

In addition, the writing must inform Cindy of the method of handling expenses. Cindy might think that a contingent fee representation means that she pays nothing unless she is successful. If Cindy is to be responsible for expenses even if she is unsuccessful, the writing must explain this and identify the expenses for which Cindy will be responsible. Second, the writing must explain which expenses Larry will subtract from any recovery. Third, the writing must state whether Larry will deduct expenses from the total recovery before calculating Larry's fee or rather that Cindy must pay the expenses from her share of the recovery.

c. *After a Matter Concludes, a Lawyer Must Provide a Written Calculation of the Fee to the Client*

After a contingent fee matter ends, a lawyer must provide the client with a written statement of the fee and the ultimate recovery for the client. The written statement must explain how the lawyer calculated the amounts. Implicit in this requirement is the additional requirement that the initial written statement of the method of calculation is the method of calculation used by the lawyer after the recovery and reflected in the later writing.

B. Fees Must Be Reasonable

Rule 1.5(a)(NE) states a very basic requirement regarding fees that takes into account the fiduciary nature of the relationship of lawyer and client. The rule states that a lawyer's fee must bc a reasonable fee and that the expenses a lawyer charges to a client must be reasonable as well. Lawyers are not disciplined often for subjecting a client to an unreasonable charge but, occasionally, they are. For example, in *In re Fordham,* 668 N.E.2d 816 (Mass. 1996), the court found excessive a fee of over $50,000 for a successful challenge to a charge of operating a vehicle under the influence.

1. Factors Regarding the Reasonableness of a Fee

Rule 1.5(a)(NE) provides a nonexclusive list of factors relevant in determining the reasonableness of the fee. The factors are:

(1) "the time and labor required,"
(2) "the novelty ... of the questions involved,"
(3) the "difficulty of the questions involved,"
(4) the expertise needed,
(5) "the likelihood, if apparent to the client, that the acceptance" of the representation will cause the lawyer to not be able to handle another representation,
(6) the customary fee other lawyers in the geographic area charge for like services,
(7) the amount of money at issue,
(8) the results,
(9) the time requirements caused by the client or the situation,
(10) "the nature and length of the professional relationship with the client,"
(11) the expertise and ability of the lawyer doing the work,

(12) the reputation of the lawyer doing the work, and
(13) the fixed or contingent nature of the fee.

If Larry is a very experienced medical malpractice plaintiff's lawyer, Larry's fee may be reasonable even though it greatly exceeds what another lawyer with less experience might charge. If the fee is contingent, a larger fee might be reasonable because the lawyer takes the risk that there will be no recovery and therefore no fee payment at all. Perhaps a matter must be dealt with within three days and will require around-the-clock efforts by the lawyer during those seventy-two hours. A higher than average fee clearly would be reasonable in such a time-pressure situation.

2. Reasonable Expenses

The requirement that the expenses charged to the client be reasonable means that a lawyer cannot use copying and other sorts of expenses incurred within the law office as a means of generating profit. The lawyer may charge only a reasonable amount in light of the cost of the service to the lawyer. *ABA Formal Opinion 93-379 (1993)* opines that absent an agreement to the contrary, in-house expenses such as copying should not exceed the actual cost of making the copy along with a reasonable allocation of overhead such as a share of the photocopier operator's salary. The *Opinion* also notes that in the case of disbursements such as a court reporter's fee, in absence of an agreement on the matter, the cost charged to the client should be the court reporter's fee without any surcharge.

C. Contingency Fee Availability

A lawyer may not be paid on a contingent basis in a criminal matter. In addition, a lawyer cannot be paid on a contingent basis in a domestic relations matter if the contingency is obtaining a divorce or the contingency is the amount of a property settlement or alimony or support in a divorce.

While the criminal law prohibition lacks a strong rationale, the domestic relations rationale is that a lawyer working on a contingent basis may inhibit the rekindling of the marriage. Because there is a public policy in favor of marriage, a contingency arrangement that tends to inhibit reconciliation does not further that public policy. The prohibition generally applies to appeals of domestic relations matters as well. The prohibition does not apply, generally, to later enforcement actions. The thought is that the marriage, by that point, is beyond reconciliation.

In all other situations, a lawyer may fashion a contingency fee arrangement as a method of payment. 1.8(i)(DE) prohibits a lawyer from acquiring a proprietary interest in a cause of action the lawyer is handling or the subject matter of the litigation. Yet the rule specifically exempts contingency fee representation from this prohibition. *See Chapter 21 Conflict of Interest Rules for Particular Situations.* Contingency fees are most often used when the litigation carries with it the potential to create a positive recovery. This is not a requirement, however. So a lawyer could enter into a fee contingent on how much money the lawyer saves the defendant client.

D. Taking an Interest in a Client as a Fee or Taking a Security Interest in a Client

Rule 1.5(a)(NE) provides the procedural requirements for the initial fee arrangement. Rule 1.8(a)(DE) deals with the requirements for a lawyer doing business with a client. Rule 1.8(a)(DE) does not apply to the initial fee arrangement because the initial fee arrangement is at a time when there is a fledgling lawyer-client relationship. *ABA Formal Opinion 00-418 (2000)* has clarified, however, that the rule does apply if, in the initial arrangement, the lawyer is taking an interest in the client as a means of payment. *ABA Formal Opinion 02-427 (2002)* states that Rule 1.8(a)(DE) also applies to a transaction in which a lawyer obtains a contractual security interest to secure a fee.

Rule 1.8(a)(DE) requires the following:

(1) the "transaction and terms" are "fair and reasonable" to the client,
(2) the "transaction and terms" are "fully disclosed" to the client,
(3) the "transaction and terms" are "transmitted in writing in a manner which can be reasonably understood by the client,"
(4) the client is advised in writing of the "desirability of seeking" the advice of independent counsel,
(5) the client has "reasonable opportunity to seek the advice of independent counsel," and
(6) "the client gives informed consent, in a writing signed by the client to the essential terms of the transaction and the lawyer's role" in the deal.

See Chapter 21 Conflict of Interest Rules for Particular Situations. Following Rule 1.8(a)(DE)'s procedures does not ensure that a court will enforce the fee agreement, but compliance with the rule does ensure that the lawyer will not be subject to discipline. Following the procedures of the rule also increases the likelihood that a court will enforce the fee agreement.

E. Modifications of Fee Agreements

Recognizing that sometimes fee agreements must be modified, *ABA Formal Opinion 11-458 (2011)* states that modification of an existing fee agreement is permissible if reasonable at the time of the modification and if the client understands and accepts the modification. The lawyer must explain the modification to the client and must tell the client that the lawyer will continue the representation even if the client does not agree to the fee modification. The *Opinion* notes that unless there has been an unanticipated change of circumstances, a fee change to increase the lawyer's compensation will not likely be reasonable or enforceable. A fee modification involving a lawyer acquiring an interest in the client's business or nonmonetary assets must abide by Rule 1.8(a) (DE)'s procedures for doing business with a client. *See Chapter 21 Conflict of Interest Rules for Particular Situations.*

A typical reception for a fee modification is that in *In re Hefron,* 771 N.E.2d 1157 (Ind. 2002), the fee agreement provided that the lawyer would be paid on an hourly basis. The lawyer was to recover assets belonging to an estate. After the lawyer realized that the asset recovery was a simple task, the lawyer asked the client to agree to a contingency fee arrangement. The new arrangement would insure that the lawyer would be paid handsomely. The court found that under the modified fee agreement the fee was unreasonable. The court also found that the lawyer violated Rule 1.8(a) by renegotiating the fee unfairly at a time when the lawyer-client relationship was in place. The lawyer violated Rule 1.8(a) in that the second fee agreement was unfair, important facts were not disclosed, and the lawyer did not give his client the opportunity to consult with independent counsel.

F. Sharing Fees with Other Lawyers

There is no restriction on the sharing of fees within a firm. If lawyers are not in the same firm, Rule 1.5(e)(NE) forbids dividing the proceeds of a single billing except in two situations: a division according to work done and a situation of shared responsibility.

1. A Division According to Work Done

First, lawyers can divide a fee in accordance with the work actually performed by the lawyers. If Cindy Client comes to Larry Lawyer, the lawyer who in the past represented Cindy in a personal injury matter, and asks Larry to represent her in a tax matter, Larry sagely might suggest to Cindy that Tom Tax Lawyer would be better for the work. Cindy might ask Larry to oversee Tom since she trusts Larry and does not know Tom. If so, Larry's bill might have an entry for oversight time by him as well as an entry for Tom's time spent completing the substantive tax work. Larry would then forward Tom's portion of the compensation to him. The total fee must be reasonable. Cindy must agree to this arrangement and her agreement must be "confirmed in writing." This means, according to Rule 1.0(b)(DE), that Cindy's consent must be in writing or the writing must confirm that oral consent has been given.

2. Shared Responsibility

Lawyers who are not in the same firm may divide fees in a way other than according to the share of the work done only if the lawyers agree to be responsible for each other. This means that Larry and Tom might agree to split the fee equally though they do not perform equal work. If they do this, Tom is responsible for Larry's actions in malpractice and Larry is likewise responsible for Tom's actions. Not many lawyers want to agree to be responsible for another lawyer outside of the law firm context. If Larry and Tom want to take this path, the client, Cindy, must agree to the division. Her agreement must be "confirmed in writing." Cindy must agree to this arrangement and her agreement must be "confirmed in writing." Larry and Tom must explain to Cindy not only that they are sharing a fee but also they must tell her the share each will receive. Of course, the overall fee the lawyers charge the client must be reasonable.

3. No Other Referral Fees Allowed

A fee paid to another lawyer not in the lawyer's firm for the referral of a client or matter is not permitted if it does not fit within one of the two exceptions to Rule 1.5(e) (NE). Also, Rule 5.4(a)(NE) and Rule 7.2(NE) clarify that a lawyer may not pay a referral fee to a nonlawyer. Rule 7.2(NE) does allow a nonexclusive reciprocal referral arrangement with other lawyers or nonlawyer professionals as long as the client is aware of the referral agreement. *See Chapter 39 Professional Independence* and *Chapter 45 Communications about Lawyer Services.*

G. The Nonrefundable Fee

Lawyers sometimes refer to a fee as nonrefundable. One thing is clear. The fee is not nonrefundable simply because the lawyer labels it so. In some jurisdictions, a nonrefundable fee may not be possible. In other jurisdictions a fee may be nonrefundable but only to the extent it is reasonable as all fees are required to be by Rule 1.5(a)(NE). A nonrefundable fee might be reasonable even if the lawyer does no work if it is a payment for lost opportunity or a payment to stand available. Such amounts might be reasonable because they are earned when the lawyer-client relationship is formed. But whatever the situation and whatever the lawyer calls the fee, it is not nonrefundable if it is not a reasonable fee for services provided.

Some courts seem to say that no fee can be nonrefundable. Such a court is very skeptical of any claim that a fee is not refundable because of the concern that clients, after paying an initial, nonrefundable fee, will feel overwhelming economic pressure to not discharge that lawyer even if the client loses confidence in the lawyer. The concern is that the fee arrangement infringes on the client's right to a lawyer of the client's choice. In the case of *In re Cooperman,* 633 N.E.2d 1069 (N.Y. 1994), a New York court expressed this concern, stating that nonrefundable fee agreements "diminish the core of the fiduciary relationship by substantially altering and economically chilling the client's unbridled prerogative to walk away from the lawyer." *Id.* at 1072. The *Cooperman* court appeared to hold nonrefundable fee agreements unenforceable because such agreements contradict this important public policy.

1. The Advance Fee

Sometimes an agreement requires a client to pay an amount at the beginning of the representation and designates that amount as nonrefundable. Such an agreement might then provide that the client will be billed for the lawyer's service on an hourly basis. When the amount billed exceeds the amount paid, the client must pay an additional amount. Courts generally have noted that the allegedly nonrefundable amount is really just an advance fee—an hourly fee paid in advance. Sometimes courts call this a special retainer. Often lawyers refer to all sorts of fees paid at the beginning of the representation as retainers so use of that term is confusing rather than helpful.

Many courts have determined that such a fee is not nonrefundable until the lawyer has worked all of the hours necessary to earn the advance fee. Larry Lawyer might require Cindy Client to pay $10,000 at the beginning of the representation. The fee agreement may state that the fee is nonrefundable and that Larry will bill hourly at the rate of $200 per hour which will be charged against the $10,000. If Cindy pays the fee and then terminates the representation before Larry works 50 hours, the unearned fee is refundable. To not refund the unearned amount is to violate Rule 1.16(d)(DE), which requires that the lawyer return unearned fees to the client at the conclusion of the representation. *See Chapter 11 Refusing to Form a Lawyer-Client Relationship or Ending a Lawyer-Client Relationship.*

In this situation, the lawyer should deposit the advance fee in the client trust account until the lawyer works the hours. Only then does the advance fee become the property of the lawyer such that the lawyer may and should transfer the funds to the lawyer's own account. To do otherwise is to violate Rule 1.15(a)(NE), which requires that the property of the client be kept separate from the property of the lawyer. *See Chapter 10 Dealing with the Property of Clients and Third Parties.*

2. A Payment for Lost Opportunity Cost

Another type of fee may be a payment for lost opportunity cost. This is not an advance to cover hours later worked. Rather, it is a payment by the client for the lost opportunity of the lawyer to represent others. The lawyer incurs this cost by agreeing to represent the client. The lawyer incurs the cost when he or she enters into the representation agreement so the lawyer earns it at that time. Thus, the fee is nonrefundable because the lawyer earns it upon agreeing to handle the representation. If the fee is earned when paid, Larry should deposit it in his own account, not the client trust account. Even so, the fee must be a reasonable payment for the lost opportunity.

Perhaps Big Bank asks Larry Lawyer to represent it in a commercial litigation matter. Larry Lawyer often represents Big Bank and National Bank. Because Larry Lawyer cannot represent National Bank in the matter if he represents Big Bank because the interests of the banks may be adverse, Larry may ask Big Bank to pay $10,000 at the beginning of the representation as a nonrefundable payment for lost opportunity. Such a fee can be nonrefundable.

3. A Payment to Be Available

Sometimes a client pays a fee for the lawyer to be available for the client's needs for a certain period of time. If the need should arise, the lawyer bills the client for the work done as an additional amount. For example, Big Bank might pay Larry Lawyer a fee to ensure that Larry is available and will have no conflicts if Big Bank needs Larry's assistance in regulatory matters. Some argue that Larry earns this sort of fee when Big Bank pays it. But if Larry does not do as promised and does not stand ready for the entire contracted time, a court could conclude that even this payment is partially refundable because Larry did not fully earn it; it is not reasonable in that circumstance.

4. Flat Fees

Lawyers may charge flat fees. Is a fee nonrefundable if the lawyer requires payment of the flat fee at the beginning of the representation? If Larry charges Cindy Client a $10,000 flat fee for a matter, payable at the start of the representation, and if Cindy terminates that representation short of completion of the matter, a court might reasonably find that Larry has not earned the entire fee. Larry would be required to return the unearned portion of the fee pursuant to Rule 1.16(d)(DE).

H. Billing Honesty

In the process of presenting and explaining the fee arrangement to the client and in the process of collecting the fee, lawyers always must be mindful of Rule 8.4(c)(DE). Rule 8.4(c)(DE) states that a lawyer must not "engage in conduct involving dishonesty, fraud, deceit or misrepresentation." *See Chapter 48 General Misconduct.*

Occasionally, lawyers run afoul of this rule when communicating about fees or dealing with fees. Unfortunately, the result is damage not only to the particular client, but to lawyers in general. A 2002 report of the American Bar Association Section on Litigation entitled *Public Perception of Lawyers Consumer Research Findings,* noted that there is a direct connection between the public's low opinion of lawyers and fees. The report stated that "the greatest number of complaints arise around lawyers' fees.... Lawyers are often not upfront about their fees; and are unwilling to account for their charges or hours." The report noted client confusion about how lawyers bill and stated that two-thirds of the respondents of a survey agreed that "lawyers are more interested in making money than serving the clients." To the extent that lawyers violate ethical principles regarding fees, the public perception suffers even more.

1. The Egregious Case

One particularly egregious case of billing dishonesty is *Iowa Supreme Court Board of Professional Ethics & Conduct v. Tofflemire*, 689 N.W.2d 83 (Iowa 2004). The lawyer in the case worked as a full-time employee for the state labor office, worked as a state public defender, and had a private practice. The lawyer filed reports with the public defender's office and the labor office, that when considered as a whole, claimed that the lawyer had worked more than twenty-four hours on multiple days. She filed reports claiming that she regularly had worked more than eighteen hours. On 174 of 259 calendar days, the lawyer reported that she had worked over ten hours. The state public defender's office paid the lawyer on the basis of these reports so they were, in effect, bills for services rendered. In addition, the lawyer took sick days from the labor office job and billed time on those days to the public defender. The lawyer billed one-half an hour for each of several letters that could not have taken so much time. Finally, several of the lawyer's requests for reimbursement did not match the actual receipts. Needless to say, the errors were not in favor of the state.

The Iowa Supreme Court suspended the lawyer indefinitely with no possibility of reinstatement for two years. The Court noted that this was a case of "repeated deception." *Id.* at 94. First, the billing for the letters was a clear example of overbilling. Second, the practice of taking sick days from the labor office and billing the public defender's office for those days was "illegal conduct involving moral turpitude." *Id.* at 85. Third, the misrepresented reimbursement amounts were clearly problematic. Fourth, the lawyer admitted that she did not prepare contemporaneous billing records. The court noted that such a practice was a "recipe for disaster" and that later preparing reports with details that would lead the reader to believe that the lawyer kept contemporaneous reports was reckless disregard for the truth. *Id.* at 90. Lastly, the court noted that it had little faith in the accuracy of the billing.

2. Lawyers and Billing Generally

Unfortunately, billing impropriety is not as unusual as one might hope. A study done by Susan Saab Fortney and reported in *Soul for Sale: An Empirical Study of Associate Satisfaction, Law Firm Culture, and the Effects of the Billable Hour Requirements,* 69 UMKC L. Rev. 239 (2000), asked law firm associates whether they had engaged in double-billing. Eighty-six percent of the 487 respondents answered "no." In response to a question about whether the associates had billed clients for recycled work, eighty-three percent of the respondents answered "no." The bad news is that at least fourteen and seventeen percent of the respondents had engaged in dishonest billing practices and were willing to admit it.

3. ABA Guidance on Billing

Some lawyers may be engaging in questionable practices without knowing that the practices are improper. In an effort to provide guidance in this area, *ABA Formal Opinion 93-379 (1993)* addressed several billing issues that arise with hourly billing. The opinion presented three scenarios.

In the first scenario a lawyer spent four hours at the courthouse representing three clients. The question was whether the lawyer might bill each client four hours for a total of twelve hours. If the lawyer had been representing any one of the clients alone, the matter would have taken four hours. The *Opinion* concluded that the lawyer could not bill four hours to each of the three clients because "[a] lawyer who spends four hours of time on behalf of three clients has not earned twelve billable hours."

In the second scenario a lawyer worked on one client's matter for five hours while flying six hours to a deposition for another client. The question was whether the lawyer might bill the clients five and six hours, respectively, for the time. Once again the *Opinion* concluded that this billing would be improper. "A lawyer who flies for six hours for one client, while working five hours on behalf of another, has not earned eleven billable hours."

In the third scenario a lawyer researched a topic for a client and later used the research for a second client. The question was whether the lawyer might bill not only the first client for the time spent researching the issue but also the second client. The *Opinion* stated: "A lawyer who is able to reuse old work product has not re-earned the hours previously billed and compensated when the work product was first generated."

Related Sections of the *Restatement (Third) of the Law Governing Lawyers*

Sections 33, 34, 35, 36, 38, 44, and 47

Checkpoints

- At the beginning of a lawyer-client relationship a lawyer must disclose the details of the fee arrangement with the client, preferably in writing.
- If the fee is contingent the lawyer must explain the nature of the fee, its method of calculation, and the treatment of expenses. The fee agreement must be in a writing and the client must sign it. After the representation, the lawyer must provide the client with an explanation of the calculation of the actual fee and expenses.
- Lawyer fees and expenses charged to the client must be reasonable.
- A lawyer may receive a contingency fee in any situation other than a domestic relations matter or a criminal matter.

- A lawyer must abide by Rule 1.8(a)(DE) with regard to an initial fee agreement in which the lawyer's fee is an interest in the client and an agreement in which the lawyer obtains a contractual security interest to secure the fee.
- A fee modification must be reasonable and the client must understand and accept the modification.
- A lawyer may share fees with a lawyer not in the same firm only if the sharing is in accord with the work done by the lawyers or on some other basis if the lawyers agree to be responsible for each other. In both situations the client must know of the terms of the arrangement and the client's agreement to the plan must be confirmed by a writing.
- While in some jurisdictions a fee cannot be nonrefundable, in others a fee can be nonrefundable if it constitutes a reasonable fee for services that are actually rendered.
- A lawyer must be honest regarding hours worked and bills submitted to the client.

Chapter 10

Dealing with the Property of Clients and Third Parties

Roadmap

- Rule 1.15(NE)
- Duties regarding the property of clients and third parties
- Recordkeeping and notice requirements

A. Lawyers Possess the Property of Others Regularly

A lawyer comes into possession of the property of clients or of third parties in all sorts of ways. Perhaps Clint Client pays Lisa Lawyer an advance fee. Any unearned fee is the property of the client until the lawyer earns the fee. *See Chapter 9 Fees.* So Lisa finds herself possessing money belonging to Clint. Perhaps the opposing party sends Lisa a settlement check payable to both Lisa and Clint. A portion of the proceeds of that settlement check belongs to Clint but is in the possession of Lisa. Perhaps a hospital rendered care to Clint and now has a valid lien, of which Lisa is aware, on a portion of the proceeds of the settlement. Lisa thus possesses funds belonging to a third party, the hospital. Perhaps Clint has been sued by a creditor and gives Lisa the keys to his yacht so that Lisa can give the yacht to the creditor as an agreed partial payment of the indebtedness. Lisa is now in possession of the yacht. Perhaps Clint is the creditor and the debtor gives Lisa a diamond necklace as an agreed partial payment of the indebtedness to Clint. Again, Lisa possesses someone else's property. The possibilities are endless.

With regard to this property of clients and third parties in the possession of lawyers, the rules of professional responsibility make strict demands. The goal is to protect the property of clients and third parties and to have a system in which a lawyer's honesty is obvious, transparent, and encouraged. Such a system should prevent intentional acts of dishonesty by lawyers. Such a system should also prevent lawyer negligence that results in harm to others.

B. Keeping Property Safe and Separate

Rule 1.15(NE) requires that a lawyer keep the property of clients and others safe and separate from the lawyer's property. This requirement applies to funds as well as other sorts of property. Rule 1.15(a)(NE) states the general rule. If a lawyer keeps client funds and the lawyer's own funds in the same bank account, the lawyer might, without even thinking about the appropriateness of the action, spend all of the funds on office operating expenses. Then the client, in effect, would have paid the lawyer's operating expenses. As long as the account contains enough money to repay all clients, there is no ultimate harm. Unfortunately, the money often runs out without all of the clients receiving their due amounts. The situation is like a game of musical chairs with a client being the one left standing without a chair. The duty to keep the property of clients safe *and* separate is a prophylactic measure to prevent this sort of unintentional harm to clients and third parties. Lawyers are disciplined for violating this rule regardless of the presence or absence of harm to clients or third parties.

1. Funds: A Trust Account

a. General Duties

A lawyer must have an account in which he or she keeps funds that are not the lawyer's. This account generally is referred to as a client trust account. Any funds that come to the lawyer that belong to a client or to a third party must be kept in a trust account. A lawyer may have one account for all amounts belonging to others or may have different accounts for different clients or purposes. If Lisa Lawyer does a large amount of work for Clint Client, Lisa may establish a client trust account specifically for Clint. If not, Lisa might deposit the funds in a client trust account that Lisa uses for all her clients. If Lisa receives an advance fee from Clint Client, that fee goes into the trust account until Lisa earns it. If Clint receives a settlement check, the portion of the proceeds belonging to Clint must be placed in the trust account. This account must be in the state in which the lawyer has his or her office or may be in another state if the client consents. The lawyer may not pay office expenses out of this account because the funds in the account do not belong to the lawyer. Having the separate account makes this concept of ownership more obvious and real.

Rule 1.15(b)(NE) provides a very limited exception to the general rule against commingling the lawyer's funds with client funds. A lawyer may deposit the lawyer's own funds into a trust account to cover the administrative costs of the account. Otherwise, no funds of the lawyer may be in the client trust account. Even in this exceptional circumstance, the lawyer must keep careful records of his or her contribution to the account.

When a client pays in advance, the lawyer must deposit the advance fee in the client trust account. Rule 1.15(c) (NE) specifically requires this. After a time, the lawyer may earn the fee by working on the client's matter. If there is no dispute about the fee, the lawyer, within a reasonable period of time, must remove the earned fee amount from the client trust account. To fail to do this is to commingle the funds of the lawyer and the client—an improper act.

b. Recordkeeping

Generally, a lawyer's trust account has funds belonging to many people in it at any one time. Small and large amounts move in and out of the account on a daily basis. Rule 1.15(a)(NE) requires a lawyer to keep careful and current records of the account using generally accepted accounting principles. On any day, a lawyer should be able to say who owns every penny in the account. Typically, the lawyer must retain these records for five years after the conclusion of the relevant matter. Many lawyers never dispose of the trust records because the records prove that the lawyer has acted properly with regard to the property of others.

c. IOLTA Programs

These days many types of accounts earn interest. Clearly, the interest earned on a client trust account is not the lawyer's so the lawyer cannot properly pocket the interest. Dividing the interest among the clients and others whose funds pass through the account is time-consuming and not cost-effective even if such precision is possible. Many states have developed programs in which interest earned on client trust accounts goes to special funds for the improvement of the law or the legal system, or for the provision of legal services for those who cannot afford to pay for legal services. These programs are usually called Interest on Lawyer Trust Account (IOLTA) programs.

IOLTA programs have been the subject of several constitutional challenges, the last being *Brown v. Legal Foundation of Washington,* 538 U.S. 216 (2003), in which the United States Supreme Court evaluated the state of Washington's IOLTA plan. The Court determined that though the interest earned by client trust accounts is the property of the clients, the state of Washington did not have to pay the clients anything in exchange for the interest since the clients suffered no compensable loss as a result of the interest being used by the IOLTA plan.

2. Other Property: Safe and Separate

Property other than funds must be kept safe and separate as well. If Lisa Lawyer has a diamond necklace belonging to a client or a third party, Lisa must promptly put the necklace in a safe place such as the office safe or a safe deposit box. Likewise, if Lisa possesses keys to a yacht belonging to another, Lisa must place the keys in a safe place like the office safe or a safe deposit box. She must also take steps to ensure that the yacht itself is in a secure and safe place. The keys and necklace must be clearly labeled and/or identified on the safe or safe deposit box inventory with the name of the owner. As is true with a trust account, a lawyer must keep records of the property of others, typically, for at least five years.

3. Notice

When a lawyer comes into possession of the property of another, except in the advance fee situation, the lawyer must promptly notify the owner that the lawyer has the property and promptly deliver the property to the owner. If asked, the lawyer must provide a "full accounting." These actions are required by Rule 1.15(d)(NE). Perhaps Lisa Lawyer receives a $100,000 settlement check in which Lisa and Clint Client both have an interest. Lisa should promptly deposit the check in the client trust account. Perhaps Lisa calculates that $25,000 of the $100,000 belongs to her as her fee while $75,000 belongs to Clint. Lisa must promptly notify Clint of the fact of receipt of the check and the calculation of the division. Lisa should make arrangements to promptly deliver the $75,000 to Clint according to Clint's instructions. Lisa should not withdraw the $25,000 from the client trust account and place it in her own account until Clint has had a reasonable opportunity to object to the amount as Lisa's fee. Once a reasonable time has passed without an objection from Clint, Lisa should move the $25,000 from the client trust account because it then belongs to Lisa.

4. A Dispute as to Ownership

a. Disputes between a Lawyer and a Client

Rule 1.15(e)(NE) deals with the situation in which there is a dispute as to the ownership of funds or other property in the possession of the lawyer. Perhaps Lisa Lawyer receives a $100,000 settlement check in a matter she handled for Clint Client. She deposits it in a client trust account. Lisa notifies Clint and explains that she calculates that $25,000 of the settlement is Lisa's fee and $75,000 belongs to Clint. Clint responds by challenging Lisa's claim. Clint asserts that Lisa should receive only $15,000. Lisa must send $75,000 to Clint because there is no dispute about $75,000. Lisa must move $15,000 from the client trust account to her own account because there is no dispute about her ownership of it. Lisa must keep the $10,000 that is in dispute in the client trust account until the disagreement can be resolved. The lawyer should suggest a method of resolving the dispute in a timely manner.

b. Disputes between a Client and a Third Party

Occasionally, a lawyer holds funds or other property to which a third party has a claim that is not frivolous and yet the client demands that the funds or other property be given to the client. In such a situation the lawyer must not release the property to the client. Rather, the lawyer must hold the property until the matter has been resolved. If necessary, a lawyer may file an action to have a court resolve the question of ownership. Perhaps Lisa Lawyer is aware of a valid lien held by the hospital in the amount of $30,000. When Lisa receives a settlement check of $100,000 in the matter, Lisa notifies Clint that Lisa's fee is $25,000 and the hospital has a right to $30,000, leaving $45,000 for Clint. Clint directs Lisa to take her fee but that he wants her to send him the rest. Lisa cannot honor Clint's instructions. She may send Clint $45,000 but must hold the remaining $30,000 until the right to it is resolved.

Related Sections of the *Restatement (Third) of the Law Governing Lawyers*

Sections 44 and 45

Checkpoints

- A lawyer must keep the property of clients and others in the lawyer's possession safe.
- A lawyer must keep the property of clients and others in the lawyer's possession separate from the lawyer's property.

- When the property of clients or others is in the form of funds, the lawyer must deposit the funds in a trust account.
- A lawyer may deposit his or her own funds in the client trust account to cover the administrative expenses of the account.
- The lawyer must keep careful records of the trust account transactions and any other property of others in the lawyer's possession.
- A lawyer must promptly notify the owner of the property that the lawyer has the property.
- A lawyer must promptly take steps to deliver the property to the owner.
- A lawyer must hold property that is the subject of a dispute as to ownership until the dispute is resolved.

Chapter 11

Refusing to Form a Lawyer-Client Relationship or Ending a Lawyer-Client Relationship

Roadmap

- Rule 1.16(DE)
- Rule 6.2(DE)
- Situations of mandatory refusal of a representation or mandatory withdrawal from a representation
- Situations of permissive withdrawal from a representation
- Permission of the tribunal for withdrawal
- Protecting the client's interest when ending a representation
- A client's right to the file at the representation's termination
- Refusal of court appointment

A. Refusing to Enter into a Representation or Ending a Representation When the Lawyer is Not Appointed by a Tribunal

The vast majority of legal representations occur not because a tribunal appoints a lawyer to represent a client but rather because a person asks a lawyer to represent him or her. Lawyers have significant freedom in such situations to accept the representations or not, subject to the lawyer's general pro bono publico requirement of Rule 6.1(ID). *See Chapter 43 Pro Bono Service.* There are some limits on a lawyer's discretion, however.

1. Situations in Which a Lawyer Cannot Undertake a Representation and Any Already Existing Representation Must End

As stated by Rule 1.16(DE), there are three situations in which the lawyer may not allow a representation to occur. In these three situations, a lawyer must not accept a representation, and if a lawyer is already in the midst of the representation, the lawyer must act to terminate the representation.

a. *The Representation Violates the Rules of Professional Conduct or Other Law*

First, a lawyer may not accept a representation if to do so would violate law or the rules of professional conduct. Perhaps Larry Lawyer represents Clint Client in a personal injury matter in which Clint has a claim of gross negligence against Big Bus Corporation. Larry cannot accept the representation of Big Bus Corporation in the same matter because representing Big Bus and Clint, adverse parties in the same litigation matter, would violate Rule 1.7(DE), a conflict of interest provision of the rules of professional conduct. No lawyer in Larry's firm can handle the representation of Big Bus in the same matter either. *See* Rule 1.10(ID). *See Chapter 18 Conflicts and Current Clients.* In this day of extremely large firms, it is perhaps possible that Lance, another lawyer at Larry's firm, might accept the representation of Big Bus Corporation without becoming aware of Larry's representation of Clint. This oversight, would, of course, be negligence and below the standard of care owed to clients such as Clint and Big Bus and required by Rule 1.1(DE). *See Chapter 5 Competence and Diligence.* Once Lance and Larry are aware of the conflict of interest problem, they and their firm must withdraw from the representation of at least one and probably both clients to avoid violating the conflicts rules. *See Chapter 18 Conflicts and Current Clients* and *Chapter 19 Conflicts and Former Clients.*

b. *Physical or Mental Disability of the Lawyer*

The second situation in which a lawyer may not accept a representation of a client is if the lawyer is not physically or mentally able to handle the matter competently. If Larry Lawyer knows that his own mental condition "materially impairs" his representation of Clint Client, Larry cannot accept the representation. If Larry already represents Clint and becomes aware of a physical or mental condition that "materially impairs" his representation of Clint, Larry must act to end the representation.

c. *The Client Discharges the Lawyer*

The third situation in which a lawyer cannot handle a representation is when the client has discharged the lawyer. This is an issue regarding ending a representation already in existence. The courts of all jurisdictions recognize that a client has the right to terminate a lawyer for whatever reason. The rationale for the rule is that the client must be able to rid himself or herself of the lawyer if the client feels that the bond of trust and loyalty no longer exists between the client and the lawyer. If the client indicates that the client wishes the lawyer-client relationship to end, the lawyer must honor that wish and take steps to terminate the relationship. As a Massachusetts court stated in *Salem Realty Co. v. Matera,* 410 N.E.2d 716 (Mass. App. Ct. 1980), "A client's right to change his lawyer at any time for any cause or no cause at all is inherent in the characteristics of trust and confidentiality in the lawyer-client relationship." *Id.* at 719. If Clint Client tells Larry Lawyer that he no longer wants Larry's services, Larry must take whatever steps are necessary in the particular representation to end his relationship with Clint.

2. Situations in Which a Lawyer May End a Representation

A lawyer is free to refuse a representation that is not the result of a judicial appointment for any reason not prohibited by law. Once a lawyer agrees to represent a client, that lawyer's right to withdraw from the representation is more constrained. Rule 1.16(b)(DE) deals with the issue of permissive, as opposed to mandatory, withdrawal from the representation of a client. The rule allows a lawyer to withdraw for any reason if there is no "material adverse effect" on the client. Even if the withdrawal will cause "material adverse effect," a lawyer may withdraw from a representation in certain specific settings. Finally, even if the withdrawal will cause "material adverse effect," a lawyer may withdraw from a representation if "other good cause" for withdrawal exists.

a. *A General Provision: No "Material Adverse Effect"*

A lawyer may withdraw for any reason if there is no "material adverse effect" on the client. Perhaps Larry Lawyer agrees to represent Clint Client in a personal injury matter. A week or so later Big Corporation offers Larry a job as an in-house lawyer and Larry accepts. Larry has done nothing in the matter for Clint other than the engagement letter. No tribunal is yet involved. Larry may withdraw from the representation of Clint; Clint will suffer little adverse effect. Clint must simply hire another lawyer.

b. The Specific Provisions

Rule 1.16(b)(DE) lists specific settings in which a lawyer may withdraw from a representation regardless of the adverse effect on the client. Of course, if the matter is already before a tribunal, the lawyer must request permission from the tribunal for the withdrawal. The tribunal might not permit the withdrawal if the client will suffer an adverse effect.

1. Client Crime or Fraud

First, a lawyer may withdraw from a representation of a client if the client is pursuing what the lawyer "reasonably believes is criminal or fraudulent" conduct and the lawyer's services are involved in the conduct. Second, a lawyer may withdraw if the client has used the lawyer's services to commit a crime or fraud.

Larry Lawyer may have discovered that Clint Client has been using documents prepared by Larry to commit a fraud. Perhaps Clint used documents prepared by Larry to obtain loans from banks and Larry has discovered that the loans are part of a scheme to defraud the banks. Larry might wish to withdraw from the representation even if Clint promises to stop because now Larry does not trust Clint. If Clint does not promise to stop, Larry may be required to withdraw so as to avoid knowingly assisting a crime or fraud. Knowingly assisting a crime or fraud would violate Rule 1.2(d)(DE). *See Chapter 8 Scope of the Representation and Communication with the Client.* Thus, the mandatory withdrawal provision of Rule 1.16(a)(DE) would require withdrawal. Even if Larry is not required to withdraw, he could choose to withdraw on the basis that he "reasonably believes" Clint will continue to pursue a path of fraudulent conduct involving Larry's services.

2. The Client Chooses a "Repugnant" Path

A lawyer may withdraw from a representation if the client insists on action with which the lawyer "fundamentally" does not agree or considers "repugnant." Usually, a lawyer becomes aware of these sorts of issues before the representation begins and can simply decline the representation. Occasionally, however, the lawyer is already in the process of the representation before discovering the client's plan and the lawyer's disagreement with it. For example, Larry Lawyer may have agreed to represent Clint Client in a litigation matter. Only after discovery is in progress does Larry realize that Clint intends to abuse the discovery process by delaying the disclosure of documents clearly subject to discovery. Larry might withdraw because he does not want to be a part of this type of conduct. Of course, Larry should first attempt to convince Clint of the error of his ways.

3. The Client Does Not "Fulfill an Obligation to the Lawyer"

A lawyer may withdraw from a representation if the client fails "substantially to fulfill an obligation" owed to the lawyer. Rule 1.16(b)(5)(DE), the provision of the rules that contains this permissive withdrawal situation, is loaded with qualifiers. First, the client must fail "substantially to fulfill an obligation to the lawyer." Second, the obligation must relate to the lawyer's services. Third, the lawyer must first give the client warning that the lawyer is considering withdrawal if the client fails to fulfill the obligation.

The most obvious example of an unfulfilled obligation is the client's failure to pay the lawyer as the client has agreed to do. Perhaps Clint agreed at the beginning of the representation to pay Larry monthly at a rate of $200 per hour. Perhaps Clint has not paid Larry anything for a year despite the fact that Larry has worked on the matter and billed Clint for hundreds of hours of work. Clint does not have any dispute with the fact that he owes Larry a certain substantial amount. Larry may explain to Clint that he will no longer represent Clint if Clint does not pay the past due amount within thirty days. If Clint does not pay Larry, Larry may withdraw. If Clint pays a part of the amount due, Larry must evaluate whether Clint has failed "substantially" to fulfill his obligation to Larry. Only if the answer to this question is "yes" may Larry withdraw from the representation.

4. The Representation Creates an "Unreasonable Financial Burden" for the Lawyer or the Client Has Made the Representation "Unreasonably Difficult"

A lawyer may withdraw from a representation if continuing the representation causes the lawyer to suffer an "unreasonable financial burden." Perhaps Larry Lawyer agreed to represent Clint at an extremely discounted rate. The matter becomes more complicated than Larry anticipated and takes up a huge percentage of Larry's time. Thus, Larry is not able to do more remunerative work and is in danger of becoming incapable of paying bills. Larry could withdraw from the representation of Clint.

A lawyer also may withdraw if the client has made the representation "unreasonably difficult." Perhaps Clint Client has retained Larry Lawyer to handle the negotiation for the sale of Clint's business. After a time Clint no longer communicates with Larry about conversations with the potential purchaser, does not inform Larry of meeting dates with the purchaser, and generally ignores Larry. Larry could withdraw from the representation because Clint has made the representation "unreasonably difficult" if not impossible.

c. A General Catch-All Provision: "Other Good Cause"

Rule 1.16(b)(DE) concludes with a final situation of permissive withdrawal: a lawyer may withdraw when "other good cause" exists. The implication of this language is that the preceding specific permissive withdrawal provisions are examples of good cause and that a lawyer may withdraw from a representation when any other situation arises that equals the situations specifically listed in the rule.

3. Permission of the Court for Withdrawal

A lawyer representing a client in a matter that does not involve a tribunal may terminate a representation by notifying the client that the lawyer will no longer be representing the client after a stated reasonable period of time. In contrast, if a lawyer represents a client in a matter that involves a tribunal, the lawyer must ask the tribunal for permission to withdraw as counsel of record for the client. The court may, or may not, permit the lawyer to withdraw. The court has discretion over this issue. This is true regardless of whether the lawyer seeks to withdraw because the rules of professional conduct demand withdrawal or whether the rules simply allow the lawyer to withdraw.

Moving for permission to withdraw is sometimes difficult because the lawyer must not improperly disclose confidential information protected by Rule 1.6(DE). *See Chapter 15 The Duty of Confidentiality.* This means that the lawyer may not be able to fully explain to the court the reason the lawyer requests permission to withdraw. For example, the best that the lawyer might be able to do in a situation in which the rules of professional conduct require withdrawal is to state that the lawyer seeks to withdraw because of the demands of the rules of professional conduct.

If the tribunal denies a lawyer permission to withdraw, Rule 1.16(c)(DE) requires the lawyer to continue with the representation. For example, in *V.H. v. J.P.H.*, 815 N.E.2d 1096 (Mass. App. Ct. 2004), the court reviewed a lower court's denial of a lawyer's motion to withdraw. The lawyer sought to withdraw because the client failed to pay. The court affirmed the denial of the motion to withdraw, noting that a court may consider the amount of work performed and paid for in comparison to the work remaining, the fees already paid, the effect of the withdrawal on the client, and the interest of the court. The lawyer in *V.H.* was required to abide by the court's ruling and continue the representation of the client. If a court does not permit the withdrawal, the lawyer must continue with the representation.

4. Facilitating the Withdrawal

a. Protecting the Client

When a lawyer withdraws from a representation, the lawyer must take, as Rule 1.16(d)(DE) states, "reasonably practicable" action to protect the client. The lawyer must give the client "reasonable notice" of the withdrawal so that the client may obtain a replacement counsel. The lawyer must return all property of the client that the lawyer has, such as an unearned advance fee or an advance on expenses not yet incurred. The lawyer must give the client papers to which the client is entitled. The lawyer may retain papers only "to the extent permitted by other law." The lawyer must take any other action necessary to protect the client's interests if that action is "reasonably practicable."

b. The Client's File

1. Generally

One question that often arises in the setting of withdrawal is exactly how the lawyer must treat the client's file in the lawyer's possession. Items in the lawyer's file that the client gave to the lawyer to assist in the representation are the property of the client and must be returned. With regard to all else, the rules do not provide much guidance. The *Restatement (Third) of the Law Governing Lawyers (2000)* section 46 notes that a lawyer should allow clients or former clients, upon request, to have copies of everything in the lawyer's file "unless substantial grounds exist to refuse." Section 46 further provides that a lawyer must "promptly after the representation ends," deliver any documents or copies of documents to the client that the client "reasonably needs." Comment c to section 46 notes that a lawyer need not disclose "law-firm documents reasonably intended only for internal review." As examples of such documents that a lawyer need not disclose to the client, the comment mentions a staffing memorandum, a memorandum discussing whether the representation must cease because of client misconduct, or a memorandum discussing potential malpractice liability to the client.

Many courts share this general view. In *Swift, Currie, McGhee & Hiers v. Henry*, 581 S.E.2d 37 (Ga. 2003), the Georgia Supreme Court evaluated a client's right to a memorandum prepared by the lawyer in the course of the representation of the client. The court noted: "A majority of courts have ruled that a document created by an attorney belongs to the client who retained him." *Id.* The court then noted that there were situations in which that statement would not necessarily require disclosure of the document to the client if "good cause" existed for the nondisclosure. As an example of "good cause," the court pointed to the situation in which the lawyer would violate a duty to a third party by the disclosure to the client. *Id.* Some jurisdictions have ethics opinions regarding the treatment of the file. These opinions are not necessarily in agreement with the *Restatement.*

Perhaps Larry Lawyer decides to no longer represent Clint in his estate planning. When Larry makes this determination, Clint's file is rather thick. Larry has Clint's birth certificate, drafts of several documents not yet complete, and a memorandum about why Larry should no longer represent Clint because of conflict of interest problems the representation of Clint creates for other lawyers in the firm. Larry must return the birth certificate; it is Clint's property. Larry must give the draft documents to Clint because he reasonably needs these to complete his estate planning work with another lawyer without having to pay the second lawyer to do the work from scratch. Larry need not disclose the conflict of interest memorandum to Clint.

2. Retaining Liens

Some states have, historically, allowed a lawyer to refuse to deliver a client's file to the client when the representation ends if the client has not paid for the lawyer's services. This right to hold the client's file is a retaining lien. It allows the lawyer to hold the file hostage in an attempt to encourage the client to pay the lawyer's bill. Even in states recognizing such a retaining lien, some courts have not allowed the lawyer to keep the file from the client if to do so would prejudice the client. If Larry Lawyer withdraws from the representation of Clint Client in a litigation matter because Clint has not paid his bill for services rendered, Larry might, in a jurisdiction recognizing a retaining lien, refuse to turn over anything relating to the litigation. Many courts would not allow Larry to retain anything of import to the litigation because the court would not allow Larry to cause prejudice to Clint. The *Restatement (Third) of the Law Governing Lawyers (2000)* in section 43 disapproves of retaining liens. Some jurisdictions, such as Kentucky, do not recognize retaining liens.

B. Refusing Appointed Representation or Ending Appointed Representation

A lawyer has an obligation to provide legal services to those who cannot otherwise afford legal services or those who cannot otherwise obtain legal services. *See Chapter 43 Pro Bono Service.* One way a lawyer can shoulder this responsibility is to accept appointed representation in cases in which the compensation for the services is low or nonexistent or in cases in which the client's cause is unpopular. Because of this responsibility as well as because of a lawyer's general role as an officer of the court, when a court or other tribunal appoints a lawyer to represent a client, the lawyer's rights regarding his or her choice of clientele are significantly different than in other situations.

Rule 6.2(DE) states that a lawyer must not avoid an appointed representation unless the lawyer has "good cause." The rule does not provide a definition of "good cause" but does provide a nonexclusive list of situations that present "good cause" for a lawyer to avoid the appointment. Because at the time of the appointment the exact effect of the appointment may not be clear, the "good cause" situations are ones in which one can say that a certain result is "likely."

1. When the Representation "Likely" Will Violate the Rules or Other Law

First, a lawyer may seek to avoid an appointment if representing the client is "likely to result in violation of the Rules of Professional Conduct or other law." In this circumstance the lawyer may know that the representation will create a violation of the rules of professional conduct. Yet, the lawyer may seek to avoid the appointment even if the violation is not certain but only "likely."

Lisa Lawyer represents Cindy Client, a defendant in a criminal matter. A court may attempt to appoint Lisa to represent Cleo, another defendant in the same matter. Perhaps Lisa has already discussed the matter with Cindy and knows that Cindy's defense will be inconsistent with the best interests of Cleo. At the time of the appointment Lisa knows that representing Cindy and Cleo will violate the conflict of interest provisions of the rules of professional conduct. *See Chapter 18 Conflicts and Current Clients.* Rule 1.16(a)(DE) requires Lisa to decline such a representation and Rule 6.2(DE) allows her to decline such a representation by seeking to avoid the appointment.

2. When the Representation "Likely" Will Result in an "Unreasonable Financial Burden"

Second, a lawyer may seek to avoid the appointment if the representation "likely" will result in an "unreasonable financial burden." An appointment for a lawyer to handle a routine criminal matter without compensation would not result in such a burden. The result might be quite different if a court appoints a lawyer to represent a defendant in a murder case in which the prosecution seeks the death penalty. Such a representation could result in an "unreasonable financial burden" even if the lawyer is to receive some compensation. The expenses for experts and investigation of such a matter are large and the number of lawyer hours likely to be involved is great. The financial burden in such a case is increased not only by the hours and other expenditure the lawyer must make on the case, but also by the other remunerative representations the lawyer is unable to handle because the lawyer must spend so much time on the death penalty case.

3. When the Repugnance of the Client or Cause "Likely" Will Result in a Material Limitation on the Representation

As Rule 1.2(b)(DE) states, a lawyer does not endorse a client's actions or beliefs by representing a client. *See Chapter 8 Scope of the Representation and Communication with the Client.* Most, if not all, lawyers represent some clients they do not like or clients who hold views with which the lawyers do not agree or clients who take actions of which the lawyers do not approve. This is all normal in the practice of law as long as lawyers are thinking actors in the process and not robotic arms of clients. In the context of appointed representation, a lawyer must not seek to avoid an appointment for these run-of-the-mill situations even if the lawyer might not choose to represent the client if the matter did not involve a court appointment. But if the client or the client's cause is so "repugnant" to the lawyer that the lawyer cannot have a proper lawyer-client relationship and cannot render appropriate legal representation, then the lawyer may seek to avoid the appointment.

Perhaps Lisa Lawyer is African-American. Perhaps a court has sought to appoint her to represent Clint, a defendant in a cross-burning incident. Lisa does not believe that she can have a proper lawyer-client relationship with Clint. In fact, Lisa believes that representation of Clint may violate Rule 1.7(DE), the conflict of interest rule for current clients, because she believes that there is a "significant risk" that her own opinions will materially limit her representation of Clint. *See Chapter 18 Conflicts and Current Clients.* Rule 6.2(DE) would permit Lisa to seek to avoid the appointment.

Related Sections of the *Restatement (Third) of the Law Governing Lawyers*

Sections 31, 32, 33, 43, 45, and 46

Checkpoints

- A lawyer may not accept a representation and may not continue a representation if one already exists if
    1. the representation violates the rules of professional conduct or other law,
    2. the lawyer's mental or physical state prevents appropriate competent representation, or
    3. the client discharges the lawyer.
- A lawyer may withdraw from a representation if
    1. the client will suffer no "material adverse effect,"
    2. the client is engaging in activity and using the lawyer's services in activity that the lawyer "reasonably believes is a criminal or fraudulent,"
    3. the client has committed a crime or fraud using the lawyer's services,
    4. the client wishes to pursue action the lawyer finds "repugnant" or with which the lawyer "fundamentally" does not agree,
    5. the client has failed "substantially to fulfill an obligation to the lawyer" related to the lawyer's services,
    6. the lawyer will suffer an "unreasonable financial burden" by continuing the representation or the representation will be "unreasonably difficult," or
    7. "other good cause" for terminating the relationship exists.
- A lawyer must request permission from the tribunal to withdraw if the matter involves a tribunal. If the tribunal refuses, the lawyer must continue the representation.
- A lawyer must take all "reasonably practicable" steps to protect the client's interests when ending a representation.
- A client or former client has the right to everything in his or her file in the lawyer's possession except documents, as the *Restatement* states, "intended only for internal review."
- Some jurisdictions recognize a retaining lien and allow a lawyer to hold the client's file until the client pays for the lawyer's services. Even if a jurisdiction recognizes a retaining lien, some courts may not allow a lawyer to withhold the file if the result would be prejudice to the client.
- A lawyer must not seek to avoid an appointed representation unless
    1. the representation would "likely" violate the rules of professional conduct or other law,
    2. the representation would "likely" cause an "unreasonable financial burden" for the lawyer, or
    3. the lawyer finds the client or the client's cause so "repugnant" that the lawyer's ability to have a proper lawyer-client relationship with the client and ability to adequately represent the client "likely" will be impaired.

Chapter 12

Sale of a Practice

Roadmap

- Rule 1.17(KS)
- Process for selling a law practice

A. A Little History

A lawyer leaving the practice of law may sell his or her practice to another lawyer. Rule 1.17(KS), the rule clearly providing this, came into existence in 1990s. The rule was created so sole practitioners would be on an equal footing with lawyers in firms with regard to transferring a law practice to another lawyer and leaving the practice of law.

Before the creation of the rule, the lack of the ability to sell a practice was not an issue for lawyers practicing in law firms. Firms could require lawyers joining the firm to make an equity payment to the firm. Then lawyers leaving the practice of law received a retirement payment of sorts. Indirectly, there was a sale of a law practice. The clients of the leaving lawyer generally stayed with the firm and the leaving lawyer received a payment. In contrast, sole practitioners had no approved method of transferring a practice to another lawyer. To achieve the desired result, the sole practitioner had to associate with a successor lawyer for a year or so as a partnership. Then the original lawyer could leave and collect a pay out. This was a significantly more burdensome approach than for lawyers in established law firms.

To level the playing field for all lawyers, a rule was developed to allow the sale of a law practice. The sale of a practice under Rule 1.17(KS) is not an impermissible payment under the advertising rules. Rule 7.2(NE) makes this clear.

Lawyers are not the only entities whose interests are tied up in such a situation. A sale of a practice necessarily touches upon the interests and rights of the clients whose matters constitute the practice. Any rule allowing a sale of a practice must, therefore, contains provisions to protect a client's interests.

B. The Selling Process

1. Leaving Private Practice in a Jurisdiction or a Subject Area

A lawyer cannot sell a law practice unless the lawyer

1. is leaving the private practice of law entirely,
2. is leaving the private practice of law in a particular jurisdiction or geographic area (depending on how a jurisdiction chooses to limit the right), or
3. no longer plans to practice in the subject matter area of the kind of cases the lawyer is selling.

A lawyer might leave the private practice of law to retire entirely, to take up another occupation, to become a judge, to work for the government, or to become an in-house lawyer. Lisa Lawyer may decide to leave the practice of law to retire. She might sell her entire practice to Larry. A lawyer may sell her practice even if she plans to practice in another jurisdiction. Perhaps Lisa lives in Indiana. Lisa might decide that she would like to move to Arizona and practice law there. Lisa may sell her entire Indiana practice to Larry.

A lawyer may sell the entire practice or a subject area of the practice. A lawyer cannot, however, sell certain cases while keeping others of the same kind. Perhaps Lisa's practice neatly divides into personal injury cases and divorce cases. If Lisa is leaving the practice of law, Lisa may sell her entire practice to Larry. Perhaps Larry specializes in personal injury representation. Larry is not interested in buying Lisa's divorce practice. Lisa may sell the personal injury practice to Larry and the divorce practice to Lance, a lawyer specializing in family law. Perhaps Lisa is not leaving the private practice of law but she has decided to specialize only in divorce work. She no longer wishes to handle personal injury cases. Lisa may sell her personal injury practice to Larry. If Lisa does this, she must no longer practice personal injury law. Lisa cannot sell some personal injury cases and keep others.

2. Good Faith

If a lawyer sells his or her practice and later decides to return to private practice, the lawyer commits no ethical breach if the lawyer at all times acts in good faith. No one can guarantee the future. A retired lawyer may suddenly need to return to private practice because of financial considerations. A lawyer who moves in-house may become dissatisfied with the management of the company and may decide to open a private practice again. A lawyer who becomes a judge may not be re-elected and may decide to move back into private practice. These lawyers may return to the private practice of law even though each one earlier sold a practice if the lawyers sold their practices with the good faith belief that the lawyer was leaving the private practice of law.

In an effort to protect the value of what the buyer is purchasing, the parties may enter into an agreement limiting the selling attorney's right to reenter the market of which the practice sold is a part. While restrictions on a lawyer's right to practice generally are prohibited by Rule 5.6(DE), restrictions that are part of a sale of a practice under Rule 1.17(KS) are permitted. *See Chapter 41 Restrictions on a Lawyer's Right to Practice Law.*

3. No Fee Increase

The purchasing lawyer must honor the fee arrangement to which the client and the selling lawyer agreed. The fee charged to the clients cannot increase as an incident to the sale. Rule 1.17(KS) states that the fee "shall not be increased by reason of the sale."

4. Notice to and Approval from Clients

The selling lawyer's duty of confidentiality to his or her clients under Rule 1.6(DE) does not evaporate simply because that lawyer seeks to sell the practice. In negotiating the sale of the practice, the selling lawyer may reveal information necessary for the buying lawyer to evaluate conflicts of interest that might arise from the purchase. This limited disclosure can occur only if it will not harm any attorney-client privilege protections and will not otherwise harm the client. This type of disclosure is in accord with Rule 1.6(b)(7). *See also Chapter 15 The Duty of Confidentiality.* The selling lawyer cannot give the potential purchaser detailed information relating to a client's representation absent client consent.

Once the selling and buying lawyers agree on the sale, the selling lawyer must give all clients whose matters are part of the sale notice of the sale. The selling lawyer must tell the clients of their right to counsel of their choice, which could be someone other than the lawyer buying the practice. The selling lawyer must tell the clients that they can take possession of their files themselves if they desire. Finally, the selling lawyer must tell the clients that their consent to the transfer of representation from the selling lawyer to the buying lawyer will be presumed if they do not take any action or object within ninety days of their receipt of the notice.

If the selling lawyer is not able to give the requisite notice, the lawyer must obtain court authorization for the transfer of the representation. The lawyer may disclose confidential client information to the court in camera in an effort to obtain court authorization for the transfer. The lawyer may disclose only that information necessary to the court's decision-making.

5. Court Approval for Counsel of Record

If a matter is already before a tribunal, the tribunal must be petitioned to allow the substitution of the buying lawyer for the selling lawyer as counsel of record in that matter. Recall that the courts have significant discretion to approve or not approve of a substitution. *See Chapter 11 Refusing to Form a Lawyer-Client Relationship or Ending a Lawyer-Client Relationship.*

6. Sale of a Practice of a Deceased Lawyer

Though Rule 1.17(KS) does not specifically so provide, the comments to the rule clarify that a representative of a deceased lawyer may sell the law practice of the deceased lawyer by following the procedures of Rule 1.17(KS). Rule 5.4(a)(2)(NE) clarifies that a purchaser who pays a representative of a deceased lawyer in a sale of a law practice pursuant to Rule 1.17(KS) does not violate the prohibitions of Rule 5.4(NE) regarding sharing legal fees with a nonlawyer. *See Chapter 39 Professional Independence.*

7. Competence of the Seller in Choosing a Buyer

Part of the selling lawyer's duty of competence owed to his or her clients under Rule 1.1(DE) is the proper choice of a buyer for the practice. The selling lawyer must exercise competence and diligence in determining that the purchaser is qualified to handle the clients' matters that comprise the selling lawyer's practice. The selling lawyer can satisfy this obligation by assuring himself or herself that the purchaser has the requisite skill and expertise in the subject area of the selling lawyer's practice or is capable of developing that skill and expertise. *See Chapter 5 Competence and Diligence.* If Lisa Lawyer has an intellectual property practice that consists of many extremely complex matters, Lisa might breach her duty of competence to her clients by agreeing to sell to Larry, a divorce lawyer with no intellectual property experience.

Checkpoints

- A lawyer may sell his or her law practice or a subject area of his or her practice if the lawyer is leaving the private practice of law in the jurisdiction or no longer plans to practice in the subject area.
- A lawyer may return to the private practice of law after a sale of a practice if the lawyer, at the time of the sale, in good faith believed he or she was leaving the private practice of law.
- A lawyer selling a practice must fulfill the duty of competence owed to all his or her clients to exercise competence in selecting a buyer.
- The buying lawyer must abide by the fee arrangements made between the selling lawyer and the clients and may not increase the fee as an incident of the sale.
- The selling lawyer must not violate the duty of confidentiality owed to all clients in the negotiation of the sale of the practice. The selling lawyer can reveal to the buying lawyer only information reasonably necessary for an evaluation of conflicts of interest. Disclosure of detailed information about a client's matter requires client consent.
- The selling lawyer must give every affected client
    1. notice of the sale,
    2. notice that the client may choose the buying lawyer or another lawyer,
    3. notice that the client may choose to take the client's file, and
    4. notice that a failure to take action or object within ninety days will be presumed to be assent to the transfer of representation.
- If a selling lawyer cannot notify a client, the lawyer must obtain a court order approving the transfer of the representation from the selling lawyer to the buying lawyer.
- If a client's matter is already before a tribunal, the selling lawyer must obtain
    1. the court's permission to withdraw as counsel of record and
    2. the court's permission for the buying lawyer to become counsel of record.
- The representative of a deceased lawyer may sell the deceased lawyer's practice and the buying lawyer may pay the representative. Such a payment is not improper sharing of legal fees with a nonlawyer.

Section III
Special Types of Clients

Chapter 13

Organizational Clients

Roadmap

- Rule 1.13(NE)
- Representing an organizational client
- Dealing with organizational constituents
- Internal and external reporting of misconduct
- The Sarbanes-Oxley Act

A. The Organization is the Client

1. The Lawyer Represents the Organization

A lawyer retained by an organization such as a corporation represents the organization. This is the lesson of Rule 1.13(a)(NE). The form of the organization is irrelevant if the intent is that the lawyer is to represent the organization. This concept applies to government entities as well as private entities. Of course, a corporation or other organization has no voice of its own and can speak to its lawyer only through its constituents such as officers, directors, employees, shareholders, and such.

The lawyer-client relationship in this setting has three parties: the lawyer, the organizational client, and the constituent of the organization who acts as the human agent for the organization but is not, individually, a client. Larry Lawyer may represent Big Bus Corporation, but the face of Big Bus to Larry is Bob, the Chief Executive Officer of Big Bus. Bob originally hired Larry to represent Big Bus, and Bob calls Larry with questions, tasks, and concerns on behalf of Big Bus. If Larry's representation of Big Bus does not please Bob, Bob may have the authority to look elsewhere for legal representation for the corporation. This is a confusing relationship on a day-to-day basis. Larry might come to think of Bob as his client in place of Big Bus or come to think of both Bob and Big Bus as his clients. Yet Larry's client is the entity only.

2. The Lawyer Does Not Represent the Constituents

The negative implication is that a lawyer representing an organization does not represent any particular constituent even though the lawyer may have many communications and repeated contact with constituents. Though Larry Lawyer may deal with Bob, the Chief Executive Officer of Big Bus, every day, Larry does not represent Bob. Larry's representation of Big Bus may cause him to have many conversations with employees, directors, shareholders, and the like. Perhaps Bob has asked Larry to investigate whether Sam, a bus driver supervisor, is abusing illegal drugs on the job. Larry may have numerous conversations with bus drivers in an effort to gather information. Larry does not, by virtue of this contact with the drivers, represent any of these employees.

3. The Duty to Clarify the Lawyer's Role

Unfortunately, these constituents may not understand the nature of the lawyer's role. A lawyer may be held to be in a lawyer-client relationship with a person if the person reasonably believes that the lawyer is his or her lawyer. *See Chapter 4 Basis of Duty: The Lawyer-Client Relationship.* The organizational representation setting presents a context in which a constituent of the organization may believe the lawyer represents the constituent. Bob may believe that Larry represents him. The employees Larry interviews when investigating Sam, the bus driver supervisor, may believe that Larry represents them. Confusion is especially likely when the lawyer is an in-house lawyer.

In order to defeat such a misconception, a lawyer such as Larry must always be wary of confusion on the part of the constituent with which he deals and must clarify the relationship. If the lawyer "knows or reasonably should know" that the person is unrepresented and misunderstands the lawyer's relationship to the person in the matter, Rule 4.3(DE) requires the lawyer to "make reasonable efforts to correct the misunderstanding." *See Chapter 37 Respect for the Rights of Nonclients.*

Rule 1.13(f)(NE) adds a slightly different requirement for a lawyer. If a lawyer "knows or reasonably should know" that the interests of the person and the interests of the organization are adverse, the lawyer must explain to the person that the lawyer represents the organization. Larry Lawyer may have evidence that Sam has abused illegal drugs on the job. When Larry talks with Sam, Larry should explain to him that Larry represents Big Bus Corporation, not Sam, so that Sam does not say something to Larry that he might later regret.

In dealing with constituents on behalf of an organization, a lawyer must take care not to give legal advice to the constituents but rather to give legal advice only to the entity. If a lawyer gives legal advice to a constituent, that person might reasonably believe that the lawyer represents him or her. Also, Rule 4.3(DE) provides that a lawyer, when dealing with an unrepresented person, must not give legal advice to that person other than the advice to engage counsel "if the lawyer knows or reasonably should know that the interests of such a person are or have a reasonable possibility of being in conflict with the interests of the client," the organization. *See Chapter 37 Respect for the Rights of Nonclients.*

If a lawyer gives advice to the constituent in such a situation, the lawyer may then be representing two clients with conflicting interests and such representation may violate Rule 1.7(DE), the rule regarding conflicts of interest and current clients. In the midst of interviewing Sam, the driver supervisor, Larry may become aware that Sam's interests and the interests of Big Bus are conflicting. Larry must not give Sam legal advice. *See Chapter 18 Conflicts and Current Clients*

4. The Lawyer May Choose to Represent a Constituent in Addition to Representing the Organization

There are times when a lawyer may choose to represent both the organization and a constituent. A lawyer may choose to represent an organization and a constituent in a related matter or the matters could be completely distinct. A lawyer may represent both an organization and a constituent if the representations present no impermissible conflicts of interest under Rule 1.7(DE). *See Chapter 18 Conflicts and Current Clients.* Bob may be exceedingly impressed with the work Larry does for Big Bus Corporation. Bob may ask Larry to handle a personal matter involving a disagreement Bob has had with his neighbor over a property boundary. If representing Bob in this matter creates no conflict with Big Bus that is impermissible, Larry may represent Bob in the property boundary dispute.

A fairly typical scenario in which a lawyer might represent both an organization and a constituent is the following. Suppose that Penny Plaintiff has sued Big Bus Corporation. Penny Plaintiff claims a Big Bus vehicle negligently collided with a car driven by Penny. Penny also has sued Dave Driver, the driver of the bus that collided with Penny and an employee of Big Bus then and now. Larry may represent both Big Bus and Dave if the conflict of interest rules do not render the representation impermissible.

The conflict of interest rules dictate that in certain conflict-laden situations clients or prospective clients must give "informed consent" to the representation. If an organization must consent to a representation of a constituent such as Bob or Dave, that constituent cannot be the source of the organization's consent. Rule 1.13(g)(NE) so provides. So if Big Bus must consent to Larry Lawyer's representation of Bob, Larry Lawyer must obtain the organization's consent from an agent of the organization other than Bob even though Bob might otherwise be the agent of the organization authorized and empowered to consent to a representation on behalf of the organization. If Larry must obtain the organization's consent to a representation involving Dave, the driver, Bob may be the source of the organization's consent. Dave cannot be the source of consent as a matter of professional responsibility because he is the involved constituent. Moreover, Dave probably cannot be the source of consent as a matter of corporate law because a low-level employee usually does not have authority from the organization to so act.

5. Confidentiality and the Attorney-Client Privilege

Any communication a lawyer representing an organization has with the various constituents relating to the organizational representation is subject to the lawyer's duty of confidentiality owed to the organization pursuant to Rule 1.6(DE). *See Chapter 15 The Duty of Confidentiality.* Because the lawyer does not represent the constituents in these encounters, the lawyer does not owe the constituents any duty of confidentiality.

Because the client is the organization, the attorney-client privilege is that of the organization even though the communications that ultimately are privileged are communications between individual constituents and the lawyer. Big Bus Corporation may claim that the attorney-client privilege protects conversations in which Bob, the Chief Executive Officer, asks Larry for legal advice or assistance for Big Bus. Big Bus also may claim that the attorney-client privilege protects Larry's conversations about Sam, the driver supervisor, that he had with employee drivers. Not all communications between lawyers and organizational constituents are protected by the privilege. There are complicated rules governing the attorney-client privilege's application to organizational constituents. *See Chapter 16 The Attorney-Client Privilege and the Work-Product Doctrine.* What is clear is that if the privilege applies to the communications, the privilege is that of the organization, Big Bus, not the individuals if Larry is clear when communicating to the individuals what his role is. Neither Bob nor the driver employees can successfully claim that the statements are privileged as to them. Thus, if Big Bus wishes to disclose a driver's statements, the driver cannot block the disclosure. If Larry interviews Sam about Sam's use of illegal drugs on the job, Larry may gain information that Sam would not want disclosed to law enforcement authorities. Yet Sam cannot block disclosure if Big Bus chooses that path. Big Bus has the right and power to invoke the privilege and the right and power to waive the privilege; the constituent, individually, does not.

6. Requesting Employees and Other Organizational Constituents Not to Voluntarily Reveal Information to Others

Perhaps Penny Plaintiff has sued Big Bus and a driver, Dave, claiming that she was injured as the result of a collision of a car she was driving and a Big Bus vehicle driven by Dave. Earl, also an employee of Big Bus, was in the Big Bus vehicle at the time of the collision. Larry Lawyer, representing Big Bus in the matter, interviews Earl. Unlike the usual situation regarding witnesses, Larry may request that Earl not voluntarily give information to Penny or Penny's lawyer. Rule 3.4(f)(DE) allows a lawyer such as Larry to make such a request if the request is made to an employee or other agent of the client. There is a caveat. Even if the request is to an employee or other agent, the lawyer cannot make such a request unless the lawyer "reasonably believes" that not talking to the other party or the other party's lawyer will not adversely affect the person's interest. *See Chapter 29 Fairness.* Earl is an employee of Big Bus so Larry may ask Earl not to talk voluntarily to Penny or Penny's lawyer if Larry "reasonably believes" such a course of action will not adversely affect Earl. On these facts, an adverse effect is not likely.

7. Opposing Counsel's Right to Contact an Organizational Constituent

A related issue is that opposing counsel may not contact some categories of organizational constituents if the lawyer knows the organization is represented in the matter. Penny Plaintiff has sued Big Bus Corporation claiming that she was injured as the result of a collision of a car she was driving and a Big Bus vehicle. Earl, also an employee of Big Bus, was in the Big Bus vehicle at the time of the collision. Penny's lawyer knows that Larry Lawyer represents Big Bus in the matter. Penny's lawyer may not contact Earl if he meets certain criteria.

Rule 4.2(DE) provides that a lawyer may not contact a represented party regarding a matter pertaining to the representation. In the context of an organization, the organization is the represented party and so Rule 4.2(DE) limits whom a lawyer may contact if those persons are affiliated with the represented organization. Penny's lawyer cannot speak with Earl if Earl is, as comment seven to Rule 4.2 (DE) states, "a constituent of the organization who supervises, directs or regularly consults with the organization's lawyer concerning the matter or has authority to obligate the organization with respect to the matter or whose act or omission in connection with the matter may be imputed to the organization for purposes of civil or criminal liability." *See Chapter 36 Contact with Represented Persons.*

8. Shareholder Derivative Actions

Shareholders of corporations sometimes bring suits claiming that officers or directors or some other constituent of a corporation is harming the corporation. The shareholders bring the action to enforce the rights of the corporation. Usually, the shareholder action claims that officers or directors have breached or are breaching a duty owed to the corporation. The corporation is a nominal defendant in such a matter and the alleged wrongdoers are defendants as well.

The corporation's lawyer naturally might take on the representation of both the corporation and the alleged wrongdoers without a thought about conflicts of interest. This would be an unfortunate oversight. The lawyer must determine whether he or she may represent the alleged wrongdoers as well as the corporation by considering Rule 1.7(DE), the conflict of interest rule for current clients. *See Chapter 18 Conflicts and Current Clients.* If the parties in the shareholder action are realigned so that the corporation is viewed as a plaintiff, the lawyer cannot represent both the corporation and the other defendants because the lawyer would be representing adverse parties in a single matter. Rule 1.7(DE) prohibits this representation. If the corporation and the other defendants are viewed as co-defendants, the lawyer may represent them all, but only if the circumstances do not otherwise present an impermissible conflict. If the corporation must consent for the representation of all defendants to occur, Rule 1.13(g)(NE) states that a constituent who is to be represented by the organization's lawyer cannot consent to the representation on behalf of the corporation.

B. The Responsibilities of Representing an Organization

As is true with any other client, a lawyer for an organization always must act in the best interests of the organization and otherwise render competent and diligent representation to the organization. An organizational client has the same decision-making authority as a client who is an individual. Ordinarily, the lawyer for the organization follows the direction of those who speak for the organization. Larry, as a lawyer for Big Bus Corporation, follows the instruction and direction of Bob, the Chief Executive Officer and Larry's primary management contact. If Larry is an outside lawyer as opposed to an in-house lawyer, Larry's contact might be an in-house lawyer at Big Bus. Both outside lawyers and in-house lawyers have the same professional responsibilities.

1. Acting in the "Best Interest" of an Organization: The Reporting Up the Organizational Hierarchy Process of Rule 1.13(b)

a. Improper Conduct by Constituents

A lawyer's responsibility to report within the organization does not arise unless the lawyer knows that one of two situations is occurring. The first situation implicating a duty to report is when the lawyer knows that an organizational actor such as an officer, director, or employee is acting or plans to act in a manner that is a breach of duty owed to the organization. The second situation implicating a duty to report is when the lawyer knows that an organizational actor such as an officer, director, or employee is acting or plans to act in a manner that is "a violation of law that reasonably might be imputed to the organization."

A lawyer for an organization might become aware of problematic activity by officers, directors, employees, or another constituent of the organization. A lawyer might discover that an officer or other employee of a corporation, for example, is acting in a way or plans to act in a way that violates duties that officer or other constituent owes to the organization. Perhaps Lisa Lawyer represents Tech Corporation. Lisa discovers that Ted, an employee of Tech Corporation, is stealing trade secrets from Tech and selling them to a competitor for personal gain.

Or a lawyer might discover that an officer, director, employee, or another constituent of the organization is engaging in conduct or intends to engage in conduct that is a violation of law imputable to the organization. As a lawyer for Tech Corporation, Lisa might discover that Ted, an employee of Tech Corporation, is allowing a pharmaceutical product made by Tech that violates federal standards of quality to be shipped to customers. Ted's action easily may be deemed to be the action of Tech Corporation. As a result, Tech Corporation could be subject to criminal sanctions.

b. "Substantial Injury to the Organization"

Even if the lawyer is aware of such misconduct, the lawyer has no duty to report unless the lawyer believes the misconduct is, as Rule 1.13(b)(NE) states, "likely to result in substantial injury to the organization." Lisa might very well conclude that Ted's sale of trade secrets to a competitor is a breach of a legal duty owed to Tech Corporation and also that Ted's conduct is "likely" to cause "substantial injury" to Tech Corporation. After all, if the competitor has Tech Corporation's trade secrets, it can perhaps make the same products better and more inexpensively. Tech Corporation's market share might shrink. Likewise, Ted's action in allowing the sale of the substandard pharmaceutical product may expose Tech Corporation to substantial criminal fines and civil liability. Tech Corporation would suffer "substantial injury."

c. *What to Do: The Reporting Up Process*

If a lawyer knows of the requisite misconduct "likely to result in substantial injury to the organization," Rule 1.13(b)(NE) provides the lawyer with a process to follow to protect the organization. The rule specifically states that the lawyer must report the matter to a "higher authority" within the organization "[u]nless the lawyer reasonably believes that it is not necessary in the best interest of the organization to do so." The default rule is reporting up the organizational hierarchy. The rule clarifies that the reporting may reach, if the circumstances demand it, the "highest authority that can act on behalf of the organization." Ordinarily, this authority is the board of directors if the organization is a corporation. The lawyer reports to higher and higher authority if the lower authority does not appropriately deal with the lawyer's concerns.

A lawyer must abide by the duty of confidentiality of Rule 1.6(DE) owed to the organization in the midst of this process. A lawyer does not violate the duty by disclosing information within the organization but *does* violate the duty by disclosing the information outside of the organization in the midst of this process unless the exception for disclosure in Rule 1.13(c)(NE) applies. *See Chapter 15 The Duty of Confidentiality.*

If Lisa Lawyer represents Tech Corporation and becomes aware that Ted, an employee of Tech Corporation, is stealing and selling trade secrets, conduct in breach of Ted's duties owed to Tech Corporation and likely to cause "substantial injury" to Tech Corporation, Lisa must report Ted's activities to a corporate constituent who has the power and authority to act to protect Tech Corporation. Likewise, if Lisa becomes aware of Ted's action of allowing the sale of a pharmaceutical product below federal quality thresholds, illegal conduct reasonably likely to be imputed to Tech Corporation, and conduct that will cause "substantial injury" to Tech Corporation, Lisa must report Ted's activities to a corporate constituent who has the power and authority to act to protect Tech Corporation. Perhaps Lisa reports to Gina, the General Counsel for Tech Corporation. If Lisa believes that Gina does not deal with the matter in the best interests of the organization, Lisa must take the matter to the Chief Executive Officer or even the board of directors. In both of these scenarios, Lisa has no duty to report up if she "reasonably believes that it is not necessary in the best interest of the organization to do so."

2. Acting in the "Best Interest" of an Organization: The Reporting Out Option of Rule 1.13(c) and 1.13(d)

To protect against situations of wholesale organizational impropriety, lawyers representing organizations also have a very limited right, but not obligation, to report wrongdoing outside of the organization. This right is in addition to the permissive disclosures allowed by Rule 1.6(DE). A lawyer representing an organization has the same duty of confidentiality as a lawyer representing an individual client. Like any other lawyer, a lawyer representing an organization may disclose confidential information in the exceptional situations described in Rule 1.6(b)(DE). *See Chapter 15 The Duty of Confidentiality.*

Because of several situations of extreme impropriety that occurred in the late 1990s and early 2000s in organizations such as Enron and WorldCom, much attention focused on the role of lawyers in such debacles. At the time, a lawyer for an organization could not report wrongdoing to anyone outside of the organization unless the situation fit one of the exceptions of Rule 1.6(DE). At that time, Rule 1.6(DE) did not contain exceptions for disclosure to prevent or mitigate financial or other property injury. So a lawyer at such an organization might report up the hierarchy within the organization but could do no more to remedy the situation. Rule 1.6(DE) was modified to broaden a lawyer's ability to disclose confidences. Likewise, Rule 1.13(NE) was modified with the same goal in mind.

Rule 1.13(c)(NE) and 1.13(d)(NE) provide that a lawyer representing an organization may disclose confidential information to entities outside the organization even if the disclosure is not otherwise permitted by Rule 1.6(DE) if

1. the lawyer has followed the Rule 1.13(b)(NE) process described for reporting within the organization,
2. the "highest authority" has failed to deal with the misconduct in an "appropriate manner,"
3. the misconduct is "clearly a violation of law,"
4. the lawyer "reasonably believes" that the misconduct is "reasonably certain" to create a "substantial injury to the organization,"
5. the lawyer "reasonably believes" disclosure is necessary to prevent the "substantial injury," and
6. the information does not relate to the lawyer's investigation or defense of the organization or a constituent of the organization if the organiza-

tion has entrusted the lawyer with the investigation of an alleged violation of law or the defense of the organization or a constituent against a claim of violation of law.

When making such a disclosure, a lawyer must match the disclosure with the necessity. In other words, a lawyer should disclose only what is necessary to prevent the injury—and no more.

Perhaps Lisa Lawyer, in her representation of Tech Corporation, has discovered employee Ted's actions in allowing the sale of a product not in compliance with federal law. Lisa has followed the reporting inside process. Lisa has presented the matter to the board of directors and the board has chosen to ignore Ted's actions. Ted's actions are a violation of law for which Tech Corporation is responsible criminally and civilly. Lisa "reasonably believes" that Ted's actions are "reasonably certain" to result in "substantial injury" to Tech Corporation. Lisa also "reasonably believes" that disclosure to the Federal Drug Administration will prevent substantial criminal and civil liability. Finally, Lisa did not discover Ted's actions as part of an investigation of an allegation that Ted, or some other organizational constituent, had improperly approved marketing the product. Also, Lisa did not discover Ted's actions as part of a defense of Ted or Tech Corporation against a claim of marketing a substandard product. With these facts, Lisa may, but is not required to, disclose Ted's actions to an outside entity such as the Federal Drug Administration.

3. Notice of the Lawyer's Discharge or Withdrawal

A lawyer representing an organization must take action that at times may be very difficult. The reporting up requirement may mean that the lawyer must report the misconduct of his or her constituent contact. The rule may require a lawyer to report the misconduct of other actors in the organization linked to the constituent contact. A lawyer embarking on the process of reporting up must understand that, though the path is required, it is a path fraught with professional danger. The constituents acting on behalf of the organization may not be receptive to the message the lawyer must convey. Sometimes the messenger becomes a target. If the lawyer is in private practice, an agent of the organization may choose to no longer look to the lawyer for legal services and may discharge the lawyer from any continuing representation. If the lawyer is an in-house lawyer, an agent of the organization might take steps to terminate the lawyer's employment. The stakes of reporting organizational misconduct for the in-house lawyer, therefore, are very high.

Rule 1.13(e)(NE) contains an attempt to protect a lawyer who suffers such misfortune as a result of trying to protect the best interests of the organization. If a lawyer "reasonably believes that he or she has been discharged" as a result of the lawyer's actions in reporting up or out, the lawyer must ensure that the "highest authority" of the organization is informed of the situation. This duty to inform the "highest authority" of the organization applies even if the lawyer has not been discharged but has withdrawn from the representation of the organization "under circumstances that require or permit the lawyer to" report up or report out.

Perhaps Lisa reports Ted's wrongful conduct regarding the marketing of the pharmaceutical product. Shortly thereafter, Lisa is informed that Tech Corporation will no longer require her services. Lisa must inform the board of directors for Tech Corporation that she "reasonably believes," if she in fact does, that she was discharged because of her report of Ted's activities.

4. The Sarbanes–Oxley Act

Congress, in 2002, in response to the corporate scandals of Enron, WorldCom and the like, enacted the Sarbanes–Oxley Act. Congress and the public were concerned that lawyers had been aware of some of the corporate wrongdoing in the scandals but that those lawyers had believed that the rules of professional responsibility required that they remain silent. The Sarbanes–Oxley Act, in section 307, 15 U.S.C. 7245, required the Securities Exchange Commission (SEC) to create regulations governing the professional responsibility of lawyers representing corporations who issue publicly-traded securities. As directed by the Act, the SEC created regulations that require a lawyer who becomes aware of evidence of a material violation of securities laws or a material breach of fiduciary duty to report up the ladder of control within the corporation.

The Sarbanes–Oxley regulations provide a step-by-step guide to the reporting lawyer and the chief legal officer, usually known as the General Counsel, as to the procedure to follow in reporting. For example, the regulations require the reporting lawyer to report to the chief legal officer or both the chief legal officer and the chief executive officer, unless such a move would be futile. In the futile situation, the reporting lawyer must report to an authorized committee of the board of directors or to the full board of directors. If the reporting lawyer reports to the chief legal officer, that officer must then report up to one of several entities identified in the regulations. The regulations specify the required conduct for each actor for each step of the reporting scheme.

The regulations also provide, as a last resort, a permissive right for a lawyer to report out of the corporation to the SEC. A lawyer may disclose confidential information to the SEC if the lawyer reasonably believes such conduct is necessary to prevent, rectify, or mitigate the consequences of a material violation. This permissive right should be read in conjunction with Rule 1.13(NE) and Rule 1.6(DE).

Related Sections of the *Restatement (Third) of the Law Governing Lawyers*

Sections 96 and 97

Checkpoints

- A lawyer representing an organization does not, by that fact alone, represent the constituents of the organization.
- A lawyer must take care to clarify to others, such as employees and other constituents of the organization, that the lawyer represents the organization and not the employees or other constituents. This is especially true if the lawyer has reason to know of confusion or if the lawyer has reason to know that the interests of the constituent with whom the lawyer is dealing are adverse to the interests of the organization.
- A lawyer may represent a constituent as well as the organization if the representation does not violate conflict of interest rules. If a lawyer must obtain consent of an organization for the representation to occur, the prospective client constituent cannot provide the consent on behalf of the organization.
- A lawyer's communications with constituents in the context of the representation of the organization are protected by the duty of confidentiality the lawyer owes the organization. The communications also may be protected by the organization's attorney-client privilege.
- A lawyer representing an organization can request an employee or other agent of the organization to refrain from revealing information to others if the lawyer "reasonably believes" such a course will not adversely affect the person.
- A lawyer representing an opposing party may not contact a constituent of the organization if the lawyer knows the organization is represented in the matter and the constituent "supervises, directs or regularly consults with the organization's lawyer concerning the matter or has authority to obligate the organization with respect to the matter or whose act or omission in connec-

tion with the matter may be imputed to the organization for purposes of civil or criminal liability."

- In the context of a shareholder derivative action, conflict of interest concepts may dictate the parameters of the lawyer's representations.
- When a lawyer knows that a constituent is engaging in conduct or planning to engage in conduct in a matter relating to the representation and such conduct
    1. is a breach of a legal duty or obligation the constituent owes to the organization or is "a violation of law that might reasonably be imputed to the organization" and viewed as the act of the organization, and
    2. is "likely to result in substantial injury to the organization,"

  the lawyer must act "as is reasonably necessary in the best interest of the organization."
- The "best interest of the organization" is served by the lawyer reporting up the hierarchy of the organization unless the lawyer "reasonably believes" such conduct is not warranted. The lawyer should go so far as to report to the "highest authority" that can act for the organization.
- A lawyer may report to an entity outside of the organization if the following is true:
    1. the lawyer has followed the process described for reporting within the organization,
    2. the "highest authority" has failed to deal with the misconduct in an "appropriate manner,"
    3. the misconduct is "clearly a violation of law,"
    4. the lawyer "reasonably believes" that the misconduct is "reasonably certain" to create "substantial injury" to the organization,
    5. the lawyer "reasonably believes" disclosure is necessary to prevent the "substantial injury" to the organization, and
    6. the information does not relate to the lawyer's investigation or defense of the organization or a constituent of the organization if the organization has entrusted the lawyer with the investigation of an alleged violation of law or with the defense of the organization or a constituent against a claim of violation of law.
- A lawyer who "reasonably believes" that he or she has been discharged as a result of abiding by the lawyer's reporting responsibilities or who withdraws under the same circumstances must notify the "highest authority" who can act on behalf of the organization.
- The Sarbanes-Oxley Act provides additional reporting responsibilities for a lawyer who represents an issuer of publicly-traded securities.

Chapter 14

Clients with Diminished Capacity

Roadmap

- Rule 1.14(DE)
- Representing a client with diminished mental capacity
- Providing emergency legal assistance to a person with diminished mental capacity

A. Maintaining a Normal Lawyer-Client Relationship with a Client with Diminished Mental Capacity

In the typical relationship between a lawyer and a client, the client establishes the objectives of the representation and participates in many of the decisions regarding the matter. Rule 1.2(a)(DE) makes clear that, as between the lawyer and the client, the client sets the objectives. In addition, Rule 1.2(a)(DE) clarifies that the client decides whether to settle a civil matter. In a criminal matter, the client decides the plea to enter, whether to waive a jury trial, and whether to testify. The client typically participates in all sorts of lesser decisions as well. The ideal relationship of lawyer and client is one of comfortable, mutual consultation and collaboration. *See Chapter 8 Scope of the Representation and Communication with the Client.*

Sometimes lawyers represent clients who have diminished mental ability. The client might be a young child or a teenager or an older adult. The client might be a middle-aged person with cognitive limitations. Just as the population in general is varied and diverse, so is the population of clients and their mental abilities. A lawyer must be mindful of the mental capacities of clients. Only by understanding the limitations of a client can a lawyer provide the best possible representation for that client.

When a lawyer determines that he or she has a client who has diminished capacity to make the kind of decisions required in the representation, that lawyer must consider the guidance of Rule 1.14(DE). Rule 1.14(a)(DE) states that a lawyer in such a circumstance must take care, if "reasonably possible," to have a "normal client-lawyer relationship with the client."

Perhaps Lisa Lawyer represents Clint Client, an elderly man, with regard to estate planning matters. Lisa discovers that Clint is sometimes a very clear thinker and sometimes seems very disoriented. In an effort to have a normal working relationship with Clint, Lisa has several conversations with him about matters to be decided. She puts everything in writing so that Clint has the opportunity to review the matter repeatedly in the midst of reaching a decision.

Clients such as Clint sometimes prefer to have family members present to help them understand matters. As comment three to the rule explains, the presence of a party who is necessary to the representation does not destroy the attorney-client privilege. Be aware, however, that the necessity of the other person's presence might be disputed later. Also, the lawyer must ensure that the client makes the decision, not the family member.

B. Protecting a Client with Diminished Mental Capacity

Unfortunately, a lawyer occasionally has a client for whom the lawyer must provide more significant assistance. If a lawyer "reasonably believes" that a client

1. suffers from a mental disability,
2. "is at risk of substantial physical, financial or other harm," and
3. cannot act to protect his or her own interests,

the lawyer may take "reasonably necessary protective action." Perhaps Lisa discovers that Clint has not been eating properly, has lost weight suddenly, and appears unable to discuss solutions to the problem of adequate nutrition. In such a situation, Rule 1.14(b)(DE) permits, but does not require, that a lawyer such as Lisa take action to assist Clint in resolving his problems.

Lawyers are not always the best judges of the parameters of the client's mental limitations; lawyers are not doctors. Comment six to the rule notes that a lawyer may need to consult with someone with more expertise in an effort to determine the client's limitations and the appropriate protective action to pursue. While the lawyer has the duty expressed in Rule 1.6(DE) to protect the confidentiality of information relating to the representation, *see Chapter 15*

The Duty of Confidentiality, Rule 1.14(c)(DE) provides that the lawyer may make disclosures of protected information if "reasonably necessary" to obtain protection for the client and the client's interests. This disclosure, says comment eight, is "impliedly authorized," even if the client denies permission to disclose.

In defining "reasonably necessary protective action," Rule 1.14(b)(DE) expressly mentions the possibility of the lawyer consulting with persons or entities that are able to protect the client. The rule also explicitly states that the lawyer may seek the appointment of a guardian, guardian ad litem, or conservator, if such appointment is appropriate. Generally, a conservator is appointed when the client needs someone to make financial decisions. A guardian is appointed to take care of all decisions relating to the person and the property of another. A guardian ad litem is appointed to make decisions regarding a particular legal matter such as a litigation matter. If Lisa is worried that Clint is not eating properly, a guardian might be the best protection for him.

The lawyer always must give great weight to the desires and values of the client. The lawyer must attempt to maximize client autonomy in choosing the path to take in acting in the best interest of the client.

C. Emergency Assistance

The comments to Rule 1.14(DE) also address the situation of a person of diminished capacity seeking a lawyer's assistance on an emergency basis. The emergency basis must be, as stated in comment nine, a situation in which the person's "health, safety or a financial interest of a person with seriously diminished capacity is threatened with imminent and irreparable harm." The rule itself does not deal with the issue of emergency assistance. Comments nine and ten allow a lawyer to act for the person even if no lawyer-client relationship can be established because of the lack of capacity and the person is not otherwise capable of exercises of judgment. The lawyer may act as is "reasonably necessary" to avoid harm if there is no one else to act to protect the person and no other alternative. The lawyer must protect the confidences of the person and disclose only what is necessary to prevent harm.

Related Sections of the *Restatement (Third) of the Law Governing Lawyers*

Section 24

Checkpoints

- A lawyer must attempt to "maintain a normal lawyer-client relationship" with a client with diminished mental capacity.
- If a lawyer "reasonably believes" that a client
    1. suffers from a mental disability,
    2. "is at risk of substantial physical, financial or other harm," and
    3. cannot act to protect his or her own interests,

  the lawyer may take "reasonably necessary protective action."
- A lawyer may assist a person with diminished mental capacity on an emergency basis even if a proper lawyer-client relationship is not possible if the person's "health, safety or a financial interest" is subject to "imminent and irreparable harm."

Section IV
Confidentiality

Chapter 15

The Duty of Confidentiality

Roadmap

- Rule 1.6(DE)
- The general duty of confidentiality
- Situations in which a lawyer may reveal or must reveal otherwise confidential information

---

A. The Duty Not to Disclose Information Relating to a Client's Representation

1. When the Duty Exists

Lawyers have a duty to maintain confidences of clients during and after the representation. The duty of confidentiality exists with regard to prospective clients even if they never become clients. *See Chapter 20 Conflicts and Prospective Clients.* Unlike the attorney-client privilege, which protects certain communications from compelled disclosure, and unlike the work-product doctrine, which protects materials prepared in anticipation of litigation from compelled disclosure, the duty of confidentiality is not so limited. *See Chapter 16 The Attorney-Client Privilege and the Work-Product Doctrine.* A lawyer has a duty to not reveal, as Rule 1.6(a)(DE) states, "information relating to the representation of a client." The duty applies to information received from a client in any form as well as to information that comes to a lawyer from any other source.

If Larry Lawyer represents Cindy Client in a divorce matter and discovers, in a conversation with a bartender, information relating to Cindy's relationship with her husband, Larry has a duty not to reveal that information. This duty not to reveal is a duty not to reveal to anyone in or out of the divorce proceeding. Larry cannot share the information with opposing counsel or Larry's best buddy, Joe, or even Larry's wife. This is in contrast to the attorney-client privilege in that the privilege would not protect the conversation with the bartender because it is not a communication between lawyer and client. *See Chapter 16 The Attorney-Client Privilege and the Work-Product Doctrine.*

1.6(DE) states the general duty of confidentiality. This section is reinforced by Rule 1.9(c)(DE), which restates a lawyer's duty not to reveal information after the representation has concluded and by Rule 1.18(b)(DE), which clarifies that the lawyer has a duty not to reveal information even when a prospective client does not become a client. *See Chapter 19 Conflicts and Former Clients* and *Chapter 20 Conflicts and Prospective Clients.*

In addition to the duty not to disclose information relating to the representation of a client, a lawyer also has a duty not to *use* the information to the disadvantage of a client. Rule 1.8(b)(DE) states the duty regarding current clients, a duty not to use information in a way that harms the client. *See Chapter 21 Conflict of Interest Rules for Particular Situations.* Rule 1.9(c)(DE) states the duty regarding former clients, a duty not to use the information in a way that harms the client unless the information is generally known. *See Chapter 19 Conflicts and Former Clients.* The rule regarding prospective clients is the same as that for former clients—a lawyer must not use information in a way that harms the client unless the information is generally known. *See Chapter 20 Conflicts and Prospective Clients.*

The rationale for protecting information is that clients must be free to tell their lawyers everything so they may obtain the best and most appropriate legal advice and representation for the situation. A client must trust that his or her lawyer will not disclose what the lawyer knows about the client's representation during the representation and even long after the representation ends.

2. The Duty to Use "Reasonable Efforts" to Safeguard Confidentiality

Rule 1.6(c) (DE) provides that a lawyer must use "reasonable efforts" to ensure that the lawyer does not disclose confidential information inadvertently. In addition, a lawyer must use "reasonable efforts" to ensure that unauthorized third parties do not gain access to confidential information. For example, *ABA Formal Opinion 11-459 (2011)* opines that, in fulfilling his or her duties, a lawyer should warn a client about potential confidentiality leaks such as the access the client's employer may have to the client's email account. Larry Lawyer should explain to his client, Clint, that Clint's employer likely has access to Clint's email correspondence so Clint should keep that in mind when communicating with Larry. In addition, Larry might explain that such access may rob the correspondence of attorney-client privilege protection. *See Chapter 16 The Attorney-Client Privilege and the Work-Product Doctrine.* A warning would be especially vital if Larry represents Clint with regard to an employment dispute with Clint's present employer. Taking such precautions is, simply put, a measure of competence. *See Chapter 5 Competence and Diligence.*

A lawyer must also use "reasonable efforts" to ensure that the lawyer's staff understands and abides by this duty as well. *See Chapter 38 Supervision and Responsibility for Other Lawyers, Nonlawyer Employees, and Other Assistants.* A lawyer might do this by having office seminars about the lawyer's duty of confidentiality, by monitoring employee behavior, and by having employees sign confidentiality agreements.

B. When Lawyers May Disclose: In Furtherance of a Client's Interests

1. Disclosure with "Informed Consent"

Lawyers may disclose otherwise confidential information in certain circumstances explicitly stated in 1.6(DE). An obvious situation in which a lawyer may disclose confidential information is when the client gives "informed consent" to the disclosure. Rule 1.0(e)(DE) defines "informed consent." In the context of consent to disclosure of confidential information, "informed consent" occurs if the lawyer "communicated adequate information and explanation about the material risks of and reasonably available alternatives" to the planned disclosure to the client and the client then agrees to the disclosure.

Perhaps Larry Lawyer represents Clint Client in a criminal matter. Clint may obtain a better result for himself if he discloses to the prosecution information he has implicating other individuals. Clint might authorize Larry to disclose to the prosecution the general import of the information Clint possesses. Clint might agree to such a disclosure by Larry as a way to determine whether the prosecution is inclined to pursue a lighter penalty in exchange for Clint's agreement to provide more detailed information. Clint's consent to the disclosure is an informed one if Larry first discusses with Clint the risks that Clint takes by allowing Larry to indicate that Clint knows anything about the matter. Larry might, for example, explain to Clint that he could be putting himself in danger if the people Clint wishes to implicate learn of his plan. Larry also must discuss any viable alternatives to such a disclosure.

2. "Impliedly Authorized" Disclosure

Another exception to the duty of a lawyer not to reveal confidential information of the client is if the client authorizes the disclosure by implication.

When a client engages a lawyer, the client impliedly authorizes the lawyer to make certain disclosures of confidential information, as Rule 1.6(a)(DE) states, "in order to carry out the representation."

Unfortunately, the rule itself does not give guidance as to when a disclosure might be "impliedly authorized." Comment five is a little more helpful. The comment states that a lawyer is "impliedly authorized" to disclose information to other lawyers in the firm. For example, when Cindy Client engages Larry Lawyer to represent her in a matter and Cindy knows that Larry works in a firm with other lawyers, Cindy is impliedly authorizing Larry to disclose confidential information to other lawyers in the firm as necessary for the representation. The same is true for disclosures to paralegals and other employees. Cindy may specify that Larry is not authorized to disclose confidential information to others in this setting, but absent a statement denying authorization, Larry is "impliedly authorized" to disclose.

The comment also states that a lawyer *may* be "impliedly authorized" to admit a fact that cannot be disputed in good faith. Lastly, the comment states that a lawyer *may* be "impliedly authorized" to make a disclosure that assists reaching a positive outcome in the matter. Almost any disclosure can arguably be justified as a disclosure to assist in reaching a positive outcome.

C. When Lawyers May Disclose: Disclosures Adverse to a Client's Interests

Rule 1.6(b)(DE) provides a list of situations in which a lawyer may disclose confidential information without client authorization of any kind. In these situations, the disclosure almost certainly harms the client. The lawyer is not acting as an agent of the client in these situations. The interest in preventing injury to others, to the lawyer, or to the judicial system creates the motivation for allowing the lawyer's disclosure. In each situation the lawyer may disclose upon a reasonable belief that disclosure is "necessary"; the lawyer need not be certain. In these circumstances, the lawyer *may* disclose but is not *required* to disclose. In other words, the lawyer can act in accordance with Rule 1.6(DE) by remaining silent, though some other rule, statute, or court order may require disclosure. Even if a lawyer has the right to disclose confidential information, the lawyer should disclose only the information absolutely needed to protect the interest addressed by the exception to the duty of confidentiality.

1. Disclosure to Prevent "Death or Substantial Bodily Harm" to Another

If a lawyer "reasonably believes" that a disclosure of otherwise confidential information is necessary to prevent "reasonably certain death or substantial bodily harm," Rule 1.6(b)(1)(DE) allows that lawyer to disclose the confidential information. If Larry Lawyer represents Cindy Client in a divorce and child custody matter and Larry learns from a credible third party that Cindy plans to toss her children into the river rather than lose custody of them, Larry may notify the authorities of the danger.

A lawyer has the discretion to disclose information in any situation involving "reasonably certain death or substantial bodily harm" even though no crime may be involved. Perhaps Larry Lawyer represents Clint Client in a criminal matter. Clint confides to Larry that Clint killed a woman several years earlier. Larry recalls that another man was found guilty of the murder of the woman and has been sentenced to death. The state's execution of the man would not be a crime. The rule allows Larry's disclosure.

This disclosure exception is preventive only. If the death or bodily harm has already occurred, there is no possibility of ethical disclosure.

2. Disclosure Related to Injury to a Person's "Financial Interests or Property"

Two of the disclosure exceptions relate to harm to a person's "financial interests or property." These exceptions are relatively recent additions to the rules. The first of the two financial interest exceptions to the duty of confidentiality, Rule 1.6(b)(2)(DE), allows a lawyer to disclose information if the lawyer "reasonably believes" the disclosure is "necessary" to prevent the client's commission of a crime or fraud if the crime is "reasonably certain to result in substantial injury to the financial interests or property of another," and the lawyer's services were used or are being used to further the crime or fraud.

The second of the two financial interests exceptions to the duty of confidentiality, Rule 1.6(b)(3)(DE), allows a lawyer to disclose information if the lawyer "reasonably believes" the disclosure is "necessary" to "prevent, mitigate or rectify substantial injury to the financial interests or property of another" if the injury is "reasonably certain to result or has resulted from the client's commission of a crime or fraud," and the lawyer's services were used to further the crime or fraud.

While the first exception allows disclosure to prevent the commission of a crime or fraud, the second exception deals with the situation in which a crime or fraud has already occurred. In this second scenario, the lawyer may disclose to prevent the injury, to mitigate the injury, or even to rectify the injury.

Both exceptions require that the client use the lawyer's services to further a crime or fraud. Rule 1.2(d)(DE) proclaims that a lawyer acts unethically by knowingly counseling a client to engage in criminal or fraudulent conduct or knowingly assisting a client in such activity. *See Chapter 8 Scope of the Representation and Communication with the Client.* Yet a client may use a lawyer's services in furtherance of a crime or fraud without the lawyer's knowledge. Recall that fraud, as defined in Rule 1.0(d)(DE), is conduct fraudulent according to relevant state law and that "has a purpose to deceive."

The financial interest exceptions apply as follows. Suppose that Larry Lawyer represents Clint Client in Clint's attempt to raise money to pursue a product idea. Larry has prepared documents that Clint shows to potential investors in an attempt to interest the investors in his venture. Larry discovers that the documents he prepared for Clint contain false information about the ownership of patents and the rights to ideas necessary to the success of Clint's venture. Larry discovers that Clint has known about the falsehoods from the beginning of his contact with Larry. Clint never planned for his venture to succeed. Rather, he has moved forward on the venture as a fraudulent scheme to obtain the money of others so that he can retire to a remote Caribbean island. Larry discovers Clint's true plan before Clint is scheduled to meet and present his idea to Venture Capitalist, a person who has a reputation for investing large sums of money without significant investigation.

Rule 1.6(b)(2)(DE) allows Larry to disclose confidential information to Venture Capitalist to prevent Clint from committing a crime or fraud. Clint is using Larry's services, the documents he prepared, to succeed in the fraudulent scheme. If Clint makes the presentation to Venture Capitalist, Larry reasonably believes that there is a good probability that Capitalist will give significant sums to Clint and that Capitalist will be unable to recover the investment. Larry "reasonably believes" disclosing Clint's plan to Capitalist is "necessary" to prevent the fraud.

Perhaps at the time Larry discovers Clint's plan, Clint has already convinced Ron Richguy to invest and Ron has given Clint $50,000. Larry may disclose to Ron so that Ron may act quickly to recover his money before Clint becomes hard to find. Clint already may have committed the crime or fraud with regard to Richguy, but Rule 1.6(b)(3)(DE) allows Larry to disclose to prevent, mitigate or rectify the financial injury to Richguy even though Clint has already committed the fraudulent or criminal act.

3. Disclosure to Obtain Ethics Advice

Every lawyer, from time to time, has concern that a course of conduct may be improper. In order to encourage lawyers to consult with others about the appropriate path, Rule 1.6(b)(4)(DE) provides that a lawyer may disclose client confidences if the lawyer "reasonably believes" the disclosure is "necessary" to obtain legal advice about the lawyer's obligations.

Perhaps Larry Lawyer, upon discovering Clint's fraudulent scheme as described in the earlier hypothetical, is uncertain whether he must disclose to Venture Capitalist and to Ron Richguy. Larry is also unsure about whether he may or must withdraw from the representation of Clint. Larry has the discretion to discuss the matter with another lawyer in an effort to obtain advice about what the professional responsibility rules demand. The bar associations of some states offer a service to lawyers for this purpose. For example, the bar may have a list of lawyers that other lawyers may contact for advice on professional responsibility matters. Rule 1.6(b)(4)(DE) simply clarifies that a disclosure of confidences is allowed in such a setting. Of course, often a lawyer may obtain advice by using hypothetical questions and thus perhaps without any disclosure of confidential information.

4. Disclosure "to Establish a Claim or Defense" for the Lawyer

Rule 1.6(b)(5)(DE) provides that a lawyer may disclose client confidences in situations in which the lawyer's actions in representing the client have been called into question. The rule allows disclosure by the lawyer if the lawyer "reasonably believes" such disclosure is "necessary"

1. "to establish a claim or defense on behalf of the lawyer in a controversy between the lawyer and the client";
2. "to establish a defense" to a civil or criminal claim that is based on the lawyer's conduct relating to the client; or
3. "to respond to allegations in any proceeding concerning the lawyer's representation of the client."

The first portion of the exception for disclosure allows a lawyer to defend himself or herself. Perhaps Clint Client sues Larry Lawyer for legal malpractice. Larry may disclose client confidences to defend himself against the allegation that Larry provided substandard representation to Clint.

Likewise, the first portion of the exception to the duty of confidentiality also allows a lawyer to make disclosures in an action to recover a fee owed by a client. The fee action is a controversy between the lawyer and the client. The lawyer may disclose confidences as needed to establish the lawyer's entitlement to the fee. In this setting the disclosure needed is probably a skeletal disclosure of the fact of services rendered.

The second portion of the exception allows a lawyer to disclose a client's confidences "to establish a defense" to a civil or criminal claim based on the lawyer's conduct relating to the client. If Larry Lawyer is prosecuted criminally for fraud in the representation of Clint, Larry may disclose confidential information about Clint in an effort to defend himself.

The last portion of the exception allows a lawyer to disclose a client's confidences "to respond to allegations in any proceeding concerning the lawyer's representation of the client." This is really a catch-all provision that allows the lawyer to defend against any allegation of impropriety.

5. Disclosure "to Comply with Other Law or a Court Order"

Occasionally, other federal or state laws require certain disclosures. For example, a state statute may require all persons with reason to believe that a child is in danger of physical abuse to report that potential abuse to a social services entity. Larry Lawyer may come upon information in the course of representing Clint and related to the representation of Clint that indicates that a child is in such danger. Rule 1.6(b)(6)(DE) permits a disclosure if other relevant law requires it. Larry could disclose as the state abuse statute mandates. Larry would not be acting contrary to the duty of confidentiality he owes to Clint.

A lawyer also may disclose confidential information if ordered to do so by a court. A typical setting in which this issue arises is when a lawyer asserts and argues that a particular communication need not be produced in response to a request for production of documents because the attorney-client privilege protects the communication. If the court disagrees, the lawyer must consult with the client in accordance with the duty of Rule 1.4(DE) regarding communicating with the client as to whether the client desires to appeal the order to produce. *See Chapter 8 Scope of the Representation and Communication with the Client.* If the client does not appeal the order, the lawyer must disclose the communication. Rule 1.6(b)(6)(DE) allows the lawyer to make this disclosure.

6. Disclosure to Evaluate Conflicts of Interest Related to Law Practice Changes

In today's world lawyers, upon occasion, move from one firm or other employer to another. Firms merge and split, and, as Rule 1.17(KS) provides, lawyers sell law practices. In such an environment, lawyers need the ability to evaluate whether such moves will create conflicts of interest before making a final decision on the change. Without the ability to evaluate conflicts before the contemplated change, lawyers would forego positive moves or would implement the changes only to discover that unknown conflicts of interest create disruptions of representation.

A very new addition, Rule 1.6(b)(7)(DE), allows lawyers to disclose confidential information so that conflicts of interest created by a lawyer's contemplated employment change, by a contemplated merger, or by a sale of a practice can be evaluated. Only a limited amount of confidential information needs to be disclosed for conflicts evaluation purposes. A comment to the rule states that usually the only needed disclosure is a short description of the matter, a statement of whether the matter is ongoing or complete, and identification of the parties involved. No disclosure should occur until the contemplated change has become the subject of substantive discussions. No disclosure can occur if the result is harm to the client or the attorney-client privilege's application.

D. Disclosure Required by Other Provisions of the Rules of Professional Conduct

1. Disclosure Required But Trumped by the Duty of Confidentiality

Other rules of professional conduct deal with various sorts of disclosures. Unlike Rule 1.6(DE), which provides that a lawyer *may* disclose in certain circumstances, these other rules generally *require* disclosure but require this disclosure only if the information is not within the confines of the duty of confidentiality stated in Rule 1.6(DE) or if the client consents. So, for example, Rule 8.3(ID) requires a lawyer to report another lawyer known to have engaged in dishonesty because such action violates the rules of professional conduct and raises a "substantial question" as to the lawyer's honesty. Yet Rule 8.3(ID) specifically exempts the lawyer from a duty to report if the reporting would require a disclosure of information protected by the duty of confidentiality of Rule 1.6(DE). *See Chapter 49 The Duty to Report Misconduct.* Rule 4.1(b)(DE), which deals with truthfulness to others, and Rule 8.1(DE), which deals with disclosure in the context of bar admission and disciplinary matters, are other examples of rules that state duties to disclose but then limit the duty to disclose by the duty of confidentiality of Rule 1.6(DE). *See Chapter 35 Truthfulness to Third Parties; Chapter 2 Admission to the Bar; Chapter 3 The Discipline Process and Jurisdiction for Discipline.*

2. Disclosure Required Regardless of the Duty of Confidentiality

The duty of a lawyer to be candid with the tribunal is different. In Rule 3.3(DE) there are various requirements of disclosure to ensure candor to the tribunal. This rule specifically states that the disclosures are required *even if* the duty of confidentiality otherwise protects the information. The judicial system's interest in seeking justice trumps the client's duty of confidentiality in the narrow circumstances described by Rule 3.3(DE). *See Chapter 28 Honesty and Candor.*

E. Disclosure Permitted By Rule 1.13

There is another situation of permissive disclosure not stated in Rule 1.6(DE). Rule 1.13(c)(NE) states that a lawyer representing an organization may disclose confidential information to entities outside the organization even if Rule 1.6(DE) does not otherwise permit the disclosure if certain circumstances are true. First, the lawyer must have become aware of a situation requiring the lawyer to report internally within the organization. In other words, the lawyer knows that a constituent of the organization is acting or plans to act in a manner that violates a legal obligation to the organization or is a violation of law that may be imputed to the organization. The lawyer also must believe that this misconduct is likely to substantially harm the organization.

Second, the lawyer must have followed the process for internal reporting described in Rule 1.13(b)(NE). Third, the "highest authority" for the organization must have failed to address in an "appropriate manner" the misconduct reported. Fourth, that misconduct clearly must be a violation of law. Fifth, the lawyer must "reasonably believe[ ]" that the improper act is "reasonably certain" to create a "substantial injury" to the organization. Lastly, the lawyer must "reasonably believe[ ]" disclosure is needed to "prevent substantial injury to the organization."

Rule 1.13(d)(NE) contains a limitation on this right to disclose. A lawyer may not disclose confidential information if the confidential information relates to the lawyer's investigation or defense of the organization or a constituent of the organization if the organization entrusted the lawyer with the investigation of an alleged violation of law or with the defense of the organization or a constituent against a claim of violation of law. When making a disclosure, a lawyer must match the disclosure with the need. In other words, a lawyer may disclose only what is needed to prevent the injury—and no more. *See Chapter 13 Organizational Clients.*

Related Sections of the *Restatement (Third) of the Law Governing Lawyers*

Sections 59–67

Checkpoints

- A lawyer has a duty not to disclose information relating to the representation of a client, a former client, or a prospective client.
- A lawyer must use "reasonable efforts" to prevent disclosure of such information by the lawyer or any member of the lawyer's staff. A lawyer must use "reasonable efforts" to ensure no one has "unauthorized access" to confidential information and there is no "unauthorized disclosure" of confidential information.
- A lawyer has a duty not to *use* information relating to a client's representation to the disadvantage of the client, former client, or prospective client. With regard to former and prospective clients, this duty evaporates if the information is "generally known."
- A lawyer may disclose confidential information if the lawyer "reasonably believes" the disclosure "necessary"
    1. to prevent "death or substantial bodily harm" to another;
    2. to prevent a client's commission of a crime or fraud if the crime or fraud is "reasonably certain to result in substantial injury to the financial interests or property of another" and if the lawyer's services were used or are being used to further the crime or fraud;
    3. to "prevent, mitigate or rectify substantial injury to the financial interests or property of another" that is "reasonably certain to result" from a client's commission of a crime or fraud if the lawyer's services were used to further the crime or fraud;
    4. to obtain legal advice about the lawyer's ethical obligations;
    5. "to establish a claim or defense on behalf of the lawyer in a controversy between lawyer and client";
    6. to establish a defense to a civil or criminal claim based on the lawyer's conduct relating to the client;
    7. "to respond to allegations in any proceeding concerning the lawyer's representation of the client";

8. to comply with other state or federal law or an order of a court; or
9. to allow for evaluation of conflicts of interest relating to a contemplated change of employment for a lawyer, or a change of firm ownership such as a merger, or a sale of a practice, only if the disclosure does not harm the client or affect attorney-client privilege application.

- A lawyer must disclose otherwise confidential information to a tribunal in accord with Rule 3.3(DE).
- A lawyer may disclose otherwise confidential information in the context of the representation of an organizational client if
  1. the lawyer has become aware of a situation requiring the lawyer to report internally,
  2. the lawyer has followed the process for internal reporting described in Rule 1.13(b)(NE),
  3. the "highest authority" for the organization has failed to address in an "appropriate manner" the misconduct reported,
  4. the misconduct is "clearly a violation of law,"
  5. the lawyer "reasonably believes" that the act is "reasonably certain" to create a "substantial injury to the organization,"
  6. the lawyer reasonably believes disclosure is necessary to prevent "substantial injury" to the organization, and
  7. the confidential information does not relate to the lawyer's investigation or defense of the organization or a constituent of the organization if the organization has entrusted the lawyer with the investigation of an alleged violation of law or with the defense of the organization or a constituent against a claim of violation of law.

Chapter 16

The Attorney-Client Privilege and the Work-Product Doctrine

Roadmap

- The attorney-client privilege
- Waiver of the attorney-client privilege
- The attorney-client privilege as applied to organizational clients
- The work-product doctrine
- Rule 26(b)(3) & (5)(B) of the Federal Rules of Civil Procedure

A. The Attorney-Client Privilege

1. Protection from Compelled Disclosure

The attorney-client privilege is an evidentiary principle that has existed for centuries. The privilege protects certain communications from compelled disclosure. The privilege is the client's, but counsel or other agents of the client may assert it on behalf of the client. Neither a lawyer nor a client can be required to testify at trial, in a deposition, or otherwise, about privileged communications. Neither a lawyer nor a client can be required to produce privileged communications in the discovery process or otherwise. If a communication is privileged, it is absolutely privileged. No showing of need or hardship or cost will result in a court compelling disclosure. The privilege survives the end of the lawyer-client relationship and survives after the client has died. The privilege protects communications but not underlying facts. Cindy Client might not have to disclose what Cindy said to her lawyer, Lisa, about the price of a particular stock on June 1. Cindy might be required, however, to testify as to her knowledge of the price of the stock on June 1.

2. Rationale

The privilege encourages discussion and disclosure between a lawyer and a client. A client can receive the best legal advice for the situation if the client feels free to disclose all relevant details to the lawyer. The lawyer then can discuss and advise the client without fear of disclosure of the discussion. Full disclosure to the lawyer is necessary for the lawyer to adequately counsel the client so that the client may remain within the bounds of the law. This preventive effect encourages legal and proper conduct and discourages illegal and improper conduct. As the United States Supreme Court stated in *Upjohn Company v. United States,* 449 U.S. 383 (1981), the privilege's "purpose is to encourage full and frank communication between attorneys and their clients and thereby promote broader public interests in the observance of law and administration of justice." *Id.* at 389.

Nondisclosure of relevant information has its costs, however. A court may not become aware of the full story. The privilege may thwart discovery of the truth. Society accepts this cost as reasonable given the benefit created by the lawyer-client relationship. Because the privilege often reduces access to relevant information, courts scrutinize the privilege's applicability and apply the privilege narrowly.

3. Scope of the Privilege

a. A Communication between a Lawyer and a Client

To be privileged, a communication must be between a lawyer and client or between their respective agents. Communications between a lawyer's paralegal and a client may be privileged even though no lawyer is a party to the communication. A client's communications with a lawyer are privileged regardless of whether the lawyer is an in-house lawyer or a lawyer in private practice. Other countries may treat in-house attorneys differently.

b. A Communication Intended to be Confidential

To be privileged, the communication must be intended to be confidential. Communicating in the presence of others indicates a lack of intent to keep the communication confidential. When a client consults a lawyer in the presence of others who are not a part of the lawyer's team and are not people necessary to assist the client, the implication is that the communication is not confidential. If Cindy Client talks to her lawyer, Lisa, at a party and several other people are participating in the conversation, the communications between Cindy and Lisa are not privileged even though Cindy is seeking legal advice and counsel from Lisa and Lisa may be rendering such advice and counsel. Communicating with Lisa in the presence of others shows a lack of intent on Cindy's part that the communication be confidential.

c. A Communication Made for the Purpose of Obtaining or Rendering Legal Service or Advice

To be protected from compelled disclosure, a communication must be made for the purpose of obtaining or rendering legal advice. Sometimes a client consults a lawyer regarding nonlegal matters. This is not surprising since, if a lawyer is doing his or her job properly, a client should respect the judgment of the lawyer. The attorney-client privilege does not apply to the communications, however, because they are not communications for the purpose of obtaining or rendering legal service. This issue often arises when the client is a business. In such a setting the party seeking disclosure typically argues that the business consulted the lawyer for business advice, not legal advice, or that the lawyer rendered business advice, not legal advice.

d. A Communication Not Used in Furtherance of a Crime or Fraud

If a client consults with a lawyer and then uses the lawyer's advice to commit a crime or fraud, the communication between the lawyer and the client is not privileged even though the communication might otherwise satisfy the requirements of the privilege. The lawyer need not know of the client's purpose or actions for the communication to be robbed of privileged status. Recall that Rule 1.2(d)(DE) states that a lawyer may not knowingly assist a crime or fraud. *See Chapter 8 Scope of the Representation and Communication with the Client.* Fraudulent conduct generally requires reckless or intentional misrepresentation. The definition of fraud for purposes of professional responsibility is conduct that is fraud under state laws and, as stated by Rule 1.0(d)(DE), "has a purpose to deceive."

Perhaps Cindy Client comes to Lisa Lawyer to discuss various ways Cindy can structure a particular transaction. Cindy might present the matter to Lisa and Lisa might counsel Cindy that taking one path would be fraudulent and illegal, that taking another path would be legal and proper, and that Cindy should take the legal path. Cindy might then use Lisa's advice to structure the transaction in a fraudulent and illegal way. The attorney-client privilege does not protect the communication between Lisa and Cindy. This is true even if Cindy did not consult with Lisa with the purpose of discovering the fraudulent path but rather decided after Lisa rendered the advice that she would act fraudulently and illegally.

Courts treat the issue of whether a communication is used to further of a crime or fraud as an exception to the general application of the attorney-client privilege. The effect of the exception status is that the party claiming the privilege first must prove that the privilege protects the communication. Then the party claiming that the communication furthered a crime or fraud must exhibit a reasonable basis for the claim. Usually, a court requires the party to make this showing using evidence other than the communication itself. The court then determines the correct resolution without disclosure of the communication to the party claiming that the privilege does not protect the communication.

4. Waiver of the Privilege

a. General Rule: Disclosure is Waiver

If a client discloses a communication to third parties, the communication no longer enjoys the privilege's protection. The disclosure waives the privilege that otherwise applies. Perhaps Cindy Client goes to Lisa Lawyer's office and, in confidence, discusses with Lisa the possibility of divorcing her husband. In this setting, Lisa gives Cindy legal advice about the possible divorce. If Cindy then leaves Lisa's office and goes to a bar and discusses with a friend the substance of her conversation with Lisa, Cindy has waived the privilege with regard to her communications with Lisa.

If Cindy discloses a part of the communication, a court might find that Cindy has waived the privilege as to all of the communication which dealt with the issue to which the disclosed portion related. Since the attorney-client privilege is a shield to encourage disclosure between lawyer and client, the courts are wary of a partial disclosure. The courts fear that the client may selectively disclose so as to present half-truths.

Rule 502 of the Federal Rules of Evidence provides that an intentional waiver in a federal setting waives the privilege as to an undisclosed communication only if the undisclosed communication concerns the same subject matter as the disclosed communication and the communications "ought in fairness to be considered together."

b. The Selective Waiver Concept

In the context of a government investigation, a client sometimes discloses privileged communications to assist the investigation and defend the client but also so that the government entity conducting the investigation will take the client's cooperation into account for purposes of evaluating an appropriate punishment. Later, a third party may claim that the client waived any privilege by disclosing the communications to the government entity.

Some have argued for the recognition of the concept of selective waiver. Selective waiver is the notion that the disclosure of communications in one context does not waive the privilege as to all the world in any context. With selective waiver a disclosure of communications to a government entity in the midst of an investigation does not waive the privilege as to those communications for purposes of a later private litigation matter.

The majority of courts dealing with such issues have rejected the concept of selective waiver. For the vast majority of courts, disclosure in one context waives the privilege for all contexts. The waiver of the privilege in the investigation waives the privilege for the disclosed communication for any context such as a later private litigation matter.

A typical case in which a party urged the court to apply the selective waiver concept is *In re Qwest Communications International Inc.*, 450 F.3d 1179 (10th Cir.), *cert. denied sub nom. Qwest Communications International Inc. v. New England Health Care Employees Pension Fund,* 549 U.S. 1031(2006). Qwest shareholders filed a federal securities fraud class action against Qwest and others claiming that Qwest and the other defendants made false statements about Qwest's finances. The shareholders requested production of certain documents Qwest had already produced to the government in the course of Securities and Exchange Commission (SEC) and Department of Justice (DOJ) investigations. Qwest asserted that the privilege protected these documents from disclosure. In the context of the government investigations, Qwest produced some privileged documents so as to be perceived as cooperating. Qwest obtained confidentiality agreements from the SEC and the DOJ as part of the disclosure. The agreements stated that Qwest did not intend to waive the attorney-client privilege or the work-product doctrine. The district court held that Qwest had waived the privilege for the disclosed documents. The Tenth Circuit Court of Appeals agreed and the United States Supreme Court denied certiorari.

Rule 502(d) of the Federal Rules of Evidence provides that a federal court can issue an order that disclosures relating to matters before it do not waive the privilege. If a court issues such an order, there is no waiver for purposes of any state or federal proceeding. Rule 502(e) provides that parties to a federal proceeding can agree to the effect of a disclosure but such an agreement binds only the parties to the agreement.

c. *Putting a Communication at Issue*

A person cannot make communications an issue in a matter and then refuse to disclose them because of privilege. For example, perhaps Cindy Client ultimately is displeased with the advice rendered by Lisa Lawyer. Cindy might sue Lisa for her lousy advice. In such a situation, Cindy cannot claim privilege for the communications with Lisa that constitute the problematic advice.

d. *A Lawyer May Waive the Privilege on Behalf of a Client*

A client can be held to have waived the privilege by the failure of the client's lawyer to object in a timely manner to disclosure or by the lawyer's disclosure of the communication. A recurring scenario is one in which one party in a litigation matter requests documents as part of a discovery request. The lawyer responding to the request then refuses to produce all or some of the documents on the basis of privilege. Occasionally, the responding lawyer fails to file a privilege log properly recording the claims of privilege. A privilege log is often the proper established procedure for a claim of privilege. A privilege log identifies the communications for which the party claims privilege and states the basis for the claim for each document. In some of these cases, courts have held that the failure of a lawyer to follow established procedure regarding the filing of a privilege log waives the privilege.

e. *Inadvertent Disclosure*

Occasionally, a disclosure occurs not as the result of a conscious choice to disclose but rather inadvertently. A client may disclose otherwise privileged communications inadvertently but the usual setting is a disclosure by a lawyer. Perhaps Lisa Lawyer discloses a privileged communication in the midst of a disclosure of many unprivileged communications in response to a discovery request. Perhaps Lisa Lawyer misdirects a communication such as a letter meant for Cindy Client to the opposition or the opposition's lawyer.

Inadvertent disclosure raises several issues. First is the issue of the proper level of care the disclosing lawyer must exercise in protecting against such disclosure. Recall that Rule 1.1(DE) requires competence in representing a client and competence requires the lawyer to use "reasonable efforts" to avoid inadvertent disclosure. *See Chapter 5 Competence and Diligence.* Second is the issue of proper conduct of the receiving lawyer if the disclosure is made to a lawyer. Rule 4.4(b)(DE) provides that the receiving lawyer must, if he or she knows or reasonably should know that the communication is disclosed inadvertently, notify the disclosing party. *See Chapter 37 Respect for the Rights of Nonclients.*

Finally is the issue of whether the inadvertent disclosure waives the attorney-client privilege.

1. Federal Rules of Civil Procedure Guidance

Rule 26(b)(5)(B) of the Federal Rules of Civil Procedure and similar rules in many states provide the procedure that the disclosing lawyer must follow to assert the privilege for disclosed material and also the procedure that the receiving lawyer must follow upon notice of the privilege assertion. The rule states:

> If information produced in discovery is subject to a claim of privilege or of protection as trial-preparation material, the party making the claim may notify any party that received the information of the claim and the basis for it. After being notified, a party must promptly return, sequester, or destroy the specified information and any copies it has; must not use or disclose the information until the claim is resolved; must take reasonable steps to retrieve the information if the party disclosed it before being notified; and may promptly present the information to the court under seal for a determination of the claim. The producing party must preserve the information until the claim is resolved.

2. The Approach to Inadvertent Disclosure in the Federal Rules of Evidence

A recent addition to the Federal Rules of Evidence addresses the conundrum of inadvertent disclosure. Rule 502(b) provides that an inadvertent disclosure in a federal context is not a waiver of the privilege if "the holder of the privilege or protection took reasonable steps to prevent disclosure" and the party "promptly took reasonable steps the rectify the error, including (if applicable) following Federal Rules of Civil Procedure 26(b)(5)(B)." Rule 502(e) provides that the parties can enter into an agreement about the effect of a disclosure that will bind the parties to the agreement but not third parties.

3. Inadvertent Disclosure May or May Not Waive the Privilege: A Factor Analysis

Historically, many courts have determined whether disclosure waives the privilege by looking at certain factors. One such factor is the steps the disclosing lawyer takes to avoid inadvertent disclosure. If the disclosing lawyer is careful in preventing inadvertent disclosure, a court is less likely to find that a disclosure waives the privilege. A second factor courts consider is the extent of the disclosure in terms of amount of privileged material. For example, was this a disclosure of one privileged document in a sea of 10,000 produced documents or was it one document in a group of ten? A court is less likely to find waiver if the inadvertent disclosure is one document in a group of 10,000. A third factor is the import of the disclosed communications to the litigation. If the inadvertent disclosure goes directly to the core of the litigation, a court may be more likely to find waiver. A fourth factor is the response of the discloser when the discloser realizes what has occurred. Courts consider the steps taken by the discloser and the speed with which the discloser acts after the disclosure to minimize the effect of the error. A fifth factor is the effect on justice of finding waiver or not finding a waiver. This factor is really a wild card that allows a court to reach what the court perceives to be a just result. With this factor approach, disclosure is not dispositive. A communication can be disclosed and yet be privileged.

4. An Inadvertent Disclosure is a Waiver

Some courts take the position that in the inadvertent disclosure setting, any disclosure waives the privilege for the disclosed communication. No privilege exists regardless of how the disclosure occurs. For example, in *Ares-Serono, Inc v. Organon International B.V.*, 160 F.R.D. 1 (D. Mass 1994), in the context of disclosure of privileged documents relating to a patent dispute, the court held that inadvertent disclosure waived the privilege for the disclosed documents. The court noted that "'[m]istake or inadvertence is, after all, merely a euphemism for negligence, and, certainly ... one is expected to pay a price for one's negligence.'" *Id.* at 4 (quoting *International Digital Systems Corp. v. Digital Equipment Corp.*, 120 F.R.D. 445, 450 (D. Mass. 1988) (other citation omitted)).

5. An Inadvertent Disclosure is Not a Waiver

A few courts have taken the position that any inadvertent disclosure by a lawyer cannot be a waiver of the client's privilege for that communication. For example, in *Premiere Digital Access, Inc. v. Central Telephone Co.*, 360 F. Supp. 2d 1168 (D. Nev. 2005), the court evaluated an inadvertent disclosure of a privileged communication, an email, disclosed in a document production of 1,280 pages. The email was from an in-house lawyer to the client and it offered advice about a contract. The client discovered the disclosure a year later when the opposition mentioned it in a response to a motion for summary judgment. The client claimed that it was an inadvertent disclosure by litigation counsel. The court refused to find a waiver on the basis of the inadvertent disclosure, stating: "waiver of the privilege may only occur due to a voluntary disclosure, and that disclosure must be made by the client." *Id.* at 1174.

Some courts espousing this position also may refuse to find a waiver when the client is the discloser if the disclosure is inadvertent. For example, in *Mendenhall v. Barber-Greene Co.*, 531 F. Supp. 951 (N.D. Ill. 1982), a case of inadvertent production by a lawyer, the court found no waiver because it believed a waiver required an intentional abandonment of a known right. An inadvertent disclosure, even by the client, cannot be intentional.

The rationale of such a case seems tied to an erroneous view of the standard for waiver of the privilege. The generally accepted position on the standard of required mental state is that waiver of the attorney-client privilege is an event of lesser moment than a waiver of constitutional rights. The waiver must be voluntary but not necessarily intentional and knowing. The *Restatement (Third) of the Law Governing Lawyers* section 79 comment g states: "To constitute waiver, a disclosure must be voluntary. The disclosing person need not be aware that the communication was privileged, nor specifically intend to waive the privilege."

f. Other Disclosures That Are Not Waivers

The professional responsibility rule with regard to confidentiality, Rule 1.6(DE), provides that a lawyer may disclose confidential information in certain narrow situations. *See Chapter 15 The Duty of Confidentiality.* Might a lawyer waive the attorney-client privilege by disclosing information that Rule 1.6(DE) specifically allows the lawyer to disclose?

Suppose Lisa Lawyer reports that Cindy Client discussed killing her own children. Lisa had good reason to believe Cindy will act on her statements. Lisa's disclosure of Cindy's statements is ethical because Rule 1.6(b)(1)(DE) allows a lawyer to disclose confidential information if the lawyer "reasonably believes" such disclosure is needed to prevent the client from acting in a way that would result in "reasonably certain death or substantial bodily harm" of another. If Lisa reports her conversation with Cindy, has she waived the privilege regarding that communication? In *Newman v. State*, 863 A.2d 321 (Md. 2004), the court faced a similar situation and refused to find that the lawyer's disclosure defeated the privilege. The court reasoned that the lawyer was not acting as the agent of the client in making the disclosure. While the confidentiality rule authorized the lawyer to disclose, the lawyer did not disclose on behalf of the client and the client did authorize the disclosure. This is a logical application of agency concepts.

5. Organizational Clients

A lawyer representing an organization is in a more complicated situation in terms of the application of the attorney-client privilege. There is no doubt that the attorney-client privilege protects communications when the client is an organization, such as a corporation. But who is the client's representative for purposes of the privilege? If the client is a corporation, do all employees represent the corporation in communications with the lawyer? Are all communications between the lawyer for the corporation and corporate representatives privileged? The law must protect the right of the organization to obtain legal advice in a confidential atmosphere similar to that for individuals, without creating a vast black hole of privilege that swallows all that organizational actors do or say.

The privilege is not so broad. If the privilege applies to a communication between an employee and the lawyer for the organization, the privilege applies because the employee is viewed as an agent of the organization such that the lawyer, in communicating with the employee, is communicating with the client, the organization. *See Chapter 13 Organizational Clients.*

a. The Upjohn *Case*

In *Upjohn Co. v. United States*, 449 U.S. 383 (1981), the United States Supreme Court evaluated the application of the attorney-client privilege in the context of a corporate client. In *Upjohn*, the corporation's lawyers conducted an internal investigation. The lawyers talked to all sorts of employees about whether the corporation had been paying bribes to foreign government officials. Later, as part of an Internal Revenue Service investigation, the government sought documentation from the internal bribery investigation such as interview notes from the meetings between the legal staff and Upjohn employees. Upjohn claimed that such materials were privileged. The Supreme Court looked at the issue after the Sixth Circuit Court of Appeals ruled that the privilege did not apply to most of the communications or notes of communications. In reaching this conclusion, the Sixth Circuit applied a narrow control group test to determine who was an agent of the corporation for purposes of the privilege. With this test, the control group consisted of the senior management of the corporation—those individuals who were substantially involved in the management of the corporation. According to the Sixth Circuit, the privilege applied only to communications between the lawyer for the corporation and this narrow control group.

The Supreme Court rejected the Sixth Circuit's application of the attorney-client privilege for purposes of federal evidence law. According to the Supreme Court, the Sixth Circuit's narrow control group test failed to protect many communications that the privilege should protect given the privilege's rationale. The privilege should encourage disclosure to the lawyer so that the lawyer can know the complete story and can render appropriate legal advice. With the narrow control group test, a lawyer for a corporation or other organization cannot speak confidentially with many of the employees who may have important information regarding the conduct of the organization. Thus, disclosure to the lawyer suffers and the lawyer cannot render the best possible legal advice.

Though the *Upjohn* Court disapproved of the narrow control group test, it did not replace that test with another. Rather, the Supreme Court discussed a laundry list of relevant factors to consider, such as whether the communication deals with information within the scope of the employee's duties.

*b. Post-*Upjohn *Developments*

The *Upjohn* opinion cast the narrow control group test in a disapproving light as a matter of federal evidence law. The opinion did not provide a clear replacement. Outside of the federal system, each state has its own evidence principles, including its own analysis or test for application of the attorney-client privilege in the entity context.

1. Broad Control Group Test

Some jurisdictions have used a broader version of the control group test. With this sort of analysis, the privilege applies to any communication that otherwise satisfies the requirements of the attorney-client privilege and is between the lawyer and an employee of the organization who has authority to obtain legal advice on behalf of the organization or has authority to act on legal advice rendered on behalf of the organization. Employees other than senior management often have authority to act on legal advice rendered to the entity. In *Upjohn,* management employees throughout the company might have had authority to implement the lawyer's advice to terminate bribery payments immediately. Yet, these management employees were not senior management in terms of speaking to overall policy for the corporation. While the privilege would not apply to communications with them under a narrow control group test, the privilege would apply under a broader control group test.

2. Subject Matter Tests

Some jurisdictions use a subject matter test. There are a variety of subject matter tests. For example, the test used in *Diversified Industries, Inc. v. Meredith,* 572 F.2d 596 (8th Cir. 1977), focuses on whether the communication of the employee with the lawyer for the corporation was for the purpose of securing legal advice for the corporation, whether the employee communicated at the direction of a superior, and whether the subject matter of the communication was within the scope of the employee's duties. Comment d to section 73 of the *Restatement (Third) of the Law Governing Lawyers* defines a subject matter test as one that grants the privilege to any communication with an employee or other agent of the entity if the communication "relates to the subject matter of the representation."

3. Other Approaches

Other courts or jurisdictions apply variations on these tests. Others use totally different analyses. Some states use tests that combine elements of the control group approach and the subject matter approach. For example, a state might have a test that has as alternatives a broad control group test and a subject matter test.

4. An Example

Larry Lawyer represents Big Corporation, a manufacturer of furniture. Ed is an employee of Big Corporation. Ed drives Big's delivery truck. Unfortunately, Ed, while driving the truck on his delivery route, collided with a car driven by Penny Plaintiff. After the accident Ed discussed the collision with Larry. Ed and Larry talked so that Larry might obtain the facts about the accident and appropriately advise Big Corporation about its potential liability to Penny. Ed's superiors, of course, told him to talk with Larry. Are Larry and Ed's conversations protected by the attorney-client privilege?

With a narrow control group analysis like that rejected by the Supreme Court in *Upjohn*, the privilege does not apply to the communication because Ed is not a member of senior management. With a broader control group analysis, the communication is not privileged because Ed, a delivery truck driver, is not an employee with authority to obtain legal advice on behalf of the entity and likely does not have authority to act on any legal advice rendered to Big Corporation.

With a subject matter test, the communication may be privileged. If the court uses the approach of the *Diversified Industries* case, the privilege applies to the communication between Ed and Larry. The communication was for the purpose of securing legal advice for the corporation, a superior directed Ed to talk with Larry about the collision, and the communication about the collision undoubtedly involved Ed's driving of the delivery truck. This matter was within the scope of Ed's employment with Big Corporation. Thus, the communication was a communication between a lawyer and a client for the purpose of obtaining or rendering legal advice. On the stated facts the communication does not appear to be in furtherance of a crime or fraud. If the communication was intended to be confidential and if there has been no waiver of the privilege, the privilege protects the communication between Ed and Larry. Likewise, if the subject matter analysis focused on whether the communication between Ed and Larry related to the subject of the representation, as the *Restatement* suggests, the communication is privileged because the communication relates to the collision and Larry is investigating so as to advise Big Corporation about its rights regarding the collision between Ed and Penny.

c. Waiver of the Organization's Privilege

While in a particular situation the privilege may protect communications between the organization's lawyer and rank-and-file employees, those same employees do not have the right to waive the privilege for the organization. Only employees with authority to make legal representation decisions for the organization have the authority to waive the organization's privilege.

B. The Work-Product Doctrine

1. The Rule Generally

The work-product doctrine protects against disclosure of documents and other tangible evidence prepared in anticipation of litigation by a party or a party's representative, such as a lawyer. Unlike the attorney-client privilege, the protection provided by the work-product doctrine is narrow and is not absolute. The United States Supreme Court established the modern work-product doctrine in the case of *Hickman v. Taylor,* 329 U.S. 495 (1947). The Court noted the tension between the efficient revelation of all pertinent information and protecting a lawyer's right to represent a client without intrusion into the lawyer-client relationship. The *Hickman* Court recognized a limited protection for materials prepared by a lawyer in anticipation of litigation. The court thought the rule was necessary in the interest of fairness so that a lawyer's work in preparing a matter would not easily be accessible by the opposition and thus moot the work. The teachings of *Hickman* have been codified in Rule 26(b)(3) of the Federal Rules of Civil Procedure and in state rules, statutes, and judge-made law. Rule 26(b)(3) states, in part:

> Ordinarily, a party may not discover documents and tangible things that are prepared in anticipation of litigation or for trial by or for another party or its representative (including the other party's attorney, consultant, surety, indemnitor, insurer, or agent). But, subject to Rule

> 26(b)(4), those materials may be discovered if (i) they are otherwise discoverable under Rule 26(b)(1); and (ii) the party shows that it has substantial need for the materials to prepare its case and cannot without undue hardship, obtain the substantial equivalent by other means.... If the court orders discovery of those materials, it must protect against disclosure of the mental impressions, conclusions, opinions, or legal theories of a party's attorney or other representative concerning the litigation.

Thus, Rule 26(b)(3) protects from disclosure documents and tangible things if these items were prepared in anticipation of litigation unless the one seeking disclosure can prove "substantial need" of the document and that the party cannot access the equivalent of the materials without "undue hardship." Even if the party can successfully show "substantial need" and "undue hardship," the court must protect the mental processes of the lawyer.

2. Materials Prepared in Anticipation of Litigation

The work-product doctrine applies to documents or other tangible things prepared in anticipation of litigation by or for a party or a party's representative. The doctrine can protect an electronic file.

Often, a party's lawyer prepares the document in question but lawyer preparation is not a requirement. If Lisa Lawyer directs Cindy Client to write a narrative explaining all Cindy remembers about an automobile collision, the doctrine can apply to the writing. If Lisa responds with a letter to Cindy analyzing the facts as Cindy describes them, the work-product doctrine can apply to the letter. The same is true for a memorandum to the file that Lisa writes in which Lisa provides a through analysis of the weaknesses of Cindy's position.

None of the documents Lisa and Cindy prepare are protected by the work-product doctrine if the documents are not prepared in the reasonable anticipation of litigation involving the collision. A matter need not yet be in progress when the documents are created for the doctrine to protect them from disclosure, but litigation must be reasonably anticipated. One can argue that everything a lawyer creates is in anticipation of litigation but, obviously, that argument goes too far.

3. "Substantial Need" and "Undue Hardship"

A party can obtain work product of an opposing party that does not involve the mental impressions and processes of a lawyer if the party can prove "substantial need" of the materials and that the party cannot obtain the substantial equivalent of the material without "undue hardship." Perhaps Lisa Lawyer represents Cindy Client in a litigation matter involving a transaction. Lisa wishes to have access to the notes of several of the parties to the transaction and the notes of their counsel resulting from a meeting at which the transaction was planned and discussed. Lisa claims that she needs these notes to prove the motivation for the transaction. Assume that the motivation is relevant to the litigation at hand. Assume also that the court determines that the notes do not involve opinion work product. Lisa has deposed the people present at the meeting and none remember the details of what the attendees of the meeting discussed. The court in such a situation might hold that the sought-after notes are work product but that Lisa, on behalf of Cindy, has shown "substantial need" for the information contained in the documents and also has shown that she cannot access that information by alternative means such as deposing the people who attended the meeting. The court might, in such a case, require disclosure of the documents.

4. The Special Treatment of Opinion Work Product

Opinion work product garners a different protection. Courts disagree somewhat about the limits of the protection. Opinion work product is the thoughts, opinions, strategies, and legal conclusions of a lawyer. Courts often state that opinion work product is discoverable only upon a showing of extraordinary justification. Some courts state that opinion work product deserves nearly absolute protection. Other courts state that opinion work product is, simply, not discoverable.

Related Sections of the *Restatement (Third) of the Law Governing Lawyers*

Sections 68–93

Checkpoints

- The attorney-client privilege protects against compelled disclosure of communications
  1. between a lawyer or the lawyer's agents and the client or the client's agents,
  2. intended to be confidential,
  3. for the purpose of obtaining or rendering legal advice,
  4. if the communication is not used to further a crime or fraud.
- The privilege provides absolute protection from disclosure and cannot be overcome by a showing of need or hardship.
- The client or lawyer acting on behalf of the client may waive the attorney-client privilege.
- Generally, intentional disclosure of a communication waives the privilege.
- Courts have not recognized the doctrine of selective waiver; a disclosure in one context waives the privilege in all contexts.
- Rule 26(b)(5)(B) of the Federal Rules of Civil Procedure provides a procedure for dealing with claims of privilege for inadvertently disclosed materials.
- To determine whether an inadvertent disclosure waives the privilege, many courts use a factor analysis. Other courts find that an inadvertent disclosure always waives the privilege. A few courts find that an inadvertent disclosure does not waive the privilege.
- Rule 502(b) of the Federal Rules of Evidence provides that an inadvertent disclosure in a federal context is not a waiver of the privilege if "the holder of the privilege or protection took reasonable steps to prevent disclosure" and that party "promptly took reasonable steps to rectify the error, including (if applicable) following Federal Rules of Civil Procedure 26(b)(5)(B)."
- The attorney-client privilege applies to organizations as well as individuals.
- In determining who is a representative of an organization for purpose of applying the attorney-client privilege, jurisdictions often follow a control group test or a subject matter test or a combination of the two.
- The work-product doctrine protects against compelled disclosure of materials prepared in anticipation of litigation by or for a party or a party's representative, such as a lawyer.
- Work product protection can be overcome by a showing of "substantial need" and "undue hardship" in accessing the information through an alternative source.
- If work product contains the thoughts, opinions, strategies or legal conclusions of a lawyer, the protection of the work-product doctrine can be overcome, if at all, only with a showing of extraordinary justification.
- Rule 26(b)(3) of the Federal Rules of Civil Procedure states the word product doctrine for purposes of federal law. States generally apply a state rule that mirrors the federal rule.

Section V
Conflicts of Interest

Chapter 17

Introduction to Conflicts of Interest Concepts

Roadmap

- Introduction to conflicts of interest rules and policies
- The effect of conflicted representation

A. Introduction

Perhaps the most consistently present professional responsibility issue for the practicing lawyer is conflicts of interest. No matter what kind of law a lawyer practices, conflicts of interest possibilities are present. Every representation presents the possibility of impermissible conflicts of interest. For this reason, it is vital that law students develop a nuanced understanding of conflicts of interest principles. In addition, law students must develop a keen eye for identifying potential conflict situations so that when they become lawyers, they can avoid conflicts and the problems that often accompany conflicts.

What makes a conflict impermissible? The rules of professional responsibility provide guidance with regard to conflicts between current clients, conflicts between current clients and prospective clients, conflicts between current clients and former clients, conflicts between former clients, conflicts between current clients and third parties, and conflicts between a lawyer's own interest and the interest of a current client. Rules also deal with conflicts created by judges moving to private practice and by lawyers moving into or out of government employ.

Some of the conflicts rules, like Rule 1.7(DE), the rule governing current clients, is generally a process rule. It provides lawyers with a process to use in evaluating whether representations are conflicted but provides few absolute answers. *See Chapter 18 Conflicts and Current Clients.* Some conflicts rules, like 1.8(j)(DE), provide more bright-line guidance. Rule 1.8(j)(DE) prohibits a lawyer from initiating a sexual relationship with a current client. *See Chapter 21 Conflict of Interest Rules for Particular Situations.*

B. A Balance of Interests

All of the conflicts rules represent a balance of sometimes inconsistent policies and interests. An overarching theme of the conflict of interest rules is a desire to protect the ideal of the lawyer's loyalty to the client. Clients must trust their lawyers. To achieve an adequate level of trust, the lawyer must have relatively undivided loyalty to the client. Indeed, this loyalty is a part of the fiduciary duty the lawyer owes to a client apart from any set of professional responsibility rules. Conflicts rules are designed to protect that loyalty.

A part of the lawyer's duty of loyalty is the lawyer's duty to keep the client's matters confidential. The conflicts rules protect confidentiality by not allowing representation in situations in which a lawyer might be tempted to disclose or use confidential information disadvantageously to the client.

Absolute priority for the loyalty principle and the notion of client confidentiality would lead to rules preventing many representations. If the rules are too draconian, a lawyer's ability to practice law might be limited significantly. For example, if a lawyer could never sue a former client on behalf of another client, a lawyer in a small town might eventually have very few matters he or she could assume. A lesser concern is the narrowing of the pool of possible lawyers. This narrowing somewhat constrains the ability of potential clients to have a lawyer of their own choosing.

Occasionally, the interest of the judicial system comes into play. The conflicts rules reflect a desire to protect the judicial system from conflicts situations that might affect, or appear to affect, the value of the justice rendered.

The conflict of interest rules are an attempt to balance all these concerns. The balancing process has resulted in some rules that require a lawyer to follow a specified process in evaluating a potential conflict. These rules often do not provide bright-line answers to the question of the propriety of a particular conflict. The balance of competing policies and interests is struck, then, in the composition of the rules and also in the application of those rules to particular fact scenarios.

C. Imputation of Conflicts

In recognition of the joint endeavor nature of law firms and other organizations in which lawyers work, the rules impute many conflicts to all lawyers in the firm. Rule 1.0(c)(DE) defines a firm as "a lawyer or lawyers in a law partnership, professional corporation, sole proprietorship or other association authorized to practice law." A legal services organization is considered to be a firm as is an in-house legal department.

D. Cure of Conflict by "Informed Consent"

The conflicts rules also strike a balance of competing interests by allowing clients, former clients, and such to consent to some conflicts of interest. Clients may even waive prospective conflicts in some contexts. Consent must be "informed consent" as defined by Rule 1.0(e)(DE). This means that any consent or waiver can occur only with full disclosure of the "material risks" accompanying the situation and the alternatives to the conflicted representation.

Assuming proper disclosure occurs such that "informed consent" can occur, a former client can consent to a conflicted representation. *See Chapter 19 Conflicts and Former Clients.* Likewise, a prospective client who is never represented by the lawyer can consent to a conflicted representation. *See Chapter 20 Conflicts and Prospective Clients.* A current client can consent to a conflicted representation

only if no law prohibits the representation,
only if the representation will not involve a lawyer representing adverse parties in the same litigation, and
only if the lawyer "reasonably believes" that he or she can "provide competent and diligent representation" to all involved parties.

See Chapter 18 Conflicts and Current Clients.

With regard to imputation involving current or former client conflicts, Rule 1.10(c)(ID) states that consent can cure the conflict "under the conditions stated in Rule 1.7." A comment clarifies that "informed consent" is required. The comment also states that the lawyer must "determine that the representation is not prohibited by Rule 1.7(b)." The comment notes that in some situations "the risk may be so severe that the conflict may not be cured by client consent."

Consent must always be "informed consent, confirmed in writing." The requirement that the consent be "confirmed in writing" means, as explained by Rule 1.0(b)(DE), that the client must give consent in writing or the lawyer must prepare a writing confirming the client's oral consent and must send the writing to the client promptly, at the very least within a reasonable time after the client gives oral consent. The requirement of a writing includes, as explained by Rule 1.0(n)(DE), "a tangible or electronic record of a communication or representation, including handwriting, typewriting, printing, photostating, photography, audio or videorecording, and electronic communications."

E. Cure of Conflict by Screening

Rule 1.0(k)(DE), defines "[s]creened" as "isolation" of a conflicted lawyer by the "reasonably adequate" processes and procedures taken to isolate the conflicted lawyer so as to "protect information that the isolated lawyer is obligated to protect" under the rules of professional responsibility or other law. Lawyers and other personnel should be told that they are prohibited from communicating with the conflicted lawyer about the matter and the conflicted lawyer should agree to the prohibition as well. Everyone should be reminded of the issue on a periodic basis. The conflicted lawyer should have no access to anything relating to the problematic matter, including electronic files.

The rules recognize screening as a method of eliminating an impermissible conflict only in five very specific situations:

1. the former judge situation of Rule 1.12(DE),
2. the former government employee situation of Rule 1.11(DE),
3. the prospective client situation of 1.18(DE),
4. the situation involving a former client represented by the lawyer while the lawyer worked at another firm, and
5. the situation involving a client of a lawyer's former firm but not represented by the lawyer but about whom the lawyer has confidential information material to a current matter.

The last two situations are the subject of Rule 1.10(a)(2)(ID). *See Chapter 19 Conflicts and Former Clients; Chapter 20 Conflicts and Prospective Clients; Chapter 22 Conflicts and Lawyers Who Are Public Officials or Other Government Employees;* and *Chapter 23 Conflicts and Former Judges, Other Adjudicative Officers, Law Clerks, and Third-Party Neutrals.*

In any other conflict setting, screening cannot cure the conflict. It can, however, be used to convince a party to consent to a conflicted representation. A former client might be reticent to agree to a conflicted representation but might agree if the former client knows that the lawyer who has confidential information about the client will be screened from the current matter.

F. The Effect of a Representation with an Impermissible Conflict of Interest

1. Discipline

As is true with other professional responsibility rules, the rules dealing with conflicts of interest provide guidance. Lawyers can be and are disciplined for stepping afoul of the conflicts provisions of the rules. Often, however, discipline is not the only concern or primary concern of lawyers.

2. Court Disqualification

A more immediate issue for litigators is court disqualification. A court might disqualify a lawyer from representing a particular client or handling a particular matter on the basis of an impermissible conflict of interest. Courts have the inherent power to regulate those who appear before them in a representational capacity. In deciding whether to disqualify lawyers on the basis of conflicts of interest, the courts are not limited to following the rules of professional conduct, though generally courts do give the rules special weight. Of course, courts often consider other issues as well, such as the effect the disqualification will have on the orderly resolution of the matter.

3. Malpractice Liability

Another concern of lawyers surrounding conflicts of interest is malpractice liability. A lawyer representing a client while the lawyer has an impermissible conflict of interest breaches the duty of loyalty to the client. In addition, a client so represented might have a stronger claim of breach of the duty of reasonable care regarding other aspects of the representation. Such a claim of breach of duty of care has more purchase viewed against a backdrop of conflict of interest.

4. An Example

Perhaps Larry Lawyer represents Cindy Client in a divorce matter. Perhaps Larry, inexplicably, takes leave of his senses and represents Clint Client in a personal injury matter against Cindy while the divorce matter is still in progress. Larry does not obtain "informed consent" from anyone. By so acting, Larry violates Rule 1.7(a)(1)(DE) in that his representation of Clint is directly adverse to Cindy, a current client. *See Chapter 18 Conflicts and Current Conflicts.* Larry is subject to discipline for this violation. In addition, the court in the personal injury matter might disqualify Larry from the representation of Clint. Lastly, Clint may become disillusioned with Larry when Clint discovers Larry also represents Cindy. Clint might sue him for malpractice, claiming that Larry represented Clint with divided loyalty and in fact subordinated Clint's interests to Cindy's interests. Clint might claim that Larry therefore failed to use reasonable care and competence in his representation.

Checkpoints

- Conflict of interest rules protect the general duty of loyalty and the more specific duty of confidentiality a lawyer owes to a client.
- Former client and prospective client conflicts can be cured by "informed consent, confirmed in writing" of the former or prospective clients.
- A current client can consent to a conflicted representation by "informed consent, confirmed in writing"
    1. *only if* no law prohibits the representation,
    2. *only if* the representation will not involve a lawyer representing adverse parties in the same litigation, and
    3. *only if* the lawyer "reasonably believes" that he or she can "provide competent and diligent representation" to all involved parties.
- Generally, conflicts are imputed to all lawyers in the conflicted lawyer's firm.
- A client can consent to an imputed conflict representation by "informed consent, confirmed in writing" and in accordance with Rule 1.7(DE).
- Screening cures a conflict in the following situations:
    1. the former judge situation of Rule 1.12(DE),
    2. the former government employee situation of Rule 1.11(DE),
    3. the prospective client situation of 1.18(DE),
    4. the situation involving a former client represented by the lawyer while the lawyer worked at another firm (Rule 1.10(a)(2)(ID)), and
    5. the situation involving a client of a lawyer's former firm but not represented by the lawyer but about whom the lawyer has confidential information material to a current matter (Rule 1.10(a)(2)(ID)).
- A lawyer who represents a client in an impermissible conflict situation
    1. is subject to discipline,
    2. may be disqualified by the court before whom the lawyer appears in the conflicted representation, and
    3. may be sued for malpractice related to the conflict.

Chapter 18

Conflicts and Current Clients

Roadmap

- Rule 1.7(DE)
- Rule 1.10(ID)
- Identifying conflicts of interest involving current clients
- Permissible representations even with conflicts of interest
- "Informed consent" to conflicts
- Waivers of future conflicts
- Imputation of current client conflicts

A. Overview

Lawyers owe loyalty to clients. A client must believe that his or her lawyer will keep the interests of the client foremost, will protect the client's confidences, and will exercise independent professional judgment to further the client's interests. Lawyers should be wary, therefore, of anything, such as a conflict of interest, which threatens to impair this loyalty. When a lawyer has a conflict of interest, there is a danger that the lawyer's divided loyalty will result in harm to the client. The conflict of interest rules assist lawyers in identifying situations in which the potential for harm to a client is real. Rule 1.7(DE) provides guidance with regard to conflicts that have the potential to injure *current* clients.

Rule 1.7(DE) divides the universe of possible current client conflict situations into three categories. First is the set of situations in which, under the conflicts test of Rule 1.7(a)(DE), there is no problematic conflict of interest. If there is no conflict, the lawyer may take the representation without raising the issue with the client. Second is the set of situations in which there is a conflict under 1.7(a)(DE), but the representation can occur with the client's "informed consent, confirmed in writing." Third is the set of situations in which there is a conflict under 1.7(a)(DE) and that conflict prevents the representation from occurring. In this last set of situations the representation cannot occur regardless of the consent of the involved parties.

Rule 1.7(DE) assists lawyers in determining in which of these three categories a particular situation falls. The first step in the analysis must be a determination of whether there is a conflict of interest. If the situation presents a conflict, the next question is whether the representation with the conflict is permissible with client consent or, rather, not possible regardless of client consent.

B. Is There a Conflict of Interest?

The starting point in the analysis is determining whether a particular situation presents a conflict of interest. A lawyer must evaluate a potential representation for conflicts before accepting the representation. If a lawyer concludes that a particular representation presents no conflict, that lawyer may take the representation but must continually be wary of developing conflicts that were not present at the beginning of the representation. If a conflict of interest develops, the lawyer may be required to withdraw from the representation.

A conflict of interest regarding a current client exists in two situations. First, a lawyer has a concurrent conflict of interest, as provided by Rule 1.7(a)(1)(DE), if the lawyer represents a client and that representation is "directly adverse" to another client. Second, a lawyer has a concurrent conflict of interest, as provided by Rule 1.7(a)(2)(DE), if the lawyer's representation of a client may be "materially limited" by the lawyer's own interest, or by the lawyer's responsibilities to another client, a former client, or another person. A slim chance of a material limitation does not create a conflict; rather, there must be a "significant risk" that the representation of the client will be "materially limited."

1. "Directly Adverse" Representation

In the first concurrent conflict of interest situation, the lawyer's representation of a client is "directly adverse" to another client. The conflict is between two *current* clients. Perhaps Larry Lawyer represents Cindy Client in an employment dispute with her employer. Perhaps Superstore has asked Larry to represent it in a debt collection matter against Cindy. In the debt collection matter Lance Lawyer represents Cindy. Larry's representation of Superstore against Cindy presents a conflict of interest because Larry is suing a current client, Cindy. Thus, Larry's representation of Superstore is "directly adverse" to another current client, Cindy.

Advocating against a current client does such a tremendous injury to the concept of loyalty. This is true even though the matter in which the lawyer is advocating against the client is an entirely different subject matter from the one in which the lawyer represents the client. The fact that the employment dispute is wholly unrelated to the Superstore debt collection action is irrelevant. If Larry represents Superstore against Cindy, Cindy will likely feel betrayed. She might no longer trust Larry in his role as her lawyer in the employment matter. Larry also might have confidential information about Cindy gained in the employment matter that Larry might be tempted to use in the debt collection matter.

A representation can be "directly adverse" even when the matter is not a litigation matter but rather is transactional. Perhaps Larry Lawyer represents Big Corporation in various trademark matters. Ed Executive, an employee of Big Corporation, has always been impressed with Larry's work and asks Larry to represent Ed in his negotiation of a new employment contract with Big Corporation. Lance Lawyer represents Big Corporation in the employment contract negotiation matter. Larry's representation of Ed would be "directly adverse" to a current client, Big Corporation, in a negotiation. Thus, the representation would create a conflict of interest.

In a "directly adverse" setting, the risk that the representation of one client will be detrimentally affected creates the conflict. Actual harm need not be proved to have a conflict of interest.

2. "Materially Limited" Representation

The second situation in which there is a conflict of interest involving a current client is if a "significant risk" exists that a lawyer's "personal interest" or a lawyer's responsibilities to another current client, to a former client, or to any other person will materially limit the lawyer's representation of a client. No actual harm to the client must occur or be proven. The conflict exists if there is "significant risk" that the lawyer's representation will be circumscribed by differing interests of other clients, of former clients, of third parties, or of the lawyer. Recognizing the conflict does not mean that the representation cannot occur; it simply means that the lawyer must analyze the situation further.

a. Sources of Limitation: Other Clients

Other clients are a fertile source of conflicts of interest. Perhaps Lisa Lawyer is considering the representation of Development Corporation in a project to develop a forested area near City. Perhaps Lisa also represents Limited Growth

Group, a community action group that opposes development of forest land around City. Lisa must consider whether there is a "significant risk" that her representation of Development Corporation may be "materially limited" by her representation of Limited Growth Group. Likewise, Lisa must consider whether there is a "significant risk" that her representation of Limited Growth Group may be "materially limited" by her representation of Development Corporation. Since Lisa represents both entities, it is possible that she will learn or has learned confidential information in the representation of one that would be useful in representing the other. Yet Lisa cannot share the information with the second client because of the duty of confidentiality of Rule 1.6(DE). *See Chapter 15 The Duty of Confidentiality.* If the possibility of a "materially limited" representation of either or both parties is a "significant risk," Lisa has a conflict in representing both entities.

A very common scenario in which conflicts arise is when a lawyer represents two clients in the same litigation matter. Perhaps Lisa Lawyer is considering the representation of Dan Driver and Paige Passenger, the passenger in the car Dan was driving at the time of a collision. Both Dan and Paige would like Lisa to represent them in an action against Dora Defendant, the driver of the other car in the collision. Dan suffered minor injuries while Paige suffered significant injuries with lasting effects. Lisa should recognize that at some point she might come to know confidential information about Dan or Paige that could be useful to the other in the action against Dora or in a claim against the other client. Lisa may come to know facts about Dan that would support a claim by Paige against Dan. In such a situation Lisa has a duty to disclose the information to Paige and yet Lisa is bound by the duty of confidentiality to Dan and thus cannot disclose the information to Paige. In deciding whether to accept such a representation, Lisa must consider whether there is a "significant risk" that her representation of Paige may be "materially limited" by her representation of Dan, or vice versa.

b. Sources of Limitation: Former Clients

Another source of conflicts of interest regarding the representation of current clients is former clients. While lawyers do not owe former clients the same loyalty-based duties lawyers owe current clients, *see Chapter 19 Conflicts and Former Clients,* the duty of confidentiality of Rule 1.6(DE) does not wane simply because the lawyer-client relationship ceases. *See Chapter 15 The Duty of Confidentiality.* Perhaps Lisa Lawyer is considering representing Cindy Client in an action against Clint. Lisa represented Clint in the past with regard to several employment issues that arose in Clint's restaurant. Lisa no longer represents Clint on such matters. Cindy would like Lisa to represent her in an employment matter against Clint. While Rule 1.9(DE), the professional responsibility rule relating to former clients, may or may not prevent Lisa from representing Cindy against Clint, *see Chapter 19 Conflicts and Former Clients,* Lisa may have a current client conflict of interest under Rule 1.7(a)(DE) because she may have confidential information from Clint that would be useful to Cindy and yet Lisa cannot share that information with Cindy. Lisa's representation of Cindy may be "materially limited" by her duties, such as the duty of confidentiality, Lisa owes Clint. In addition, Lisa may think fondly of Clint and thus may not be as aggressive in advocating for Cindy as she would otherwise be. At the time Lisa considers representing Cindy, Lisa must consider whether there is a "significant risk" that her representation of Cindy may be "materially limited" by her former representation of Clint. If there is a "significant risk," Lisa has a conflict of interest.

c. Sources of Limitation: A Lawyer's "Personal Interest"

Another source of conflicts of interest is the lawyer's own interests. Perhaps Lisa Lawyer is considering representing Cindy Client on a claim against the City Girls' Club. Perhaps Lisa feels that she owes her success to the mentoring and guidance she received from the Club when she was a teenager. Lisa's personal loyalty to the Club may interfere with Lisa's ability to render independent professional judgment on behalf of Cindy. Lisa may not pursue Cindy's claim as aggressively as she would otherwise. Or Lisa may limit the possible avenues Cindy might take. Lisa must consider whether there is a "significant risk" that her representation of Cindy may be "materially limited" by her loyalty to the Club. If there is a "significant risk," Lisa has a conflict of interest.

Other sources of personal conflicts include the lawyer's business involvements and relationships with other lawyers involved in a matter. For example, the fact that in a matter Lisa represents Cindy and Lisa's mother represents the opposing party may create a "significant risk" that Lisa's representation of Cindy will be "materially limited." Likewise, if Lance Lawyer represents Lisa in a minor contract matter, Lisa's relationship with Lance may affect her representation of her own clients in matters in which Lance is the opposing counsel.

When a matter involves a question of the propriety of the lawyer's conduct, the lawyer's own interest in defending himself or herself might interfere with the representation rendered the client. A lawyer serving on the board of directors of a corporation may not be able to represent the corporation with regard to certain matters because of a "significant risk" that the representation will be "materially limited." For example, the lawyer may not be able to handle a matter involving a board of directors decision because the lawyer was involved in the decision-making process as a member of the board.

d. Sources of Limitation: A Third Person

A conflict of interest can exist when the source of the limitation on the client's representation is a third person. Perhaps Lisa Lawyer is considering the representation of Cindy Client in a divorce matter. Cindy's father, Fred, is a good friend of Lisa. Fred first contacted Lisa and explained that he would like Lisa to represent Cindy and handle the matter aggressively. Fred says that he has never liked his soon-to-be former son-in-law and wants to punish him for treating Cindy so badly. In the beginning of the relationship, if Lisa believes that there is a "significant risk" that Fred will interfere with the lawyer-client relationship and if Lisa believes that the result of Fred's intrusion will be a material limitation of Lisa's representation of Cindy, Lisa has a conflict of interest that requires more attention.

e. Positional Conflicts

Occasionally, a lawyer is called upon to argue inconsistent legal positions for different clients. Lisa Lawyer may argue on behalf of Cindy Client that the product liability statute of limitations should be based on actual knowledge of a defect or injury. Lisa may argue on behalf of Giant Corporation that the product liability statute of limitations should be based on a should-have-known standard. Representing clients in this manner does not usually create a "significant risk" of a "materially limited" representation for either client.

The analysis is different, however, if in representing Cindy, Lisa creates precedent that could negatively affect Giant Corporation's position. If Lisa argues for a statute of limitations based on actual knowledge, and if Lisa makes this argument in the Supreme Court for the state in which Giant also has product liability matters pending against it, then the precedent created in Cindy's matter could cause the statute of limitations in the Giant matters to be evaluated on an actual knowledge of injury basis. This standard could significantly extend the length of time in which a plaintiff might bring a claim against Giant and, thus, be harmful to Giant. Such a situation may present a conflict of interest under Rule 1.7(DE).

C. If There is a Conflict of Interest, Is the Representation Permissible with Client Consent?

There are some conflicted representations a lawyer may not undertake even if the client is inclined to give "informed consent." If a representation presents a concurrent conflict as described by Rule 1.7(a)(DE), the lawyer cannot represent the client in the matter if the representation is prohibited by law, if the representation is of two or more adverse clients in the same litigation matter, or if the lawyer "reasonably believes" that he or she cannot render "competent and diligent representation" to the client. If none of these three situations are present, the lawyer may represent the client if each affected client renders "informed consent, confirmed in writing."

1. Representation Prohibited by Law

There are certain representations that the law prohibits. If the representation is not allowed by law, then the representation cannot occur with or without client consent to the conflict of interest! Rule 1.7(b)(2)(DE) states this principle. For example, some states have laws prohibiting a lawyer from representing two defendants in a capital murder case. The legislatures of those states justify such bans by noting the risk of adverse impact on the representations that such a conflicted representation might create, and the appeals such representations would generate. Likewise, federal criminal statutes forbid certain representations by former government lawyers.

2. Representation of Two or More Adverse Clients in the Same Litigation Matter

Rule 1.7(b)(3)(DE) presents another situation in which a conflicted representation cannot occur. A lawyer in a litigation matter or in any other matter before a tribunal, cannot represent two clients asserting claims against each other. Lisa Lawyer cannot represent Cindy in pursuing a personal injury claim against Dora and also defend Dora against Cindy's claim. There is simply no way that a lawyer such as Lisa can honor her duties of confidentiality and loyalty, which she owes to both Cindy and Dora, in such a situation.

3. No Reasonable Belief in "Competent and Diligent Representation"

Even if no law prevents the representation in the conflict situation and even if the representation does not involve a lawyer representing adverse parties in a litigation matter, Rule 1.7(b)(1)(DE) states that a lawyer can handle a representation only if the lawyer "reasonably believes" that the lawyer can provide "competent and diligent representation" to the client or clients whose representation presents the conflict of interest. Rule 1.1(DE) and Rule 1.3(DE) define competence and diligence. *See Chapter 5 Competence and Diligence.* If a lawyer does not reasonably believe that he or she can provide "competent and diligent representation" to the client, the lawyer cannot ask the client to give "informed consent" to the conflict.

Perhaps Lisa Lawyer is considering the representation of Cindy Client on a claim against the City Girls' Club. Lisa believes that she owes her success to the mentoring and guidance she received from the Club when she was a teenager. Lisa's personal loyalty to the Club may interfere with Lisa's ability to render independent professional judgment on behalf of Cindy to the point that not only is a conflict created, but also the conflict is not one to which Cindy can consent. Lisa may not reasonably believe that she can render "competent and diligent representation" to Cindy because of her allegiance to the City Girls' Club.

When a lawyer considers representing two or more plaintiffs or two or more defendants, the lawyer may decide that the risk of a material limitation is so great that the lawyer cannot request consent from the potential clients. This is especially true in the criminal context. Comment twenty-three to Rule 1.7(DE) notes that in the criminal context a lawyer should not "ordinarily" represent more than one defendant. Lisa Lawyer should avoid representing Dave and Don, defendants charged with robbery of a gas station. The risk is simply too great that Dave may, at some point, wish to point the finger of blame at Don. The prosecution may seek a deal with Don at the expense of Dave. Dave and Don may tell inconsistent stories. Lisa would be unable to adequately represent both clients in such a scenario. Any of these conflict situations can create viable claims of ineffective assistance of counsel. *See Chapter 7 Ineffective Assistance of Counsel.*

D. "Informed Consent"

1. "Informed Consent, Confirmed in Writing"

If a representation presents a conflict of interest under Rule 1.7(a)(DE), and if no law prohibits the representation, if the representation does not involve the lawyer representing adverse parties in the same litigation matter, and if the lawyer "reasonably believes" that the lawyer can render "competent and diligent representation" to the client, then the lawyer may request that the client consent to the conflicted representation. Rule 1.7(b)(4)(DE) provides that the consent must be informed and must be "confirmed in writing." The requirement of the writing assists clients in understanding the seriousness of the issue of consent to conflicts of interest.

To give "informed consent" a client must first be aware of all the reasonably foreseeable ways that the conflict could adversely affect the client. As Rule 1.0(e)(DE) states, the lawyer must explain to the client the "material risks" and "reasonably available alternatives." The requirement that the consent be "confirmed in writing" means, as explained by Rule 1.0(b)(DE), that the client must give consent in writing or the lawyer must prepare a writing confirming the client's oral consent and must send the writing to the client promptly, at the very least within a reasonable time after the client gives oral consent. The requirement of a writing includes, as explained by Rule 1.0(n)(DE), "a tangible or electronic record of a communication or representation, including handwriting, typewriting, printing, photostating, photography, audio or videorecording, and electronic communications."

If the lawyer seeks to represent two or more clients in the same matter as a common representation, the lawyer must explain to the clients that there will be no recognized attorney-client privilege between the clients. This means that in the future, if the parties become adverse, any information from the representation that the attorney-client privilege might otherwise protect from disclosure would not be protected. This consequence may be a significant negative to proceeding with the common representation.

If there is a conflict between two current clients, both clients must give consent for the representation to occur because both of their interests are at issue. If Lisa plans to represent both Dan Driver and Paige Passenger in an action against Dora, Lisa must obtain the "informed consent" of both Dan and Paige. Lisa must explain to both Dan and Paige the burdens of the common representation. Lisa must explain the loyalty issues that might arise as well as the confidentiality issues such a situation presents.

In seeking "informed consent" of one client, a lawyer may need to disclose another client's or former client's confidential information. Yet that other client or former client may not agree to the disclosure. Without the disclosure, the lawyer cannot obtain consent to the conflict so the representation cannot occur.

Perhaps, because of a prior representation of Dan, Lisa knows the details of Dan's driving history, including Dan's arrests for driving while impaired. Lisa may believe that she has a conflict and that in order to obtain Paige's consent to the representation, Lisa must disclose the fact that she represented Dan in the past and also Dan's driving history. Lisa cannot disclose this information to Paige without Dan's consent because it is confidential under Rule 1.6(DE). *See Chapter 15 The Duty of Confidentiality.* Dan might consent to the multiple representation and yet not consent to the disclosure of information. Without Dan's consent to the disclosure, Lisa cannot make the required disclosure to obtain Paige's "informed consent" and, as a result, cannot represent Paige.

If the concurrent conflict of interest results from the involvement of a former client or a prospective client, the former or prospective client's "informed consent" to the representation may be necessary under the requirements of Rule 1.9(DE). *See Chapter 19 Conflicts and Former Clients.* Thus, the lawyer may be required to obtain the consent of two current clients if that is the nature of the conflict or the consent of a current client and a former client if the conflict involves a current client and a former client. If the conflict involves a prospective client, the lawyer may need to obtain the "informed consent" of a current client and a prospective client not ultimately represented by the lawyer.

2. Revocation of Consent

A client can revoke consent to a representation at any time. This is consistent with the client's right to terminate a representation at any time and seek another lawyer's services. *See Chapter 11 Refusing to Form a Lawyer-Client Relationship or Ending a Lawyer-Client Relationship.* If a client's consent has been necessary for the lawyer to represent another client, the client's revocation of consent means that the lawyer must take steps to end the problematic representation. If the lawyer is already counsel of record in a matter before a tribunal, the lawyer must ask to withdraw. In such a situation courts are careful to consider the fact that representation of a client has begun in reliance on another person's consent. Fairness to the relying party is an important factor. In deciding questions of disqualification, a court might consider the harm that a disqualification might cause to another who properly relied on the consent. A court might also consider such factors as whether the circumstances of the situation have changed materially since the party gave "informed consent."

E. Waiver: Consent to Future Conflicts of Interest

Lawyers sometimes seek to have a client waive conflicts that might arise later. At the beginning of a representation there may be no situation of direct adversity and no "significant risk" of a "materially limited" representation. Thus, there is no conflict of interest. Yet a lawyer may want to ensure that if a conflict arises, the lawyer will not be forced to withdraw from this or another representation.

Perhaps Lisa Lawyer has represented General Factory Corporation for years in all sorts of matters. Sam Supplier has now asked Lisa to represent him in supply contract disputes. Sam supplies General Factory Corporation as well as other manufacturing entities. At the time of the representation initiation, Sam has no contract disputes with General Factory. Lisa worries, however, that if Sam does have a dispute with General Factory, Sam will not consent to allowing Lisa to represent General Factory against Sam. Sam would be represented by another lawyer in such a matter. Lisa wants to be sure that the representation of Sam does not create conflicts for the representation of General Factory because Lisa earns from General Factory ten times annually what Lisa believes she might earn from representing Sam. To solve her problem, Lisa might seek a waiver from Sam. Lisa might ask Sam to agree, at the time Lisa first agrees to represent Sam, that if Sam ever has a dispute with General Factory Corporation, Lisa can represent General Factory Corporation against Sam.

If a conflict of interest does materialize, such a waiver of conflict may be enforceable if the conflict of interest is not one for which consent is not possible under the limitations of Rule 1.7(b)(DE). If consent is possible, then an advance waiver may, or may not, be valid. The waiver is more likely to be valid if the waiving party, at the time of agreeing to the waiver, understands the risks involved in the representation and waiver. Factors in favor of enforcing a future waiver include the following:

1. the waiving party is a sophisticated user of legal services,
2. the waiving party has the benefit of the counsel of an independent lawyer,
3. the waiver occurs after a full explanation of the conflict of interest possibilities and risks, and
4. the waiver does not relate to the subject matter of the present representation.

ABA Formal Opinion 05-436 (2005) clarifies that this factor approach means that a waiver of future conflict may be valid even if it is very general. This can occur if the waiving party is a sophisticated user of legal services, the party has separate and independent counsel on the waiver issue, and the waiver does not relate to the same subject matter as the current representation. Waivers of future conflicts are especially viable, therefore, with regard to corporate clients who have the benefit of legal advice.

For example, in *Galderma Labs, L.P. v. Actavis Mid Atlantic LLC*, 927 F. Supp. 2d 390 (N.D. Tex. 2013), the court enforced an advance waiver by Galderma, a global company and sophisticated user of legal services. The court enforced the waiver and refused to disqualify the law firm because Galderma was a sophisticated user of legal services, was a party to many such advance waivers in other matters, and Galderma's general counsel, an experienced lawyer, signed the waiver on behalf of the company.

A waiver of a future conflict is, in fact, consent to the conflict, so the waiver must, if it is to be enforceable, be an "informed consent" as discussed above. In addition, the waiver must, like any other "informed consent" to a conflict of interest, be "confirmed in writing." Thus, the waiver itself must be in writing or there must be a written confirmation of an oral waiver. Waivers of future conflicts are often a part of the initial engagement agreement. Thus, it is often in writing and often the waiving party signs the waiver agreement as part of the overall engagement agreement.

F. When Things Go Wrong

1. Withdrawal

If a lawyer undertakes a representation in which consent is not required or undertakes a representation in which consent is required and obtained, the conflict situation may change as the representation progresses. Perhaps the lawyer no longer reasonably believes that the lawyer can competently and diligently represent the client or clients. Perhaps a conflict becomes apparent and the client refuses to consent to the representation with the conflict. In these scenarios, the lawyer must withdraw. Rule 1.16(a)(DE) requires withdrawal because continued representation would violate Rule 1.7(DE). *See Chapter 11 Refusing to Form a Lawyer-Client Relationship or Ending a Lawyer-Client Relationship.*

If a lawyer represents multiple plaintiffs or defendants in a single matter, the lawyer generally must withdraw from representing all of the clients. Perhaps in representing Dan Driver and Paige Passenger in a matter against Dora Defendant based on an automobile collision, Lisa Lawyer discovers information about Dan's substance abuse that could be helpful to Paige in asserting a claim against Dan. Lisa has a duty to disclose this information to Paige but also owes Dan a duty of confidentiality and cannot disclose the information to Paige without Dan's permission. Dan does not give permission for the disclosure. Lisa cannot continue the representation of Paige and may not be able to continue the representation of Dan.

A similar result must occur in many other conflict situations. For example, perhaps Lisa has never represented General Factory Corporation. General Factory asks Lisa to represent it in an employment matter against Cindy. Lisa sees this as a great opportunity because General Factory could be a steady stream of very interesting and well-paying work. Unfortunately, Lisa already represents Cindy in a personal injury matter against Dora Defendant. The personal injury matter arose from an automobile collision. Absent Cindy's consent, Lisa cannot represent General Factory in the matter against Cindy because the General Factory representation would be "directly adverse" to Cindy, a current client. If Lisa is not diligent in her client conflict detection, she might begin the representation of General Factory before realizing that the General Factory matter is adverse to a current client, Cindy. When Lisa discovers the conflict, the only question is whether she must withdraw from the representation of one or both clients.

2. The "Hot Potato" Doctrine

In the General Factory scenario above, one can argue that Lisa must withdraw from only one of the representations. Lisa should withdraw from the representation of General Factory because Lisa has confidential information about Cindy that might be useful to General Factory and yet Lisa's duty of confidentiality would bar disclosure to General Factory. The confidential information she has about General Factory, in contrast, would not be useful to Cindy in the personal injury matter so there would be no continuing conflict. In effect, General Factory would be a former client. Rule 1.9(DE), which governs conflicts with former clients, would not prohibit the representation of Cindy unless the matter was the same or "substantially related" and the interests of the two parties were "materially adverse." This rule would not demand withdrawal from the representation of Cindy. *See Chapter 19 Conflicts and Former Clients.*

The general rule applied by many courts when dealing with disqualification questions, however, values the loyalty a lawyer owes a client. If a lawyer or law firm discovers that it is representing a client in a matter adverse to another current client, the lawyer or law firm must withdraw from both representations. This is especially true if the lawyer or law firm seeks to terminate a current client so as to take on a new, more financially advantageous client. This "hot potato" rule prevents any manipulation of the rules by sharp lawyers. As the court in *Picker International Inc. v. Varian Associates Inc.*, 670 F. Supp. 1363

(N.D. Ohio 1987), *aff'd*, 869 F.2d 578 (Fed. Cir. 1989), stated "A firm may not drop a client like a hot potato, especially if it is in order to keep a far more lucrative client." *Id.* at 1365. In the view of the *Restatement (Third) of the Law Governing Lawyers*, a lawyer should receive the benefit of the more lenient former client conflict rule only when, as comment c to section 132 provides, withdrawal "occurs at a point that the client and lawyer had contemplated as the end of the representation."

G. Imputing the Conflict

Rule 1.10(ID) provides for the imputation of conflicts in all but a small set of situations. Rule 1.10(a)(ID) states that if a lawyer has a conflict of interest under Rule 1.7(DE), all lawyers in the same firm have the same conflict unless the conflict is personal to the lawyer. If Lisa Lawyer cannot represent Cindy Client because Rule 1.7(DE) forbids it, no lawyer in Lisa's firm can knowingly represent Cindy. A firm is defined in Rule 1.0(c)(DE) as "a lawyer or lawyers in a law partnership, professional corporation, sole proprietorship or other association authorized to practice law." A legal services organization is considered to be a firm as is an in-house legal department.

The conflict is *not* imputed if

1. the basis of the disqualification is a "personal interest" of the original lawyer, and
2. the situation does not "present a significant risk of materially limiting the representation."

Perhaps Lisa Lawyer concludes that she cannot handle the representation of Cindy Client because the opposing lawyer is Lisa's mother. Lisa concludes that a "significant risk" exists that the representation of Cindy will be "materially limited." Lisa also concludes that she does not reasonably believe that she can render Cindy "competent and diligent representation." Thus, Lisa has a conflict of interest and cannot ask Cindy to consent to the representation. Yet Lisa's conflict of interest is based on a "personal interest" and is not imputed to Lena, Lisa's law partner, if Lena does not believe that there is a "significant risk" that the representation will be "materially limited." Lena could then handle the representation of Cindy. It is possible, however, that Lena could share the conflict if she feels that the fact that the opposing counsel is Lisa's mother would affect her representation of Cindy. This would be true, for example, if Lena has a close personal relationship with both Lisa and Lisa's mother.

In an imputed disqualification situation, the problem can be cured by the client's "informed consent, confirmed in writing" and otherwise in accord with Rule 1.7. Rule 1.10(c)(ID) so provides. As Rule 1.0(e)(DE) states with regard to "informed consent," the lawyer must explain to the client the "material risks" of the representation and the "reasonably available alternatives." The requirement that the consent be "confirmed in writing" means, as explained by Rule 1.0(b)(DE), that the client must give consent in writing or the lawyer must prepare a writing confirming the client's oral consent and must send the writing to the client promptly, within a reasonable time after the client gives oral consent. The requirement of a writing includes, as explained by Rule 1.0(n)(DE), "a tangible or electronic record of a communication or representation, including handwriting, typewriting, printing, photostating, photography, audio or videorecording, and electronic communications."

Perhaps Lisa Lawyer cannot represent Cindy Client in an employment matter against Big Corporation because Lisa represents Big Corporation in similar employment matters. Lisa has a conflict of interest and does not believe she can ask Cindy and Big Corporation to consent. Such a conflict is imputed to Lisa's firm, so Lena, Lisa's partner, cannot represent Cindy either. However, Lena could perhaps obtain the "informed consent" of both current clients, Cindy and Big Corporation, if she "reasonably believes" she can represent Cindy competently and diligently and the continued representation of Big Corporation by Lisa will also be competent and diligent.

Rule 1.10(d)(ID) clarifies that Rule 1.11(DE), the rule dealing with government lawyers, rather that Rule 1.10(ID), governs the issue of imputation when government lawyers are involved. *See Chapter 22 Conflicts and Lawyers Who Are Public Officials or Other Government Employees.*

Related Sections of the *Restatement (Third) of the Law Governing Lawyers*

Sections 121–123, 125, 128–131, and 135

Checkpoints

- A lawyer has a concurrent conflict of interest
    1. if the lawyer represents a client and that representation is "directly adverse" to another client or
    2. if there is a "significant risk" that a lawyer's representation of a client may be "materially limited" by the lawyer's own interest or by the lawyer's responsibilities to another client, a former client, or another person.
- If a lawyer has a conflict of interest regarding a representation, the lawyer may not represent the client
    1. if law forbids the representation,
    2. if the representation results in the lawyer representing one client against another in the same litigation matter,
    3. if the lawyer does not reasonably believe that the lawyer can represent the client competently and diligently, or
    4. if the client affected by the conflict does not give "informed consent, confirmed in writing."
- Clients may waive future conflicts of interest. Factors in favor of enforcing a future waiver are:
    1. the waiving party is a sophisticated user of legal services,
    2. the waiving party has the benefit of the counsel of an independent lawyer,
    3. the waiver occurs after a full explanation of the conflict of interest possibilities and risks, and
    4. the waiver does not relate to the subject matter of the present representation.
- If a lawyer undertakes a representation and if the situation changes so that the lawyer no longer "reasonably believes" that the lawyer can competently and diligently represent the client or clients, or if a conflict becomes apparent and the client now refuses to consent to the representation, ordinarily, the lawyer must withdraw from both representations.
- If a lawyer has a conflict of interest under Rule 1.7(DE), Rule 1.10(a)(ID) states that all lawyers in the same firm have the same disqualifying conflict unless
    1. the basis of the disqualification is a "personal interest" of the original lawyer, and
    2. the situation does not "present a significant risk of materially limiting the representation."
- An imputed disqualification can be waived by "informed consent, confirmed in writing" and otherwise in accord with Rule 1.7(DE).

Chapter 19

Conflicts and Former Clients

Roadmap

- Rule 1.9(DE)
- Rule 1.10(ID)
- Identifying conflicts of interest involving former clients
- Imputation of former client conflicts
- Use or disclosure of confidential information of former clients
- Conflict situations involving lawyers who move from one practice setting to another

A. Introduction

As is true with current clients, a lawyer owes former clients a duty of loyalty and all the subparts of that duty, such as the duty to keep the former client's confidences. Yet the duties owed are of a lesser intensity than is true with current clients.

B. The Duty of Confidentiality

With a current client, a lawyer has a duty not to reveal client information relating to the representation. *See* Rule 1.6(DE). *See also Chapter 15 The Duty of Confidentiality.* Likewise, Rule 1.9(DE) provides that a lawyer has a duty not to reveal client information relating to the representation of a former client.

With regard to a lawyer's *use* of confidential information relating to current clients, Rule 1.8(b)(DE) provides that a lawyer may not use a client's information to the disadvantage of the client unless the client consents or a rule otherwise allows or requires the disclosure. *See Chapter 21 Conflict of Interest Rules for Particular Situations.* In contrast, Rule 1.9(c)(DE) provides that a lawyer cannot use information relating to a former client's representation to that former client's disadvantage unless

1. the rules otherwise permit the use,
2. the rules otherwise require the use, or
3. "when the information has become generally known."

C. The Basic Former Client Conflict of Interest Rule

1. The Rule and Rationale

The loyalty interest recognized and protected by Rule 1.7(DE), the current client conflict of interest rule, *see Chapter 18 Conflicts and Current Clients*, is less when the lawyer no longer represents the client. Rule 1.9(DE), the former client conflict of interest rule, is less constraining on the lawyer as a result. Rule 1.9(DE) prohibits representations in which former client confidential information might be in danger of use or disclosure and situations in which the lawyer appears to have switched sides in a matter.

Rule 1.9(a) provides that a lawyer may not represent a client in the following scenario:

1. the interests of the client are "materially adverse" to the interests of a former client,
2. the representation is in the "same or a substantially related matter" as the representation of the former client, and
3. the former client does not give "informed consent, confirmed in writing" for the representation.

If the representation is in the "same or a substantially related matter," and if the client is "materially adverse" to the former client, the lawyer likely has confidential information relating to the former client that can be of assistance to the current client. If the lawyer has such information, the lawyer has a duty to the current client to disclose the information and an inconsistent duty to the former client to keep the information confidential. Rule 1.9(DE) prevents this circumstance from occurring without an analysis of the actual confidential information of the former client the lawyer possesses. In addition to protecting confidential information, the rule prevents a lawyer from, in effect, switching sides in a matter. At the same time, the rule accomplishes the competing goal of not unduly constraining lawyers in the private practice of law.

2. "Same or a Substantially Related Matter"

With the rule's goals in mind, it is no surprise that comment three to the rule states that matters are the "same" or are "substantially related" "if they involve the same transaction or legal dispute or if there otherwise is a substantial risk that confidential factual information as would normally have been obtained in the prior representation would materially advance the client's position in the subsequent matter." If Lisa Lawyer represented Cindy Client in recent years but represents Cindy no longer, and if Lisa learned intimate details about Cindy's financial situation during that representation, Rule 1.9(DE) prohibits Lisa from later representing Hugh, Cindy's husband, in a divorce matter. The confidential information Lisa might have about Cindy could significantly advance Hugh's position in the divorce and so the matter is the "same or a substantially related matter." Rule 1.9(DE) prohibits the representation without Cindy's "informed consent, confirmed in writing." If Lisa represented Cindy many years ago, the confidential information Lisa might have relating to Cindy's finances would likely be too dated to assist Hugh in the divorce. Thus, the matter would not be the "same or a substantially related" one. The representation could occur without Cindy's consent. Likewise, if the local newspaper has published prominently anything Lisa knows, the matter may not be deemed the "same" or "substantially related." Comment three notes that information disclosed to the public may not be disqualifying.

In all of these scenarios there is also the issue of whether, even if there is no conflict as to Cindy or even if there is a conflict as to Cindy and Cindy consents, whether there is a current client conflict as to Hugh. Rule 1.7(DE) must be analyzed to determine whether there is a concurrent conflict and whether Hugh must consent to the representation for it to occur. Might there be a "significant risk" that Lisa's representation of Hugh will be "materially limited" as a result of the prior representation of Cindy? *See Chapter 18 Conflicts and Current Clients.* If so, Lisa has a current client conflict of interest.

Occasionally, the issue of a former client conflict of interest arises when the information the lawyer has is general business practice information or general litigation strategy information. Perhaps Lisa represented General Factory Corporation on employment matters in years gone by and so knows all about how General Factory deals with employee complaints and issues. Perhaps Lisa knows how General Factory approaches employment litigation. This sort of generalized information, sometimes called playbook information, often does not create a conflict of interest.

In contrast, if, in the past, Lisa represented General Factory in an employment matter in which an employee claimed sexual harassment by a supervisor, and if Lisa now seeks to represent Elaine, another employee with a sexual harassment claim against General Factory, and if Elaine alleges that the harassment was at the hand of the same supervisor, Lisa may have a conflict of interest. The matter may be the "same or a substantially related" one. Lisa likely had access to this supervisor's employment file and other confidential information that would advance Elaine's claim against General Factory.

Aside from analysis of conflicts of interest for purposes of ethics, courts apply this same sort of analysis to the question of disqualification in a particular litigation matter. In *HealthNet, Inc. v. Health Net, Inc.*, 289 F. Supp. 2d 755 (S.D. W. Va. 2003), a trademark infringement action, HealthNet sought disqualification of the law firm representing the opposition. A member of the opposition's law firm, Guthrie, had once participated in the representation of HealthNet when another firm employed Guthrie. At that earlier time, Guthrie had written a letter to HealthNet advising it about the use of the trademark at issue. In discovery in the current trademark litigation, Guthrie's letter was noted on a privilege log. Because Guthrie wrote the letter, as opposed to another lawyer in his earlier firm, it is clear that Guthrie individually represented HealthNet at that time. At the time of the motion to disqualify, Guthrie's new firm represented the opposition. So Guthrie represented HealthNet on the trademark issue in the past and then Guthrie's new firm represented the opposition on the trademark issue. The two entities clearly have "materially adverse" interests. In determining whether Guthrie's prior representation of HealthNet was the "same or a substantially related matter" as the current one, the court applied the test of the *Restatement (Third) of the Law Governing Lawyers.* Section 132 of the *Restatement* states in part:

> The current matter is substantially related to the earlier matter if: (1) the current matter involves the work the lawyer performed for the former client; or (2) there is a substantial risk that representation of the present client will involve the use of information acquired in the course of representing the former client, unless that information has become generally known.

The *HealthNet* court then concluded, "It seems entirely likely that the defendant would benefit from the use of information acquired by Mr. Guthrie in the course of representing the plaintiff, and it does not appear to the court that the information has become generally known." *HealthNet*, 289 F. Supp. 2d at 759–60.

3. Who Is a Former Client?

One of the most difficult questions in this area is the question of whether a party is a current client or rather a former client. If the party is a current client, Rule 1.7(DE) applies whereas if the party is a former client, the more lenient Rule 1.9(DE) applies. A lawyer-client relationship may exist if a party reasonably believes that a lawyer represents the party. *See Chapter 4 Basis of Duty: The Lawyer-Client Relationship.* This standard informs the analysis of whether a client may be a current or former client of a lawyer. If a lawyer has represented a client in the past, that client is a current client, not a former client, if the client reasonably believes that the lawyer still represents the client. The lawyer's belief is not relevant. If a lawyer sends a client a letter clearly stating that the representation has concluded, however, then the party could not have a reasonable belief that the lawyer-client relationship continues to exist. Such a disengagement letter clarifies that the client is a former client. Lawyers often do not wish to terminate their relationship definitively when particular matters end because they hope that their clients will return with future business. As a result, there is often no certainty with regard to the status of the party as a current or former client.

4. "Informed Consent"

If a representation presents a conflict of interest under 1.9(a)(DE), a lawyer may not handle the representation unless the former client gives "informed consent, confirmed in writing." "Informed consent," as defined by 1.0(e)(DE), requires the lawyer to explain to the former client the "material risks" and the "reasonably available alternatives" to the conflicted representation. The requirement that the consent be "confirmed in writing" means, as explained by Rule 1.0(b)(DE), that the former client must give consent in writing or the lawyer must prepare a writing confirming the former client's oral consent and must send the writing to the former client within a reasonable time after the former client gives oral consent. The requirement of a writing includes, as explained by Rule 1.0(n)(DE), "a tangible or electronic record of a communication or representation, including handwriting, typewriting, printing, photostating, photography, audio or videorecording, and electronic communications."

A former client usually has little to lose by refusing consent. The refusal most likely has no negative effect on the former client and simply prevents the lawyer from representing someone else. If the former client consents to the representation, the lawyer must evaluate whether there is a concurrent conflict of interest such that the current client's "informed consent, confirmed in writing" is necessary under Rule 1.7(DE). *See Chapter 18 Conflicts and Current Clients.*

5. Imputing the Conflict

a. *The General Rule*

Rule 1.10(ID) provides the general rule for the imputation of former client conflicts identified by Rule 1.9(DE). Rule 1.10(a)(ID), states that if a lawyer has a conflict of interest under Rule 1.9(DE), all lawyers in the same firm have the same conflict. The imputation rule results from the view that, as comment two to Rule 1.10(ID) states, "a firm of lawyers is essentially one lawyer." If Lisa Lawyer cannot represent Cindy Client because Rule 1.9(DE) forbids it, no lawyer in Lisa's firm knowingly can represent Cindy. Rule 1.0(c)(DE) defines a firm as "a lawyer or lawyers in a law partnership, professional corporation, sole proprietorship or other association authorized to practice law." A legal services organization and an in-house legal department are also firms.

b. *The Exception for "Personal Interest" Conflicts Is Not Applicable to Former Client Conflicts*

There is an exception to this general imputation rule. No imputed disqualification occurs if

1. the basis of the disqualification is a "personal interest" of the original lawyer, and
2. the situation does not "present a significant risk of materially limiting the representation."

However, this exception is not really applicable in the former client scenario because the nature of a former client conflict is a conflict with the interests of a current client, not the lawyer's own interests. This "personal interest" is an exception for current client conflict situations. *See Chapter 18 Conflicts and Current Clients.*

c. *The Consent Cure*

Another ameliorator of the general imputation rule is that, according to Rule 1.10(c)(ID), an imputed disqualification can be waived by "informed consent, confirmed in writing" if consent can be requested under the standards of Rule 1.7(DE).

Perhaps Lisa Lawyer represented Cindy Client in her purchase of a business. That matter concluded in two years ago. Lisa has not done any legal work for Cindy or the business since then. Assume that Cindy is a former client. Now Lisa would like to represent Ed Entrepreneur in a matter in which Cindy and her business are adverse parties. Ed, who provided financing to Cindy for the purchase of the business in the earlier transaction, claims that Cindy misled him at the time of the business purchase. Lisa cannot represent Ed because Ed's current matter and the matter Lisa handled for Cindy arise from the same transaction. There is substantial risk that Lisa has confidential information from Cindy's representation that could materially assist Ed in the current matter. Absent Cindy's "informed consent, confirmed in writing," Lisa cannot represent Ed. If Lisa cannot represent Ed, then as a matter of professional responsibility, Rule 1.10(a)(ID) does not permit Lena, another lawyer in Lisa's firm, to represent Ed. Lena can represent Ed only if Lena properly can request Cindy's consent under Rule 1.7(DE) and Cindy gives "informed consent, confirmed in writing."

d. Does Screening Prevent Imputation?

If the former client conflict does not involve a migratory lawyer, a lawyer who represented the former client at a different firm than the one he or she works now, screening the lawyer with the conflict does not prevent imputation of the conflict to every lawyer in the firm. According to Rule 1.0(k)(DE), screening is the "isolation of the lawyer from any participation in a matter." This isolation occurs through procedures designed to protect information the lawyer has a duty to protect. If Lisa has a conflict of interest involving former client Cindy which prevents her representation of Ed, the conflict is imputed to all lawyers in Lisa's firm. If Lisa represented Cindy while Lisa worked at another firm, another lawyer at Lisa's current firm could represent Ed if the firm screens Lisa. But screening does not block the imputation of the conflict if Lisa represented Cindy while Lisa worked at her current firm. The rules that apply to the migratory lawyer situation are discussed in the next section.

D. Conflicts and Migratory Lawyers

1. When a Lawyer Represents a Client, Moves to Another Practice Setting, and No Longer Represents the Client: Conflicts for the Lawyer and the New Firm

A lawyer may not represent a client with "materially adverse" interests to a former client in the "same or a substantially related matter" regardless of where the lawyer practices. So if Lisa Lawyer cannot represent Ed Entrepreneur because the representation is "materially adverse" to the interests of Cindy, a former client, and the matter is the "same or a substantially related matter," it is irrelevant to the conflicts analysis that Lisa represented Cindy while affiliated with Best Firm and is affiliated with Good Firm when she wants to represent Ed. Lisa can represent Ed only if Cindy gives "informed consent, confirmed in writing."

If Lisa was still with Best Firm, no lawyer at Best Firm could represent Ed absent such consent. The question is whether the same is true with regard to the lawyers at Good Firm, the firm Lisa joined after her representation of Cindy concluded. Rule 1.10(a)(2)(ID) provides that the lawyers at the second firm can avoid imputation of a conflict created by a lawyer joining the firm by doing the following:

1. "timely screen[ing]" the joining conflicted lawyer "from any participation in the matter";
2. giving to the conflicted lawyer none of the fee (the lawyer's salary or partnership share, agreed to independent of the particular matter, can include funds derived from the representation);
3. giving prompt "written notice" to the former client (so that the former client can assure that the screening is properly within the bounds of the rules of professional conduct) that should include the following:
    a. a description of the procedures used,
    b. a statement of the firm's and the conflicted lawyer's compliance,
    c. a reminder that review by a tribunal is possible, and
    d. an agreement from the firm to answer promptly any of the former's client's written questions about the screening and to respond promptly to any of the former client's written objections; and
4. "at reasonable intervals upon the former client's written request and upon termination of the screening procedures,"providing "certifications of compliance with the[] Rules and with the screening procedures" to the former client by the conflicted lawyer and a partner with the firm.

According to Rule 1.0(k)(DE), screening is the "isolation of the lawyer from any participation in a matter." This isolation occurs through procedures designed to protect information the lawyer has a duty to protect. Lawyers and other personnel must be told that they are prohibited from communicating with the conflicted lawyer about the matter and the conflicted lawyer must agree to the prohibition as well. Everyone should be reminded of the issue on a periodic basis. The conflicted lawyer must have no access to anything relating to the problematic matter, including electronic files.

So Good Firm, Lisa's second firm, can avoid the imputation of her disqualifying conflict by screening Lisa. Lisa must be "timely screened." Lisa must receive no part of the fee Good Firm earns from representing Ed other than a salary or partnership share arranged by a separate agreement. Good Firm must give Cindy prompt "written notice" of the screening procedures used by Good Firm, a statement that Good Firm and Lisa are in compliance with the screening procedures, a reminder that Cindy can take the matter to a tribunal if she is not satisfied, and an agreement from Good Firm to promptly respond to Cindy's written questions and objections. Good Firm and Lisa must also provide "certifications of compliance" if Cindy requests such in writing.

Good Firm might simply decide that screening is too onerous and forgo representing Ed unless Cindy consents to the representation.

2. When a Lawyer Did Not Represent a Client But Another Lawyer in the Firm Did, and the First Lawyer Moves to Another Practice Setting: Conflicts for the Lawyer and the New Firm

Now consider the situation of a moving lawyer who *did not* individually represent the former client. Assume that Lisa practiced law with Best Firm two years ago. Lisa, a newly minted lawyer at the time, worked in the trusts and estates department of the firm. She spent her time drafting wills and trust documents under the tutelage of more senior lawyers. At that time Best, a partner in the firm, represented Cindy in her purchase of a business. Lisa had no involvement whatsoever with Cindy's matter. Now Lisa practices law in Good Firm. She still does trusts and estates work. Lena, a partner at Good Firm, would like to represent Ed in his claims against Cindy arising our of Cindy's purchase of the business.

Rule 1.9(b)(DE) applies to the situation in which a lawyer's former firm represented a client, but the moving lawyer did not individually work on the matter. This is Lisa's situation. Lisa did not represent Cindy but other members of Lisa's former firm did represent Cindy while Lisa worked there. Rule 1.9(b)(DE) provides that a lawyer cannot represent a person in the following scenario:

1. the matter is the "same or a substantially related matter" as the prior firm's representation if the former client,
2. the current person has "materially adverse" interests to the former client, and
3. the moving lawyer has information material to the current matter that is protected from use or disclosure by Rule 1.6(DE) and Rule 1.9(c)(DE).

The representation is possible with the former client's "informed consent, confirmed in writing."

Ed's current matter and Cindy's representation two years ago are the "same or a substantially related" matter. In addition, the interests of Cindy and of Ed are "materially adverse." Without Cindy's consent, Lisa cannot represent Ed if Lisa possesses confidential information, protected by Rules 1.6(DE) and 1.9(c)(DE), material to Ed's matter. This is not likely given that Lisa's work did not involve work on corporate change matters. Lisa could have such information, however, as a result of occurrences such as lunch conversations with lawyers working on Cindy's matter, access to Cindy's file, or even general office conversation. Lisa's knowledge can be inferred from general office practices. For example, if all lawyers in a five-person firm have access to all firm files and all lawyers routinely participate in conversations about all cases, one can infer that all the lawyers have protected information. If Lisa has protected information about Cindy, she cannot represent Ed without Cindy's consent.

Likewise, if Lisa has a conflict under Rule 1.9(b)(DE) because she has problematic information, her conflict is imputed to all the lawyers at Good Firm, her new firm, unless Good firm screens Lisa pursuant to the directives of Rule 1.10(a)(2)(ID) or unless Cindy gives "informed consent, confirmed in writing" and in accord with Rule 1.7(DE). Rule 1.10(a)(2)(ID) requires the following for a proper screening:

1. "timely screen[ing]" the joining conflicted lawyer "from any participation in the matter";
2. giving to the conflicted lawyer none of the fee (the lawyer's salary or partnership share, agreed to independent of the particular matter, can include funds derived from the representation);
3. giving prompt "written notice" to the former client (so that the former client can assure that the screening is properly within the bounds of the rules of professional conduct) that should include the following:
    a. a description of the procedures used;
    b. a statement of the firm's and the conflicted lawyer's compliance;
    c. a reminder that review by a tribunal is possible; and
    d. an agreement from the firm to answer promptly any of the former's client's written questions about the screening and to respond promptly to any of the former client's written objections; and
4. "at reasonable intervals upon the former client's written request and upon termination of the screening procedures," providing "certifications of compliance with the [...] Rules and with the screening procedures" to the former client by the conflicted lawyer and a partner with the firm.

According to Rule 1.0(k)(DE), screening is the "isolation of the lawyer from any participation in a matter." This isolation occurs through procedures designed to protect information the lawyer has a duty to protect. Lawyers and other personnel should be told that they are prohibited from communicating with the conflicted lawyer about the matter and the conflicted lawyer should agree to the prohibition as well. Everyone should be reminded of the issue on a periodic basis. The conflicted lawyer should have no access to anything relating to the problematic matter, including electronic files.

Good Firm, Lisa's second firm, can avoid the imputation of her disqualifying conflict by screening Lisa. Lisa must be "timely screened." Lisa must receive no part of the fee Good Firm earns from representing Ed except her usual salary or partnership share. Good Firm must give Cindy prompt "written notice" of the screening procedures used by Good Firm, a statement that Good Firm and Lisa are in compliance with the screening procedures, a reminder that Cindy can take the matter to a tribunal if she is not satisfied and an agreement from Good Firm to promptly respond to Cindy's written questions and objections. Good Firm and Lisa must also provide "certifications of compliance" if Cindy requests such in writing.

3. When a Lawyer at a Firm Represents a Client and the Lawyer and the Client Leave the Firm: Conflicts for the Firm

Another former client scenario occurs when a lawyer who personally represents a client leaves the firm. What responsibilities do the lawyers remaining at the firm have to the former client, assuming that the client either leaves with the leaving lawyer or otherwise terminates the relationship with the firm? Perhaps Lisa Lawyer represented Cindy in the purchase of a business two years ago. At the time Lisa practiced at Best Firm. Shortly thereafter, Lisa moved to Good Firm. Since then Cindy has not employed any lawyer at Best Firm. Now Lisle, a lawyer at Best Firm, wishes to represent Ed in a matter arising from Cindy's purchase. Ed claims that Cindy misled Ed regarding the purchase of the business.

Rule 1.10(b)(ID) governs this situation. The rule applies if a lawyer leaves a firm and a client of that lawyer is no longer represented by the firm. In such a situation, a lawyer at the firm cannot represent a client if the following is true:

1. the client's interests are "materially adverse" to those of a former client,
2. the current representation is the "same or a substantially related matter," and
3. any lawyer still at the firm has information material to the current matter that is protected by Rules 1.6(DE) and 1.9(c)(DE).

Representation is possible with "informed consent, confirmed in writing" and in accordance with Rule 1.7(DE).

If Lisle of Best Firm represents Ed, Ed's interests in the matter will be "materially adverse" to Cindy's interests. In addition, the representation is the "same or a substantially related matter" to Lisa's earlier representation of Cindy. Ed's claim arises from the transaction with regard to which Lisa represented Cindy while Lisa was working at Best Firm. Even so, Lisle can represent Ed if no lawyer present at Best Firm now has material information about Cindy protected by Rules 1.6(DE) and 1.9(c)(DE). An important question is whether any lawyers assisted Lisa in the representation of Cindy and if any of those lawyers are still with Best Firm. If there is a lawyer at the firm who worked on the matter, then the representation of Ed by a Best Firm lawyer such as Lisle cannot occur unless Cindy provides "informed consent, confirmed in writing" and that is in accord with Rule 1.7(DE).

Related Sections of the *Restatement (Third) of the Law Governing Lawyers*

Sections 121–124 and 132

Checkpoints

- A lawyer may not disclose information relating to a former client representation unless the rules otherwise permit or require the disclosure.
- A lawyer may not use information relating to a former client's representation to that former client's disadvantage unless
    1. the rules otherwise permit the use,
    2. the rules otherwise require the use, or
    3. "when the information has become generally known."
- A former client can consent to a conflict with "informed consent, confirmed in writing."
- Absent consent, a lawyer may not represent a client in the following circumstance:
    1. the client's interests are "materially adverse" to the interests of a former client of the lawyer, and
    2. the representation is in the "same or a substantially related matter."
- If a lawyer has a former client conflict of interest, all lawyers in the same firm have the same conflict.

- A client can give "informed consent, confirmed in writing" to an imputed conflicted representation if the consent is in accord with rule 1.7(DE).
- If a lawyer has a former client conflict and the lawyer represented the former client while working at another firm, and the former client does not consent, the lawyers in the conflicted lawyer's new firm may avoid imputation of the conflict by screening the conflicted lawyer. To properly screen, the firm must do the following:
    1. "timely screen" the joining conflicted lawyer "from any participation in the matter";
    2. give to the conflicted lawyer none of the fee;
    3. give prompt "written notice" to the former client (so that the former client can assure that the screening is properly within the bounds of the rules of professional conduct) that should include the following:
        a. a description of the procedures used,
        b. a statement of the firm's and the conflicted lawyer's compliance,
        c. a reminder that review by a tribunal is possible, and
        d. an agreement from the firm to answer promptly any of the former's client's written questions about the screening and to respond promptly to any of the former client's written objections; and
    4. "at reasonable intervals upon the former client's written request and upon termination of the screening procedures," provide "certifications of compliance with the [...] Rules and with the screening procedures" to the former client by the conflicted lawyer and a partner with the firm.
- If a lawyer practiced with a firm and other lawyers in the firm represented a client but the lawyer did not individually represent the client, and if the lawyer leaves the firm and joins another firm, absent consent, the lawyer may not represent a party in the following situation:
    1. the party's interests are "materially adverse" to the client of the former firm,
    2. the matter is the "same or a substantially related matter," and
    3. the lawyer has information protected by Rule 1.6(DE) or 1.9(c)(DE) that is material to the current matter.
- In such a circumstance and even if the former client does not consent, the lawyers in the conflicted lawyer's new firm may avoid imputation of the conflict by screening the conflicted lawyer. To properly screen, the firm must do the following:
    1. "timely screen" the joining conflicted lawyer "from any participation in the matter";
    2. give to the conflicted lawyer none of the fee;
    3. give prompt "written notice" to the former client (so that the former client can assure that the screening is properly within the bounds of the rules of professional conduct) that should include the following:

a. a description of the procedures used;

b. a statement of the firm's and the conflicted lawyer's compliance;

c. a reminder that review by a tribunal is possible; and

d. an agreement from the firm to answer promptly any of the former's client's written questions about the screening and to respond promptly to any of the former client's written objections; and

4. "at reasonable intervals upon the former client's written request and upon termination of the screening procedures," provide "certifications of compliance with the [...] Rules and with the screening procedures" to the former client by the conflicted lawyer and a partner with the firm.

- If a lawyer at a firm represents a client and then leaves the firm, and if no lawyer at the firm continues to represent the client, absent consent, no lawyer at the firm may represent a client in the following situation:

  1. the interests of the client are "materially adverse" to the former client,
  2. the matter is the "same or a substantially related matter," and
  3. any lawyer at the firm has material information protected by Rules 1.6(DE) and 1.9(c)(DE).

Chapter 20

Conflicts and Prospective Clients

Roadmap

- Rule 1.18(DE)
- Definition of a prospective client
- Use or disclosure of prospective client information
- Conflict of interest rules for prospective clients

A. Introduction

In the modern practice of law, lawyers often communicate with potential clients about the possibility of performing legal work. If a lawyer-client relationship forms, the lawyer owes that client all the duties and must abide by all conflict of interest requirements for a current client. If the lawyer decides not to represent the potential client, or if the potential client decides not to use the services of the lawyer, the question arises as to the responsibilities the lawyer owes the potential client who does not ripen into a true client. The answer depends on the character of the interaction between the potential client and the lawyer.

Jurisdictions have different tests for the point at which a lawyer-client relationship forms. As discussed in *Chapter 4 Basis of Duty: The Lawyer-Client Relationship*, if a person has a reasonable belief that a lawyer represents him or her, a court may recognize that there is a lawyer-client relationship and all duties a lawyer owes a client attach. In the time before such a belief would be reasonable, when the person is considering forming a lawyer-client relationship and consults with a particular lawyer, the person is not a full-fledged client but may be a prospective client under the definition of Rule 1.18(a)(DE). A lawyer owes a prospective client a more limited set of duties because the relationship does not justify more.

B. What Is a Prospective Client?

Rule 1.18(a)(DE) defines a prospective client as "[a] person who consults with a lawyer about the possibility of forming a client-lawyer relationship with respect to a matter." This consultation is the key to the recognition of prospective client status. The comment to the rule elaborates on this statement by noting that whether a consultation has occurred depends on the circumstances. As an example, the comment notes that a consultation can occur if a lawyer, by any medium, invites "the submission of information about a potential representation without clear and reasonably understandable warnings and cautionary statements that limit the lawyer's obligations, and a person provides information in response." So a prospective client relationship can form without the lawyer and potential client having in-person contact or real-time or other exchanges. The prospective client status can be created by a person responding to a website invitation to submit information. The comment notes, however, that a person who provides information in response to advertising that has only basic information about the lawyer is not a prospective client because "[s]uch a person communicates information unilaterally to a lawyer, without any reasonable expectation that the lawyer is willing to discuss the possibility of forming a client-lawyer relationship." The comment, by stating that there is no prospective status if the person has no "reasonable expectation that the lawyer is willing to discuss the possibility of forming a client-lawyer relationship," implies that there is a prospective client-lawyer relationship if the person has a "reasonable expectation that the lawyer is willing to discuss the possibility of forming a client-lawyer relationship."

Some courts, applying standards developed before the concept of a prospective client became recognized by the professional responsibility rules, state that a lawyer-client relationship exists if a lawyer renders legal advice to a person. Other courts may focus on the disclosure of confidential information. Yet, a comment to Rule 1.18(DE) notes that "[p]rospective clients, like clients, may disclose information to a lawyer, place documents or other property in the lawyer's custody, or rely on the lawyer's advice." Thus, for purposes of Rule 1.18, the disclosure of confidential information and the rendering of legal advice are not the bright-line beginnings of a full lawyer-client relationship. These court statements reflect standards developed at a time when recognition of a full lawyer-client relationship was necessary if a lawyer was to owe *any* duties to the party. There was no middle ground of prospective client status. With recognition of a prospective client to whom limited duties are owed, there is room for more subtlety with regard to the beginning of a lawyer-client relationship and the recognition of prospective clients.

A typical setting for recognition of prospective client status is the following. A lawyer meets with a person to discuss the possibility of the lawyer representing the person. The lawyer warns the person before the meeting that the lawyer does not represent the person yet because the lawyer must analyze whether any conflicts of interest prevent the representation. In such a situation, the person *would not* be reasonable in believing himself or herself to be a client of the lawyer. The person *would* be reasonable in believing that the lawyer may represent the person in the future. Such a person would be a prospective client under Rule 1.18(a)(DE).

If Larry Lawyer agrees to meet with Clint to discuss representing Clint in a personal injury matter, and if Larry explains in a telephone conversation before the meeting that he does not yet represent Clint but that he is considering doing so, Clint would not be reasonable in concluding that Larry represents him. Clint would be reasonable in believing that he is a prospective client. Clint should properly have the benefit of the protections of Rule 1.18(DE), the rule applicable to prospective clients. In contrast, a person is not a prospective client if the person has no reasonable belief that the lawyer would consider a representation. For example, perhaps Dora, the person against whom Clint has a personal injury claim, hears that Larry, a well-known plaintiff's counsel, is representing Clint. Dora telephones Larry's office and leaves a voice mail message containing confidential information. Dora cannot later claim that she should benefit from the protections of Rule 1.18(DE). Dora garners no protection because she disclosed the information without the reasonable expectation that Larry would consider representing Dora. Requiring a reasonable expectation of representation prevents a person wishing to create a conflict of interest for a lawyer from doing so by trickery.

C. The Duty of Confidentiality

Only by the prospective client's disclosure of relevant information can the lawyer determine whether he or she may take the matter and whether he or she chooses to assume the representation. Likewise, by discussing the matter with the lawyer, the prospective client can better decide whether to engage the lawyer. In recognition of the need for this disclosure, a lawyer owes a prospective client a duty of confidentiality. A lawyer may not reveal information relating to the representation of the prospective client unless the rules otherwise would permit or require disclosure if the prospective client were a former client. Recall that Rule 1.6(DE) permits disclosure in certain circumstances and other rules require disclosure in narrow circumstances. *See Chapter 15 The Duty of Confidentiality* and *Chapter 28 Honesty and Candor.*

Rule 1.18(b)(DE) limits use of information as well. The rule provides that a lawyer may not use information of the prospective client to the disadvantage of the prospective client unless the rules otherwise would permit or require such use if the prospective client were a former client or unless the information has become "generally known." The comment provides that a lawyer can condition a consultation on the party agreeing that the lawyer is free to use any information disclosed in the consultation. Of course, the prospective client's advance agreement to such use must take the form of "informed consent." As Rule 1.0(k)(DE) explains, this means that any consent or waiver can occur only with full disclosure of the risks accompanying the situation and the alternatives to the situation.

D. Conflicts of Interest

1. The Basic Rule

A lawyer must acquire information from the prospective client to determine whether the lawyer has a conflict of interest that prohibits representation and to evaluate whether to accept the representation. Yet, that information can create conflicts of interest for future matters for the lawyer. Unlike the conflict of interest rules for current and former clients, Rule 1.18(c)(DE), the conflict of interest rule for prospective clients, does not recognize a conflict unless the lawyer *actually* receives "significantly harmful" information from the prospective client. A lawyer cannot represent another client if

1. the matter is the "same or a substantially related matter" as the prospective client consultation,
2. the client's interests are "materially adverse" to the interests of the prospective client, and
3. the prospective client gave the lawyer information "that could be significantly harmful" to the prospective client.

If a lawyer has a prospective client conflict of interest, all lawyers in the firm have the same conflict of interest.

Perhaps Clint comes to Larry Lawyer seeking Larry's assistance in a divorce proceeding. During the consultation Clint tells Larry that he is seeking a divorce from his wife, Cindy, because he wishes to pursue a relationship with another woman, Rachel. Clint tells Larry that he would like to proceed with the divorce without revealing Rachel's involvement. Larry ultimately decides not to represent Clint because he feels Clint may not be able to pay Larry. Later,

Cindy, Clint's wife calls Larry to determine whether Larry will represent her in the divorce. Larry cannot represent Cindy. Cindy and Clint have "materially adverse" interests in the divorce proceeding. Larry would be representing Cindy in the same matter as the one about which Clint consulted with Larry. Finally, Larry has information about Clint that "could be significantly harmful" to Clint if Larry told Cindy. Larry would have a duty to tell Cindy this information. *See Chapter 8 Scope of the Representation and Communication with the Client.* Larry could not represent Cindy without Clint's consent. No lawyer in Larry's firm could represent Cindy if Larry could not represent Cindy without consent or screening.

2. Obtaining Advance Consent

Because the identification of a conflict of interest in the prospective client setting and the subsequent disqualification depends on the information actually transmitted to the lawyer, lawyers have the ability to control somewhat the extent of future problems. Lawyers can seek to limit the information the prospective client gives to the consulted lawyers. Ideally, the prospective client provides to the lawyer only the minimum information necessary for the lawyer to properly evaluate the matter.

In addition, as noted in a comment to the rule, before any consultation a lawyer may obtain a prospective client's "informed consent" that any information disclosed in the consultation cannot be the basis for future disqualification. A prospective client's "informed consent" might be appropriate if the prospective client is asking many law firms to, in effect, bid on the legal work of the prospective client. Recall that Rule 1.0(e)(DE) provides that "informed consent" requires that the person be told of the risks and alternatives to the planned conduct before expressing agreement. Even so, the "informed consent" may be difficult to enforce if the prospective client is an unsophisticated user of legal services or if the consent is not evidenced by a writing.

3. Obtaining Consent after Disclosure

Even if a lawyer does not obtain the prospective client's consent *before* the disclosure to the lawyer, the lawyer may avoid disqualification later. A lawyer can represent a client whose interests are "materially adverse" to the prospective client in the "same or a substantially related matter" even if the lawyer has "significantly harmful" information about the prospective client if the lawyer obtains the prospective client's "informed consent, confirmed in writing" as well as the client's "informed consent, confirmed in writing" and otherwise in accordance with Rule 1.7(DE). To give "informed consent" a client must first be aware of all the reasonably foreseeable ways that the conflict could adversely affect the client. As Rule 1.0(e)(DE) states, the lawyer must explain to the client the "material risks" and "reasonably available alternatives." The requirement that the consent be "confirmed in writing" means, as explained by Rule 1.0(b)(DE), that the client must give consent in writing or the lawyer must prepare a writing confirming the client's oral consent and must send the writing to the client promptly, at the very least within a reasonable time after the client gives oral consent. The requirement of a writing includes, as explained by Rule 1.0(n)(DE), "a tangible or electronic record of a communication or representation, including handwriting, typewriting, printing, photostating, photography, audio or videorecording, and electronic communications."

Even if the prospective client will not consent to the involvement of the lawyer with the information, the prospective client may consent to the involvement of another lawyer in the firm.

4. Screening

Even if a lawyer has a prospective client conflict that disqualifies the lawyer, and even if the prospective client does not consent to the representation by the lawyer or any other lawyers in the firm, the other lawyers in the firm are not disqualified if the requirements of Rule 1.18(d)(DE) are fulfilled. Rule 1.18(d)(DE) provides a procedure to limit the harsh effect of the general imputation of disqualification rule given the prospective nature of the client. Another lawyer in the firm can represent another client in a situation in which all of the lawyers would otherwise be disqualified by a prospective client conflict if the following is true.

First, the lawyer who received the problematic information at the time of the prospective client consultation, must have taken "reasonable measures to avoid exposure to more disqualifying information than was reasonably necessary" to decide to accept the representation or refuse it.

Second, the lawyer with the prospective client conflict must be screened in a timely fashion from any participation in the later representation. Screening, as Rule 1.0(k)(DE) explains, is isolation of the lawyer so that information that lawyer has is protected from disclosure. This isolation occurs through procedures designed to protect information the lawyer has a duty to protect. Lawyers and other personnel should be told that they are prohibited from communicating with the conflicted lawyer about the matter and the conflicted lawyer should agree to the prohibition as well. Everyone should be reminded of the issue on a periodic basis. The conflicted lawyer should have no access to anything relating to the problematic matter, including electronic files.

Third, the lawyer with the prospective client information must not receive a fee from the later representation. The lawyer's salary or partnership share, agreed to independent of the particular matter, can include funds derived from the representation.

Fourth, the prospective client must be given prompt written notice of the later representation.

Perhaps Clint consults with Larry Lawyer about Larry representing Clint in a divorce matter. During the consultation, Clint tells Larry about his interest in another person, Rachel, and his desire to keep that information secret. Larry refuses the representation. Cindy, Clint's wife, then requests Leo, Larry's law partner, to represent Cindy in the divorce matter. As established earlier, Larry could not represent Cindy because of the information he has about Clint. Leo could represent Cindy, however,

1. if Larry behaved reasonably in attempting to limit the information Clint disclosed to Larry in the initial consultation to only the information required for the representation decision,
2. if the firm screens Larry from Cindy's matter,
3. if Larry receives no fee from the representation of Cindy, and
4. if the firm notifies Clint in writing promptly after Leo decides to represent Cindy.

E. The Duty of Competence

Rule 1.18(DE) is silent about whether a lawyer owes a prospective client a duty of competence. Yet a comment notes that Rule 1.1(DE), the basic duty of competence owed to clients, applies to prospective clients as well. This is logical given the recognition in another comment that it is theoretically possible for a lawyer to render legal advice to a prospective client.

Related Sections of the *Restatement (Third) of the Law Governing Lawyers*

Section 15

Checkpoints

- A prospective client is "[a] person who consults with a lawyer about the possibility of forming a client-lawyer relationship with respect to a matter."
- If a person does not have a reasonable belief that the lawyer represents him or her, but does have the reasonable belief that such a relationship may result, then the person may be a prospective client.
- A lawyer may not reveal information relating to the representation of the prospective client unless the rules would permit or require disclosure if the prospective client were a former client.
- A lawyer may not use information of a prospective client to the disadvantage of the prospective client unless the rules would permit or require such use if the prospective client were a former client or unless the information has become "generally known."
- A lawyer cannot represent a client if
    1. the matter is the "same or a substantially related matter" as a prospective client consultation,
    2. the client's interests are "materially adverse" to the interests of the once-prospective client,
    3. the prospective client gave the lawyer information "that could be significantly harmful" to the prospective client, and
    4. the prospective client has not waived the conflict of interest in advance nor have the prospective client and the other client consented to the conflicted representation by "informed consent, confirmed in writing" and in accordance with Rule 1.7(DE).
- A prospective client conflict of interest is imputed to all lawyers in the firm.
- Another lawyer in the firm can represent a client in a situation in which all of the lawyers would otherwise be disqualified if the following is true:
    1. the lawyer who received the problematic information must have taken "reasonable measures to avoid exposure to more disqualifying information than was reasonably necessary" to decide to accept the representation or refuse it,
    2. the lawyer with the prospective client information must be screened in a timely fashion from any participation in the later representation,
    3. the lawyer with the prospective client information must not receive a fee from the later representation, and
    4. the prospective client must be given prompt written notice of the representation.
- A lawyer owes a prospective client the duty of competence.

Chapter 21

Conflict of Interest Rules for Particular Situations

Roadmap

- Rule 1.8(DE)
- Business transactions between a lawyer and a client
- Use of client information
- Gifts from clients and preparing instruments effectuating gifts from clients
- Obtaining literary or media rights during a representation
- Financial assistance to clients
- Third party payment of fees
- Aggregate settlements
- Agreements prospectively limiting malpractice liability
- Agreements settling claims or potential claims of malpractice against a lawyer
- Acquiring an interest in a cause of action or the subject matter of litigation in matter which a lawyer represents a client
- Sexual relationships with clients
- Imputation of these conflicts

A. Introduction

There are some particular conflict settings that are treated separately from the general analysis of Rule 1.7(DE), the current client rule, Rule 1.9(DE), the former client rule, and Rule 1.18(DE), the prospective client rule. Rule 1.8(DE) contains these more-particularized statements of guidance. The situations dealt with by the provisions of Rule 1.8(DE) generally involve conflicts between a client's interest and a lawyer's interest. These are situations in which a lawyer might be tempted to subordinate a client's interests to his or her own interests. The provisions of Rule 1.8(DE) are designed to remove such temptation. Thus, the danger of injury to a client is eliminated or at least lessened. A lawyer is more likely to honor the duties of loyalty and confidentiality owed to a client. The prohibitions and requirements contained in Rule 1.8(DE), except the sexual relationship prohibition of Rule 1.8(j)(DE), are imputed to all lawyers in the firm.

B. Business Transactions with a Client

1. The Rule

Lawyers often enter into contracts with clients. The most obvious contract is the initial fee agreement. Lawyers also enter into contracts with clients that are unrelated or at least not directly related to the matter the lawyer is handling for the client. A lawyer might sell a house to a client or buy the client's car. The client might loan money to the lawyer. The possibilities are endless. None of these transactions are prohibited. They are, however, substantially regulated by professional responsibility rules and other law.

Rule 1.5(NE) provides special requirements for fee agreements between a lawyer and a client. *See Chapter 9 Fees.* Rule 1.8(a)(DE) provides more general requirements for any business transaction between a lawyer and a client and especially for any transaction in which the lawyer knowingly obtains "an ownership, possessory, security or other pecuniary interest adverse to a client." In addition to these professional responsibility strictures, the law of contracts also provides guidance about contracts between two parties in a fiduciary relationship such as a lawyer and a client. All of these restrictions are imposed because in such a situation there is a temptation for a lawyer to put his or her own interest above that of a client. In addition, the fiduciary nature of the lawyer-client relationship and the powers of persuasion of lawyers make the temptation relatively easy to act upon.

Rule 1.8(a)(DE) states that a lawyer may enter into a business transaction with a client or knowingly obtain "an ownership, possessory, security, or other pecuniary interest adverse to a client" if

1. the "transaction and terms" are "fair and reasonable" to the client;
2. the "transaction and terms" are "fully disclosed to the client";
3. the "transaction and terms" are "transmitted in writing to the client in a manner that can be reasonably understood by the client";
4. the lawyer in writing advises the client of the advantages of consulting with an independent lawyer about the deal;
5. the client has "reasonable opportunity to seek" the counsel of an independent lawyer; and

6. the client gives "informed consent," in a signed writing, to the "essential terms" of the deal, and to the role the lawyer assumes in the deal.

Specifically, the rule requires the client's consent to include consent to the lawyer serving as a lawyer for the client in any such deal. To obtain "informed consent," Rule 1.0(e)(DE) provides that the lawyer must explain the "material risks" of the deal and all "reasonably available alternatives" to the deal. In a situation in which the lawyer is representing the client for purposes of the deal, the lawyer must tell the client of the risk created by the lawyer's dual role as lawyer for the client and also as a participant in the transaction. This means that the lawyer must explain to the client the risk that the lawyer will favor himself or herself over the client in the deal.

In addition, in the situation in which the lawyer represents the client and himself or herself in the deal, a lawyer must abide by Rule 1.7(DE) as well as Rule 1.8(a)(DE). The lawyer's own interest in such a representation may create such a conflict that under Rule 1.7(DE) the lawyer cannot request client consent even if the lawyer otherwise abides by Rule 1.8(a)(DE). *See Chapter 18 Conflicts and Current Clients.*

2. Initial Fee Agreements

Rule 1.8(a)(DE) generally does not apply to the initial fee agreement. The lawyer is not yet in a lawyer-client relationship at the time of the initial fee agreement. Though there is a cognizable relationship even so, the infancy of the relationship means that the lawyer may have less influence over the other party. Rule 1.5(NE) provides a separate set of requirements for that initial arrangement. *See Chapter 9 Fees.* Yet, *ABA Formal Opinion 00-418 (2000), ABA Formal Opinion 02-427 (2002),* and comment one to Rule 1.8(a)(DE) clarify that Rule 1.8(a)(DE) *does apply* if the lawyer obtains a contractual security interest to secure a fee or, in the initial arrangement, accepts any nonmonetary asset, such as stock, as a fee.

3. Modification of Fee Agreements

ABA Formal Opinion 11-458 (2011) addresses the modification of an existing fee agreement. The *Opinion* does not state that all such agreements require compliance with Rule 1.8(a)(DE); the *Opinion* does state that all such agreements must be reasonable at the time of the modification and the client must understand and accept the modification. The lawyer must explain the modification to the client and must tell the client that the lawyer will continue the representation even if the client does not agree to the fee modification. The *Opinion* notes that unless there has been an unanticipated change of circumstances, a fee change to increase the lawyer's compensation will not likely be reasonable or enforceable. The *Opinion* also states that a fee modification involving a lawyer acquiring an interest in the client's business or nonmonetary assets must abide by the requirements of Rule 1.8(a)(DE) for doing business with a client.

Clearly, a careful lawyer seeking to obtain a proper fee modification might follow Rule 1.8(a)(DE) in every case. A typical reception for a fee modification is that in *In re Hefron*, 771 N.E.2d 1157 (Ind. 2002). In that case a lawyer agreed to represent a client on an hourly basis in an effort to recover assets belonging to an estate. Soon the lawyer realized that the asset recovery was very easy. The lawyer then presented to the client a contingency fee contract. A contingency fee would pay the lawyer a handsome sum and the lawyer already knew that the risk of failure was slim. The Indiana Supreme Court found that the fee was unreasonable. The court also found that by renegotiating the fee unfairly at a time when the lawyer-client relationship already existed, the lawyer did not follow the required path for a transaction with a client. The court opined that the contingency fee agreement was far from "fair and reasonable." Further, the lawyer did not disclose important facts. Lastly, the lawyer did not provide the client with time to discuss the matter with another lawyer.

4. Other Transactions

Transactions unrelated to the lawyer's fee that a lawyer has with a client must be done in accord with Rule 1.8(a)(DE)'s procedures with the exception of routine consumer transactions. Think of the ridiculousness of requiring these procedures when a lawyer dines at his or her client's restaurant or buys a television at a client's store. Comment one to Rule 1.8(DE) clarifies that the rule does not apply to "standard commercial transactions" that the client offers to others and lists as examples "banking or brokerage services, medical services, products manufactured or distributed by the client, and utilities' services."

The procedures of Rule 1.8(a)(DE) apply to any other transactions that are not "standard commercial transactions" and are not fee agreements for legal services. So, for example, a lawyer must follow the procedures when purchasing a house or a car from a client, when loaning money to a client, when receiving a loan from a client, and when investing in or with a client if these transactions are not "standard commercial transactions." This list is, of course, not exclusive.

Perhaps Lisa Lawyer represents Cindy Client. Cindy desires to open a restaurant in a developing area of town. Lisa believes that Cindy has a good concept and would like to invest $20,000 in Cindy's endeavor in exchange for a twenty percent ownership share of the restaurant. Note that the interest in the restaurant is not one given to Lisa in exchange for services; it is not a fee. Lisa may invest in Cindy's restaurant and Lisa may receive in return an interest in the restaurant. To enter into such a transaction, Lisa must confirm that the terms of the deal are "fair and reasonable." An exchange of $20,000 for a twenty percent interest in the restaurant must be a "fair and reasonable" trade. Second, Lisa must disclose fully the terms to Cindy. Lisa must tell Cindy, for example, that Lisa is not simply loaning Cindy the money for the restaurant but rather that Lisa will own twenty percent of the restaurant as a result of the $20,000 payment. Third, Lisa must convey all of this information to Cindy in writing in a manner that she can understand. Fourth, Lisa must explain to Cindy in writing that Cindy might benefit from discussing this deal with another lawyer who is not involved in the deal or affiliated with Lisa since Lisa is the other party to the deal. Fifth, Lisa must give Cindy time to consult with such a lawyer. Finally, Cindy must give her "informed consent" in a signed writing. Cindy must consent to all essential terms—that Lisa is giving Cindy $20,000 for use in starting a restaurant business and that Lisa is receiving twenty percent ownership of the restaurant business in return. Cindy also must consent to Lisa's role in the transaction—as the opposing party in the deal and as Cindy's counsel on the deal if that is the case. Lisa must be certain, as Rule 1.7(DE) requires, that she reasonably believes that she can render competent and diligent representation to Cindy if she plans to represent Cindy in the deal. If Lisa takes all these steps, she has acted properly.

5. Contract Doctrine: Undue Influence Prevents Enforcement

In *Mayhew v. Benninghoff*, 53 Cal. App. 4th 1365, 62 Cal. Rptr. 2d 27 (Cal. App. 1997), the California Court of Appeals stated, "Attorneys wear different hats when they perform legal services on behalf of their clients and when they conduct business with them. As to the latter, the law presumes the hat they wear is a black one." Independent of Rule 1.8(a)(DE) or any other rule of professional responsibility is the contract doctrine of undue influence. As applied to a lawyer and client transaction, the doctrine holds that any contract between a lawyer and client is presumed to be the result of undue influence. Such a contract is voidable at the option of the client unless the lawyer can overcome the presumption of undue influence. A typical statement is that in *Hunt v. Picklesimer*, 162 S.W.2d 27, 30 (Ky. 1942). The court stated: "Even where a conveyance by a client to his attorney is fair upon its face, it is presumptively invalid, and the burden of establishing its fairness is upon the attorney." *Id.* at 30.

Following the requirements of Rule 1.8(a)(DE) assists a lawyer in proving that a contract is not the product of the lawyer's undue influence and should be enforced. Abiding by Rule 1.8(a)(DE) does not guarantee enforcement, however. Looking at all the circumstances, a court must decide that a transaction is not the product of undue influence if the contract is to be enforced.

In the situation of Lisa and Cindy and the restaurant, assume that Lisa has abided by Rule 1.8(a)(DE) regarding the transaction with Cindy. If Cindy later refuses to honor the contract and refuses to recognize Lisa's ownership interest in the restaurant, Lisa might bring an action claiming breach of contract and seeking damages or even specific enforcement. Because the contract is one between a lawyer and her client, the court will presume that the contract is unenforceable as the product of undue influence. To have the court honor the contract, Lisa must prove that Cindy entered the transaction without undue influence. Lisa's ability to prove that the transaction was in accord with Rule 1.8(a)(DE) greatly assists Lisa in overcoming the undue influence presumption.

C. Use of Client Information

1. No Use Disadvantageous to a Client

Rule 1.6(DE) prohibits disclosure of information relating to the representation of a client. *See Chapter 15 The Duty of Confidentiality.* Rule 1.8(b)(DE) provides that a lawyer may not *use* information relating to a client's representation in a way that disadvantages the client. There are two exceptions to the prohibition. First, a lawyer may use client information if the client gives "informed consent." A lawyer seeking to obtain such consent must explain to the client, as stated in Rule 1.0(e)(DE), the "material risks" of the proposed action and all "reasonably available alternatives." How likely is it that a client would consent to the lawyer using the information in a way that would hurt the client? Second, a lawyer may use information relating to the representation to the disadvantage of the client if another rule allows or requires it.

There are companion provisions regarding former and prospective clients. Rule 1.9(c)(DE) provides that a lawyer may not use information relating to a representation of a former client to the disadvantage of that former client. That rule allows disadvantageous use, however, if the rules otherwise require or permit such use or the information has become "generally known." *See Chapter 19 Conflicts and Former Clients.* Rule 1.18(b)(DE), the prospective client rule, allows use or disclosure of prospective client information only if such use or disclosure is allowed with former clients. *See Chapter 20 Conflicts and Prospective Clients.*

2. No Prohibition If the Use Is Not Harmful to a Client

While a lawyer may not use information in a way disadvantageous to a client, Rule 1.8(b)(DE) does not prohibit the use of information relating to a client's representation if the use does not negatively affect the client. Perhaps Cindy Client is planning to buy property in a particular area of the city and to develop the property as a condominium complex. Lisa represents Cindy in the endeavor. Lisa discovers, in the context of the representation, that property that is perfect for Cindy's purpose is for sale and so Lisa buys it before Cindy is able to buy it herself. Then Lisa offers the property to Cindy at a much higher rate. In addition to ensuring that Cindy will end the representation, Lisa has violated 1.8(b)(DE) because her purchase of the property has increased Cindy's cost; the use of the information is disadvantageous to Cindy.

In contrast, if Cindy discovers that the property is for sale and decides to buy property elsewhere, then Lisa may purchase the property even though she discovered the property in the context of the representation. Lisa's purchase of the property does not injure Cindy. There is no rule violation.

D. Gifts from a Client

1. Soliciting Gifts

Rule 1.8(c)(DE) states that a lawyer may not seek a "substantial gift" from a client. This prohibition includes testamentary gifts. This rule is based on a fear that lawyers have such outstanding powers of persuasion and the opportunity to use those powers that they can convince clients to give them anything. Perhaps Lisa Lawyer represents Cindy Client in many matters. Lisa cannot ask Cindy to give her a house or a car. Lisa cannot ask Cindy to leave her the house in Cindy's will. Note that Lisa can accept a gift from a client, but Lisa cannot "solicit" the gift.

2. Preparing Instruments for Gifts

On behalf of a client, a lawyer may not prepare any instrument giving the lawyer or the lawyer's spouse, child, grandchild, parent, or grandparent a "substantial gift." Also, a lawyer cannot prepare such an instrument if the gift is to go to a person with whom the lawyer enjoys a "close, familial relationship." Lisa Lawyer may not prepare a will for her client, Cindy, that names Lisa or Lisa's husband, child, grandchild, parent, or grandparent as a beneficiary to receive a "substantial gift" such as a house. Lisa may not prepare a will for Cindy that names Lisa's aunt, Ida, as a beneficiary to receive Cindy's house if Ida and Lisa have a "close, familial relationship."

3. An Exception for Relatives of the Client

There is an exception to these prohibitions if the recipient of the gift is related to the client as a spouse, child, grandchild, parent, or grandparent or if the client and the person enjoy a "close, familial relationship." If Cindy is Lisa's client and if Cindy is Lisa's mother, Lisa may seek a substantial gift and may prepare any necessary instrument to effectuate that gift. Lisa also may prepare Cindy's will even if the will names Lisa's son, Lou, as a beneficiary, since Lou is Cindy's grandson.

4. Seeking to Be Named by a Client as Executor or Other Fiduciary

A lawyer may ask a client to appoint the lawyer as the executor of the client's estate or to appoint the lawyer to some other fiduciary role. Even though the lawyer may enjoy great financial benefit from such an appointment, there is no ban to seeking such a role. The lawyer's interest in seeking such a position can create a conflict of interest in that there is a danger that the lawyer will not fully counsel the client about the advantages and disadvantages of other options to the appointment of the lawyer. The lawyer must be mindful of Rule 1.7(DE) in terms of any conflict created. *See Chapter 18 Conflicts and Current Clients.*

E. Literary and Media Rights Regarding a Representation

Rule 1.8(d)(DE) forbids a lawyer from entering into or negotiating an agreement with a client, before the end of a representation, that gives the lawyer the right to write about and publish or otherwise put forth in the media a work based "in substantial part" on the client's representation and information relating to that representation. A lawyer can enter into such as agreement after the representation has concluded but cannot enter into such an agreement before the representation ends.

The rationale is that a lawyer might be swayed by the prospect of a best-selling work. That lawyer might tailor the representation so that it makes a good tale. Even without a contract in existence during the representation, however, a lawyer might make tactical decisions in part based on how the situation might be portrayed in a book or other media account. A lawyer might hope to obtain the right to publish an account after the matter concludes.

Perhaps Lisa Lawyer represents Cindy Client with regard to Cindy's product liability claim against Bad Corporation. If Cindy has agreed that when the matter concludes Lisa has the right to write a book about the matter, Lisa might not encourage settlement. Lisa might think a trial would make a better story than a settlement. The rule is designed to prevent this sort of effect.

F. Providing Financial Assistance to a Client

Because a lawyer who has a financial interest in a client's matter might be inclined to favor protection of his or her financial interest rather than using independent professional judgment on behalf of the client, a lawyer's ability to provide financial assistance in a litigation setting is significantly limited by Rule 1.8(e)(DE). The general rule is that a lawyer may not provide financial assistance to a client in a pending or planned litigation matter. There is no prohibition to providing financial assistance to a client the lawyer represents in a non-litigation matter.

There are two exceptions to the general prohibition. First, a lawyer may pay court costs and litigation expenses with the understanding that the client will repay the lawyer later. The repayment can be contingent on the successful conclusion of the matter. Second, if a client is indigent, a lawyer may pay the client's court costs and litigation expenses without a promise of repayment.

Litigation expenses include the costs of marshalling the evidence for the case. The cost of a medical examination of the client is also a litigation expense payable by the lawyer. General living expenses are not litigation expenses. Lisa Lawyer may not pay the rent or buy groceries for her client, Cindy, but Lisa may pay for Cindy's medical examination for a matter in which Cindy claims that she was injured by the potential defendant. Cindy must agree to repay Lisa unless Cindy is indigent or unless Lisa and Cindy agree that the repayment will occur only if Cindy's claim is successful.

This rule limits interference with a lawyer's exercise of independent judgment on behalf of a client. The rule also prevents any sort of inappropriate encouragement of litigation. Ancient common law prohibitions of maintenance, champerty, and barratry were particularly concerned with inappropriate encouragement of litigation. Maintenance was defined as lending money for the purpose of maintaining a legal action. Champerty was defined as purchasing a cause of action or an interest in a cause of action. Barratry was loosely defined as stirring up litigation. The importance of these doctrines has faded somewhat but the doctrines still exist as does the wariness of anything that improperly encourages litigation.

The constraint on a lawyer providing financial assistance also prevents lawyers from competing for clients on the basis of financing offerings. Clients must choose a lawyer on some other basis, such as competence.

G. Payment of a Lawyer by Someone Other than the Client

When a third party pays a lawyer's fees, there are two dangers. One danger is that the lawyer will allow the third party to interfere in the lawyer-client relationship. The third party may believe that paying the bills gives him or her the right to direct the lawyer's services. For example, a father paying the lawyer's fee for his daughter in a divorce matter may feel that the lawyer should consult him regarding strategy. It is an application of the adage that whoever pays the piper calls the tune.

The second danger is that the lawyer's interest in securing payment in the matter or in securing future work might lead the lawyer to act in the third party's interest to the detriment of the client. For example, a lawyer paid by an insurer to defend an insured may be inclined to act to protect the interests of the insurer so that the insurer will send more work to the lawyer.

To limit these interferences on the lawyer's exercise of independent judgment, Rule 1.8(f)(DE) provides that a lawyer may accept payment from someone other than a client. To do so properly the lawyer must ensure that three requirements are satisfied.

First, the lawyer must obtain the client's "informed consent." As noted in Rule 1.0(e), the lawyer must explain the "material risks" of the payment scheme and the "reasonably available alternatives" of the plan to the client. Then the client can give truly "informed consent."

Second, the lawyer must not disclose information to the third party that the duty of confidentiality of Rule 1.6(DE) protects. *See Chapter 15 The Duty of Confidentiality.* In the example of the father paying the lawyer's fees for his daughter's divorce, the lawyer must not disclose confidential information to the father unless the daughter consents to the disclosure.

Third, the lawyer must conduct the representation so that there is no interference with the lawyer's independent professional judgment or with the lawyer-client relationship. A lawyer paid by an insurer to defend an insured may have a continuing relationship with the insurer. The insurer pays the lawyer not only in this matter, but in others. The insurer sends the lawyer other work. The lawyer must remind himself or herself constantly to keep the interests of the client, the insured, foremost. The lawyer must not sacrifice the insured client in an attempt to please the insurer so as to capture future work from the insurer.

It is possible that a situation presents a conflict of interest that is impermissible under Rule 1.7(DE), the general conflicts rule. *See Chapter 18 Conflicts and Current Clients.* If there is a "significant risk" of a "materially limited" representation of the client, and if the lawyer does not reasonably believe he or she can represent the client diligently and competently, then Rule 1.7(DE) prohibits the representation regardless of any client consent.

H. Aggregate Settlements

1. The Setting

Whenever a lawyer represents more than one client in a matter and there is an offer to settle with more than one of the clients as part of the same transaction, there is an offer of "aggregate settlement." A typical setting is a mass tort scenario. For example, assume that many people sue Plus Pharmaceutical Corporation claiming that Zing, a drug made and marketed by Plus, caused them injury. Lisa Lawyer represents several hundred of these claimants. If the matter becomes a class action, any settlement must follow the special rules for class action settlements. The class action rules call for court approval of any settlement.

Many matters, however, do not become class actions. In the Zing matter, Plus Pharmaceutical Corporation might decide to offer to settle with all claimants. Plus might propose a formula for awarding monetary amounts to each of the claimants on the basis of the degree of injury each suffered. Plus Pharmaceutical Corporation might state that the settlement can occur only if eighty-five percent of the claimants accept its terms. This would be an offer of "aggregate settlement."

In the mass tort setting there is a danger that Lisa Lawyer will subordinate the interests of any one claimant to the interests of the group and Lisa's own interest in resolving the matter. Lisa might overlook the poor result the settlement gives some of the claimants she represents because the settlement is favorable for most of the claimants she represents. Lisa might be swayed by what she might recover from the settlement even though the settlement is not a great deal for all of her clients.

Aggregate settlements also occur in run-of-the-mill litigation when a defendant settles with several defendants, two of whom are represented by the same lawyer. In litigation surrounding an automobile crash, a defendant might offer to settle with all four plaintiffs, all represented by one lawyer. The settlement offer might provide for all four plaintiffs to receive equal amounts. This is an offer of an "aggregate settlement." In this setting the lawyer might overlook that the deal is not great for one party because it is great for the other three. Also, the lawyer may desire to conclude the matter quickly with the settlement offered so that the lawyer obtains a profitable result short of extended litigation.

In the criminal context, the prosecutor may offer two defendants represented by the same lawyer a deal regarding guilty pleas or *nolo contendere* pleas. These are also offers of aggregated resolution of the matter. Again, there is a risk that the interests of the two defendants would not receive equal treatment by the lawyer.

2. The Rule

Because of the complicated nature of these "aggregate settlement" settings and the danger of the conflicts of interest inherent in such settings, Rule 1.8(g)(DE) clarifies the disclosure necessary for such arrangements. A lawyer may not participate in an "aggregate settlement" unless he or she explains the settlement to the client. The lawyer must discuss with the client the "existence and nature of all the claims or pleas." The lawyer must also discuss with each client the participation of every other participant in the settlement. *ABA Formal Opinion 06-438 (2006)* and comment thirteen to Rule 1.8(DE) states that each client must be told what every other client is receiving and how the deal affects every other client. To make such disclosures the lawyer must have consent from all affected clients giving permission for the sharing of confidential client information. After receiving this information, a client may exercise his or her Rule 1.2(a)(DE) right to accept or decline the settlement or agreement. *See Chapter 8 Scope of the Representation and Communication with the Client.* The client's "informed consent" to the settlement or agreement must be in writing and signed by the client.

I. Agreements Limiting a Lawyer's Liability

1. Prospective Limitations on Liability

When a lawyer asks a client to contract away the right to sue the lawyer for possible future acts of malpractice, the lawyer does not act in the best interest of the client. Rarely, if ever, would foregoing a right to recover for a lawyer's possible malpractice be advantageous to a client. The prospective waiver removes a significant check on the lawyer's conduct such that the lawyer could be less than careful and diligent in the representation.

A situation in which it might be beneficial to a client is if a lawyer agreed to represent a client at a tremendously reduced fee in exchange for a liability waiver. Or perhaps the matter is so risky and complicated that the client may not obtain representation at all if the client does not agree to forego a malpractice recovery. Or perhaps a sophisticated user of legal services wishes to engage the lawyer to handle a discrete part of a litigation matter, relying, perhaps, on research or other information provided by the client or another lawyer. A lawyer might not feel comfortable with such limitations if the lawyer might be subject to malpractice for not doing what the client actually tells the lawyer not to do.

A lawyer, in proposing a prospective waiver, protects the lawyer's own interest and cannot be thought of as representing the client on this matter. The lawyer can easily imagine the future scenarios that might implicate the prospective waiver. The client may not be able to understand or anticipate those future scenarios. To provide protection for clients, Rule 1.8(h)(DE) requires that a client have independent representation for purposes of the contract prospectively limiting liability.

This requirement, in practical terms, eliminates the possibility of obtaining a client's agreement to prospective limit a lawyer's liability. First, no client will like having to consult another lawyer just to continue the representation by the first lawyer. A client might well decide to have another lawyer do all the work. This is especially true since a prospective waiver agreement generally would be discussed early in the lawyer-client relationship before there are many ties to bind the parties together. Only if the client is an organization with in-house counsel would this requirement not be extremely burdensome. Second, if a client consults a second lawyer about the prospective waiver, the second lawyer probably would advise the client to reject it. Prospective waivers are, therefore, not common.

Perhaps Clint Client asks Lisa Lawyer to represent him in a business litigation matter. Lisa asks Clint to agree that Lisa will not be liable to Clint for any acts of malpractice. In order for the agreement to be proper, Clint must be independently represented regarding the agreement.

2. Settlement of Already Existing Claims

Occasionally, a lawyer, though acting in complete good faith, errs in a representation. Perhaps the lawyer misses a deadline or misunderstands the law relevant to a particular matter or discloses certain documents that are privileged and very harmful to the client. Each of these errors by the lawyer might ripen into a claim of malpractice. The lawyer often is the first person to realize the mistake. Such a lawyer might wish to resolve the problem quickly by settling any possible claim the client might have against the lawyer.

While malpractice is not a good thing, a lawyer's desire to resolve the matter without ado is a virtuous path. Any limitation of the lawyer's ability to settle the matter must take into account the value of such a settlement.

Rule 1.8(h)(DE) does not forbid settlement agreements between a lawyer and a client regarding claims or potential claims. The rule does state several conditions for the settlement agreements. If the client already has separate and independent counsel with regard to the malpractice claim, the malpracticing lawyer has no additional requirements. If, however, the lawyer seeks to settle and the client has not engaged a separate and independent lawyer, the lawyer must advise the client in writing that having an independent lawyer regarding this matter would be desirable. The lawyer also must give the client a "reasonable opportunity" to engage an independent lawyer and obtain that lawyer's advice. Clearly, the malpracticing lawyer does not represent the client with respect to the agreement; the client is represented by another lawyer or is unrepresented.

A settlement agreement is, in fact, a transaction with a client so a lawyer is best served by following the requirements of Rule 1.8(a)(DE) regarding business transactions with a client. Taking such steps might later be helpful to the lawyer in proving that the lawyer handled the matter in a professionally responsible matter. Following Rule 1.8(a)(DE) might also strengthen a lawyer's claim that the agreement should be enforced because it was not the product of undue influence.

3. Limited Liability Entities

Some practice forms in which lawyers associate themselves provide for limited liability for the lawyers not involved in the particular representation. One might think that a limitation of liability might be contrary to Rule 1.8(h)(DE). A comment to the rule clarifies that this is not so. Practicing in limited liability forms is not contrary to the rules of professional responsibility if the lawyer doing the work for the client remains responsible.

Perhaps Lisa and Lara practice in a firm that takes the form of a professional limited liability company. The nature of a professional limited liability company is that if Lisa commits malpractice in her representation of Clint, Lisa is personally responsible for that malpractice. All her assets are fair game. The firm's assets are also at risk. But if Lara did not participate in any way in the representation of Clint, Clint cannot reach Lara's personal assets such as her house and car.

Note that Rule 7.5(d)(DE) requires lawyers to be clear about practice form. *See Chapter 45 Communications about Lawyer Services.*

4. Agreements to Arbitrate

Lawyers are permitted to provide, prospectively or otherwise, for arbitration of lawyer-client disputes in agreements with clients. When a client agrees to arbitrate, the client is not agreeing to a limitation of liability. Rather, the client is agreeing to a process for dealing with the dispute. A lawyer must explain the arbitration provision to the client so that the client fully understands. Comment fourteen to Rule 1.8(DE) clarifies this. *ABA Formal Opinion 02-425 (2002)* also indicates that agreements providing for mandatory arbitration do not contradict professional responsibility rules.

Courts sometimes refuse to enforce lawyer-client agreements to arbitrate on the basis that the provision is unconscionable. For example, in *Hodges v. Reasonover*, 103 So. 3d 1069 (La. 2012), the court refused to enforce an arbitration clause because the lawyer did not explain and client did not understand that the clause was to apply to malpractice claims as well as fee disputes.

5. Agreements to Limit the Scope of a Representation

Rule 1.2(c)(DE) allows a lawyer and client to define the parameters of the representation. For example, Clint Client might engage Lisa Lawyer to research and write an appellate brief and engage Larry Lawyer to handle the oral argument of the matter on the basis of Lisa's research and brief. A corporate entity such as Plus Pharmaceutical Corporation might engage Lisa to represent Plus on a workers compensation claim but not on other related tort claims. The prohibition on prospectively limiting liability in Rule 1.8(h)(DE) does not prohibit the types of representational limitation permitted by Rule 1.2(c)(DE). It is true that liability is limited by the Rule 1.2(c)(DE) scope of representation limitations, but that liability limitation is simply incidental to the scope of representation limitation. *See Chapter 8 Scope of the Representation and Communication with the Client.* Rule 1.2(c)(DE) allows only such limitations as are "reasonable under the circumstances" and requires the client's "informed consent."

J. Acquiring a "Proprietary Interest" in a "Cause of Action or Subject Matter of Litigation"

1. The General Rule

A lawyer who acquires an interest in a cause of action or in the subject matter of a litigation matter the lawyer is handling for the client might have his or her independent professional judgment clouded by self-interest. A lawyer might be tempted to act in a way that protects the lawyer's investment even if that path is not optimal for the client. To minimize the risk of such temptation, Rule 1.8(i)(DE) forbids a lawyer from acquiring a "proprietary interest" in a cause of action or a "proprietary interest" in the subject matter of a litigation matter regarding which the lawyer represents the client. Lisa Lawyer cannot give Clint Client $5,000 in exchange for a twenty-five percent share of the proceeds of a litigation matter. Also, if the matter involves, for example, a dispute regarding the ownership of a patent, Lisa cannot buy an interest in the patent from Clint, her client who claims that he owns the patent. The patent is the subject matter of the litigation.

If a lawyer already possesses the interest before the representation begins, the lawyer must analyze whether the conflict created by the ownership precludes representation. The provisions of Rule 1.7(DE) apply. Also, the prohibitions in Rule 1.8(i)(DE) apply only in the litigation context so Rule 1.7(DE) must be considered regarding any investment in a non-litigation matter. *See Chapter 18 Conflicts and Current Clients.*

2. The Exceptions

a. Liens

There are situations in which a lawyer may acquire an interest that would otherwise appear to be prohibited by Rule 1.8(i)(DE). First, a lawyer may acquire a lien to ensure payment of the legal fee and expenses. Commonly, states, by statute or case law, recognize a charging lien. This is recognition of a lawyer's claim to be paid for the lawyer's services out of the recovery in the matter. Some states also recognize a retaining lien. A retaining lien gives a lawyer the right to withhold materials in the lawyer's possession until the client pays the lawyer's fee. Even in states that recognize a retaining lien, some courts do not allow a lawyer to retain anything that could prejudice a client. The *Restatement (Third) of the Law Governing Lawyers,* in section 43, does not approve of retaining liens. *See Chapter 11 Refusing to Form a Lawyer-Client Relationship or Ending a Lawyer-Client Relationship.*

Liens are recognized, or not, as a matter of law separate from professional responsibility rules. Rather than making such liens unethical and thus creating conflict with long-existing law, the rules of professional responsibility simply recognize liens as an exception to the general prohibition.

b. Contingent Fees

The second exception to the rule prohibiting acquisition of a "proprietary interest," in a litigation matter is that a lawyer may contract for a "reasonable contingent fee." *See Chapter 9 Fees.* In the United States contingent fee representation is thought necessary so that people with limited means may have access to justice. Other countries do not look so kindly upon contingent fees.

K. Sexual Relationships with Clients

1. The Dangers

When a lawyer becomes sexually involved with a client, the relationship creates several complications. First, there is always the possibility that the client's involvement with the lawyer is the product of the lawyer's undue influence. Clients are vulnerable, emotionally and otherwise. Lawyers are assumed to be, and are, very persuasive people. Often, after the personal relationship sours, a client claims that a lawyer took advantage of the client in establishing the sexual relationship.

The second complication is that the relationship creates a conflict of interest for the lawyer. The lawyer may not be able to exercise independent professional judgment because the personal relationship clouds the lawyer's judgment. If Lisa Lawyer becomes sexually involved with Clint Client, Lisa might not give Clint candid advice because she may worry about the effect such advice might have on the personal relationship.

A third complication is that a client may not be as candid with a lawyer as a result of the sexual relationship. Clint Client may not fully disclose his extramarital affairs to Lisa because he worries that the information might affect the personal relationship. Yet Lisa might need that information to properly represent Clint.

2. The Rule

In years gone by, the question of the appropriateness of sexual relationships with clients was decided by applying the general conflicts rule, Rule 1.7(DE). Because of the recurring nature of the issue and the conclusion in the vast majority of situations that sexual relationships between lawyers and clients are problematic, Rule 1.8(j)(DE) was created. Rule 1.8(j)(DE) provides that a lawyer may not have a sexual relationship with a client unless that relationship existed before the lawyer-client relationship began. The rule does not prohibit a lawyer from having a sexual relationship with a former client.

The beauty of this rule, as compared to the situation before its creation, is that the rule is clear; a lawyer can easily determine the path of proper conduct. The rule guards against the undue influence complication of sexual relationships between lawyers and clients. The effect that such a relationship has on the lawyer's advice and the client's candidness continues to exist in relationships formed before the lawyer-client relationship. These situations must be evaluated using the general conflicts of interest rule, Rule 1.7(DE). Rule 1.8(j)(DE) simply reduces the number of situations in which a sexual relationship might negatively affect the lawyer-client relationship.

L. Imputation to the Lawyer's Firm

If any one of the provisions of Rule 1.8(DE) applies to a lawyer, except Rule 1.8(j)(DE), the provision also applies to all lawyers in the firm. Rule 1.8(k)(DE) states that the prohibitions and requirements of Rule 1.8(a)(DE) through Rule 1.8(i)(DE) apply to all lawyers associated in a firm. A firm is any association of lawyers organized for the practice of law. According to Rule 1.0(c)(DE), a firm is made of lawyers in "a law partnership, professional corporation, sole proprietorship or other association authorized to practice law," or lawyers in a "legal services organization" or "legal department" of an entity. For example, if Lisa Lawyer must abide by Rule 1.8(a)(DE)'s procedures in contracting with her client, Cindy, then Lisa's law partner, Lara, also must abide by the procedures in contracting with Cindy.

Rule 1.8(j)(DE), the provision stating that a lawyer may not become sexually involved with the lawyer's client, does not apply to other lawyers in the firm. If Lisa Lawyer represents Clint Client, Lisa may not become sexually involved with Clint. Lisa's law partner, Lara, who does no work on Clint's matter, violates no rule by becoming sexually involved with Clint unless the relationship creates an impermissible conflict of interest under Rule 1.7(DE).

Related Sections of the *Restatement (Third) of the Law Governing Lawyers*

Sections 36, 43, 54, 60, 125, 126, 127, and 134

Checkpoints

- A lawyer may enter into a business transaction with a client or knowingly obtain "an ownership, possessory, security or other pecuniary interest adverse to a client" if
  1. the "transaction and terms" are "fair and reasonable" to the client,
  2. the "transaction and terms" are "fully disclosed" to the client,
  3. the "transaction and terms" are "transmitted in writing in a manner which can be reasonably understood by the client,"
  4. the lawyer in writing advises the client of the advantages of consulting with an independent lawyer about the deal,
  5. the client has "reasonable opportunity to seek" the counsel of an independent lawyer, and
  6. the client gives "informed consent" in a signed writing to the "essential terms" of the deal and to the lawyer's role in the deal.
- Unless the client gives "informed consent," a lawyer may not use information relating to a client's representation in a way not otherwise permitted or required by the rules if the use is disadvantageous to the client.
- A lawyer may accept gifts from a client. A lawyer may not seek a "substantial gift" from a client or prepare any instrument on behalf of the client giving the lawyer or the lawyer's spouse, child, grandchild, parent, or grandparent, or person in a "close, familial relationship" with the lawyer, a "substantial gift," unless the recipient is related to the client as spouse, child, grandchild, parent, grandparent, or the client and the other person are in a "close, familial relationship."
- A lawyer may ask a client to appoint the lawyer to be the executor of the client's estate or to hold some other fiduciary role.
- During a representation, a lawyer may not enter into an agreement or negotiate an agreement with a client that gives the lawyer "literary or media rights" to tell the client's story or any story "based in substantial part" on the client's story regarding the representation matter.
- A lawyer may not provide financial assistance to a client except a lawyer may
  1. advance the expenses of litigation and court costs to a client even if the repayment is contingent on a positive outcome of the matter, and

2. pay the expenses of litigation and court costs to an indigent client without a promise of repayment.

- A lawyer may accept from another person payment for representation of the client only if
    1. the client gives "informed consent,"
    2. the paying party does not interfere with the lawyer-client relationship or the lawyer's rendering of independent professional judgment, and
    3. the lawyer protects confidential client information.
- If a lawyer represents more than one client in a matter, the lawyer may participate in an "aggregate settlement" or an aggregate plea in the criminal context only if the clients give "informed consent" in a signed writing after the lawyer explains to each client
    1. the "existence and nature of all the claims" and
    2. how each client will be affected by the settlement.
- A lawyer may enter into an agreement with the client limiting in advance the lawyer's malpractice liability only if the client has the benefit of advice from an independent lawyer.
- A lawyer may enter into a settlement agreement with the client of a claim for malpractice only if
    1. the client is represented by independent counsel or
    2. the lawyer
        a. in writing informs the client of the desirability of consulting with an independent lawyer, and
        b. provides the client with a "reasonable opportunity" to consult with an independent lawyer.
- In conjunction with a litigation matter, a lawyer may not acquire a "proprietary interest" in
    1. the cause of action in which the lawyer represents the client or
    2. the subject matter of the litigation in which the lawyer represents the client,

    except that a lawyer may acquire

    1. a recognized lien to ensure payment or
    2. a contingent fee.
- The prohibitions and requirements regarding the following apply equally to other lawyers in the lawyer's firm:
    1. Business transactions with the client.
    2. Use of information relating to the representation.

3. Gifts from the client.
4. Literary and media rights.
5. Financial assistance to the client.
6. Fees paid by someone other than the client.
7. Aggregate settlements.
8. Agreements limiting liability.
9. Acquisition of proprietary rights to the cause of action or the subject matter of the litigation.

- A lawyer may not begin a sexual relationship with a client after the formation of the lawyer-client relationship unless the lawyer-client relationship terminates. Another lawyer in the firm may have a sexual relationship with the client; there is no imputation.

Chapter 22

Conflicts and Lawyers Who Are Public Officials or Other Government Employees

Roadmap

- Rule 1.11(DE)
- Responsibilities of lawyers who move from public office or other government employment to private practice
- Responsibilities of lawyers who move from private practice to public office or other government employment
- Responsibilities of lawyers who are public officers or are other government employees
- Conflicts of interest and government employee lawyers and public officers
- Negotiation of future employment

A. Responsibilities of Lawyers Who Move from Public Office or Other Government Employment to Private Practice

1. Introduction

a. Moving from a Government Job to the Private Sector Is Common

New lawyers often begin their careers in government employment. These lawyers do so for all sorts of reasons. For some lawyers, government service is the reason they went to law school; they desire a career of public service. For others, a government job may be a way to gain valuable expertise that will assist them in succeeding in the private sphere. Many lawyers work in the government sector for a few years in the beginning of their professional life and then move to the private sector.

b. Applicable Law

A lawyer who makes such a move from the public sector to the private sector must take note of Rule 1.11(DE), the rule of professional responsibility that specifically deals with current and former public officials and other government-employed lawyers. Because of the public interest involved in government settings, other statutes, rules, or regulations also exist. These other laws may apply generally or to very specific contexts. For example, a law might apply only to United States Attorneys who move to private practice. If other law sets a standard of behavior different from Rule 1.11(DE), the other law governs.

2. What Is a Matter?

Several of the provisions of Rule 1.11(DE) deal with the concept of a matter. Rule 1.11(e)(DE) defines a matter as "any judicial or other proceeding, application, request for a ruling or other determination, contract, claim, controversy, investigation, charge, accusation, arrest or other particular matter involving a specific party or parties." A matter also includes any other matter the conflict of interest rules of the government entity covers. A matter might be the same as another if it involves the same facts, if it is close in time to the other, and if it involves the same parties.

3. The Prohibition of Use or Disclosure of Information

A lawyer who works as a public officer or other government employee and who leaves that job must not use information of a client relating to the representation to the disadvantage of that client. Rule 1.11(a)(DE) makes this clear by stating that the lawyer in the situation must abide by Rule 1.9(c)(DE). *See Chapter 19 Conflicts and Former Clients.* The lawyer may use such information only if the rules permit the use or require the use or if the information becomes "generally known." For example, the client could consent to the lawyer's use of the information.

A lawyer cannot disclose information about the representation unless the rules permit or require such disclosure. For a lawyer who worked in a state or federal agency on behalf of the agency, the former client is the agency. For a lawyer who worked as a public defender, the former clients are the people represented by the lawyer in the defender capacity.

4. The Prohibition of Adverse Representation with "Confidential Government Information"

a. The Prohibition

Rule 1.11(c)(DE) contains a specific provision relating to "confidential government information." "Confidential government information" is information gained by "governmental authority." It must be information that the "government is prohibited by law from disclosing to the public or has a legal privilege not to disclose." The information must not be "otherwise available to the public." Rule 1.11(c)(DE) constrains a lawyer's conduct if the lawyer *knows* he or she has "confidential government information" about someone that the lawyer gained while a public officer or other government employee. If a lawyer knows he or she has such information, that lawyer cannot "represent a private client whose interests are adverse to that person in a matter in which the information could be used to the material disadvantage of that person." This provision is prophylactic in that it prohibits representing another when the danger of use presents itself.

b. The Effect on the Lawyer's Firm

In current client and former client conflict settings, Rule 1.10(a)(ID) imputes the disqualification of a lawyer to all lawyers in the firm. *See Chapter 18 Conflicts and Current Clients* and *Chapter 19 Conflicts and Former Clients.* In an attempt to avoid erecting too many barriers to moving from government employment to the private sector and vice-versa, the general imputed disqualification provision of Rule 1.10(a)(ID) does not apply to the government lawyer context. Rule 1.10(d)(ID) specifically excludes application to Rule 1.11(DE) situations.

Rule 1.11(c)(DE) provides that other lawyers in the disqualified lawyer's firm can handle the representation even if one lawyer in the firm is disqualified because he or she has "confidential government information" that could be used to the "material disadvantage" of a person while representing a client with adverse interests. If a lawyer cannot handle a representation because the lawyer has "confidential government information," another lawyer in the firm *can* handle the representation if two conditions obtain. First, the lawyer with the information must be screened from the matter in a timely manner. Screening, as Rule 1.0(k)(DE) explains, is isolation of the lawyer so that information that lawyer has is protected from disclosure. Second, the lawyer cannot receive a fee from the matter, though the lawyer can receive a previously agreed-upon salary or partnership share that is, in part, based on the matter. Unlike many screening situations, no notice must be given to the government entity or the affected party.

Perhaps Larry, while a lawyer at the Department of Justice, participated in an investigation of Technology Corporation. In that role he was privy to trade secrets of Technology Corporation, "confidential government information." A year later, Larry finds himself in private practice. His firm represents MegaTech Inc. in a litigation matter against Technology Corporation. Larry has "confidential government information" about Technology Corporation that could be used against Technology Corporation. Larry cannot represent MegaTech Inc. although a member of Larry's firm can if Larry is screened from the MegaTech Inc. matter and Larry receives no part of the fee.

5. The Prohibition Regarding Matters in Which the Lawyer Was Involved "Personally and Substantially"

a. The Prohibition

When a lawyer has participated "personally and substantially" in a matter as a public officer or other government employee, the lawyer cannot later represent "a client in connection with" the matter unless the government entity gives "informed consent, confirmed in writing." Rule 1.0(e)(DE) states that "informed consent" means that the risks involved and the alternatives available must be clearly explained before the consent is given. "Confirmed in writing," according to Rule 1.0(b)(DE), means that the consent must be in writing or the consenting party must be given a confirmation in writing of an earlier oral consent promptly after the oral consent. Rule 1.0(n)(DE) defines a "writing" as "a tangible or electronic record of a communication or representation, including handwriting, typewriting, printing, photostating, photography, audio or videorecording and electronic communications."

The prohibition of Rule 1.11(a)(DE) applies regardless of whether the client is adverse to the government entity or another former client. The rule prevents the lawyer from using the public office or other government employment for the substantial benefit of a later client. A lawyer hopes to be able, in the private sector, to use the general expertise he or she amassed while a public official or other government employee. This ability is part of the motivation for government employment in the first instance. The prohibition on activity relating to matters the lawyer was involved in "personally and substantially" simply removes the situations in which the lawyer might have and might be able to trade on specific client information and thus removes the situations in which the exploitation of the public office is most egregious.

If Larry Lawyer is a public defender, he is a government employee. His clients, however, are the people he defends. Assume Larry represents David Defendant in a criminal matter in which David is charged with robbery. After Larry moves to the private sector, Larry cannot represent Doug Defendant, a person facing criminal charges related to the charges faced by David unless the government entity, the public defender agency, gives "informed consent, confirmed in writing." Of course, Doug's representation also is subject to Rule 1.7(DE), the rule governing conflicts of interest and current clients and Rule 1.9(DE), the rule governing conflicts of interest involving former clients. *See Chapter 18 Conflicts and Current Clients* and *Chapter 19 Conflicts and Former Clients.*

b. The Effect on the Lawyer's Firm

Rule 1.11(b)(DE) provides that other lawyers in the firm may handle a representation presenting a Rule 1.11(a)(DE) conflict if the firm screens the problem lawyer. Screening, as Rule 1.0(k)(DE) explains, is isolation of the lawyer so that information that lawyer has is protected from disclosure. The former government lawyer must not receive a fee from the later representation. The lawyer's salary or partnership share, agreed to independent of the particular matter, can include funds derived from the representation. Also, the government entity must be given prompt written notice of the representation and screening. This notice must be sufficient so that the government entity can determine compliance with this rule.

B. Responsibilities of Lawyers Who Move from Private Practice to Public Office or Other Government Employment

1. Current and Former Client Conflicts

The typical career path is for a lawyer to work in a government job early in the lawyer's career and then to move to private practice with an expertise developed in the government job. Sometimes, however, a lawyer tires of the demands of private practice or for other reasons moves from private practice to a government job. Rule 1.11(d)(DE) deals with this sort of movement.

A lawyer who moves from private employment to a government job owes his or her former clients all the duties the lawyer would owe those clients if the lawyer simply had moved to another private practice setting. A lawyer moving from one firm to another takes with him or her duties of confidentiality and loyalty and the same is true when the lawyer moves to a government job. Rule 1.11(d)(1)(DE) clearly states that a lawyer moving from private to public practice settings is subject to Rule 1.7(DE) and Rule 1.9(DE), the conflict of interest rules for current and former clients. *See Chapter 18 Conflicts and Current Clients* and *Chapter 19 Conflicts and Former Clients.* Perhaps Larry Lawyer, a criminal defense lawyer, successfully defends David Defendant on charges of robbery. Shortly after the conclusion of the trial, Larry takes a job with the prosecutor's office. In his new job Larry cannot prosecute David on a charge related to the robbery because he would, in effect, be representing a party with interests "materially adverse" to David's interests in the "same or a substantially related" matter. Rule 1.9(DE) precludes the representation.

2. The Prohibition Regarding Matters in Which the Lawyer Was Involved "Personally and Substantially"

A lawyer who moves from a private practice setting to being a public officer or other government employee may not participate in a matter in which the lawyer was involved "personally and substantially" in the prior employment unless the government entity gives "informed consent, confirmed in writing." There is no imputation of disqualification and no screening requirement. Assume Larry Lawyer represented Big Corporation in an effort to have the government open certain federal lands to mining. Larry then becomes a lawyer in the federal agency entrusted with administering such lands. Even if Big Corporation is no longer involved in the effort to have the specific lands opened, Larry cannot work on the issue because he was involved "personally and substantially" in the matter when he worked in the private sector. The federal agency could consent, however, to Larry's involvement. Larry's obligations to Big Corporation are governed by Rule 1.7(DE) and Rule 1.9(DE).

C. General Responsibilities of Lawyers Who Are Public Officials or Other Government Employees

1. Current and Former Client Conflicts

A government lawyer has the same general ethical duties as any other lawyer. The rules of professional responsibility on the whole do not distinguish between types of lawyers. In-house lawyers, big firm lawyers, small-town solo practitioners, and government lawyers are all the same. Because Rule 1.11(DE) provides a special rule with regard to conflicts for lawyers moving in and out of government employment, and thus might lead some to believe that no other conflicts rules apply, Rule 1.11(d)(DE) clarifies that Rule 1.7(DE), the current client conflict rule, and Rule 1.9(DE), the former client conflict rule, apply to government lawyers.

The situation of a public defender illustrates this notion well. A public defender is a government employee employed to defend people accused of crimes but who do not have the ability to provide their own lawyer. A public defender must always be cautious of conflicts between current clients that might violate Rule 1.7(DE), *see Chapter 18 Conflicts and Current Clients*, and be cautious of conflicts with former clients that might violate Rule 1.9(DE). *See Chapter 19 Conflicts and Former Clients.* Being a government employee does not eliminate the evil these rules are designed to prevent and so does not eliminate the applicability of Rule 1.7(DE) and Rule 1.9(DE).

2. Negotiating Private Employment

As discussed above, a typical career path for a lawyer is to work in a government job early in the lawyer's career and then move to private practice with an expertise developed in the government job. The time of the transition from government employment to private employment presents its own issues. A public officer or other government employee seeking future employment with a private firm might have the incentive to give lawyers with that firm or the firm's clients special treatment so as to curry favor with the firm and secure the private sector job.

Rule 1.11(d)(DE) provides a guard against such an effect. This rule provides that a government lawyer may not negotiate for employment in the private sector with anyone who is a party or lawyer in a matter in which the lawyer is involved "personally and substantially." This rule applies the same standard to government lawyers as Rule 1.12(DE) applies to judges. *See Chapter 23 Conflicts and Former Judges, Other Adjudicative Officers, Law Clerks, and Third-Party Neutrals.* If Larry Lawyer is prosecuting Clint, who is represented by Lance, Larry cannot negotiate with Lance for employment until Clint's prosecution is complete.

If, at the time of the prosecution of Clint, Larry has already decided that in the future he will be seeking a job with Lance, the incentive for Larry to act in the Clint matter so as to please Lance is still present to a degree. The rule cannot take away the entire danger without making employment after the government job virtually impossible. The standard as it exists now is a significant constraint on certain types of government lawyers such as prosecutors. With a typical caseload, a state prosecutor may have matters pending at any time against all the criminal defense firms the prosecutor might want to work with after the prosecutor ends government service.

Law clerks, though they are government employees, are governed by the more specific provisions of Rule 1.12(DE). A law clerk may interview or otherwise negotiate employment with a party or lawyer in a matter in which the law clerk is involved "personally and substantially." The law clerk must notify the judge or other adjudicative officer the law clerk assists before any negotiation. The judge or other adjudicative officer can monitor the law clerk to ensure that no untoward effects occur. *See Chapter 23 Conflicts and Former Judges, Other Adjudicative Officers, Law Clerks, and Third-Party Neutrals.*

Related Sections of the *Restatement (Third) of the Law Governing Lawyers*

Section 133

Checkpoints

- Because public interests are at stake with a government lawyer, other statutes or regulations may apply.
- A lawyer who works as a public official or government employee and who leaves that job must not use information of a client relating to the representation to the disadvantage of that client unless the rules permit the use or require the use or unless the information becomes "generally known."
- A lawyer may reveal information of a client relating to a representation only if the rules allow the disclosure or require it.
- If a lawyer knows the lawyer has "confidential government information" about someone gained while the lawyer was a public officer or other government employee, the lawyer cannot "represent a private client whose interests are adverse to that person in a matter in which the information could be used to the material disadvantage of that person."
- If a lawyer cannot handle a representation because the lawyer has "confidential government information," another lawyer in the firm can handle the representation if

1. the lawyer with the information is screened from the matter in a timely manner, and
2. the lawyer does not receive a fee directly from the matter.

- When a lawyer is involved "personally and substantially" in a matter as a public official or other government employee, the lawyer later cannot represent a client in the same matter, unless the government entity gives "informed consent, confirmed in writing."
- If a lawyer cannot handle a matter because he or she participated "personally and substantially" in that matter as a public officer or other government employee, other lawyers in the firm may handle the representation if
  1. the firm screens the former government employee,
  2. the lawyer does not receive a fee from the later representation, and
  3. the government entity is given prompt written notice of the representation.
- A lawyer moving from a private to a public practice setting is subject to Rule 1.7(DE) and Rule 1.9(DE).
- A lawyer who moves from a private to a public practice setting may not participate in a matter in which the lawyer was involved "personally and substantially" in the prior employment unless the government entity gives "informed consent, confirmed in writing."
- Rules 1.7(DE) and 1.9(DE) apply to lawyers who are public officials or other government employees.
- A public officer or other government employee may not negotiate for employment in the private sector with anyone who is a party or lawyer in a matter in which the public officer or other government employee is involved "personally and substantially."
- A law clerk may interview or otherwise negotiate employment with a party or lawyer in a matter in which the law clerk is involved "personally and substantially" but must notify the judge or other adjudicative officer the law clerk assists before any such contact.

Chapter 23

Conflicts and Former Judges, Other Adjudicative Officers, Law Clerks, and Third-Party Neutrals

Roadmap

- Rule 1.12(DE)
- Conflicts of interest rules for by lawyers who serve as judges, other adjudicative officers, law clerks, or third-party neutrals such as arbitrators and mediators
- Negotiation of future employment

A. Lawyers as Former Judges, Other Adjudicative Officers, Law Clerks, and Third-Party Neutrals Such as Arbitrators and Mediators

Lawyers move from the practice of law to the bench and back again in the course of a career in law. Lawyers who become judges may move back to the private practice of law because they tire of the bench or the public does not reelect them. Occasionally, a lawyer might move back and forth several times. For example, a lawyer employed as a prosecutor might be appointed to complete an open judgeship and then might have to stand for election. If the public does not elect the lawyer, the judge might become a lawyer in private practice. Perhaps such a lawyer runs for election once again and is elected this second time. Then the lawyer moves back to the bench. Generally, lawyers are either in private practice or are judges at any one time, but they are not both at once.

Lawyers serving as third-party neutrals may have a different movement. A lawyer serves as a third-party neutral if the lawyer acts as an arbitrator, mediator, conciliator, or evaluator, or takes any other role in which the lawyer is assisting parties, as Comment one to Rule 2.4(DE) states, "in the resolution of a dispute or in the arrangement of a transaction." *See Chapter 25 A Lawyer as a Third-Party Neutral.* Some lawyers become arbitrators or mediators and no longer represent clients. Other lawyers may serve as arbitrators or mediators or in some other third-party neutral capacity in some matters and represent clients in other matters at the same time. On any given day, a lawyer may act as a third-party neutral in one matter and represent a client in another matter.

Some lawyers may serve as judges *pro tempore*, part-time judges, special masters, referees, hearing officers, or other parajudicial officers. These lawyers may be akin to judges in career movement while others may be more like third-party neutrals. For purposes of this discussion, such a lawyer is an adjudicative officer. Comment one to Rule 1.12(DE) so defines them.

The situation of law clerks is a bit different in that usually a lawyer becomes a clerk after law school and before practicing law. This is not always the case, of course. The law clerk serves as a clerk for a year or so and then moves on to practice law in a private setting or in a different government setting than the clerkship.

B. Conflict of Interest Concerns

Justice is best served if a judge or other adjudicative officer decides the matters before him or her on the basis of the merits of the matter alone. Justice is best served if a third-party neutral deals with the matters before him or her on the basis of the facts and law relating to those matters. Similarly, because law clerks play an influential role in the decision-making of judges and other adjudicative officers, law clerks should not be swayed by concerns other than those presented by the merits of the matter.

How a judge or other adjudicative officer treats a matter before him or her might be affected by self-interest concerns generated by the judge looking forward to the time when the judge will be a practicing lawyer. For example, Jane Judge might be tempted to decide a matter in favor of the client represented by Fine Firm so that Fine Firm might be inclined to employ Jane at the conclusion of the judgeship.

The interest in securing future employment might be even more intense for law clerks who are at the beginning of their work life as lawyers. Clara Clerk might be inclined to present issues relating to the case involving Fine Firm favorably to Fine Firm if Clara seeks to work at Fine Firm in the future. Likewise, a third-party neutral might be affected by self-interest concerns generated by the third-party neutral looking past the end of the proceeding. Melinda Mediator might handle a mediation differently if Melinda believes that she might represent one of the parties to the mediation after the mediation concludes. *See Chapter 25 A Lawyer as a Third-Party Neutral.*

Even if judges, other adjudicative officers, law clerks, and third-party neutrals are beyond temptation, there is the issue of the public perception. The system of justice works if the public believes in the fairness of the process. If the public believes that the actors in the process are acting in self-interest and with bias, then there is great injury to the system and to the value of the justice delivered.

In recognition of the potential danger, one might expect an absolute prohibition of representation on employment involving parties or lawyers in contact with the lawyer as judge, other adjudicative officer, law clerk, or third-party neutral. Yet, a rule making the transition from judge or other adjudicative officer to lawyer impossible would greatly limit the pool of lawyers interested in serving in those capacities. A rule placing too great a constraint on law clerks' careers after they leave clerkships would result in a decline in interest in working as a clerk. A rule making a lawyer's service as a third-party neutral too costly in terms of limits on future activities regarding the practice of law would significantly decrease the interest of lawyers in serving as third-party neutrals. The relevant rule attempts to protect against improper effects on a judge's, other adjudicative officer's, law clerk's, or third-party neutral's actions while at the same time not unduly constraining the lawyer's activities.

C. The Basic Conflict Constraint

Rule 1.12(DE) provides guidance to any lawyer who has acted as a judge, other adjudicative officer, law clerk to a judge or adjudicative officer, or third-party neutral. A judge who has moved off the bench and now represents clients, according to Rule 1.12(a)(DE), cannot represent a client in a matter in which the lawyer participated "personally and substantially as a judge." The same standard of disqualification applies to other adjudicative officers, law clerks to judges and other adjudicative officers, and third-party neutrals.

The only exception to the disqualification is if the lawyer obtains the "informed consent" of *all* of the parties to the proceeding. The "informed consent" must be "confirmed in writing." To obtain such consent, the lawyer must, as Rule 1.0(e)(DE) directs, discuss the "material risks" of the representation and the "reasonably available alternatives" with all parties. A "reasonably available" option in most situations is that the party be represented by another lawyer. While the "informed consent" must be "confirmed in writing," this requirement does not mean that the consenting person must give "informed consent" in writing. Rule 1.0(b)(DE) clarifies that a confirmation can take the form of a writing prepared by the lawyer and promptly sent to the consenting person confirming an oral "informed consent." A writing can be a traditional writing or can be in another form. Rule 1.0(n)(DE) states that a "writing" is "a tangible or electronic record of a communication or representation" and states as examples of a writing audio and video recording and electronic communications.

This rule means that if a lawyer serving as a judge, other adjudicative officer, law clerk, or third-party neutral deals with the substance of a matter, that lawyer has participated "personally and substantially" in the matter. If Jane Judge presided over the trial of a matter involving Cindy Client, she participated "personally and substantially" in the matter as a judge. Jane cannot represent Cindy in the appeal without "informed consent, confirmed in writing" from all parties.

A lawyer does not participate "personally and substantially" if he or she is a judge on a court that has many judges and he or she does not preside in a matter before the court. Perhaps Jane Judge is on the state court of appeals and the court sits in panels of three judges. A panel of the court of appeals hears a matter involving Cindy Client. Jane, however, is not a member of the three-judge panel. Jane has not participated "personally and substantially" as a judge and thus is not prohibited from representing Cindy in the matter. No "informed consent" is required.

This standard of participation applies similarly to other adjudicative officers, law clerks, and third-party neutrals. Other codes of conduct applicable to the particular role a lawyer might assume may constrain the lawyer's conduct more severely than this ethics rule. So, for example, a judge should be aware of constraints contained in the relevant Code of Judicial Conduct.

D. Imputed Disqualification and the Screening Cure

Rule 1.12(c)(DE) provides that if a lawyer is disqualified because of participation in the matter as a judge, other adjudicative officer, law clerk to a judge or adjudicative officer, or third-party neutral, the other lawyers in the lawyer's firm cannot knowingly represent a party in the matter unless the firm takes certain steps to isolate the conflicted lawyer. This isolation helps to ensure that the conflicted lawyer protects the information the lawyer may be obligated to protect. Rule 1.0(c)(DE) states that a firm is a "law partnership, professional corporation, sole proprietorship, or other association authorized to practice law." A firm can also be lawyers in a legal services organization or in-house legal department in an entity such as a corporation.

The lawyers in the firm are imputedly disqualified even if a lawyer in the firm has represented the client before the conflicted lawyer joins the firm. A lawyer in the firm must not represent the client. If the representation is already in progress, the lawyer must withdraw from the representation pursuant to Rule 1.16(a)(DE) unless the firm takes the proper steps to isolate the conflicted lawyer. To properly isolate the lawyer, the firm must

1. "timely screen" the conflicted lawyer from participation in the matter,
2. apportion the conflicted lawyer no part of the fee from the representation (although the regular salary or partnership share is allowed), and
3. give prompt written notice to all parties and the tribunal so that everyone can determine whether these requirements are followed.

To screen the lawyer, Rule 1.0(k)(DE) directs that the firm must put in place procedures that are "reasonably adequate" to ensure that the lawyer protects the information the lawyer may be obligated to protect. To give proper notice, the firm should explain the nature of the disqualification and the steps taken to screen the conflicted lawyer.

Perhaps Jane Judge moves from the bench to Fine Firm. While a judge, Jane presided over the trial of a matter involving Cindy Client. Cindy has now come to Larry, a lawyer at Fine Firm, asking that Larry represent her in her appeal of the matter. Because Jane participated "personally and substantially" in the trial of Cindy's matter while Jane was a judge, Larry may not represent Cindy in the same matter unless the firm screens Jane. The firm might do this by not allowing Jane access to Cindy's file and by cautioning all lawyers and staff working on Cindy's matter that they must not discuss Cindy's matter with Jane. Jane must not receive any direct fee from Cindy's matter though she can receive the five percent of firm profit share that Fine Firm and Jane negotiated when she became a part of Fine Firm. Lastly, all parties and the court, in writing, must be made aware of Jane's conflict and that the firm is screening Jane. Fine Firm should explain the steps being taken to isolate Jane. With such notice, there can be monitoring to assure that the required isolation of Jane continues during the matter.

E. A Partisan Arbitrator on a Panel of Arbitrators

Rule 1.12(d)(DE) identifies one type of adjudicator not governed by these disqualification rules. Occasionally, a panel of arbitrators conducts the arbitration. Occasionally, some of these arbitrators are selected by parties to the arbitration as partisans. A typical procedure is that each party selects partisan arbitrators and then the selected arbitrators choose additional arbitrators. Rule 1.12(d)(DE) states that an arbitrator who is selected by a party as a partisan member of a panel of arbitrators is not disqualified from later representing the party who selected the arbitrator. At no time in the arbitration or after it is there an illusion that such an arbitrator is unbiased.

F. Negotiating for Future Employment

1. Judges, Other Adjudicative Officers, and Third-Party Neutrals

A lawyer who is participating "personally and substantially" in a matter in the role of judge, other adjudicative officer, or third-party neutral may not discuss employment with a party in the matter or with a lawyer representing a party in the matter. This prohibition of Rule 1.12(b)(DE) eliminates an incentive for the lawyer to curry favor with the parties or lawyers in the matters before him or her.

Perhaps Jane Judge is presiding over a matter involving Penny Plaintiff and David Defendant. Larry Lawyer, a lawyer with Fine Firm, represents Penny in the matter. Lance Lawyer, a lawyer with Other Firm, represents David in the matter. Jane cannot negotiate for employment with Penny, David, Larry, Fine Firm, Lance, or Other Firm.

2. Law Clerks

The rule regarding the negotiation of employment by law clerks is a bit more relaxed than the rule applying to judges, other adjudicative officers, and third-party neutrals. Law clerks may discuss employment with a party or lawyer in a matter in which the law clerk is participating "personally and substantially." Rule 1.12(b)(DE) provides that a law clerk must first, however, inform the judge or other adjudicative officer with whom the clerk is employed that the clerk will be having such discussions.

Perhaps Clara Clerk works for a state court of appeals judge, Jane Judge. Clara's clerkship ends soon and so she has decided to seek a job with large firms in Capital City. Many of these firms have matters pending in the court of appeals. Several have matters in progress before Judge Jane. Clara must provide Judge Jane with a list of all of the firms she intends to contact that also have matters before Judge Jane.

The more relaxed rule for law clerks is a recognition that a law clerk is never the ultimate decision-maker in any matter. At all times the judge or other adjudicative officer supervises the law clerk so any untoward bias by the law clerk can be monitored and tempered by the supervising judge or other adjudicative officer.

Checkpoints

- Without the "informed consent, confirmed in writing," of *all* parties to the proceeding, a lawyer cannot represent a client in a matter in which the lawyer participated "personally and substantially" as a judge, other adjudicative officer, law clerk, or third-party neutral.
- If a lawyer is disqualified because of participation in the matter as a judge, other adjudicative officer, law clerk, or third-party neutral, the other lawyers in the lawyer's firm cannot knowingly represent a party in the matter unless the firm
    1. "timely screen[s]" the conflicted lawyer from participation in the matter,
    2. apportions the conflicted lawyer no part of the fee from the representation (except the usual salary or partnership share), and
    3. gives prompt written notice to *all parties and the tribunal* so that everyone can determine whether these requirements are followed.
- An arbitrator a party selects as a partisan member of a panel of arbitrators is not disqualified from later representing the selecting party.
- A lawyer participating "personally and substantially" in a matter in the role of judge, other adjudicative officer, or third-party neutral may not discuss employment with a party in the matter or with a lawyer representing a party in the matter.
- After first informing the judge or other adjudicative officer for whom a law clerk works that the clerk will be having such discussions, a law clerk may discuss employment with a party or lawyer in a matter in which the law clerk is participating "personally and substantially."

Section VI
When a Lawyer Is Not in an Advocate Role

Chapter 24

Lawyer Evaluation of a Client's Matter for a Third Party

Roadmap

- Rule 2.3(DE)
- A lawyer's role evaluating a client's matter when a third party may use the evaluation
- Negative evaluations
- Adequate disclosure
- Liability to third parties

A. Internal Reports

Occasionally, a lawyer's client may ask the lawyer to investigate a matter and report findings. For example, Big Corporation may suspect that its employees are bribing government inspectors. Big may ask its lawyer, Larry, to investigate and report his findings to Big. In completing this assignment, Larry is investigating and evaluating the client, Big, for the client. Larry provides his evaluation of the situation to no third parties. There are no issues of disclosure of confidential information. Larry is simply performing typical tasks in representing a client. No special rules are necessary.

B. Evaluative Reports for Use by Third Parties

Sometimes a different scenario occurs. A client such as Big Corporation might ask its lawyer, Larry, to investigate a matter and provide a report of his findings to a third party. A corporation might ask its lawyer to provide an evaluation of the propriety of its incorporation to a potential lender. A corporation might ask its lawyer to provide an evaluation of the corporation's compliance with environmental laws to a potential purchaser of the business. A corporation might ask its lawyer to provide to potential investors an evaluation of the tax consequences of a particular planned transaction that would interest those investors. A corporation might ask its lawyer to provide an evaluation of its legal liability for use by its auditors in the routine corporate accounting audit. Sometimes these sorts of evaluations are referred to as opinion letters.

In some areas of the law, specific guidance exists regarding the issuance of these opinions. For example, regarding responding to an auditor's request for information about legal issues involving the client, the *American Bar Association Statement of Policy Regarding Lawyers' Responses to Auditors' Requests for Information* provides helpful guidance.

1. An Evaluation Compatible with Other Aspects of the Relationship with the Client

Perhaps Big Corporation wishes to sell a piece of real estate to Thelma Thirdparty. In order to convince Thelma to agree to buy the property, Big asks Larry to investigate the title to the property and report his findings to Thelma. If Larry investigates the title, finds that the title is clear, and reports such to Thelma, Larry assists Big in obtaining the sale of the real estate. In this scenario, Larry evaluates the title for the client, Big, but Larry knows that the evaluation ultimately will be given to a party Larry does not represent, Thelma.

When a lawyer's evaluation is destined for the hands of a third party, a lawyer such as Larry must take care to understand the situation. Rule 2.3(a)(DE) directs that if a lawyer "reasonably believes" that evaluating an issue and having the evaluation used by a third party is compatible with the lawyer's duties owed to the client, the lawyer may provide such an evaluation to a third party. In contrast, in situations in which the disclosure of the evaluation "is likely to affect the client's interests materially and adversely," the lawyer must obtain the client's "informed consent." In any situation, the lawyer may not disclose any other information related to the evaluation unless the client has consented to the disclosure. Rule 2.3(c)(DE) makes clear that the Rule 1.6(DE) duty of confidentiality remains in place. *See Chapter 15 The Duty of Confidentiality.* After Larry investigates the title of the property as Big Corporation requested and discovers that the title is clear, he can safely say that disclosure of his evaluation of the title issue will not harm his client, Big. Larry may, therefore, provide the title report to Thelma.

2. An Evaluation Likely to Affect the Client "Materially and Adversely"

Perhaps Big Corporation asks its lawyer, Larry, to evaluate its compliance with environmental laws and to provide the evaluation to Thirdparty Corporation, a potential purchaser of the business. Larry completes the investigation and determines that his report could significantly harm Big. Rule 2.3(b)(DE) states that when a lawyer "knows or reasonably should know" that the disclosure of the evaluation to a third party "is likely to affect the client's interests materially and adversely," the lawyer must obtain "informed consent" of the client for the disclosure to the third party. "Informed consent," as defined in Rule 1.0(e)(DE), requires that the client consent after the lawyer explains the "material risks" the conduct entails and the "reasonably available alternatives" to the conduct. Because Larry concludes that providing the environmental law evaluation to Thirdparty Corporation is likely to have a material and adverse effect on Big, Larry must explain the situation to Big. Larry must spell out the inherent danger of the disclosure as well as any possible alternatives. Then Big must consent to the disclosure for the disclosure to occur.

3. Disclosure of the Scope of the Evaluation and Report

A client may ask a lawyer to perform an investigation that is limited in scope. Big Corporation might ask Larry Lawyer to investigate, evaluate, and provide a report, for use by a third party, of Big Corporation's compliance with certain environmental laws but not all environmental laws. Big might ask Larry to consider only Big Corporation's behavior in the last two years in the evaluation. Big might ask Larry to consider only its operation in Georgia and Alabama but not Tennessee.

A lawyer should indicate any material limitation on the investigation, evaluation, or report in the materials provided to a third party. This disclosure is necessary to prevent the lawyer's evaluation from being misleading. A lawyer must always be mindful of not making a false statement of material fact or law to the third party. Rule 4.1(DE) prohibits such conduct. *See Chapter 35 Truthfulness to Third Parties.* In addition, such statements may be the basis of criminal or civil liability for the lawyer. A lawyer may decide that the limitations are so significant that the investigation, evaluation, or report is inherently misleading regardless of explicit qualifications. Such a lawyer wisely might decide not to provide the materials on those terms so as to avoid violating Rule 4.1(DE) regarding truthfulness to others.

4. Lawyer Liability to Third Parties

A lawyer who provides an evaluation to a third party with reason to believe that the third party is likely to rely upon it may have a basis for liability to the third party. Courts have varying approaches to the issue of a lawyer's liability to third parties. While lawyers generally owe no duties to nonclients, the situation in which a lawyer provides an evaluation to a third party knowing that the third party will likely rely upon the evaluation is a situation in which courts sometimes recognize lawyer liability to the third party. If Larry Lawyer provides the title report to Thelma Thirdparty stating that the property's title is clear, and if Thelma later discovers that Larry was incorrect, Thelma may be able to successfully sue Larry on the basis of the incorrect evaluation.

Related Sections of the *Restatement (Third) of the Law Governing Lawyers*

Section 95

Checkpoints

- If a lawyer "reasonably believes" that evaluating an issue for a client and providing the evaluation to a third party is compatible with the lawyer's duties owed to the client, the lawyer may provide the evaluation.
- If a lawyer "knows or reasonably should know" that disclosure to a third party of an evaluation done for a client "is likely to affect the client's interests materially and adversely," the lawyer must obtain the client's "informed consent" for the disclosure.
- Any material limitation on an evaluation should be described in the evaluation report to avoid misleading the third party.
- A lawyer providing an evaluation to a third party at the request of a client may be liable to the third party for a faulty evaluation.

Chapter 25

A Lawyer as a Third-Party Neutral

Roadmap

- Rule 2.4(DE)
- Rule 1.12(DE)
- A lawyer's responsibilities as a third-party neutral
- Conflicts of interest rule for a third-party neutral

A. Third-Party Neutrals Do Not Act in a Representational Capacity

Lawyers are sometimes asked to provide a service in a nonrepresentational capacity. A lawyer might be asked to serve in a decision-making role such as an arbitrator or evaluator. Two parties may have a dispute and ask Lisa Lawyer to serve as the arbitrator for their matter. Lisa would then hear the positions of the two parties in the matter and render a decision resolving the dispute. A lawyer could serve in a slightly different role—that of a conflict resolution facilitator such as a mediator or conciliator. Two parties may have a dispute and ask Lisa to help them attempt to reach an agreed-upon resolution. Lisa would then facilitate the negotiation process for the parties. A lawyer might be asked to assist parties in arranging a transaction. Some of these settings have their own codes of conduct. For example, The American Bar Association and the American Arbitration Association jointly have created a *Code of Ethics for Arbitration in Commercial Disputes.*

In any of these capacities, a lawyer is serving as a third-party neutral. Rule 2.4(a)(DE) acknowledges that lawyers may serve in a third-party neutral capacity.

B. The Duty to Explain and Clarify the Neutral Role

Rule 2.4(b)(DE) warns that a lawyer serving as a third-party neutral must explain to any unrepresented parties that the lawyer does not represent those parties. The unstated assumption is that lawyers for represented parties will counsel their clients about the role of the third-party neutral lawyer. In all of the above scenarios in which Lisa serves as a third-party neutral, if the parties are not represented by counsel, Lisa must explain that she does not represent the parties. If a lawyer "knows or reasonably should know" that a participant in the matter is confused about the lawyer's role, the lawyer must explain the difference between a lawyer's typical role in representing a client and a lawyer's role in the matter as a third-party neutral.

In general a lawyer should be clear with the participants about the role the lawyer plays in the particular matter. If a lawyer is serving as a third-party neutral, the lawyer is not acting in a representational capacity. By serving as a third-party neutral, a lawyer does not establish a lawyer-client relationship with any of the actors in the matter. If a lawyer is clear as to his or her role, the lawyer represents none of the actors in the matter and owes to none of the parties the duties that the usual lawyer-client relationship creates. Recall that the existence of the relationship and thus the duties owed can depend on the reasonable belief of the person in the position of client. *See Chapter 4 Basis of Duty: The Lawyer-Client Relationship.* A lawyer may owe the parties certain duties as the result of codes that may apply to the particular type of third-party neutral the lawyer is, but the lawyer owes no duties independent of such codes.

Perhaps two parties have asked Lisa Lawyer to facilitate a settlement discussion. Perhaps in the midst of her conversations with one of the parties she realizes that the party believes that Lisa is advocating that party's position to the other party. Lisa must educate the party about the difference between Lisa representing the party and Lisa serving as a facilitator or mediator—a third-party neutral. Lisa must explain that she is not acting in an advocacy role.

Note that Rule 4.2(DE) and Rule 4.3(DE) do not apply in this context because those rules apply only when a lawyer is acting in a representational capacity and, in the case of Rule 4.2(DE), has contact with a represented party or, in the case of Rule 4.3(DE), has contact with an unrepresented party. *See Chapter 36 Contact with Represented Persons* and *Chapter 37 Respect for the Rights of Nonclients.*

C. Conflicts of Interest Created by Service as a Third-Party Neutral

1. Representation of a Party in the Matter after Service as a Third-Party Neutral

a. Generally

Occasionally, one of the parties in the matter in which the lawyer serves as a third-party neutral decides that he or she would like the lawyer to represent the party regarding the matter after the lawyer's role as a third-party neutral has concluded. This might occur if the party was particularly impressed by the lawyer's performance as a third-party neutral. Perhaps Lisa Lawyer serves as a mediator in a dispute between Penny Plaintiff and David Defendant. At the time of the mediation Lance Lawyer represents Penny. Penny may decide after the unsuccessful mediation that she would rather be represented by Lisa in the subsequent litigation of the matter.

Unfortunately for Penny, Rule 1.12(a)(DE) provides that a lawyer such as Lisa cannot represent a party in the same matter in which the lawyer "participated personally and substantially" as a third-party neutral unless all parties to the proceeding give "informed consent, confirmed in writing." *See Chapter 23 Conflicts and Former Judges, Other Adjudicative Officers, Law Clerks, and Third-Party Neutrals.* The rule is an attempt to prevent a lawyer, while serving as a third-party neutral, from succumbing to the temptation to act so as to improve the third-party neutral's opportunities for future employment with the actors in the proceeding.

Rule 1.0(e)(DE) explains that to obtain "informed consent," a lawyer must fully explain the "material risks" and "reasonably available alternatives" to the conduct proposed. Because Lisa has served as a mediator in the dispute between Penny and David, Lisa has obviously participated in the matter "personally and substantially" as a third-party neutral. Lisa cannot represent Penny in the later litigation of the matter unless both Penny and David consent after Lisa explains to both of them the "material risks" involved and any "reasonably available alternatives." Rule 1.0(b)(DE) clarifies that a confirmation can take the form of a writing signifying consent or can be a document prepared by the lawyer and promptly sent to the consenting person confirming an earlier oral "informed consent." A writing can be a traditional writing or can be in another form. Rule 1.0(n)(DE) states that a writing is "a tangible or electronic record of a communication or representation" and states as examples audio and video recording and electronic communications.

b. A Multimember Arbitration Panel

A different situation exists if the lawyer has served as a member of an arbitration panel in a matter if the lawyer was chosen to serve as a partisan arbitrator. If Lisa is selected by Penny as a partisan arbitrator to serve on a three-member arbitration panel in the matter involving David, Lisa could represent Penny later in the matter. Rule 1.12(d)(DE) contains this exception. *See Chapter 23 Conflicts and Former Judges, Other Adjudicative Officers, Law Clerks, and Third-Party Neutrals.*

c. Imputation of the Conflict and the Screening Cure

A lawyer serving as a third-party neutral creates conflict of interest concerns for the lawyer's firm as well. If a lawyer who has served as a third-party neutral in a matter cannot later represent one of the parties in the matter, the ability of other lawyers in the third-party neutral's firm is constrained significantly as well. Rule 1.12(c)(DE) states that a member of the third-party neutral's firm cannot knowingly represent the party unless

1. the firm screens the third-party neutral in a timely manner from any participation in the matter,
2. the third-party neutral receives no part of the fee from the representation, and
3. the parties and "any appropriate tribunal" are given notice in writing so that these parties can determine whether these requirements are followed.

A lawyer is screened when the lawyer does not participate in the matter in any way and is isolated from it. Rule 1.0(k)(DE), which explains screening, notes that procedures must be imposed in a timely manner to ensure that any information the screened lawyer is obligated to protect is in fact protected. These procedures must be "reasonably adequate" to protect the information.

A screened lawyer cannot receive a fee related to the representation. Such a lawyer can receive a fee that is the result of a prior agreement unrelated to this specific matter that deals with the division of firm income or the lawyer's salary. This is true even though the some share of the money going to the lawyer may be the result of the matter from which the lawyer is screened.

Finally, the firm must give written notice to all parties to the matter and the relevant tribunal. The firm should explain the nature of the disqualification and the steps taken to screen the conflicted lawyer.

If Lisa cannot represent Penny as a result of Lisa's service as a third-party neutral in an earlier stage of the matter, no one in Lisa's firm may represent Penny unless Lisa is screened. Lisa must not receive a fee from the matter. Both Penny and David must be informed, as well as the court before whom the matter is pending. *See Chapter 23 Conflicts and Former Judges, Other Adjudicative Officers, Law Clerks, and Third-Party Neutrals.*

2. Restrictions on a Third-Party Neutral Seeking Employment

A lawyer who is serving as a third-party neutral and is "participating personally and substantially" may not discuss employment with a party in the matter or with a lawyer representing a party in the matter. This prohibition, stated in Rule 1.12(b)(DE), takes away an incentive for the third-party neutral to be less than neutral. Perhaps Lisa Lawyer is acting as the sole mediator in a matter involving Penny and David. Larry Lawyer, a lawyer with First Firm, represents Penny in the matter. Lance Lawyer, a lawyer with Finest Firm, represents David in the matter. Lisa cannot negotiate for employment with Penny, David, Larry, Lance, First Firm, or Finest Firm. *See Chapter 23 Conflicts and Former Judges, Other Adjudicative Officers, Law Clerks, and Third-Party Neutrals.*

Checkpoints

- A lawyer may serve as a third-party neutral such as an arbitrator or mediator.
- A lawyer does not act in a representational capacity when the lawyer serves as a third-party neutral.
- A lawyer serving as a third-party neutral may owe duties to the participants as a result of specific codes of conduct that may apply to the particular setting.
- A lawyer must clarify his or her role to unrepresented parties.
- A lawyer must explain the nonrepresentational nature of the third-party neutral role if the lawyer has reason to believe that a party is confused.
- A lawyer who has served as a third-party neutral in a matter and has "participated personally and substantially" cannot later represent one of the parties in the matter unless all parties give "informed consent, confirmed in writing." The only exception to this rule is when a lawyer is selected as a partisan arbitrator of a party and has served in that regard as a member of a multimember arbitration panel. Then the lawyer can later represent the party who originally selected the lawyer as a partisan member.

- If a lawyer who has served as a third-party neutral in a matter cannot later represent a party in that same matter, no one in the third-party neutral's firm can later knowingly represent one of the parties in the matter unless
    1. the firm screens the third-party neutral in a timely manner from any participation in the matter,
    2. the third-party neutral receives no part of the fee from the representation, and
    3. the parties and "any appropriate tribunal" are given notice in writing so that these parties can determine whether these requirements are followed.
- A lawyer who is serving as a third-party neutral in a matter, and is "participating personally and substantially," cannot negotiate employment with any party or lawyer for a party in the matter.

Section VII
The Lawyer as an Advocate

Chapter 26

Frivolous Positions

Roadmap

- Rule 3.1(DE)
- Rule 3.4(d)(DE)
- Rule 3.8(a)(ID)
- Frivolous positions in claims, defenses, or discovery requests
- A prosecutor's duty to not pursue a charge for which there is no probable cause
- Federal Rule of Civil Procedure 11
- Abuse of process
- Malicious prosecution

A. The Duty to Avoid Frivolous Positions

1. The General Prohibition

A lawyer may not pursue a frivolous claim or defense. Rule 3.1(DE) provides that a lawyer may not "bring or defend a proceeding, or assert or controvert an issue therein, unless there is a basis in law and fact for doing so that is not frivolous, which includes a good faith argument for an extension, modification or reversal of existing law." The rationale for the rule is that taking a frivolous position in contravention of the rule requires wasteful expenditure for other parties in the litigation. Such action also wastes the time and other resources of the judicial system.

This rule does not require lawyers to act as the judges of their clients' cases. A lawyer may take a position in furtherance of the client's goals even if the lawyer believes that the client will lose in the end. The lawyer cannot, however, take a position that has no basis in law or fact.

a. The Facts

While this standard does not require a lawyer to do a complete factual investigation before filing a matter or asserting a claim, it does require that the lawyer take no position that is contrary to the facts the lawyer knows or should know. The duty of competence and applicable rules of procedure dictate the level of investigation necessary. *See Chapter 5 Competence and Diligence.*

Assume that Lisa Lawyer's client, Cindy, has come to Lisa for representation in a medical malpractice action. Cindy claims that she was injured in a botched surgery. Cindy wants to sue the hospital and several doctors who she believes caused her injury during the surgery. Lisa obtains the hospital record of the surgery and discovers that one of the physicians Cindy has named was not present for the surgery and so could not have caused her injury. After more investigation Lisa discovers that the physician in question was not in town the week of the surgery but rather was on a humanitarian mission in South America. Lisa would violate Rule 3.1(DE) if she filed a complaint claiming that this physician injured Cindy in the surgery in question.

b. The Law

With regard to law, Rule 3.1(DE) simply requires that the lawyer not take a position in a matter unless there is a basis in law for that position. The rule even allows a lawyer to argue that the law should be changed when the law appears to be contrary to the client's position if the lawyer can make such an argument in good faith. As is true with regard to the proper factual investigation, the duties of competence and diligence and rules of procedure dictate the level of legal research necessary. *See Chapter 5 Competence and Diligence.*

Assume Lisa Lawyer discovers that the statute of limitations bars Cindy Client's medical malpractice action relating to her botched surgery. Cindy's only chance of success is a claim that the statute should not begin to run until the date Cindy was told that someone did something improper in the surgery. Lisa's legal research tells her that the supreme court of the jurisdiction reviewed this exact issue last year and stated in a unanimous published opinion that the jurisdiction would not apply this interpretation to the statute of limitations. The supreme court membership has not changed since it rendered the opinion. In such a circumstance, Lisa perhaps cannot make the argument, without violating Rule 3.1(DE), that the court should recognize the interpretation of the statute of limitations that favors Cindy.

c. *An Objective Standard*

While the rule itself is silent, courts and commentators agree that the appropriate standard for measuring a lawyer's conduct regarding frivolous claims and such is an objective one. The question is what a reasonable lawyer would do or think, not what this particular lawyer did or thought.

d. *The Criminal Law Exception*

Rule 3.1(DE) provides that a lawyer representing a defendant in a criminal proceeding or in any other proceeding that could result in incarceration of the client may "defend the proceeding as to require that every element of the case be established." This statement makes clear that the professional responsibility rule should in no way be read to interfere with the prosecution's constitutional burden in a criminal matter. The constitutional burden is that the prosecution must prove guilt beyond a reasonable doubt on all elements of the crime.

If Lisa Lawyer's client, Cindy, has been charged with murder, Lisa may assist Cindy in entering a plea of not guilty and maintaining that position even if Lisa has no evidence supporting the client defendant's denial of guilt. Lisa is simply requiring the prosecution to prove that Cindy is guilty of murder beyond a reasonable doubt.

On appeal in a criminal matter, defense counsel is held to a bit of different standard on the issue of frivolous matters than in civil cases. The United States Supreme Court, in *Anders v. California*, 386 U.S. 738 (1967), held that if a defense lawyer can file no nonfrivolous basis for an appeal, that lawyer must file a brief explaining that there are no nonfrivolous bases for appeal. This brief is now commonly called an *Anders* brief. This issue occurs, usually, in the context of appointed counsel.

2. The Discovery Conduct Rule

Rule 3.4(d)(DE) also addresses the issue of lawyers asserting frivolous positions. This rule forbids the making of a "frivolous discovery request" in the context of pretrial procedure. The term "frivolous" is not defined in 3.4(d)(DE); however, Rule 3.1(DE) is helpful in that it requires any claim to have a basis in fact or law that is nonfrivolous and includes in the definition of nonfrivolous "a good faith argument for an extension, modification or reversal of existing law." One can assume that the same standard applies to discovery requests. *See Chapter 29 Fairness.*

Lisa Lawyer may be aware that existing law says that her client is not entitled to certain information. Lisa may request that information if she can make a good faith argument that existing law is incorrect or inapplicable to her client's situation.

3. The Probable Cause Standard for Prosecutors

Another rule relates tangentially but not directly to the issue of frivolous positions. Rule 3.8(a)(ID) states that a prosecutor must not prosecute a charge that the prosecutor "knows is not supported by probable cause." While a charge lacking probable cause may not be the same as a frivolous position generally, the special role a prosecutor holds in the criminal justice system demands that the prosecutor have an independent and perhaps more stringent obligation. *See Chapter 33 The Lawyer as Prosecutor.*

B. Other Federal and State Rules

1. Generally

In addition to the professional responsibility principles applicable to frivolous matters, an additional regulator of lawyer conduct in this area is a body of federal and state rules governing procedure and discovery. Because the effect of asserting a frivolous position is most urgently felt in the litigation matter in which it occurs, the court presiding over that matter often takes heed of the conduct as a result of a motion filed by another party or simply *sua sponte*. Courts are generally reticent to sanction abuses unless they are egregious.

Rule 11 of the Federal Rules of Civil Procedure has been most influential in providing courts with a framework for policing frivolous positions. Many states have patterned a rule for their state courts using federal Rule 11 as a model. In addition, there are some state and federal rules that touch upon this conduct in particular contexts such as discovery. Finally, even absent a rule, the courts have inherent power to sanction abuse.

2. Federal Rule of Civil Procedure 11

a. The Requirement

Rule 11 of the Federal Rules of Civil Procedure requires that a lawyer sign every "pleading, written motion, and other paper." By signing such a document and presenting it to a court, the lawyer certifies that "to the best of the person's knowledge, information, and belief, formed after an inquiry reasonable under the circumstances," the following is true:

1. that the paper "is not being presented for any improper purpose, such as to harass, cause unnecessary delay, or needlessly increase the cost of litigation,"
2. that "the claims, defenses, and other legal contentions are warranted by existing law or by a nonfrivolous argument for extending, modifying, or reversing existing law or for establishing new law,"
3. that "the factual contentions have evidentiary support or, if specifically so identified, will likely have evidentiary support after a reasonable opportunity for further investigation or discovery," and
4. that "the denials of factual contentions are warranted on the evidence or, if specifically so identified, are reasonably based on belief or a lack of information."

Thus, Rule 11 targets, in part, the same conduct Rule 3.1(DE) regulates.

b. Sanctions

Rule 11 provides that a court, if it finds that a violation has occurred, may impose a punishment upon "any attorney, law firm, or party" that has violated Rule 11 or is "responsible for a violation." The opposing party may move for sanctions or the court may raise the issue *sua sponte* with a show cause order. A court may impose an appropriate sanction which is one that "suffices to deter repetition of the conduct or comparable conduct by others similarly situated." The sanction may be something other than the payment of a fine. For example, a court might order a lawyer to write an apology to opposing counsel or prepare a summary of the law of Rule 11.

The court may order the offending party to pay a monetary penalty. The court might order that the penalty be paid to the court. Or the court may order the offending party to pay an amount to the party moving for sanctions under Rule 11. If the sanction is "imposed on motion and warranted for effective deterrence," the court may enter "an order directing payment to the movant of part or all of the reasonable attorney's fees and other expenses directly resulting from the violation."

c. The Grace Period

If a party raises the Rule 11 issue by motion, that party must serve the motion and then a 21-day grace period must pass. During the grace period, the offending party may withdraw the "paper, claim, defense, contention, or denial" or may correct it. If the offending party chooses not to withdraw or correct the offending document, the moving party may then file the motion with the court.

C. Tort Actions

A lawyer who pursues a frivolous position may also be liable in tort. Assume that Cindy Client, acting with the assistance of her lawyer, Lisa, sues Dan Defendant claiming that Dan committed medical malpractice. Because Lisa, the lawyer, has a lead role in the judicial system and the particular litigation, Dan justly may develop a healthy dislike for the Lisa. For Dan, Lisa is responsible for what Dan feels is a bogus lawsuit. In addition, the zeal with which Lisa pursues the claim may cause Dan to believe that the Lisa is particularly evil. If Cindy's case ultimately fails, it is at least understandable that Dan might want to take steps to "get even."

The torts of abuse of process and malicious prosecution sit at the ready for such an aggrieved defendant as Dan. Dan could choose to sue the plaintiff's lawyer, Lisa, instead of or in addition to suing Cindy.

Because these process torts have a chilling effect on the general willingness of the public and lawyers in particular to take legal positions, they have traditionally been circumscribed so as to minimize this chilling effect. These torts are defined narrowly and applied strictly. They are extremely difficult to establish against anyone and especially against lawyers—but it is possible.

1. Abuse of Process

The tort of abuse of process occurs when one uses a legal process, as the *Restatement (Second) of Torts (1977)* section 682 states, "primarily to accomplish a purpose for which it is not designed." For example, suppose that Lisa Lawyer obtains a warrant for the arrest of a business's credit manager on the basis that the credit manager is practicing law without a license. Practicing law without a license is a crime in the jurisdiction. *See Chapter 40 The Unauthorized Practice of Law.* Suppose Lisa's real motivation in obtaining the warrant is to coerce the credit manager to dismiss a garnishment proceeding he instituted against Lisa's client. In such a situation a court could find that Lisa committed the tort of abuse of process.

2. Malicious Prosecution

Another possible area of liability is the tort of malicious prosecution. Historically, this tort has been called "malicious prosecution" even when the matter has been civil. Some jurisdictions, as does the *Restatement (Second) of Torts (1977)* in section 674, now refer to the tort in the civil context as "wrongful use of civil proceedings."

Generally the tort requires a showing

1. that a party acted without probable cause in pursuing civil proceedings,
2. that the party acted with a primary purpose other that proper resolution of the claim that is the basis of the proceedings, and
3. that the wrongful proceedings ended in favor of the target party.

Lawyers take an active part in pursuing proceedings so lawyers are an easy initial target for suits based on wrongful initiation of process, though, ultimately, actions against lawyers are not generally successful.

a. Lack of Probable Cause

The requirement that a malicious prosecution plaintiff, to prove the tort, must prove that the defendant acted without probable cause is of particular assistance to lawyer defendants. Many courts apply a loose standard to probable cause. In *Prewitt v. Sexton*, 777 S.W.2d 891, 896 (1989), the Kentucky Supreme Court, defining probable cause to be "a suspicion founded upon circumstances sufficiently strong to warrant a reasonable person in the belief that the charge is true," refused to find a lack of probable cause because there was no evidence that the lawyer in the case "failed to make a reasonable effort to investigate the basis of his client's claim before filing suit." Though the court noted that a lack of knowledge or a lack of investigation of the law could be evidence of a lack of probable cause, the *Prewitt* court concluded that "all that is required to establish probable cause is that the attorney's view of the law is a tenable position." *Id.* at 897.

b. Wrongful Purpose

A malicious prosecution plaintiff must prove that the lawyer pursued the action primarily for a purpose other than proper resolution of the claim. As in any other setting, proving motivation is an extremely daunting task. Comment d to *Restatement (Second) of Torts (1977)* section 674 states that even if a lawyer does not have probable cause and even if the lawyer is "convinced that his client's claim is unfounded," the lawyer is not liable "if he acts primarily for the purpose of aiding his client in obtaining a proper adjudication" of the claim. The comment is based on the policy that the tort should not be allowed to exert so much power over the situation that the lawyer feels compelled to prejudge the client's claim. This is true even when the lawyer knows that the client's chance of success is minimal. The delicate balance of the judicial system is maintained.

c. *Positive Outcome*

Finally, to succeed on a claim of malicious prosecution, the wrongful proceeding must have ended positively for the target of the wrongful prosecution. This is a large hurdle for many malicious prosecution plaintiffs, whether or not the defendant is a lawyer, because courts often do not accept anything other than a verdict or other dismissal in favor of the target as a positive end for the target. Some courts, for example, do not recognize a payment in settlement as a result in favor of the target. *See, e.g., Puttuck v. Gendron,* 199 P.3d 971 (Utah Ct. App. 2008).

Related Sections of the *Restatement (Third) of the Law Governing Lawyers*

Section 110

Checkpoints

- A lawyer may not assert a frivolous claim or defense or make a frivolous discovery request.
- A position is not frivolous even if contrary to existing law if there is a good faith argument for a change of that law.
- A prosecutor may not pursue a charge that the prosecutor knows lacks probable cause.
- Federal and state rules also regulate the assertion of frivolous positions.
- Federal Rule of Civil Procedure 11 requires a lawyer to sign any pleading, motion, or other paper and to certify that
    1. the presentation of the paper is not for an "improper purpose,"
    2. the "claims, defenses, and other legal contentions are warranted,"
    3. the allegations have or "likely have evidentiary support," and
    4. the "denials of factual contentions are warranted" or "are reasonably based on belief or a lack of information."
- A violation of Rule 11 or a similar state or federal rule subjects the lawyer and the client to the possibility of monetary and/or nonmonetary sanctions.
- Pursuit of frivolous positions may also create liability for the torts of abuse of process or malicious prosecution.

- Abuse of process occurs when one uses legal process primarily for a purpose for which the process was not designed.
- Malicious prosecution occurs when one
    1. pursues a matter without probable cause,
    2. the matter is pursued for a wrongful purpose, and
    3. the matter ends in favor of the target of the prosecution.

Chapter 27

The Duty to Expedite Litigation

Roadmap

- Rule 3.2(DE)
- The duty to expedite litigation

A. When Delay Benefits the Lawyer

Rule 3.2(DE) states: "A lawyer shall make reasonable efforts to expedite litigation consistent with the interests of the client." This pronouncement makes clear that a lawyer must consider the interests of clients when organizing and prioritizing litigation. This should be obvious in light of the more general duty of lawyers to represent clients competently and diligently as stated by Rule 1.1(DE) and Rule 1.3(DE). *See Chapter 5 Competence and Diligence.* The comment to the rule focuses on the duty to expedite as a duty not to improperly delay litigation.

If Lisa Lawyer is a busy and successful litigator, she often may request extensions of filing deadlines or may request that hearings be delayed. Rule 3.2(DE) is a reminder that Lisa must always consider the interests of the particular client affected. If delay is not in the best interest of the client, Lisa should not request the delay even though the delay would make Lisa's own work schedule more manageable. Lisa must take care to have a caseload that is not so onerous as to create a need for delaying cases to the extent that the delay may harm her clients.

B. When Delay Benefits the Client

The less than clear situation occurs when delay actually benefits the client. Because Rule 3.2(DE) states the lawyer's duty to expedite litigation as a duty to act "consistent with the interests of the client," a lawyer might conclude that *not* expediting the matter is the best course for the client. The comment to the rule warns, however, that not expediting a litigation matter will not "be reasonable if done for the purpose of frustrating an opposing party's attempt to obtain rightful redress or repose." The comment notes that the analysis should focus on whether the course of action has "some substantial purpose other than delay." The comment further warns that if the delay is "otherwise improper," "realizing financial or other benefit" "is not a legitimate interest of the client." Such a move is not "otherwise improper" if it is not frivolous.

Rule 3.2(DE) is consistent with Rule 4.4(a)(DE), the rule prohibiting a lawyer from using methods that have "no substantial purpose other than ... delay." *See Chapter 37 Respect for the Rights of Nonclients.*

Lisa Lawyer violates Rule 3.2(DE) if she takes a frivolous position for the sole purpose of delay and Lisa seeks delay because it creates a financial benefit for Lisa's client, Cindy. If Lisa takes a nonfrivolous position that will cause delay but Lisa does so not only for the effects of the delay but for other reasons as well, Lisa has probably not violated Rule 3.2(DE).

Checkpoints

- A lawyer must not unreasonably delay litigation if delay is contrary to the interests of the client.
- A lawyer must not unreasonably and improperly delay litigation even if delay is somehow in the interest of the client. A delay may be improper if the course of action is frivolous.

Chapter 28

Honesty and Candor

Roadmap

- Rule 3.3(DE)
- Rule 4.1(a)(DE)
- Rule 8.4(c)(DE)
- Honesty in general
- False statements of fact or law to a tribunal
- Disclosure of legal authority
- Offering false evidence
- A client's criminal or fraudulent conduct regarding a proceeding
- Disclosure in the *ex parte* context

A. Honesty and Candor Generally

Lawyers must be honest. Rule 8.4(c)(DE) provides that it is professional misconduct for a lawyer to engage in "dishonesty, fraud, deceit or misrepresentation." This is a general rule that applies whether or not a lawyer is acting in the context of a representation. Perhaps Lisa Lawyer writes a legal thriller. The book is published and is successful. Then someone proves that Lisa plagiarized the work. Since plagiarism is an act of dishonesty, Lisa has violated Rule 8.4(c)(DE) even though the book did not relate to Lisa's legal practice. *See Chapter 48 General Misconduct.*

Another honesty provision is Rule 4.1(a)(DE). The rule states that when dealing with persons who are not clients or tribunals, a lawyer knowingly may not "make a false statement of material fact or law to a third person." *See Chapter 35 Truthfulness to Third Parties.* The juxtaposition of Rule 8.4(c)(DE) and Rule 4.1(a)(DE) raises the question whether a false statement of nonmaterial fact or law which, apparently, would not violate Rule 4.1(a)(DE), would violate Rule 8.4(c)(DE). The answer from the plain meaning of the words of the rules is "yes" because even a misrepresentation that is not material violates Rule 8.4(c)(DE).

When dealing with a tribunal, a lawyer's duties with regard to honesty are a bit more stringent. This heightened duty is the result of the vital role lawyers have in the judicial system. That system cannot perform properly if the other players in the system cannot trust the lawyers. Rule 3.3(DE) has specific requirements of utmost candor when the lawyer deals with a tribunal.

Rule 1.0(m)(DE) defines a tribunal as a court or "other body acting in an adjudicative capacity." Rule 1.0(m)(DE) further states that "[a] legislative body, administrative agency or other body acts in an adjudicative capacity when a neutral official, after the presentation of evidence or legal argument by a party or parties, will render a binding legal judgment directly affecting a party's interests in a particular matter." When a lawyer deals with such an entity as this, the lawyer must act with candor as delineated by Rule 3.3(DE).

B. False Statements of Fact or Law

Rule 3.3(a)(1)(DE) provides that when dealing with a tribunal, a lawyer may not knowingly make an untrue statement of fact or law. Note that this rule is written in the absolute sense. The tribunal has to be able to trust what a lawyer says so the lawyer must speak truthfully, even about small, less than material, matters.

Perhaps Lisa has a vacation scheduled for the first week of July. At a scheduling conference in May, the judge asks Lisa whether she has a conflict with a trial date of July 1. Lisa does not want to try the case on that day because she does not want to miss her vacation. She also does not want to tell the court that her only conflict is a vacation because she fears the judge will schedule the trial on that day anyway. Lisa tells the court that she cannot try the case on that day because she already has another trial scheduled for that day. She does not. Lisa has behaved unethically because she has violated Rule 3.3(a)(1)(DE).

Occasionally, a lawyer makes untrue statements to the court about the matter before the court. Perhaps a lawyer on appeal knowingly tells the court that the lower court made certain findings when in fact the lower court did not. Or perhaps the lawyer tells the court that certain matters were discussed below when in fact the issues were not discussed at all. Perhaps the lawyer states the facts of the matter in the brief with so much spin that the recitation of facts is false. In each of these situations, the lawyer has violated Rule 3.3(a)(1)(DE).

Also, a lawyer may violate Rule 3.3(a)(1)(DE), not by an affirmative misstatement, but by a failure to disclose. A comment to the rule states: "There are circumstances where failure to make a disclosure is the equivalent of an affirmative misrepresentation." For example, if Lisa Lawyer fails to disclose to the court that her client has died and yet Lisa participates in a settlement conference with the court, the lawyer's actions lead the court to believe that the client is alive. Such conduct may be viewed as the equivalent of a false statement of fact and a violation of Rule 3.3(a)(1)(DE).

Some courts punish lawyers only by chastising them when the courts discover such lawyer dishonesty. Often, courts use Federal Rule of Civil Procedure 11 or a state version of that rule to sanction a lawyer when the lawyer exhibits a lack of candor when the true situation is that the lawyer's position is frivolous. *See Chapter 26 Frivolous Positions.* For example, in *In re Guevara*, 41 S.W. 3d 169 (Tex. Ct. App. 2001), a lawyer grossly misstated to the appellate court the procedural posture of the case, stating that there was no need for a trial on certain issues because the opposition had dismissed certain claims. The lawyer also told the court that the court below had determined the beneficiary of an insurance policy. These were false statements of fact. The court, applying a rule similar to Rule 11, required the offending lawyer to pay the other party's lawyer fees.

Lawyers must be truthful about the law as well. Occasionally, lawyers intentionally modify quotations from legal opinions to make the precedent seem more in their clients' favor. Sometimes a "not" is added or left out to reverse the original meaning of the passage. Sometimes ellipses are carefully used to convert a sentence found in an opinion to a sentence having quite a different meaning. When a lawyer does something like this knowingly, the lawyer is making a false statement about the law in violation of Rule 3.3(a)(1)(DE). When a court discovers such conduct the court may report the lawyer to the discipline authorities. Frequently, however, the court addresses the lawyer's conduct in the matter at hand by sanction or other punishment. In *Precision Specialty Metals, Inc. v. United States*, 315 F.3d 1346 (Fed. Cir. 2003), a lawyer filed a document in support of a motion for reconsideration that contained very selectively edited quotations so that the original sources appeared to support her argument when in reality they did not. The court sanctioned the lawyer under Rule 11 and noted that the court could have used its inherent power to punish the lawyer as well.

C. Duty to Correct False Statements

In addition to the duty to avoid making false statements, a lawyer must correct any untrue statement "of material fact or law previously made to the tribunal by the lawyer." If Lisa Lawyer states in an appellate argument that a witness testified to a certain material fact, and if Lisa later learns that she was mistaken about that testimony, Lisa has a duty to correct the misimpression as long as the proceeding has not concluded. A comment to the rule clarifies that a proceeding has concluded only when a final judgment has been affirmed on appeal or the time for appeal has expired. Rule 3.3(c)(DE) notes that this duty to correct a false statement may require disclosure of information for which the lawyer otherwise owes the client a duty of confidentiality under Rule 1.6(DE). *See Chapter 15 The Duty of Confidentiality.* In other words, the lawyer's duty to the court to be candid trumps the lawyer's duty to the client to protect confidences. If Lisa Lawyer states to the court that her client, Cindy, has no additional assets other than those listed on a filing with the court, and then Cindy reveals to Lisa that she has other assets, Lisa must disclose the other assets to the court even though the communication with Cindy about the assets otherwise would be protected by the duty of confidentiality.

D. Disclosure of Legal Authority

A lawyer has no duty to disclose facts relating to a matter before a tribunal unless disclosure is required by discovery processes, the court specifically orders disclosure, disclosure is necessary under Rule 3.3(a)(1)(DE) to correct an earlier statement of the lawyer, or the situation in which nondisclosure is the equivalent to an affirmative misrepresentation. A lawyer's duty regarding the law is greater.

Rule 3.3(a)(2)(DE) requires a lawyer to disclose to the tribunal "legal authority in the controlling jurisdiction known to the lawyer to be directly adverse to the position of the client and not disclosed by opposing counsel." The rationale of the rule is that the failure to disclose legal authority to the tribunal simply leads to unneeded expenditure of judicial resources because judges and their staffs must research matters anew. If a court does not uncover a relevant precedent, the danger is that a superior court will reverse the lower court's decision. Another possibility is that the decision, based on an incomplete picture of relevant precedent, will create inconsistent precedent. Again, the ultimate result is waste of judicial resources.

There are several important qualifiers to this duty to disclose adverse legal authority, however. First, Rule 3.3(a)(DE) is written so that only a knowing failure to disclose is a violation. So if a lawyer is simply a poor researcher and does not find the case that is "directly adverse," the lawyer may be incompetent and liable for malpractice but the lawyer has not violated Rule 3.3(a)(2)(DE).

Because of this mental state requirement, it is very difficult to prove that a lawyer has knowingly failed to disclose authority to a tribunal. Such proof is possible. In *In re Thonert,* 733 N.E.2d 932 (Ind. 2000), the Indiana discipline authority sanctioned a lawyer for failing to abide by the Indiana equivalent of Rule 3.3(a)(2)(DE). Because the lawyer had been personally involved in the "directly adverse" authority, the lawyer had a harder time claiming that he did not knowingly omit it.

A second qualifier is that a lawyer need not disclose the legal authority unless that authority is "directly adverse." While one can often argue that particular legal authority is not "directly adverse," courts often view this as a requirement to disclose authority a court would want to be aware of before making a decision in the matter.

A third qualifier is that the lawyer need only disclose the authority if it is from the controlling jurisdiction. A lawyer need not disclose a case directly on point in a neighboring state.

Finally, there is no need to disclose if opposing counsel discloses the legal authority. One would think that opposing counsel would want to rely on a case that is "directly adverse" to the opposition's position and is from the controlling jurisdiction. So really the duty to disclose adverse authority only arises when opposing counsel fails to identify the case.

Even if a lawyer must disclose legal authority under Rule 3.3(a)(2)(DE), the lawyer is free to distinguish it or ignore it—as long as it is cited to the court. As with other duties under Rule 3.3(DE), the duty to disclose continues until the judgment has been affirmed on appeal or the time for appeal has passed.

E. Offering False Evidence

1. Offering Evidence Known to Be False

a. General Rule: Evidence and Witnesses

Lawyers are officers of the court and this role places limits on the bounds of their representation of clients. If a lawyer knows that a witness intends to testify falsely or that other evidence is false, the lawyer may not offer that witness or evidence. Rule 3.3(a)(3)(DE) prohibits the offering of evidence the lawyer *knows* to be false. A comment clarifies that this prohibition applies not only to the presentation of evidence at trial but also in depositions or any other "ancillary proceeding conducted pursuant to the tribunal's adjudicative authority."

Lisa Lawyer cannot offer a document as evidence that she knows is fraudulent even though Lisa's client, Cindy, demands that Lisa do so. Lisa should attempt to convince Cindy of the error of the urged conduct. Also, Lisa cannot put a witness on the stand if she knows the witness will testify falsely. Of course, it is very hard to know definitively what a person will or will not do.

b. When the Witness Is the Client

In a civil matter, Rule 3.3(a)(3)(DE) does not allow Lisa to offer Cindy Client's testimony if she knows it will be false testimony. Presenting Cindy's testimony would be knowingly presenting false evidence.

In a criminal matter, the issue is much more clouded. The professional responsibility prohibition on the lawyer's presentation of false evidence collides with the criminal defendant's constitutional right to testify. In *Nix v. Whiteside*, 475 U.S. 157 (1986), the Supreme Court established that a criminal defendant has no constitutional right to testify falsely. This opinion lessens the conflict between the defendant's constitutional rights and the lawyer's duty to some extent. Even so, the situation presents a very sticky wicket for lawyers representing criminal defendants.

Courts generally require that a lawyer allow a criminal defendant to testify even if the lawyer knows that the client will testify falsely. The lawyer must follow the procedure used in the locality for such situations. The lawyer must notify the court of the problem and follow the court's instructions. For example, some courts require the lawyer to put the criminal defendant on the stand. The lawyer assists the client in eliciting truthful testimony and then the defendant testifies in a narrative fashion as to the matters about which the lawyer knows the client will testify falsely. In such a proceeding, the lawyer does not participate in the presentation of the false evidence other than perhaps asking an opening question such as, "Do you have something to share with us today?" The lawyer cannot rely on the problematic testimony in the closing argument or in any other way. Some courts have required the lawyer to participate in the presentation of the false testimony. These courts believe that the trier of fact can adequately judge the credibility of all witnesses and so the proceeding is sufficiently protected. A lawyer does not behave improperly by following the direction of the court on this issue.

c. Withdrawal

Sometimes a conflict between the lawyer and the client over the lawyer's inability to present certain evidence causes a breakdown of the lawyer-client relationship. The client may desire a new lawyer. Or the lawyer may seek to end the relationship. Regardless whether the motivation to end the relationship is the lawyer's or the client's, in accord with Rule 1.16(a)(DE), the lawyer must request permission from the court to withdraw from the representation and be removed as counsel of record. If the court grants the request, the lawyer must take all other necessary steps for withdrawal from the representation. *See Chapter 11 Refusing to Form a Lawyer-Client Relationship or Ending a Lawyer-Client Relationship.* A lawyer may not disclose confidential information in seeking permission to withdraw if Rule 3.3(DE) or another rule does not otherwise permit the disclosure.

Often, however, the conflict does not occur until the trial is imminent or in progress. A court may not allow the lawyer to withdraw at that point.

If the court permits the lawyer to withdraw, the withdrawal eliminates the problem for the lawyer. The withdrawal does not eliminate the threat of injury to the judicial system that can be caused by the client having the testimony or other evidence presented by a second lawyer who is unaware of the problem. Perhaps the client simply learns what not to disclose to the new lawyer so that the new lawyer has no Rule 3.3(DE) issue.

2. A Reasonable Belief That the Evidence Is False

a. General Rule: Evidence and Witnesses

If a lawyer does not *know* that the evidence is false but, rather, has a *reasonable belief* that it is false, Rule 3.3(a)(3)(DE) states that the lawyer *may* refuse to offer the evidence. This rule gives lawyers the right to refuse to present the evidence, but does not mandate that lawyers refuse to present the evidence. Note that if the client wants the evidence presented, the client may terminate the lawyer-client relationship rather than allow the lawyer to proceed without the evidence.

b. When the Witness Is the Client

If Lisa reasonably believes that her own client, Cindy, will testify falsely in a civil matter, Lisa may refuse to put Cindy on the stand. In contrast, if Cindy is a defendant in a criminal matter, Lisa generally may not refuse to put Cindy on the stand. Denying Cindy the right to testify in her own defense infringes on her constitutional rights. Cindy Client's constitutional right to testify in her own defense limits Lisa's right to refuse to present evidence she reasonably believes is false.

3. Discovering the Falsity of Evidence Already Presented

Rule 3.3(a)(3)(DE) provides that if a lawyer offers "material evidence" that the lawyer later learns is false, the lawyer has a duty to take "reasonable remedial measures." The same is true if the lawyer later learns that his or her client has testified falsely or if a witness called by the lawyer has testified falsely. The lawyer need not have been the one to elicit the false testimony. The lawyer is responsible for any witness he or she puts on the stand. The lawyer is responsible for his or her client as well. A large qualifier on these duties is that a lawyer must take "reasonable remedial measures" only if the evidence offered is material.

If Lisa Lawyer discovers that her client, Cindy, has lied on the stand about a material matter, what must she do to remedy the situation? What are "reasonable remedial measures"? First, Lisa must discuss the matter with Cindy and attempt to convince Cindy that Cindy must correct the testimony. Once Lisa explains a lawyer's duty to take "reasonable remedial measures," Cindy may understand that the best approach is to participate in correcting the situation. If Cindy refuses, Lisa must take steps to neutralize the false statement.

Lisa might believe that withdrawal from the representation is necessary to avoid other rules violations. Note, however, that the court must approve and, given the stage of the proceeding that these issues arise, approval may not occur. Even if a court approves of the withdrawal of a lawyer such as Lisa, the withdrawal is not remedial unless it undoes the effect of the false testimony. Lisa must act to erase the effect of the false evidence. This duty may require Lisa to disclose the untruth to the court. Lisa may then follow the direction of the court as to the avenue to follow to remedy the situation. The court might declare a mistrial, might instruct the jury on the matter, or might let the matter pass unnoted.

Rule 3.3(c)(DE) clarifies that the lawyer's duty to take "reasonable remedial measures" exists until the end of the proceeding. The end of the proceeding occurs when a final judgment in the proceeding is affirmed or the time for appeal passes. Rule 3.3(c)(DE) also notes that a lawyer's duty to disclose information as part of the duty the take "reasonable remedial measures" trumps any duty of confidentiality under Rule 1.6(DE) the lawyer might otherwise have. *See Chapter 15 The Duty of Confidentiality.*

F. Criminal or Fraudulent Conduct Relating to an Adjudicative Proceeding

When a lawyer represents a client in a proceeding and knows that someone "intends to engage, is engaging or has engaged in criminal or fraudulent conduct" regarding the proceeding, Rule 3.3(b)(DE) requires the lawyer to take "reasonable remedial measures." Such measures may include disclosure of the matter to the tribunal. The lawyer may be required to disclose even if the knowledge came to the lawyer via confidential communications otherwise protected by the duty of confidentiality of Rule 1.6(DE). Rule 3.3(b)(DE) applies to conduct of the client or another person if the conduct affects the integrity of the tribunal and the adjudicative process. The type of conduct targeted includes bribing, intimidating, or improperly communicating with any actor in the adjudicative process—witnesses, jurors, or court officials. In addition, the rule applies to any sort of improper destruction or concealment of evidence. It also applies to any failure to disclose evidence when law requires disclosure.

Perhaps Lisa's client, Big Corporation, has been sued for marketing an unsafe product. Perhaps the court has ordered Big to produce all evidence relating to safety testing for the product. Lisa discovers that Big, the day after the court order, directed its employees to destroy all documents relating to safety testing that suggested that the product was unsafe. Lisa now knows that Big has engaged in criminal or fraudulent conduct relating to the proceeding. Lisa has a duty to take "reasonable remedial measures," including disclosure of Big Corporation's actions to the tribunal.

G. *Ex Parte* Proceedings

Rule 3.3(DE) generally does not require a lawyer to affirmatively disclose adverse facts. The rationale is that the adversarial system ensures that all facts are developed properly. In an *ex parte* proceeding, however, the adversarial system is hobbled. Only one side of the matter is represented. The danger is that the tribunal will hear only one version of the story and a just result will not occur. Yet the tribunal's objective is a just result. In such a setting, a lawyer has an increased duty of candor with regard to disclosure of relevant facts. Rule 3.3(d)(DE) requires a lawyer participating in an *ex parte* proceeding to disclose all known material facts "that will enable the tribunal to make an informed decision," even if the facts are adverse.

Related Sections of the *Restatement (Third) of the Law Governing Lawyers*

Sections 94, 98, 105, 111, 112, 118, and 120

Checkpoints

- A lawyer may not engage in acts of dishonesty.
- A lawyer may not knowingly make a false statement of material fact to a third person.
- A lawyer may not knowingly make a false statement of fact or law to a tribunal.
- A lawyer must correct any statements about material facts or law that the lawyer has made to a tribunal if the lawyer discovers the statements are incorrect.
- A lawyer's failure to disclose information to a tribunal can, in some situations, be viewed as a misrepresentation.
- A lawyer must disclose "directly adverse" legal authority from the controlling jurisdiction to the tribunal if the lawyer knows of the authority and the authority has not been otherwise disclosed.
- A lawyer may not present testimony or other evidence to a tribunal that the lawyer knows to be false.
- If the client is a defendant in a criminal matter and if the lawyer knows the client intends to testify falsely, the lawyer must notify the court of the issue and follow the court's instruction as to the presentation of the evidence. A lawyer behaves properly by following the court's direction.
- A lawyer may refuse to present evidence or witnesses, including the lawyer's client in a civil matter (but not the lawyer's client in a criminal matter), if the lawyer reasonably believes the evidence is false or the witnesses will testify falsely.
- If a lawyer presents "material evidence" to a tribunal and later discovers that the evidence is false, the lawyer must take "reasonable remedial measures," which may include disclosure of the falsity to the tribunal.
- If a lawyer knows that a person, even if that person is the lawyer's client, intends to engage, is engaging, or has engaged in a crime or fraud relating to an adjudicative proceeding, the lawyer must take "reasonable remedial measures," which may include disclosure to the tribunal.
- A lawyer's duty of candor to the tribunal continues to the conclusion of the proceeding and trumps the duty of confidentiality of Rule 1.6(DE).
- A lawyer must make a complete disclosure of a "material facts" in an *ex parte* proceeding.

Chapter 29

Fairness

Roadmap

- Rule 3.4(DE)
- Obstructing access to evidence, destroying evidence, or falsifying evidence
- Offering witnesses unlawful incentives to testify
- Disobeying the rules of the tribunal
- Referring to or mentioning irrelevant or inadmissible information
- Statements of "personal knowledge" of factual matters
- Statements of opinion about culpability, credibility, guilt, or justness
- Requesting others not to cooperate

A. An Atmosphere of Fairness

In the context of litigation, the rules of ethics require a lawyer to act with a basic level of fairness with regard to the opposition and the opposition's counsel. This level of fairness is necessary for the justice system to work properly. The thought is that the truth can become known with a fair, competitive search for and presentation of the facts. The rules attempt to create fairness of competition. The rules seek to ensure that the evidence is available and accessible. Only the relevant evidence, not any biased but persuasive opinions, should be a part of the competitive activity to uncover the truth.

B. Obstructing Access to Evidence or Destroying Evidence

1. Generally

For the adversarial process to work properly, both sides in a particular litigation must have equal opportunity to marshal the relevant evidence. Rule

3.4(a)(DE) forbids a lawyer from "unlawfully obstruct[ing] another party's access to evidence." Rule 3.4(a)(DE) also prohibits unlawfully "alter[ing], destroy[ing], or conceal[ing]" anything with "potential evidentiary value." Destruction, or spoliation, of evidence is a crime in most, if not all, jurisdictions. Rule 3.4(a)(DE) makes this unlawful activity also improper for purposes of professional responsibility. In addition, a lawyer may not "counsel or assist" anyone else to take such action.

A lawyer must be careful not to be perceived by the client as directing the client to destroy or conceal evidence. Clint Client might believe that Larry Lawyer is directing Clint to destroy a certain document if Larry comments to Clint, "I really wish that document did not exist; it really hurts our case." Larry must be aware how Clint might perceive his comments.

2. Possession of Physical Evidence

The duty not to obstruct, alter, destroy, or conceal evidence creates some particularly difficult situations for criminal defense lawyers. Perhaps Larry Lawyer's client, Clint, has killed his business partner and has given Larry the gun he used in the crime. Courts seem to agree that Larry may keep the gun for a reasonable period of time to perform appropriate testing if doing so does not alter the evidence. Then Larry must notify the authorities that he has the gun. In the case of *In re Ryder,* 263 F. Supp. 370 (E.D. Va.), *aff'd,* 381 F.2d 713 (4th Cir. 1967), a lawyer was disciplined because he put a weapon used in a bank robbery and money from the robbery in a safe deposit box. A client had given the weapon and the money to the lawyer. By placing the evidence in the safe deposit box, the lawyer impeded the ability of the authorities to access it.

Perhaps a client does not give the lawyer the evidence but tells the lawyer where the evidence can be located. For example, if Clint Client tells Larry Lawyer where to find a robbery victim's wallet, Larry might observe the wallet without moving it. In such a situation, Larry does not alter or destroy the evidence in any way. If, however, Larry moves the wallet, even if he returns it to the original location, he has perhaps destroyed evidence in violation of Rule 3.4(a)(DE).

C. Falsifying Evidence

1. Generally

Rule 3.4(b)(DE) provides that a lawyer must not "falsify evidence" or "counsel or assist a witness to testify falsely." A lawyer usually prepares a witness before that witness testifies in a deposition or at trial. As long as the lawyer does not tell the client to make untrue statements, this practice of witness preparation can be good, competent lawyering. Lawyers usually are careful to tell witnesses repeatedly that they should speak the truth at all times in the proceeding so that there is no misunderstanding. Problems arise if the lawyer indicates to the witness what the witness should say to assist the lawyer in obtaining a good result in the matter. With such coaching, the witness, as well as other reasonable minds, might conclude that the lawyer counseled the witness to testify falsely in violation of Rule 3.4(b)(DE).

2. Unlawful Incentives to Witnesses

Rule 3.4(b)(DE) prohibits a lawyer from offering unlawful incentives to witnesses. In most if not all jurisdictions, a lawyer cannot pay a witness for testimony because there is a fear that the payment may influence the substance of the testimony. Most jurisdictions allow a lawyer to pay a fact witness a reasonable fee for expenses related to serving as a witness. An expert witness can be paid his or her expenses and can also be paid a reasonable fee for the expert's time spent preparing to testify and for the time spent testifying. Most jurisdictions do not allow a witness payment to be contingent on the outcome of the matter or contingent on the content of the testimony. Making a payment to an expert contingent on the outcome of the matter or on the content of the testimony gives the witness an inducement to testify so as to advance the lawyer's position whether or not that testimony is truthful.

3. *Mary Carter* Agreements

Participation in the creation of a particular kind of settlement agreement has been found to violate Rule 3.4(b)(DE). This arrangement is often called a *Mary Carter* agreement. The name comes from the case, *Booth v. Mary Carter Paint Co.,* 202 So. 2d 8 (Fla. App. 1967). In a *Mary Carter* settlement arrangement, a plaintiff settles with less than all of the defendants. A typical setting is a medical malpractice action in which a plaintiff sues several physicians and perhaps a hospital. The plaintiff settles secretly with one or more defendants but does not settle with all of the defendants. The settling defendants agree to pay an amount that ultimately will be reduced if the plaintiff recovers from the remaining defendants. This agreement provides an incentive for the settling defendants to alter their testimony to assist the plaintiff.

In addition to the fact that a lawyer may violate Rule 3.4(b)(DE) by participating in or arranging a *Mary Carter* agreement, many courts also hold such agreements unenforceable because they contradict public policy. The courts find the agreements contrary to public policy because they harm the administration of justice.

4. Prosecutors

Prosecutors do not violate Rule 3.4(b)(DE) when they offer incentives to witnesses to testify. The incentive might be immunity or a reduced sentence offered to a codefendant. Courts generally view such actions by prosecutors as attempts to gain truthful testimony and evidence, not attempts to influence the substance of testimony or other evidence. As a result, these actions are not seen as unethical or otherwise improper.

D. Disobeying an Obligation under the Rules of the Tribunal

1. Obligations under the Rules

Lawyers must obey the rules of the relevant tribunal. The tribunal may sanction any lawyer who does not do this. Rule 3.4(c)(DE) makes clear that such a lawyer behaves improperly and is subject to discipline for not obeying the tribunal's rules. If a lawyer believes that the lawyer need not obey, the rule requires the lawyer to state so to the tribunal. The lawyer cannot simply fail to respond to a court's order to produce documents, for example. The lawyer must tell the tribunal that the lawyer will not obey and state the reason the lawyer believes the order need not be obeyed.

Rule 1.0(m)(DE) defines tribunal as a court or "other body acting in an adjudicative capacity." Rule 1.0(m)(DE) further states that "[a] legislative body, administrative agency or other body acts in an adjudicative capacity when a neutral official, after the presentation of evidence or legal argument by a party or parties, will render a binding legal judgment directly affecting a party's interests in a particular matter."

Perhaps in a civil matter the judge has issued an order requiring Larry Lawyer's client, Clint, to produce certain documents. Larry believes that Clint need not produce the documents that fall within the description in the court's order. Larry believes that the attorney-client privilege protects these documents from disclosure. Larry cannot refuse to produce the documents without also stating that any document responsive to the order is privileged and need not be produced. If Larry were to not produce anything without explanation, the court and the opposition would be misled. They perhaps would think that Larry's client has no documents described in the order. Larry must be forthright.

2. Pretrial Discovery

In the context of pretrial discovery, Rule 3.4(d)(DE) requires a lawyer to refrain from making a "frivolous discovery request." Rule 3.4(d)(DE) does not describe what type of request would be frivolous. Rule 3.1(DE) assists in that, with regard to frivolous claims, it requires any claim to have a basis in fact or law that is nonfrivolous and includes in the definition of nonfrivolous "a good faith argument for an extension, modification or reversal of existing law." One can assume that the same standard applies to discovery requests. *See Chapter 26 Frivolous Positions.* In addition, Rule 3.4(d)(DE) requires a lawyer "to make a reasonably diligent effort to comply" with a discovery request from the opposition. A lawyer must exert such effort only if the discovery request is a "legally proper" one.

E. Referring to Irrelevant or Inadmissible Facts

To maximize the fairness of the judicial system's operation, there are rules of evidence that govern what the tribunal may consider when deciding a matter. To ensure the full effect of these rules of evidence and thus ensure fairness of the proceeding, Rule 3.4(e)(DE) forbids a lawyer at trial from referring to facts that "the lawyer does not reasonably believe" to be relevant or that are not "supported by admissible evidence." This is simply a requirement that lawyers play by the rules of the game, the applicable rules of evidence.

In representing Clint Client in the trial of an action in which Big Corporation claims that Clint has not paid what he owes, Larry, several times over the course of the three-day trial, states that various law enforcement entities have investigated Big Corporation for making fraudulent claims of money due. In reality, no investigations have occurred. Each time Larry makes such a statement, opposing counsel objects and the judge strikes the comment and admonishes the jury to disregard the comment. Larry has acted improperly. While the judge has attempted to minimize the effect of Larry's actions, the repeated comment may affect the jury's consideration of the matter. Larry should be assisting in the quest for truth within the rules established for trial evidence.

Larry should not attempt to subvert the rules he, when being admitted to the bar, agreed to honor.

F. Stating "Personal Knowledge" of Factual Matters or Expressing an Opinion as to Culpability, Credibility, Guilt, or Justness

1. Opinion

Trial lawyers, because of their training and expertise, are very comfortable in a courtroom. There, a lawyer speaks with a voice to which the judge and jury are particularly attuned. When the lawyer speaks, the other actors in the trial listen. Because of this role, it is particularly important that the lawyer not express his or her personal opinion about the matter at hand. The lawyer is, after all, an advocate. The lawyer is not a witness and is not the trier of fact.

If Larry Lawyer, at trial, expresses his opinion about the guilt or innocence his client, Clint, a defendant in a criminal matter, the trier of fact may give Larry's opinion more weight than other, properly admitted evidence. At best, such a statement may confuse the trier of fact as to Larry's role. The trier of fact's job is to evaluate the evidence and reach a conclusion about the ultimate issue of guilt or innocence. The lawyer's opinion on the issue should not substitute for the trier's opinion.

Rule 3.4(e)(DE) provides that a lawyer may not state at trial the lawyer's opinion about the guilt or innocence of a criminal defendant. In addition, Rule 3.4(e)(DE) forbids a lawyer from stating at trial his or her opinion about the credibility of a witness, the culpability of a party in a civil matter, or the justness of a matter. All of these are issues upon which the trier of fact should reach a conclusion untainted by a lawyer's, or anyone else's, opinion.

2. "Personal Knowledge" of Facts

A lawyer should not express his or her "personal knowledge" of factual matters at trial. The lawyer, by expressing "personal knowledge," is, in effect, testifying without being sworn. Such a move confuses the lawyer's role in the proceeding and exposes the trier of fact to information that does not come into the proceeding by way of the proper channels. If the lawyer is a witness, that lawyer should be sworn, should move to the witness box or chair, and testify by way of direct examination and cross examination.

G. Requests Not to Cooperate with Others

A vital part of representing a client in any matter is explaining to the client his or her rights and responsibilities. This is especially true in the litigation context. A lawyer should explain to the client that the client should not provide any information to the opposing party or that party's lawyer without first consulting his or her own lawyer. The lawyer may explain to the client that the client should not cooperate with the opponent other than through the formal procedures of subpoenas and depositions.

These formal procedures are costly and time-consuming, however. In the interest of efficiency and competence, lawyers often seek to talk to witnesses informally. A lawyer may want to investigate the client's case before filing suit. The lawyer wants to be sure the client has a valid claim. The best way to do that may be to confirm the client's story by talking to witnesses or even the potential opposing party.

Perhaps Clint, Larry Lawyer's client, has asked Larry to help him recover for injuries he received in an automobile collision. A truck owned by Lush Landscape Service and driven by an employee, Will Worker, collided with Clint's car. Clint was injured. Lou Lawyer represents Lush Landscape. Lou has interviewed Will. Lou has also interviewed Wanda Witness. Wanda is not affiliated with Lush Landscape in any way. She simply observed the collision. Having heard Will's story and Wanda's story, Lou might want to give his client an advantage by telling Will and Wanda not to talk to Clint or Clint's counsel.

Lou cannot make such a statement to Wanda. Rule 3.4(f)(DE) prohibits a lawyer from requesting that a witness who is not an employee, agent, or relative of the client not to talk with another party. In effect, Lou, by making such a statement, is not only violating Rule 3.4(f)(DE), but also Rule 3.4(a)(DE) in that Lou is obstructing access to evidence.

Lou perhaps could ask Will not to talk with Larry or Clint. Will is an employee of Lush Landscape and Lush Landscape is a party. Will thus falls within the category of persons Lou could ask to not talk with the opposition. Rule 3.4(f)(DE) has another requirement, however. Not only must Will be an employee, agent, or relative of Lou's client, Lush Landscape, but also Lou must reasonably believe that Will would not be "adversely affected" by not talking with Clint or Larry. If Lou believes, reasonably, that Will would not be "adversely affected," Lou could request that Will not talk with Larry and Clint.

Regardless of what Lou tells Wanda or Will, Larry may not be able to talk to them. If Wanda is represented in the matter, Rule 4.2(DE) forbids such contact. If Will is individually represented in the matter, Rule 4.2(DE) forbids such contact. In addition, if Will is a certain type of agent of Lush Landscape, then contact with him is deemed contact with Lush Landscape and so is prohibited by Rule 4.2(DE) because Lou represents Lush Landscape in the matter. See *Chapter 36 Contact with Represented Persons.*

Related Sections of the *Restatement (Third) of the Law Governing Lawyers*

Sections 105, 107, 116, 117, 118, 119, and 120

Checkpoints

- A lawyer may not obstruct another party's access to evidence unlawfully or "counsel or assist" another to do so.
- A lawyer may not "unlawfully alter, destroy or conceal" potential evidence or "counsel or assist" another to do so.
- If a lawyer gains possession of physical evidence, the lawyer must turn over the evidence to the authorities within a reasonable period of time.
- A lawyer must not "falsify evidence" or "counsel or assist" another to do so.
- A lawyer may not provide unlawful incentives to witnesses. A payment to a fact witness, other than a payment of reasonable expenses for testifying, is generally unlawful. A lawyer may compensate an expert witness for the time spent on the matter. Such payments cannot be contingent on the content of the testimony or the result in the matter.
- Arranging *Mary Carter* agreements may be unethical.
- Prosecutors do not act unethically by paying informants or offering witnesses immunity or other favors.
- A lawyer must obey the rules of the tribunal. If a lawyer believes that he or she should not be required to obey, the lawyer must state the refusal openly as well as the reason for the refusal.
- A lawyer must not make "frivolous discovery requests" and should respond to discovery requests appropriately.
- A lawyer must not, at trial, refer to irrelevant or inadmissible facts.
- A lawyer, at trial, must not state an opinion about culpability, credibility, guilt, or justness.
- A lawyer must not state "personal knowledge" of factual matters at trial. A lawyer who is a witness at trial may, in that capacity, state "personal knowledge."

- A lawyer may request a witness to refrain from cooperating with another party to a matter only if the witness is a relative, employee, or other agent of the lawyer's client and the lawyer reasonably believes that not cooperating will not harm that person.

Chapter 30

Impartiality

Roadmap

- Rule 3.5(ID)
- *Ex parte* contact with judges, jurors or other officials during a proceeding
- Contact with jurors after discharge
- Disrupting a proceeding

A. Protecting the Integrity of the Judicial System

Rule 3.5(ID) provides some basic guides designed to protect the integrity of tribunals and the judicial system in general. The rule prohibits improper contact with the judge, jurors, prospective jurors, or other officials involved in the matter.

B. Contact with the Judges or Jurors, Prospective Jurors, or Other Officials

1. Seeking to Improperly Influence

Rule 3.5(a)(ID) makes improper conduct that is already condemned as illegal. The law prohibits activities intended to improperly influence a judge, a juror, a prospective juror, or another official in the judicial system. All jurisdictions have laws prohibiting the offering of bribes to such actors. Any lawyer who attempts to bribe or does bribe a juror, for example, is guilty of a crime. If a lawyer's attempt to influence an actor in the judicial system constitutes a crime, Rule 3.5(a)(ID) makes that conduct improper for purposes of professional responsibility as well.

2. *Ex Parte* Communications During a Proceeding

Rule 3.5(b)(ID) states that a lawyer may not communicate with a judge, a juror, a prospective juror, or any other official in a matter *ex parte* while the proceeding is in progress. The only exception to this rule is that a lawyer may communicate with one of these judicial actors if a law or court order specifically allows the contact. For example, a court may allow *ex parte* communications with the judge or the judge's staff for scheduling matters. Note that judges are generally subject to a prohibition on *ex parte* contact as well. While it is clear that the rule is intended to forbid substantive conversations about the matter at hand and is not aimed at pleasantries, this rule, literally read, forbids a lawyer from saying "Hello" to a juror in the hallway leading to the courtroom. Yet if a lawyer walks by a juror and does not speak at all the juror may have a negative opinion of the lawyer. A better scenario is to avoid the juror entirely if possible.

In *ABA Formal Opinion 14-466(2014),* the ABA Standing Committee on Ethics and Professional Responsibility addressed the question of whether a lawyer's review of a juror's or potential juror's internet presence constitutes improper *ex parte* contact under Rule 3.5(b)(ID). *Opinion 14-466* states that a lawyer's review of the internet presence of such an actor is not improper *ex parte* contact even if the actor receives notice of the review. Rule 3.5(b)(ID) prohibits a lawyer from requesting access to the actor's internet site or making such a request though another.

3. Communications with Jurors or Prospective Jurors after the Court Discharges the Jury

Lawyers often like to talk to jurors after the conclusion of the trial. By talking with jurors, a lawyer can learn about how the jury perceived the lawyer and the lawyer's case. The lawyer can use that information to improve his or her performance in future representations or even in the appeal of the matter at hand.

Rule 3.5(c)(ID) states that generally such contact with jurors or potential jurors is proper. There are limits on this contact, however. First, a lawyer cannot have such contact if a law or court order forbids such. Occasionally, a court may have a standing rule that prohibits such contact unless the court specifically allows it. A lawyer must inform himself or herself of such laws and rules.

Second, a lawyer may not communicate with a juror who has indicated to the lawyer that the juror does not wish to communicate with the lawyer. Any attempt to talk with the juror under these circumstances may be viewed as harassment.

Lastly, a lawyer must conduct himself or herself appropriately in the context of such a communication. Rule 3.5(c)(ID) forbids communication involving "misrepresentation, coercion, duress or harassment."

C. Conduct Done with the Goal of Disrupting a Proceeding

Because a lawyer has a vital role in an adjudicative proceeding, a lawyer must not act in a way that harms the integrity of the proceeding. Rule 3.5(d)(ID) states that a lawyer has acted unethically if the lawyer engages "in conduct intended to disrupt a tribunal." The important qualifier in this rule is the scienter requirement. The lawyer, to violate Rule 3.5(d)(ID), must intend that the conduct disrupt the tribunal. It is not enough that the conduct is, in fact, disruptive.

A lawyer can violate Rule 3.5(d)(ID) by conduct during a deposition as well as conduct in a courtroom. The conduct can be words of a brief or memorandum filed with the court. In the case if *In re Abbott*, 925 A.2d 482 (Del.), *cert. denied sub nom. Abbott v. Office of Disciplinary Counsel of the Supreme Court of Delaware*, 552 U.S. 950 (2007), the Delaware Supreme Court reprimanded a lawyer for violating Rule 3.5(d)(ID). The lawyer filed appellate briefs containing many comments about opposing counsel. In the brief the lawyer commented that opposing counsel had presented a "fictionalized account" of the hearing below and that opposing counsel's arguments were "ridiculous." The lawyer also implied that the appellate tribunal would rule on the basis of bias. In ordering a public reprimand, the Delaware Supreme Court noted that civility and professionalism were integral to fair and just results and that the comment about bias impugned the integrity of the tribunal. Rule 8.2(a)(DE) also protects the integrity of tribunals with regard to statements made about judges. *See Chapter 47 Judicial Candidates and Statements about Judges.*

Related Sections of the *Restatement (Third) of the Law Governing Lawyers*

Sections 113 and 115

Checkpoints

- A lawyer may not act unlawfully to influence a judge, a juror, a prospective juror, or any other official in a proceeding.
- A lawyer may not have *ex parte* contact with a judge, a juror, a prospective juror, or any other official during a proceeding unless a court order or other law permits such contact.
- A lawyer may communicate with jurors and prospective jurors after the court has discharged the jury unless the court or law forbids the practice or the person indicates an unwillingness to communicate with the lawyer. The communication is improper if it constitutes "misrepresentation, coercion, duress or harassment."
- A lawyer may not "engage in conduct intended to disrupt a tribunal."

Chapter 31

Publicity Relating to Trials

Roadmap

- Rule 3.6(DE)
- Rule 3.8(f)(ID)
- Public statements that have a "substantial likelihood of materially prejudicing" a proceeding
- Permissible public statements
- Prosecutors' public statements that have a "substantial likelihood" of increasing the public's condemnation of the accused

A. The Damage Created by Extrajudicial Statements

The justice system is organized so that matters before a court are decided on the basis of evidence properly before the trier of fact. Rules of evidence and procedure govern what is admitted at trial and what the judge and jury consider. If the trier of fact has exposure to other information about the matter to be decided, the proceeding may be tainted.

There is no way to insulate a trier of fact from all information about a matter unless the First Amendment is totally tossed on its head. That, of course, should not happen. A lawyer has free speech rights protected by the First Amendment just as all other citizens do. However, a lawyer is an integral actor in the judicial process. Lawyers should not contribute to a subversion of the system in which lawyers toil.

In an attempt to minimize the flow of information outside of the proceeding, Rule 3.6(DE) specifies the kind of information a lawyer may and may not discuss publicly and extrajudicially. This rule has not been a stranger to controversy. In *Gentile v. State Bar of Nevada*, 501 U.S. 1030 (1991), the United States Supreme Court determined that an earlier Nevada version of this rule was unconstitutionally vague as Nevada had applied that rule to the comments of a Nevada lawyer. Rule 3.6(DE) has been modified in response to the Supreme Court's analysis in *Gentile.*

B. Forbidden Extrajudicial Communications

1. A Prohibition for All Lawyers

Rule 3.6(a)(DE) forbids a lawyer who participates in a matter as part of an investigation or as part of a litigation team from making certain communications outside of the parameters of the proceeding. A lawyer may not make a communication "that the lawyer knows or reasonably should know will ... have a substantial likelihood of materially prejudicing an adjudicative proceeding in the matter" if the communication is destined for public dissemination.

Because the evil is a possible taint of the fact-finder and usually the fact-finder is a jury, the rule prohibits a lawyer from making extrajudicial statements in a situation in which the lawyer "knows or reasonably should know" that the statements will be publicly disseminated. Public dissemination creates the greatest risk of a lawyer's statements having an influence on possible members of the jury in the fact-finding process.

If Larry Lawyer is representing Clint, a suspect in a murder investigation, Larry must be very careful about making comments about the matter to a local newspaper reporter. Larry may have discovered quite a bit of information about the murder victim that paints her in a very unsympathetic light. If Larry discloses the information about the victim in an interview with the reporter, the reporter may publish Larry's comments in the newspaper or on the newspaper's website. Larry's comments could cause potential jurors to form adverse opinions about the victim and, thus, judge the accused less harshly. Larry would have a difficult time arguing that he reasonably should not have known that his comments would be disseminated publicly. Larry would also have a difficult time arguing that he reasonably should not have known that such comments would "have a substantial likelihood of materially prejudicing" any future trial.

2. Potentially Prejudicial Statements

Some lawyers avoid violating Rule 3.6(a)(DE) by making no comments whatsoever. Some lawyers worry that they may not accurately identify the communications the rule prohibits. A comment to the rule helps to limit this uncertainty. The comment identifies the types of statements that "are more likely than not to have a material prejudicial effect."

The comment warns that a lawyer's statements about the identity of a witness or the possible testimony of a witness could have a "material prejudicial effect." In addition, a lawyer's comment about the "character, credibility, reputation or criminal record" of a party or witness is problematic. The trier of fact should evaluate the parties and witnesses on the basis of the proceeding itself, not on the basis of the lawyer's comments in the newspaper or on a website.

A comment warns that if a lawyer is involved in a criminal matter or other proceeding that might result in incarceration, that lawyer should be wary of commenting about the possibility of a guilty plea or expressing an opinion about guilt or innocence. The lawyer in such a situation should also be wary of commenting about "any confession, admission, or statement given by a defendant" or potential defendant. In addition, the lawyer should avoid comments about the lack of a statement from the defendant or potential defendant.

Another type of statement that the comment identifies as potentially problematic is a comment about examinations or tests. These statements include comments about consent or lack of consent to the tests or examinations and also comments about the results of the tests. The comment further warns lawyers not to discuss physical evidence.

Rule 3.4(e)(DE) prohibits a lawyer from alluding at trial to irrelevant or inadmissible evidence. *See Chapter 29 Fairness.* Thus, it is no surprise that the comment to Rule 3.6(DE) identifies evidence "that the lawyer knows or reasonably should know is likely to be inadmissible" as information about which a lawyer should not comment upon publicly if the information would "create a substantial risk of prejudicing an impartial trial."

Finally, the comment notes that a statement that the defendant has been charged with a crime is the sort of statement that would likely have a "material prejudicial effect" on a proceeding unless the lawyer also states that the defendant is presumed innocent until proven guilty and that the charge is simply an accusation.

Before making any statement publicly, a lawyer must consider the nature of the proceeding involved. The level of prejudice arising from a statement might be different in different settings. For example, a statement might have less prejudicial effect if the fact-finder is a judge rather than a jury or if the matter is civil rather than criminal. The setting with the highest danger of prejudice from a lawyer's comments is a criminal jury trial.

3. Imputed Prohibition

Rule 3.6(d)(DE) clarifies that Rule 3.6(DE)'s prohibitions apply to all associated lawyers. If Larry would violate 3.6(a)(DE) by making a comment, no lawyer in Larry's firm may make such a comment either. Rule 1.0(c)(DE) defines a firm as lawyers "in a law partnership, professional corporation, sole proprietorship or other association authorized to practice law" and also includes lawyers working in legal services entity or in a organization's legal department.

4. Prosecutors

The prohibition on trial publicity in Rule 3.6(a)(DE) applies to prosecutors as well as to private practice lawyers. For example, the North Carolina Bar disbarred the prosecutor handling the case of the alleged rape of an exotic dancer by Duke lacrosse team members with violating the North Carolina version of Rule 3.6(a)(DE). The complaint alleged that the prosecutor made numerous public statements about the cooperativeness, character, and credibility of the defendants, the results of tests; the nature of physical evidence; and the prosecutor's personal opinion about the guilt or innocence of the accused men.

Prosecutors have an additional restraint on their speech in the form of Rule 3.8(f)(ID). Rule 3.8(f)(ID) prohibits a prosecutor from making extrajudicial comments "that have a substantial likelihood of heightening public condemnation of the accused." In the North Carolina disbarment order for the Duke lacrosse case prosecutor, the North Carolina Bar found that the prosecutor had violated the North Carolina version of Rule 3.8(f)(ID) by making statements about the indicted individuals such as referring to them as hooligans. *See Chapter 33 The Lawyer as Prosecutor.* Rule 3.8(f)(ID) states that prosecutors may make statements "necessary to inform the public of the nature and extent of the prosecutor's action and that serve a legitimate law enforcement purpose." The North Carolina Bar determined that the prosecutor in the Duke lacrosse case had not abided by this guidance.

A prosecutor has the additional duty of taking "reasonable care" to prevent people associated or employed by the prosecutor from making any statement Rule 3.8(f)(ID) forbids the prosecutor from making. A comment to the rule clarifies that if a prosecutor appropriately cautions the police and other associates with whom the prosecutor works, the prosecutor "ordinarily" has shown "reasonable care."

C. Permitted Extrajudicial Communications

1. Generally Permitted Statements

There are statements that a lawyer is specifically permitted to make. Rule 3.6(b)(DE) provides a safe harbor for certain types of public comments. If a lawyer makes a statement specifically noted in Rule 3.6(b)(DE), the lawyer has not violated the general prohibition of Rule 3.6(a)(DE).

So what kinds of public statements are clearly permitted? A lawyer may state the claim involved in a matter, the offense, the defense, and "the identity of the persons involved" in the matter if no law specifically limits such disclosure. For example, if a juvenile is involved in a criminal matter, a statute may prohibit disclosure of the identity of the juvenile.

A lawyer may state anything that is already a part of a public record and may comment about the scheduling of the matter and the result of any step in the progress of the matter. A lawyer may state that the matter is being investigated. A lawyer may also request assistance regarding locating evidence and information and may make a statement that warns the public or a particular individual of harm if the lawyer has reason to believe that there is a "likelihood of substantial harm to an individual or to the public interest."

2. Specific Statements Permitted in Criminal Matters

If the matter is criminal, the lawyer may make the statements discussed above and in addition may state that an arrest has been made and the time and place of the arrest. The lawyer may state the identity of the accused as well as the accused's residence, the accused's occupation, and the accused's family status. The lawyer may identify the investigating officer or agency and the arresting officer or agency. The lawyer may state how long the investigation has been ongoing as well. The lawyer may make a public statement containing information necessary to assist in the apprehension of the accused if the accused has not yet been apprehended. This portion of Rule 3.6(DE) is of particular importance to prosecutors.

3. A Right to Reply

Sometimes lawyers believe that they need to make public statements to level the playing field. Perhaps in a criminal matter the police or prosecutor has made statements to the press that cast a lawyer's client in an unfortunate light. Rule 3.6(c)(DE) provides that not only may a lawyer make statements otherwise permitted by Rule 3.6(DE), but also the lawyer may make a statement that would otherwise violate Rule 3.6(a)(DE) if "a reasonable lawyer would believe" that the response is needed to lessen "the substantial undue prejudicial effect" created by the statements of others. The lawyer's responsive comment must state only what is "necessary to mitigate" the effects of the earlier statements of others.

Related Sections of the *Restatement (Third) of the Law Governing Lawyers*

Section 109

Checkpoints

- A lawyer involved in a litigation matter or investigation of a litigation matter may not make statements that have a "substantial likelihood of materially prejudicing" the proceeding if the lawyer "knows or reasonably should know" that the statements will be publicly communicated.
- A statement is likely to have a "substantial likelihood of materially prejudicing" a proceeding if the statement is about one of following:
    1. The character of a party, suspect, or witness.
    2. The credibility of a party, suspect, or witness.
    3. The reputation of a party, suspect, or witness.
    4. The criminal record of a party, suspect, or witness.
    5. The identity or testimony expected of a party or witness.
    6. The "performance or results" of tests or examinations.
    7. A person's refusal to agree to an examination or test.
    8. The "identity or nature of physical evidence."
    9. "[I]nformation that the lawyer knows or reasonably should know is likely to be inadmissible" if the disclosure of the information would create a "substantial risk of prejudicing" the proceeding.
- In addition, in a criminal matter or any other matter that could result in incarceration, a statement has a "substantial likelihood of materially prejudicing" a proceeding if the statement is about one the following:
    1. The fact that a person has been charged with a crime unless there is also a statement that the person is presumed innocent until that person is proven guilty and that the charge is simply an accusation.
    2. The possibility of a guilty plea.
    3. The existence of a confession or admission or the substance of a confession or admission.
    4. The existence or the content of a statement by the defendant or suspect.
    5. The fact that the defendant or suspect has not made a statement or has refused to make a statement.

6. The lawyer's opinion about the "guilt or innocence of a defendant or suspect."

- A lawyer may state publicly the following:
  1. Information that is a part of a public record.
  2. Information about whether an investigation is in ongoing.
  3. Information about scheduling.
  4. The result of any part of the proceeding.
  5. The claim.
  6. The offense.
  7. The defense.
  8. The identity of the persons involved if other law does not forbid the disclosure.
  9. A "request for assistance" in obtaining necessary information or evidence.
  10. A "warning of danger" if the lawyer has "reason to believe" that the person involved presents a "likelihood of substantial harm" to a person or the public interest.
- In a criminal matter, a lawyer may also state the following:
  1. The identity of the accused.
  2. The residence of the accused.
  3. The occupation of the accused.
  4. The family status of the accused.
  5. Information necessary to assist in the apprehension of the accused.
  6. The time of the arrest.
  7. The place of arrest.
  8. The fact of arrest.
  9. The identity of the arresting officers or entities.
  10. The identity of the investigating officers or entities.
- If a lawyer is prohibited from making a certain statement, no lawyer in the first lawyer's firm may make such a statement.
- Even if a lawyer would ordinarily be prohibited from making a certain public statement, the lawyer may make the statement if the lawyer reasonably believes that the statement is necessary to counteract the "substantial undue prejudicial effect" of public statements by others not affiliated with the lawyer's client.
- A prosecutor must abide by Rule 3.6(DE) and Rule 3.8(f)(ID).
- A prosecutor must limit public comments to those necessary to explain the prosecutor's actions and that further law enforcement purposes.

- A prosecutor must not make a public statement that has a "substantial likelihood" of increasing the "public condemnation" of the accused.
- A prosecutor must use "reasonable care" to ensure that associates and employees of the prosecutor do not make statements publicly that the prosecutor could not make.

Chapter 32

The Lawyer Witness

Roadmap

- Rule 3.7(DE)
- Serving as an advocate at trial if the lawyer is a "necessary witness" in the matter
- Exceptions to the prohibition
- Conflicts of interest in the lawyer witness situation

A. The Prohibition Generally

May a lawyer serve as a witness in a matter in which the lawyer is also representing a client? A typical situation in which this question might arise is when the client is in a contractual dispute and the lawyer represented the client in the contract negotiation and formation. The lawyer is a possible witness as to what occurred in those negotiations. For example, assume that Lisa Lawyer represented Big Corporation in the negotiation and formation of a supply contract with Supplies Forever, Inc. Supplies Forever, Inc. later sues Big Corporation claiming that Big terminated the supply contract improperly. Lisa may be a witness regarding the negotiation of the contract terms, especially the termination provisions. Yet Big would like Lisa to represent it in the contract dispute litigation. May Lisa wear two hats—that of witness and that of lawyer in the matter?

Rule 3.7(DE) addresses the issue of the lawyer witness. Rule 3.7(a)(DE) states that a lawyer may not serve as a "necessary witness" and as an "advocate at a trial" unless the lawyer's testimony "relates to an uncontested issue," the testimony relates to the legal fee in the matter, or the client would suffer a "substantial hardship" by being deprived of the lawyer's services. Rather than robbing the fact-finder of the lawyer's testimony, the rule allows the lawyer's testimony but disapproves of the lawyer serving as the client's advocate at trial not only when the lawyer would certainly be a "necessary witness" but also when the lawyer "likely" will be a "necessary witness." The rule contains no provision for consent to dual roles. The prohibition applies only to the trial representation, not representation outside of the proceeding.

Unlike most rules of professional responsibility, this rule is given effect more often by courts than by discipline authorities. While a lawyer occasionally is disciplined in hindsight for violating this rule, more often courts use the rule as a basis for disqualifying lawyers in the midst of proceedings. This means that Lisa Lawyer must evaluate carefully whether the situation of representing Big Corporation in the contract dispute has the potential of violating Rule 3.7(DE). Even if Lisa decides that she may continue the representation, an opposing party's motion to disqualify or the court's *sua sponte* move to disqualify may require Lisa to deal with the issue formally.

B. The Rationale

The rationale for this rule of disqualification is that having a lawyer serve as both advocate and witness may confuse the finders of fact. As a comment to Rule 3.7(DE) states, "It may not be clear whether a statement by an advocate-witness should be taken as proof or as an analysis of the proof." If Lisa Lawyer serves as both a witness and an advocate, members of the jury hearing the matter might come to trust her as an advocate and then allow that trust to influence their opinion of Lisa's credibility as a witness. Perhaps the jury would not analyze Lisa's testimony as critically as it would other witnesses. Or perhaps some members of the jury develop a dislike and distrust of Lisa in her advocacy role. When she testifies, those members would tend to discount Lisa's testimony without any independent analysis of credibility as a witness. There is also the danger that the lawyer will become confused as well.

To the extent the jury's confusion causes a discrediting of the lawyer's testimony or a weakening of the lawyer's advocacy role, the lawyer's client suffers. To the extent that the confusion causes the lawyer's testimony or advocacy to have stronger impact than would otherwise occur, the opposing party suffers. In general, however, the situation has a potential negative impact on the judicial system itself in that the lawyer's multiple roles may make the proceeding seem less than impartial. In *Cottonwood Estates, Inc. v. Paradise Builders, Inc.*, 624 P.2d 296 (Ariz. 1981), the Arizona Supreme Court commented about this issue, stating that a lawyer witness "disrupts the normal balance of judicial machinery." *Id.* at 300.

C. Parameters of the Prohibition

1. The Prohibition Applies If the Lawyer is "Likely to Be a Necessary Witness"

Rule 3.7(a)(DE) provides that a lawyer may not serve as an advocate at trial if the lawyer is "likely to be a necessary witness." Courts have interpreted this requirement of necessity to mean that the lawyer's testimony "is relevant, material, not merely cumulative, and unobtainable elsewhere." *Merrill Lynch Business Financial. Services, Inc. v. Nudell,* 239 F. Supp. 2d 1170, 1173 (D. Colo. 2003).

If Lisa seeks to represent Big Corporation in the litigation against Supplies Forever, Inc. stemming from the supply contract dispute, Lisa may represent Big unless Lisa is "likely to be a necessary witness." If Lisa is a witness to the negotiations leading to the formation of the contract but has no information about the negotiation about the contract termination terms, then Lisa's testimony would likely be irrelevant or at least not material. Thus, Lisa would not "likely" be a "necessary witness" and Rule 3.7(DE) would not demand Lisa's disqualification as an advocate. Perhaps Lisa has information about the negotiation of the contract termination terms but several other witnesses are available who can testify about the same facts. Then Lisa's testimony would be cumulative or at least available otherwise. Lisa would not "likely" be a "necessary witness" and Rule 3.7(DE) would not demand Lisa's disqualification.

The requirement that the lawyer must "likely" be a "necessary witness" prevents strategic disqualification maneuvers. If a lawyer were disqualified by being a "likely" witness, the opposing party might name the lawyer as a witness as a way of strategically depriving the lawyer's client of counsel of choice. The requirement that the lawyer be proved to be "necessary" is some insurance against such a move.

Some courts do more. Some courts, when an opposing party claims that a lawyer must be disqualified as counsel because that lawyer will be a witness, require a clear showing that the lawyer is a "necessary witness" and that the testimony of the lawyer may be prejudicial to the lawyer's client. For example, in *Sargent County Bank v. Wentworth,* 500 N.W.2d 862 (N.D. 1993), the North Dakota Supreme Court required "a showing that the attorney will give evidence material to the determination of the issues being litigated, that the evidence is unobtainable elsewhere, and that the testimony is or may be prejudicial to the testifying attorney's client." *Id.* at 871. The requirement of a showing of prejudice reduces the situations in which the rule of lawyer witness disqualification can be used strategically by the opposition. If Lisa's representation of Big Corporation in the supply contract matter against Supplies Forever, Inc. occurs in a jurisdiction or court requiring a prejudice showing, Supplies Forever, Inc., cannot have Lisa disqualified on the basis of being a witness unless it can prove that Lisa's testimony is relevant, material, not cumulative, not available otherwise, and prejudicial to Big Corporation, Lisa's client. Such a burden would be difficult for Supplies Forever, Inc. to shoulder.

2. The Prohibition Applies to Representation "at a Trial"

Rule 3.7(a)(DE) prohibits a witness at trial from also being an advocate at that trial. Many courts take this statement literally and allow lawyers who will be witnesses to participate as counsel in pretrial activities and in other out-of-court ways. As the court stated in *Main Events Productions, LLC v. Lacy*, 220 F. Supp. 2d 353 (D.N.J. 2002):

> The Rule is designed to prevent a situation in which at trial a lawyer acts as an attorney and as a witness, creating the danger that the fact finder (particularly if it is a jury) may confuse what is testimony and what is argument, and otherwise creating an unseemly appearance at trial. Limiting the disqualification to advocacy at trial achieves these objectives and at the same time respects a client's right to be represented generally by an attorney of his choice.

Id. at 357. If lawyer participation in pretrial or other out-of-court activities would reveal the dual role, courts may not allow the lawyer to participate in those activities.

If Lisa Lawyer is a "necessary witness" in the litigation involving Supplies Forever, Inc.'s claim that Big Corporation improperly terminated a supply contract, Lisa cannot advocate for Big "at a trial." Since the goal of the rule is to minimize role confusion for the trier of fact, many courts have interpreted this rule to mean that Lisa can assist in the representation of Big on the matter as long as Lisa does nothing to place herself in front of the trier of fact in the role of advocate as well as witness. Lisa can do legal research and generally handle the representation of Big that takes place out of the courtroom and that will not eventually end up in the courtroom. Lisa should refrain from participating in a deposition that might be presented to the fact-finder because then the deposition would expose the finder to Lisa in two roles. The possibility of confusion would increase.

D. Exceptions

1. Testimony about an "Uncontested Issue"

Occasionally, a lawyer may be asked to testify about a matter that is not disputed. Perhaps Lisa Lawyer's testimony is necessary to establish when certain contract negotiations took place involving her client, Big Corporation. Lisa keeps precise records and can establish the dates and times involved. No one else involved in the matter can establish the dates and times with precision but no one disputes that all the negotiations took place when Lisa says they did. Rule 3.7(a)(1)(DE) permits Lisa to represent Big at trial and also be a witness as to the dates and times of the negotiations. As a comment to Rule 3.7(DE) states regarding testimony about undisputed facts, "the ambiguities in the dual role are purely theoretical."

2. Testimony about the "Nature and Value of Legal Services" in a Matter

In some matters, a lawyer may be awarded legal fees by the court if the lawyer's client is victorious. In order to establish the correct fee to award, the court must hear testimony from the lawyer who toiled on the victorious case. The lawyer's testimony generally involves an accounting of tasks done, time spent, expenses incurred, and the lawyer's usual billing rate. The testimony usually occurs after the lawyer's client has already been successful on the merits. Rule 3.7(a)(2)(DE) allows the lawyer who has handled the principal matter to testify about the collateral fee issue. The rationale for the exception is that the fee issue is a matter for the judge, not a jury, and a judge is not likely to be confounded by the lawyer switching roles for this solitary purpose, especially since the judge has been a witness to the services about which the lawyer is testifying. Requiring a second lawyer for this last stage creates significant costs with little, if any, added benefit.

3. Disqualification of the Lawyer Creates a "Substantial Hardship" for the Lawyer's Client

Even if the lawyer is a "necessary witness," Rule 3.7(a)(3)(DE) provides that the lawyer can serve as the client's advocate at trial if disqualifying the lawyer would "work substantial hardship on the client." As a comment to Rule 3.7(DE) points out, determining whether the client will suffer "substantial hardship" requires balancing the interests of the opposing party, the judicial system, and the client.

Proving "substantial hardship" is difficult, especially since Rule 3.7(b)(DE) provides that another lawyer from the lawyer witness's firm can replace the lawyer witness in the role of advocate. Thus, disruption to the representation can be minimized. The *Restatement (Third) of the Law Governing Lawyers* in section 108, Comment h (2000), attempts to shed light on the definition of "substantial hardship" as follows:

> Relevant factors include the length of time the lawyer has represented the client, the complexity of the issues, the client's economic resources, the lawyer's care in attempting to anticipate or avoid the necessity of testifying, the extent of harm to the lawyer's client and opposing parties from the blending of the roles of advocate and witness, additional expense that disqualification would entail, and the effect of delay upon the interests of the parties and the tribunal.

If a lawyer's client could foresee that the lawyer would be a "necessary witness," a court is less likely to recognize "substantial hardship" because the client perhaps could have avoided some of the hardship by replacing the lawyer earlier. On the other hand, if a lawyer has a body of knowledge of the matter that cannot be recreated easily in another and the client and lawyer have an exceptional bond of trust, perhaps disqualification of the lawyer could amount to "substantial hardship."

In Lisa Lawyer's representation of Big Corporation regarding the supply contract dispute, Lisa might argue that the court should not disqualify her because to do so would cause Big "substantial hardship." Lisa might argue that she has superior knowledge of the matter because she was intimately involved in the contract negotiation process. She might argue that no other lawyer could duplicate that knowledge. In addition, Lisa might argue that she has long worked with Big on contract matters and thus has a broad understanding of Big's business and contracting style. Lisa might argue that this lengthy relationship is one of great trust such that Big should not be robbed of her counsel of choice. Finally, Lisa might argue that any injury to the opposing party or to the judicial system would be minimal.

E. The Disqualification Is Not Imputed

Any hardship potentially created by the disqualification provision of Rule 3.7(DE) is, perhaps, less because the lawyer's disqualification is not imputed to other lawyers in the disqualified lawyer's firm. Rule 3.7(b)(DE) clarifies that a lawyer may be an advocate in a matter even if a witness is associated professionally with the advocate. If Lisa Lawyer knows that she may not act as an advocate at trial for Big Corporation because Lisa will be a "necessary witness," Lisa can minimize the disruption in the representation of Big by having Lisa's partner, Lena, represent Big in the trial of the matter. Lisa can assist, in many jurisdictions, with out-of-court aspects of the litigation.

F. Conflicts of Interest Inherent in Some Lawyer Witness Settings

Occasionally, the situation may be more complicated. Assume that Lisa may not represent Big Corporation in the matter because of Rule 3.7(DE). If Lisa is unable to represent Big in the matter because of conflicts of interest under Rules 1.7(DE) or 1.9(DE) regardless of whether Rule 3.7(DE) applied, Lisa's partner or associate cannot act as an advocate in the matter in which Lisa is a witness. The conflicts established by Rules 1.7(DE) or 1.9(DE) are imputed via Rule 1.10(ID) to all lawyers in a firm. All of the lawyer's in Lisa's firm are disqualified. *See Chapter 18 Conflicts and Current Clients* and *Chapter 19 Conflicts and Former Clients.*

When would a lawyer have a Rule 1.7(DE) or Rule 1.9(DE) conflict of interest in a lawyer witness setting? Typically, a lawyer would have such a conflict if the lawyer's testimony would be contrary to the interests of the client. Again, assume that Lisa represented Big Corporation in negotiations relating to a supply contract. Big Corporation later terminated the supply contract and is involved in a dispute about whether Big terminated the contract properly. Assume that Lisa is a "necessary witness" and the situation does not fit within any exception to Rule 3.7(DE). The rule dictates that Lisa may not represent Big in the contract dispute trial. If Lisa knows that her testimony as a witness in the contract dispute litigation will contradict Big's position, Lisa also probably has a conflict of interest under Rule 1.7(DE). Lisa wants to testify truthfully yet she knows that doing so harms her client. This Rule 1.7(DE) conflict would then be imputed to other lawyers associated with Lisa so that none of them could represent Big Corporation in the contract dispute. Even if Rule 3.7(DE) permitted Lisa to serve as a witness and also as Big's counsel at trial, Rule 1.7(DE) or Rule 1.9(DE) could block Lisa's representation of Big if Lisa's testimony might contradict Big's position.

Big Corporation might be able to consent to such a conflict, subject to the constraints of Rules 1.7(DE) and 1.9(DE), but such consent obviously would not be likely. Such consent must be informed and "confirmed in writing." Rule 1.0(e)(DE) defines "informed consent" as "the agreement by a person to a proposed course of conduct after the lawyer has communicated adequate information and explanation about the material risks of and reasonably available alternatives to the proposed course of conduct." The requirement that the consent be "confirmed in writing" means, as explained by Rule 1.0(b)(DE), that the client must give consent in writing or the lawyer must prepare a writing confirming the client's oral consent and must send the writing to the client promptly, at the very least within a reasonable time of the oral consent. A writing, as defined by Rule 1.0(n)(DE), is "a tangible or electronic record of a communication or representation, including handwriting, typewriting, printing, photostating, photography, audio or videorecording, and electronic communications."

A lawyer's role as a witness also could create a Rule 1.7(DE) conflict of interest for the lawyer's partner who steps in to handle the representation at trial. If Lisa must be a witness and Lisa's partner, Lena, handles the matter at trial, Lena may be torn between his desire to help her client and her desire to not injure her partner. If the conflict is significant, Rule 1.7(DE) may prohibit Lena's representation of Big Corporation. *See Chapter 18 Conflicts and Current Clients.*

Related Sections of the *Restatement (Third) of the Law Governing Lawyers*

Section 108

Checkpoints

- A lawyer may not represent a client at trial if the lawyer is "likely" a "necessary witness" in the matter unless
    1. the lawyer is a witness regarding "uncontested issues,"
    2. the lawyer is a witness regarding the legal fees in the matter, or
    3. depriving the client of the lawyer's services at trial causes the client "substantial hardship."
- The disqualification demanded by this rule is not imputed to other lawyers in the lawyer's firm.
- If the lawyer witness cannot serve as the client's advocate at trial because to do so would violate the general conflict of interest rules, Rule 1.7(DE) and Rule 1.9(DE), the conflict is imputed to all other lawyers in the firm of the lawyer witness.

Chapter 33

The Lawyer as Prosecutor

Roadmap

- Rule 3.8(ID)
- Prosecuting without probable cause
- Protecting the constitutional rights of the accused
- Pretrial rights
- Exculpatory evidence
- Obtaining a subpoena for a lawyer
- Public statements harmful to the accused
- Post-conviction responsibilities

A. Prosecutors are Special

When a lawyer is a prosecutor in a criminal matter, the lawyer has duties beyond those of a lawyer in a civil context or those of defense counsel in a criminal context. As a comment to Rule 3.8(ID) states, "A prosecutor has the responsibility of a minister of justice and not simply that of an advocate." As a "minister of justice," the prosecutor has a duty to protect vital constitutional rights of the accused, a duty to ensure that the accused enjoys the benefits the justice system provides, and a duty to ensure that wrongful convictions do not occur.

B. Protection of the Basic Rights of the Accused

1. No Prosecution of a Charge without Probable Cause

Rule 3.8(ID) contains four provisions that protect very basic rights of the accused. First, Rule 3.8(a)(ID) provides that a lawyer serving as a prosecutor may not pursue a charge if the lawyer knows that probable cause is lacking. This rule recognizes the incredible power the system places in the hands of the prosecutor at the charging stage and seeks to place some additional limits on that power. Prosecutors, after all, are integral actors in the decision to charge a person with a crime as well as which crime to charge. Prosecutors are the presenters of the matter to the grand jury as well. Thus, while other lawyers have a duty not to pursue frivolous positions, a prosecutor has the added duty to not pursue a charge if the prosecutor knows that probable cause is lacking. *See Chapter 26 Frivolous Positions.*

According to Rule 1.0(f)(DE), a prosecutor knows something if he or she has "actual knowledge" although knowledge can result from inference from facts.

2. Protection of the Constitutional Right to Counsel

The Sixth Amendment to the United States Constitution states that an accused has the right "to have Assistance of Counsel for his defence." Rule 3.8(b)(ID) bolsters this right by requiring a prosecutor to "make reasonable efforts to assure" that the accused is told of the right to counsel. In addition, the prosecutor must "make reasonable efforts to assure" that the accused is given "reasonable opportunity" to arrange representation by a lawyer and is told the procedure for doing so.

3. Protection of Pretrial Rights

A prosecutor must not seek a waiver of pretrial rights from an accused person who is unrepresented. Rule 3.8(c)(ID) states this prohibition. In particular, the rule mentions the accused's right to a preliminary hearing. At the preliminary hearing, the accused may test whether there is probable cause to charge the accused with the crime. Thus, this limitation on prosecutorial conduct seeks to protect the accused's right to explore formally the existence of probable cause.

While the rule states that a prosecutor must not seek waiver of "important pretrial rights" from an "unrepresented accused," an accused who decides to proceed *pro se* is not considered unrepresented. An accused person is always free to waive rights voluntarily.

4. Exculpatory Evidence Disclosure

The United States Supreme Court established in *Brady v. Maryland*, 373 U.S. 83 (1963), that a prosecutor must provide to the accused any evidence favorable to the accused and material to the issue of guilt or to punishment. *Brady* established that a suppression of such information when it is demanded is a violation of due process. Later, cases established that the prosecutor must disclose such information even absent a request for it, *United States v. Agurs*, 427 U.S. 97 (1976), and that a prosecutor has a duty to learn whatever others acting for the government in the matter know so that the prosecutor may make proper disclosure, *Kyles v. Whitley*, 514 U.S. 419 (1995). As the United States Supreme Court stated in *Brady v. Maryland,* 373 U.S. 83, 87 (1963), "Society wins not only when the guilty are convicted but when criminal trials are fair; our system of the administration of justice suffers when any accused is treated unfairly."

Rule 3.8(d)(ID) provides a professional responsibility rule to support the constitutional requirement of disclosure of exculpatory information. Rule 3.8(d)(ID) requires a prosecutor to make "timely disclosure" of any information the prosecutor knows that "tends to negate the guilt of the accused or mitigates the offense." With regard to the punishment of the accused, the prosecutor must disclose any "mitigating information" the prosecutor knows that is not subject to privilege. A prosecutor must disclose this information relevant to sentencing to the accused and to the tribunal. The prosecutor need not make such disclosures if the tribunal issues a protective order precluding the disclosure.

If Larry is a prosecutor in a rape case and the laboratory reports to Larry that no DNA of the indicted individual has been found on the alleged victim, Larry must disclose this information to the accused because it is clearly exculpatory. In addition, if the lab reports to Larry that it found DNA on the accuser but that the DNA belongs to an unidentified male, Larry must disclose this as well. Such evidence not only tends to show that the accused did not commit the crime, but it also shows that if a crime was committed, it was committed by someone else.

C. Subpoenas for Lawyers

In an effort to protect against unnecessary intrusion into the attorney-client relationship, Rule 3.8(e)(ID) limits the circumstances in which prosecutors may subpoena lawyers. The limitations apply to a grand jury proceeding or another criminal proceeding with regard to a present or past client. In such a circumstance, a prosecutor may subpoena a lawyer only if the prosecutor "reasonably believes"

1. that no privilege applies,
2. that the evidence the prosecutor seeks is "essential" to the success of the investigation or prosecution, and
3. that the prosecutor has no other "feasible alternative" avenue to obtaining the evidence sought by the subpoena.

D. Public Statements of Prosecutors

Prosecutors, like all other lawyers, must follow Rule 3.6(DE) with regard to making extrajudicial statements. In addition, Rule 3.8(f)(ID) adds to the restraint on prosecutors' statements by prohibiting statements that might increase the public's scorn of the accused. This added restraint reflects the special role of prosecutors in the justice system. Prosecutors may make public statements that "serve a legitimate law enforcement purpose" and that "inform the public of the nature and extent of the prosecutor's action." *See Chapter 31 Publicity Relating to Trials.*

A prosecutor must not only take care with his or her own statements but must also use "reasonable care" to ensure that all other persons working with the prosecutor on a matter do not make statements that the prosecutor could not properly make. A comment clarifies that if a prosecutor warns all relevant persons of the limits of proper statements, the prosecutor will have exercised "reasonable care."

E. Post-Conviction Responsibilities of Prosecutors

1. "New, Credible and Material Evidence Creating a Reasonable Likelihood that a Convicted Defendant Did Not Commit" the Offense

a. Conviction Did Not Occur in Prosecutor's Jurisdiction

A prosecutor must always seek justice. A conviction, if in error, is not a successful result for a prosecutor.

If a prosecutor comes to know of "new, credible and material evidence" which creates a "reasonable likelihood" that a person convicted of an offense did not commit that offense, and the conviction did not occur in the prosecutor's jurisdiction, the prosecutor must "promptly" reveal the evidence to "an appropriate court or authority." That authority might be the chief prosecutor in the convicting jurisdiction.

Rule 1.0(f)(DE), notes that knowledge "denotes actual knowledge" but that knowledge "may be inferred from circumstances."

b. Conviction Occurred in Prosecutor's Jurisdiction

If the conviction occurred in the prosecutor's jurisdiction, the prosecutor not only must "promptly" reveal the evidence to "an appropriate court or authority," but must also "promptly" reveal the information to the defendant through the defendant's counsel. If the defendant does not have counsel, the prosecutor should request the court to appoint counsel so that the defendant can act upon the evidence. The prosecutor may delay this disclosure only if the court orders a delay.

In addition, the prosecutor must investigate or "make reasonable efforts" to have an investigation take place to evaluate the defendant's guilt with regard to the offense of which the defendant was convicted.

2. "Clear and Convincing Evidence Establishing" a Defendant Did Not Commit the Offense

If a prosecutor knows of "clear and convincing evidence establishing" that a defendant did not commit the offense of which the defendant was convicted and if that conviction occurred in the prosecutor's jurisdiction, the prosecutor has the affirmative duty to remedy the conviction. The comment to the rule notes that "[n]ecessary steps may include" the following:

1. Notifying the defendant of the evidence.
2. Asking the court to appoint counsel for the defendant if defendant is unrepresented.
3. "[W]here appropriate notifying the court that the prosecutor has knowledge that the defendant did not commit the offense of which the defendant was convicted."

Related Sections of the *Restatement (Third) of the Law Governing Lawyers*

Sections 97 and 109

Checkpoints

- Prosecutors have duties other lawyers do not have as a result of the special role as a "minister of justice" that prosecutors play in the justice system.
- A prosecutor must not prosecute a charge if the prosecutor knows that probable cause is lacking.

- A prosecutor must use "reasonable efforts" to ensure that the accused is told about the right to counsel, and that the accused has a "reasonable opportunity" to exercise the right to counsel.
- A prosecutor must not attempt to obtain waivers of "important pretrial rights" of an "unrepresented accused."
- A prosecutor must disclose to the accused in a "timely" manner all information the prosecutor knows that "tends to negate the guilt" or "mitigates the offense."
- With regard to sentencing, a prosecutor must disclose to the accused and the court in a timely manner all "mitigating information" not protected by a privilege. A prosecutor need not disclose exculpatory information if the tribunal issues a protective order covering the information.
- A prosecutor must not seek a subpoena for a lawyer regarding a grand jury or other criminal matter unless the prosecutor "reasonably believes" that
    1. the information the prosecutor seeks is not privileged,
    2. the information sought is "essential" to success in the investigation or prosecution, and
    3. the prosecutor has no "feasible alternative."
- A prosecutor must not make extrajudicial statements that have a "substantial likelihood" of increasing the "public condemnation of the accused" and must otherwise abide by Rule 3.6(DE), the rule which sets forth guidance for public comments for all lawyers.
- A prosecutor must use "reasonable care" to assure that everyone assisting the prosecutor makes no public statement that would violate Rule 3.8(ID) or 3.6(DE) if made by the prosecutor.
- A prosecutor who knows of "new, credible and material evidence" which creates a "reasonable likelihood" that a person convicted of an offense in a jurisdiction other than that of the prosecutor did not commit that offense must "promptly" reveal the evidence to "an appropriate court or authority."
- A prosecutor who knows of "new, credible and material evidence" which creates a "reasonable likelihood" that a person convicted of an offense in the prosecutor's jurisdiction did not commit that offense, must do the following:
    1. "Promptly" reveal the evidence to "an appropriate court or authority."
    2. "Promptly" reveal the information to the defendant through the defendant's counsel unless the court orders a delay.
    3. If the defendant does not have counsel, request the court to appoint counsel so that the defendant can act upon the evidence.
    4. Investigate or "make reasonable efforts" to have an investigation take place to evaluate the defendant's guilt with regard to the offense of which the defendant was convicted.

- If a prosecutor knows of "clear and convincing evidence establishing" that a defendant did not commit the offense of which the defendant was convicted and if that conviction occurred in the prosecutor's jurisdiction, the prosecutor has the affirmative duty to remedy the conviction. The comment to the rule notes that "[n]ecessary steps may include" the following:
    1. Notifying the defendant of the evidence.
    2. Asking the court to appoint counsel for the defendant if defendant is unrepresented.
    3. "[W]here appropriate notifying the court that the prosecutor has knowledge that the defendant did not commit the offense of which the defendant was convicted."

Chapter 34

Duties in Nonadjudicative Proceedings

Roadmap

- Rule 3.9(DE)
- Disclosure of representative capacity
- Conduct in nonadjudicative proceedings

A. Special Expectations of Lawyers

1. Generally

Nonlawyers as well as lawyers may appear in nonadjudicative proceedings before legislative bodies or administrative agencies. Unlike the situation of an appearance before a tribunal, a lawyer has no monopoly on appearing in a nonadjudicative proceeding. When lawyers appear in nonadjudicative proceedings in a representative capacity, however, lawyers have duties above and beyond those required of nonlawyers or even lawyers appearing in a nonrepresentational capacity. Rule 3.9(DE) states these duties.

2. Disclosure of Representative Capacity

If a lawyer is appearing in a nonadjudicative proceeding before a legislative or administrative agency as part of the representation of a client, that lawyer must disclose the representational capacity of the appearance. The lawyer does not have to disclose the identity of the client, although generally the identity of a client is not privileged. The lawyer must, however, disclose that the lawyer appears in the proceeding in a representational capacity.

3. Abiding by Other Specific Rules

When representing a client in a nonadjudicative capacity before a legislative entity or an administrative agency, a lawyer must abide by

1. Rule 3.3(a)(DE), Rule 3.3(b)(DE), and Rule 3.3(c)(DE);
2. Rule 3.4(a)(DE), Rule 3.4(b)(DE), and Rule 3.4(c)(DE); and
3. Rule 3.5(ID).

To abide by Rule 3.3(a)(DE), Rule 3.3(b)(DE), and Rule 3.3(c)(DE), a lawyer must not knowingly

1. state facts falsely;
2. state the law falsely;
3. "fail to correct a false statement of material fact or law" that the lawyer earlier made to the entity;
4. fail to tell the entity about legal authority known to be "directly adverse" to the position of the lawyer's client and from the controlling jurisdiction;
5. offer false evidence;
6. fail to take "reasonable remedial measures" to correct the situation when the lawyer discovers that the lawyer, the client of the lawyer, or a witness called by the lawyer has presented false evidence; or
7. fail to take "reasonable remedial measures" if the lawyer knows that "a person intends to engage, is engaging or has engaged" in conduct that is criminal or fraudulent and that is related to the proceeding.

The duties continue to the end of the proceeding. The disclosures are required even if the information is protected by the duty of confidentiality of Rule 1.6(DE). *See Chapter 28 Honesty and Candor.* Given the general and pervasive duty the rules, such as Rule 8.4(c)(DE), place on lawyers to act honestly and candidly in all matters, requiring lawyers to be honest and candid in the setting of a nonadjudicative proceeding is consistent.

To abide by Rule 3.4(a)(DE), Rule 3.4(b)(DE), and Rule 3.4(c)(DE), a lawyer must not

1. "unlawfully obstruct another party's access to evidence,"
2. unlawfully conceal "a document or other material" with "potential evidentiary value,"
3. unlawfully alter or destroy "a document or other material" with "potential evidentiary value,"

4. "counsel or assist" another in obstructing access to evidence or altering, destroying or concealing "a document or other material" with "potential evidentiary value,"
5. "falsify evidence,"
6. "counsel or assist" a witness to give false testimony,
7. offer an unlawful incentive to a witness, or
8. "knowingly disobey an obligation under the rules" of the entity without openly stating that the lawyer bases the action on the belief that the lawyer has no obligation.

See Chapter 29 Fairness.

Rule 3.5(ID) requires that a lawyer not

1. unlawfully "seek to influence a judge, juror, prospective juror or other official";
2. have *ex parte* contact during a proceeding with a judge, juror, potential juror, or other official unless authorized to have such contact by law or court order;
3. have *ex parte* contact with a juror or prospective juror after the jury is discharged if such contact is unlawful or the court has prohibited it, or the juror clarifies that he or she does not want contact with the lawyer, or the lawyer, in such a communication, engages in "misrepresentation, coercion, duress or harassment"; or
4. "engage in conduct intended to disrupt a tribunal."

See Chapter 30 Impartiality.

B. What is a Nonadjudicative Proceeding?

A comment to the rule clarifies when the duties of Rule 3.9(DE) apply. The comment notes that the duties apply only when the lawyer appears in a representational capacity in an official hearing before a legislative body or government agency. The duties do not apply unless the proceeding is one in which the lawyer presents evidence or makes an argument. Representation of a client in a negotiation, in a bilateral transaction, in applying for a license or privilege, in abiding by general reporting requirements, or in participating in an examination or an investigation is not participation in a nonadjudicative proceeding.

Assume that Big Bank, Larry Lawyer's client, has asked Larry to assist it in responding to various requests for information from the government agency charged with monitoring Big Bank. The government entity is conducting a routine investigation of Big Bank's commercial loan practices. Larry, in assisting Big Bank in the investigation, is acting in a representational capacity but the proceeding is not the type to which the duties of Rule 3.3(DE), Rule 3.4(DE), and Rule 3.5(ID), as specified in Rule 3.9(DE), apply. Rather, the comment notes that Larry's conduct must comply with Rules 4.1(DE), Rule 4.2(DE), Rule 4.3(DE), and Rule 4.4(DE). The situation in which Larry works with regard to the investigation is not significantly similar to a proceeding before a tribunal, and so the duties of lawyers appearing before tribunals do not apply to the investigation situation.

Related Sections of the *Restatement (Third) of the Law Governing Lawyers*

Section 104

Checkpoints

- A lawyer must disclose that he or she is appearing in a representative capacity when appearing before a legislative or administrative body in a nonadjudicative proceeding if the lawyer in fact is appearing in representation of a client.
- A lawyer appearing in such a capacity must abide by
    1. Rule 3.3(a)(DE), Rule 3.3(b)(DE), and Rule 3.3(c)(DE);
    2. Rule 3.4(a)(DE), Rule 3.4(b)(DE), and Rule 3.4(c)(DE); and
    3. Rule 3.5(ID).
- A nonadjudicative proceeding to which Rule 3.9(DE) applies is an official hearing before a legislative body or government agency. Rule 3.9(DE) applies if in this hearing the lawyer presents evidence or makes an argument.

Section VIII
Dealing with Nonclients

Chapter 35

Truthfulness to Third Parties

Roadmap

- Rule 4.1(DE)
- Knowingly making "a false statement of material fact or law to a third person"
- Disclosure of a "material fact" to a third party to avoid assisting a client's crime or fraud

A. The General Duty of Honesty

Rule 4.1(DE) is one of the many rules emphasizing the importance of honesty to the practice of law. Other such rules include Rule 3.3(DE), which deals with the duty of candor when a lawyer interacts with the a tribunal, and Rule 8.4(c)(DE), which deals with the general requirement of lawyer honesty. *See Chapter 28 Honesty and Candor* and *Chapter 48 General Misconduct.* Rule 4.1(DE) specifically deals with a lawyer's duty of honesty when the lawyer deals with third parties such as the opposition and the opposition's lawyer. This rule applies when a lawyer is acting in a representative capacity.

B. Material False Statements

1. Affirmative Statements

4.1(a)(DE) prohibits a lawyer from knowingly making "a false statement of material fact or law to a third person." A lawyer has no general duty to disclose information, but when a lawyer speaks, the statement must be truthful. A lawyer violates the rule by incorporating or affirming a false statement of another if the lawyer knows the statement is false. Rule 1.0(f)(DE) defines "knowingly" as "actual knowledge" which may be inferred from the circumstances.

A good example of conduct that is prohibited is the lawyer's conduct in *Cleveland Bar Association v. McMahon,* 872 N.E.2d 261 (Ohio 2007). The lawyer, in an action to recover for injuries to a passenger incurred in an automobile collision, wrote to opposing counsel and quoted a colloquy from a court transcript. In the quoted transcript the driver admitted fault. In reality, the driver never appeared in court and the colloquy quoted in the letter never occurred. Clearly, the lawyer knowingly made "a false statement of material fact" to opposing counsel. The lawyer was disciplined, of course.

2. Omissions

Occasionally, a situation arises in which a lawyer faces discipline not for a statement but for a failure to make a statement—usually to correct a misimpression furthered by the lawyer. For example, assume that Lisa Lawyer represents Clint Client on a personal injury claim arising from an automobile collision. Lisa files a negligence action against Dora Driver. Larry Lawyer represents Dora. Unfortunately, Clint dies during the pretrial phase. Lisa continues to discuss settlement with Larry but does not tell Larry that Clint has died. Some courts have determined that a lawyer such as Lisa has violated Rule 4.1(DE). These courts view the lawyer's failure to disclose the death while also pursuing the matter as if the client is alive as an implied misrepresentation. If Lisa appears for a pretrial conference and does not disclose the death of Clint to the court, Lisa may have violated Rule 3.3(DE) as well. *See Chapter 28 Honesty and Candor.* The ABA, in *ABA Formal Opinion 95-397 (1995)*, stated that a lawyer in this situation must disclose the client's death to the opposition and the court in the next contact with those entities after the client's death. In addition to the professional responsibility issue, if the settlement discussions lead to a settlement agreement and Lisa does not disclose Clint's death, the settlement may be set aside as a contract formed as the result of mistake.

3. Statements in Negotiations

A topic of frequent discussion is whether a lawyer, in the course of a negotiation, may take liberties with the truth as a posturing technique. In the context of a settlement negotiation, Lisa Lawyer might desire to state that Clint Client will settle a property dispute for no less than $100,000 even though Clint will settle for much less. A comment to Rule 4.1(DE) informs this discussion. The comment states that the rule applies only to statements of fact and that some statements are not taken generally to be statements of fact. The comment explains that "[e]stimates of price or value placed on the subject of a transaction and a party's intentions as to an acceptable settlement of a claim are ordinarily in this category, and so is the existence of an undisclosed principal except where nondisclosure of the principal would constitute fraud."

According to the comment, Lisa may state that Clint will settle for no less than $100,000 when that is not true. Lisa must, however, avoid making other statements of fact that are not true. Lisa could not that state that an independent appraiser valued the property in question at $150,000 unless that was in fact the case. The ABA addressed negotiation ethics in *ABA Formal Opinion 06-439 (2006),* and affirmed that a statement of unwillingness to settle for a certain amount, even if untrue, is not improper. The *Opinion* noted that parties to a negotiation would not be expected to rely on such a statement. In contrast, the *Opinion* noted that a statement that documentary evidence exists and will be admitted at trial is improper if such evidence does not exist.

C. Disclosure of a "Material Fact" to Avoid Assisting a Client's Crime or Fraud

Rule 1.2(d)(DE) states that a lawyer may not counsel or assist a client in conduct the lawyer knows constitutes a crime or fraud. *See Chapter 8 Scope of the Representation and Communication with the Client.* When that crime or fraud takes the form of a misrepresentation, Rule 4.1(b)(DE) applies. Rule 4.1(b)(DE) requires a lawyer to disclose a "material fact when disclosure is necessary to avoid assisting" a client's crime or fraud. A lawyer acts improperly only if he or she knowingly fails to disclose. Thus, a lawyer must know of the client's criminal or fraudulent behavior. Rule 1.0(d)(DE) states that fraud is any conduct constituting fraud under the law of the relevant jurisdiction done with "a purpose to deceive."

In such a situation, a lawyer should explore all other methods to terminate assistance to the client's bad acts short of disclosure of confidential information. First, a lawyer should counsel a client not to pursue criminal or fraudulent avenues. Second, a lawyer should withdraw if necessary to avoid involvement in the crime or fraud. If the lawyer's involvement is such that continuing to represent the client is continuing to assist the crime or fraud, Rule 1.16(a)(DE) demands withdrawal. *See Chapter 11 Refusing to Form a Lawyer-Client Relationship or Ending a Lawyer-Client Relationship.* If third parties are continuing to rely on the lawyer's past work touching upon the crime or fraud, the lawyer must give notice to third parties that the withdrawal has occurred. In such situation, a lawyer might disavow documents he or she prepared.

Last, if withdrawal does not put adequate distance between the lawyer and the client's criminal or fraudulent acts, the lawyer must disclose whatever material facts are necessary so that the lawyer does not assist the client in the untoward activities. Rule 4.1(b)(DE) limits this duty by requiring disclosure only when Rule 1.6(DE) does not prohibit such a disclosure. However, Rule 1.6(DE) permits disclosure in many situations. If the client is using the lawyer's services in furtherance of a crime or fraud "reasonably certain" to result in "substantial" financial or property injury, Rule 1.6(b)(2)(DE) permits disclosure to prevent the client's crime or fraud. If the client has used the lawyer's services in furtherance of a crime or fraud "reasonably certain" to result in "substantial" financial or property injury, Rule 1.6(b)(3)(DE) permits disclosure to "prevent, mitigate or rectify" the injury. And in the rare situation in which the lawyer "reasonably believes" there is a danger of "reasonably certain death or substantial bodily harm," Rule 1.6(b)(1)(DE) allows a lawyer to disclose information necessary to prevent the injury. *See Chapter 15 The Duty of Confidentiality.*

An example makes these duties clearer. Assume Eric Entrepreneur asked Larry Lawyer to assist him in obtaining needed capital so that Eric can market his invention. Larry prepared documents that Eric then gave to Vinny Venture Capitalist. One of the documents stated that Eric holds the patent on the invention. Vinny agreed to invest substantially with an initial infusion of capital followed by future payments at six-month intervals. Larry has now discovered that Eric does not have the patent on the invention and that Eric intentionally lied about the patent so that Vinny would agree to invest. Larry reasonably believes that if Eric does not hold the patent, the venture is doomed to failure.

Larry, if possible, should first confront Eric and attempt to convince him to remedy the situation. If Eric refuses, Larry should withdraw from the representation because to continue this representation could be seen as continued assistance to Eric's fraud in violation of Rule 1.2(d)(DE). This is especially true since Vinny will be making future payments in reliance on the false information prepared by Larry.

Larry should notify Vinny of the withdrawal. Because Vinny may continue to rely on the documents provided by Larry, Larry should disavow the problematic document. Larry's disavowal should alert Vinny that there is a problem with the document but the disavowal stops short of specific disclosure.

If these disclosures do not cause Vinny to discover the patent problem or otherwise do not stop the transaction and, thus, Larry's involvement in it, Rule 4.1(b)(DE) requires that Larry disclose the fact that Eric does not hold the patent. Rule 1.6(DE) does not prohibit disclosure. Because Eric used Larry's services to further the fraud, under Rule 1.6(b)(3)(DE). Larry may disclose the patent information even though it is information that otherwise would be protected by the duty of confidentiality. Larry's disclosure would prevent "substantial" financial injury to Vinny that is "reasonably certain" to result as a consequence of Eric's fraud.

Related Sections of the *Restatement (Third) of the Law Governing Lawyers*

Section 98

Checkpoints

- A lawyer must not knowingly "make a false statement of material fact or law to a third person."
- An omission in certain contexts may amount to an impermissible implied misrepresentation.
- In the negotiation context, certain statements are not viewed as statements of fact that can be justifiably relied upon. These statements are not violations of Rule 4.1(DE).
- A lawyer must disclose a "material fact" when "necessary to avoid assisting" the client in a crime or fraud if the duty of confidentiality does not prevent disclosure.

Chapter 36

Contact with Represented Persons

Roadmap

- Rule 4.2(DE)
- Communication with represented persons
- Communication with represented organizations

A. The No Contact Rule

Rule 4.2(DE) prohibits a lawyer who is in a representational role from communicating with a person that the lawyer knows another lawyer represents with regard to the matter unless law or a court order gives the lawyer the right to such contact or unless the person's lawyer has agreed to the contact. A person obtains legal representation in a matter because he or she needs the assistance of a lawyer. Rule 4.2(DE) protects the lawyer-client relationship from interference. It helps to prevent a lawyer from overreaching and helps to prevent a represented person from disclosing information without first consulting with counsel.

1. Knowledge of the Representation

The rule makes a lawyer's contact with a represented person improper only when the lawyer knows that the person is represented in the matter. Rule 1.0(f)(DE) explains that the standard is one of "actual knowledge" but that such knowledge can be developed from the circumstances. A lawyer may know that a person is represented generally by a lawyer and yet not know that the lawyer represents the person for purposes of this specific matter. Yet, a comment to the rule states that "the lawyer cannot evade the requirement of obtaining the consent of counsel by closing eyes to the obvious."

Perhaps Lisa Lawyer represents Clint Client in Clint's personal injury claim against Speedy Delivery Corporation. Clint is claiming that a Speedy Delivery truck collided with Clint's car, causing Clint's injuries. Lisa Lawyer may know that Larry Lawyer has represented Speedy Delivery Corporation in every personal injury matter filed against it in the last five years. This knowledge of past representation does not mean that Lisa knows that Larry represents Speedy Delivery with regard to Clint's claim even though such would be a very good guess.

If Speedy Delivery tells Lisa that Larry represents it regarding Clint's claim or if Larry appears as counsel on a filing with a court regarding Clint's claim, Lisa then knows of the representation and may not communicate with Speedy Delivery without first contacting Larry. If Speedy Delivery also has an in-house lawyer working on the claim, the situation is less clear. *ABA Formal Opinion 06-443 (2006)* states that Lisa may contact the in-house lawyer without first obtaining Larry's consent as long as the in-house counsel is working as a lawyer on the matter.

2. The Represented Person Need Not Be a Party or Adverse

Rule 4.2(DE) forbids contact with a represented person even if that person is not a party in a particular litigation. In Lisa Lawyer's representation of Clint Client in Clint's personal injury action against Speedy Delivery, Lisa would like to talk to Wanda Witness about the collision. Wanda, who was standing on a street corner, saw the collision. Wanda has hired Lance Lawyer with regard to the matter. Even though Wanda is not a party to the litigation and even though Clint's interests and Wanda's interests may not be adverse, Lisa cannot talk with Wanda without first consulting Lance.

3. The Prohibition Applies Even When the Represented Person Initiates the Contact

If the lawyer knows that the person is represented in the matter, the lawyer may not communicate with the person about the matter even if the person approaches the lawyer. Perhaps in the matter involving Speedy Delivery, Lisa knows that Lance represents Wanda. Wanda comes to Lisa's office and wishes to tell Lisa what she saw regarding the collision. Lisa cannot talk with Wanda without first obtaining permission from Wanda's lawyer, Lance.

4. The Prohibition Applies Only If the Lawyer Represents a Client in the Matter

Occasionally, a person who is represented in a matter seeks to talk about the matter with a lawyer who is not representing anyone in the matter. Perhaps Clint is not pleased with his relationship with Lisa and contacts Linda Lawyer to discuss his claim against Speedy Delivery. Linda does not violate any principle by talking with Clint about the claim if Linda does not represent anyone regarding the collision in which Clint was injured.

5. The Prohibition Applies Only to Communications about the Matter in Which the Person Is Represented

Rule 4.2(DE) forbids communication with the represented person only if the communication relates to the matter with respect to which the person is represented. So Lisa Lawyer, who represents Clint, could communicate with Wanda even though Wanda is represented regarding the collision, if Lisa communicates with Wanda about an unrelated topic. Perhaps Wanda and Lisa are on the same PTA committee. Lisa could talk with Wanda about the PTA. As a practical matter, however, any contact between Lisa and Wanda is suspect, especially to Wanda's lawyer.

6. Representatives of the Lawyer

Rule 8.4(a)(DE) states that a lawyer is guilty of misconduct if he or she violates a rule of professional conduct or does so through the acts of another. *See Chapter 48 General Misconduct.* This means that if Lisa Lawyer cannot communicate with a person, Lisa cannot have her paralegal communicate with that person either.

A lawyer's client is not viewed as an agent of the lawyer in this context. While Lisa Lawyer cannot communicate with a represented opposing party in a litigation matter, Clint, Lisa's client, may communicate with the opposing party. Lisa does not violate Rule 4.2(DE) by explaining to Clint that he has this right. *ABA Formal Opinion 11-461(2011)* states that a lawyer may counsel a client about issues the client should discuss with the other party and strategies to use in the discussion. The *Opinion* warns the lawyer not to overreach by actions such as assisting the client in eliciting confidential information or admissions against interest.

7. Contact with a Government Entity When the Government Is Represented in the Matter

Rule 4.2(DE) specifically states that a lawyer may communicate with a represented party if law or a court order authorizes the communication. A major authorization of communication is the constitutional right to "petition the Government for a redress of grievances" that is a part of the First Amendment to the United States Constitution. If the Federal Trade Commission blocks Fresh Food's purchase of competitor Good Food on the basis that the combination has a significant anticompetitive effect, both Fresh Food and Good Food have the right to petition any government entity to have the decision modified even though the government is represented for purposes of the issue.

B. Investigations Conducted by Lawyers

1. Criminal Investigations

A common law enforcement technique is an undercover investigation. The police may do such an investigation with direction from lawyers or lawyers may be principal actors in the ruse. If the investigation creates a situation in which a lawyer or someone under the lawyer's direction communicates with a person who already has legal representation in the matter, the communication arguably violates Rule 4.2(DE). To the extent the ruse also involves deceit, the lawyers involved also violate Rule 8.4(c)(DE), which prohibits dishonest conduct. *See Chapter 48 General Misconduct.* Many people view this kind of law enforcement activity as being not violative of Rule 4.2(DE) because law or the language of the rule authorizes the conduct.

2. Civil Investigations

Occasionally, a lawyer takes part in an investigation as part of a civil matter. For example, Larry Lawyer, in representing Great Cola Company, might pretend to be a customer in a conversation with Drink Distributor to determine whether Distributor is offering Great Cola on terms that breach the distribution contract with Great Cola Company. If Distributor is represented by counsel regarding the contract, Larry may be violating Rule 4.2(DE) as well as engaging in dishonest conduct in violation of Rule 8.4(c)(DE). Some courts find such conduct improper on the basis of Rule 4.2(DE) or 8.4(c)(DE) or both. Other courts find no violation.

C. Organizations

When the represented person is an organization, the application of Rule 4.2(DE) can be more complex. Let's return to the scenario of Lisa Lawyer representing Clint Client in a personal injury action against Speedy Delivery Corporation. Larry Lawyer represents Speedy Delivery. Clint claims that he suffered his injuries as the result of a collision of his car with a Speedy Delivery truck driven by Don Driver. Clint claims that Don was negligent. Lisa would like to talk to Don and the President of the company, Paul. Lisa would also like to talk with Margaret, a witness to the collision. Margaret was standing at a bus stop at the time. Margaret was a receptionist at Speedy Delivery at the time of the collision but was not on duty when she witnessed the collision. Margaret is no longer an employee of Speedy Delivery. Does Rule 4.2(DE) prohibit Lisa from talking with Don, Paul, or Margaret?

1. Current Employees

In the above example, Don and Paul are current employees of the organization Speedy Delivery, which is represented by Larry Lawyer. Rule 4.2(DE) does not bar Lisa Lawyer from talking to *every* current employee, however. A comment to the rule lists three categories of employees that Lisa may not contact without the approval of Speedy Delivery's lawyer.

First, Lisa may not contact any current employee who "supervises, directs or regularly consults with the organization's lawyer concerning the matter." Paul, as the President of Speedy Delivery, may be such an employee so that Lisa must not contact Paul without Larry's consent.

Second, Lisa may not communicate with any current employee who "has the authority to obligate the organization with respect to the matter." Again, Paul, as President of Speedy Delivery, may be such an employee so that Lisa must not contact Paul without Larry's consent.

Third, Lisa may not contact any current employee "whose act or omission in connection with the matter may be imputed to the organization for purposes of civil or criminal liability." Don is such an employee as the driver of the Speedy Delivery truck. If Don tells Lisa that he was speeding through a red light at the time of the collision, then he is, in effect, testifying to negligence and that negligent conduct is imputed to Speedy Delivery. Lisa cannot talk with Don without Larry's consent.

Even if Margaret remained a Speedy Delivery employee, Lisa could talk with her without contacting Larry. Margaret, a receptionist, does not deal substantively with Speedy Delivery's lawyer. She cannot obligate the organization with respect to the collision, and her conduct at the time of the collision would not be imputed to Speedy Delivery for purposes of liability.

2. Former Employees

Since Margaret is a former employee of Speedy Delivery at the time Lisa would like to talk with her, Lisa may talk with Margaret without contacting Speedy Delivery's lawyer. Rule 4.2(DE) does not bar communication with a former employee. A comment states: "Consent of the organization's lawyer is not required for communication with a former constituent." Remember that Rule 4.2(DE) exists to protect the lawyer-client relationship. A former client is not a part of the lawyer-client relationship between the organization and the lawyer because the former client is no longer a representative of the organization. So Lisa may talk with Margaret unless Margaret has employed her own lawyer with regard to the matter.

Lisa may talk with Margaret even if Margaret would have been a member of the group of employees to which Lisa could not talk if Margaret were still employed by the organization. Lisa could talk with Don and Paul, for example, if Don and Paul were no longer employed by Speedy Delivery at the time Lisa wishes to communicate with them.

When dealing with any unrepresented person, including a former employee, Lisa must abide by Rule 4.3(DE). See *Chapter 37 Respect for the Rights of Non-clients.* In addition, a lawyer must take care not to induce the former employee to reveal privileged communications. Questioning a former employee of an opposing party so as to induce the disclosure of privileged communications may violate Rule 4.4(a)(DE) in that the lawyer is using "methods of obtaining evidence that violate the legal rights of such a person." A comment to Rule 4.2(DE) and *ABA Formal Opinion 91-359 (1991)* warn against such activity. Some courts have disqualified lawyers if the former employee disclosed privileged communications and the lawyer induced the disclosure. If Paul was a former President of Speedy Delivery but not a current employee, Lisa can talk with him. Lisa must take care to not make inquiries that are likely to lead Paul to disclose privileged communications. *See Chapter 16 The Attorney-Client Privilege and the Work-Product Doctrine.*

Related Sections of the *Restatement (Third) of the Law Governing Lawyers*

Sections 99–102

Checkpoints

- A lawyer, in a representational capacity, may not communicate about a matter with a person the lawyer knows is represented in the matter unless the lawyer obtains permission from that person's lawyer or a court or the law allows the contact.
- A lawyer may not direct a representative or allow a representative of the lawyer, such as a paralegal or investigator, to communicate with a person the lawyer may not contact.
- On behalf of a client, a lawyer may assist a client in exercising the First Amendment right to petition the government even though such contact might otherwise contradict Rule 4.2(DE).
- If the represented person is an organization, a lawyer may not communicated with any current employee who
    1. "supervises, directs or regularly consults with the organization's lawyer concerning the matter,"
    2. "has authority to obligate the organization with respect to the matter," or
    3. "whose act or omission in connection with the matter may be imputed to the organization for purposes of civil or criminal liability."
- A lawyer may communicate with any former employee of a represented organization.

Chapter 37

Respect for the Rights of Nonclients

Roadmap

- Rule 4.3(DE)
- Rule 4.4(DE)
- Forthrightness when dealing with an unrepresented nonclient
- Giving legal advice to an unrepresented nonclient whose interests may conflict with those of the client
- Using techniques that have no purpose but to "embarrass, delay, or burden" others or infringe on the rights of others
- Inadvertent disclosures

A. An Unrepresented Nonclient

In the context of representing a client a lawyer may have occasion to deal with all sorts of people. For example, a litigator may talk with witnesses and others as the lawyer investigates and prepares the case. If a lawyer, in the course of representing a client, has contact with a person who is not a client and a lawyer does not represent that person for the purpose of the matter, the lawyer must abide by several basic standards. Rule 4.3(DE) provides these restrictions.

First, the lawyer may not indicate expressly or by implication that the lawyer is disinterested. If Lisa Lawyer represents Cindy Client with regard to Cindy's personal injury claim against Big Store, Lisa may want to talk with Wanda Witness, a shopper who witnessed the injury to Cindy. Lisa cannot lead Wanda to believe that she represents Big Store or that she is not representing anyone in the matter.

In fact, Lisa has an affirmative duty to exercise "reasonable efforts to correct" any misimpression about Lisa's role that Wanda might have. Lisa has this duty if Lisa "knows or reasonably should know" that Wanda is confused.

Lisa should identify her client. She also should explain how the client's interests and Wanda's interests may diverge if such an explanation is appropriate for the situation.

A lawyer dealing with an unrepresented person always must be very careful not to create a lawyer-client relationship when the lawyer does not desire such. When a lawyer already represents a client in the matter, the lawyer must avoid creating an attorney-client relationship with unrepresented persons in the matter whose interests may conflict with the lawyer's current client. Because courts may find that a lawyer-client relationship exists, and the lawyer owes duties, if a reasonable person would think that the relationship exists, a lawyer always must be mindful not to make statements or act in ways that could lead a reasonable person to believe that there is a relationship. *See Chapter 4 Basis of Duty: The Lawyer-Client Relationship.*

In particular, a lawyer must take care not to give legal advice to the otherwise unrepresented person if the lawyer "knows or reasonably should know" that the interests of the otherwise unrepresented person have a "reasonable possibility of being in conflict" with the client's interests. If the lawyer gives the unrepresented person advice, then the lawyer may well be converting the person to the status of client. Such would be impermissible if the interest of the client and the unrepresented person conflict.

If Cindy was injured in Big Store when a shelf fell on her, and if Lisa knows that the shelf fell because Wanda, the witness, leaned against it, it is possible that Wanda's interests may conflict with Cindy's interests. Lisa should take care not to make any statements that could be construed as legal advice. Of course, Lisa may advise Wanda to retain her own lawyer. The same would be true if Lisa was negotiating, on behalf of a client, contract terms with Wanda.

B. Responsible Treatment of Everyone

Regardless of whether the person with whom the lawyer deals in representing a client is represented, the lawyer must treat such a person with a modicum of civility. Rule 4.4(a)(DE) states that a lawyer may not use "means that have no substantial purpose other than to embarrass, delay, or burden" another person. Also, a lawyer may not obtain evidence in a manner that violates the rights of a person. For example, a lawyer should not try to elicit privileged information by asking a person questions that are likely to do so. *See Chapter 36 Contact with Represented Persons.*

C. Inadvertent Disclosures

A lawyer has a duty to preserve the confidentiality of communications and to protect the privileged status of communications. *See Chapter 15 The Duty of Confidentiality.* In a modern law office, mistakes do occur, however. Perhaps in the course of responding to a discovery request a lawyer turns over 10,000 documents to the opposition. Unfortunately, two of the documents should not have been produced because the attorney-client privilege protects them. Or perhaps a lawyer, or a member of the lawyer's staff, sends an email or a fax or a package by messenger. Unfortunately, the email, fax, or package was intended to go to the client but it went to the opposition's lawyer. How do we deal with such realities of law practice?

1. The Sending Lawyer

A comment to Rule 1.6(DE) notes that a lawyer must act competently to protect against inadvertent or unauthorized disclosure of confidential information. The duty of competence contained in Rule 1.1(DE) is judged by a rule of reason. A lawyer should have procedures in place to limit the possibility of inadvertent disclosure. For example, a lawyer might have a procedure in place to scrub all metadata from electronic documents leaving the firm.

When an inadvertent disclosure occurs, it is possible that the disclosing lawyer has not acted competently to protect privileged communications of the client. It is also possible that a disclosure occurs even with competent representation.

2. The Receiving Lawyer

If a lawyer receives a communication, electronic or otherwise, relating to the representation of a client and the lawyer "knows or reasonably should know" that the communication was mistakenly sent to the lawyer, the lawyer must, as Rule 4.4(b)(DE) directs, "promptly notify" the sender. This notice allows the sender to be aware of a need to take action to protect any privilege.

If Lisa receives a letter from the opposition's lawyer, Larry, that begins with "Dear Clint Client," Lisa "reasonably should know" that the letter was misdirected to Lisa. Lisa must notify Larry that she has the letter. The comment to the rule clarifies that Lisa has no obligation to stop reading the letter or to return it simply on the basis of it being a misdirected communication. Other law, however, may require such action.

3. Rule 26 of the Federal Rules of Civil Procedure

Other applicable rules may require more than Rule 4.4(b)(DE) requires. For example, Rule 26(b)(5)(B) of the Federal Rules of Civil Procedure deals with this scenario. This rule states that if a party produces in discovery a document that the party believes to be privileged or protected by the work-product doctrine, that party must notify the receiver of the claim and its basis. The receiver must then "promptly return, sequester, or destroy" the information and any copies of it. The rule forbids the use or dissemination of the information until the court has resolved the claim of protection. If the receiving party disseminates the information before notice of the claim, it must take "reasonable steps to retrieve" it. The rule allows the receiver to present the information to the court under seal for a determination of its status.

4. "Inappropriately Obtained" Information Is Not Inadvertently Disclosed

Rule 4.4(b)(DE) addresses inadvertently disclosed documents or "electronically stored information." The Rule can apply to metadata but only if the lawyer knows or should know that the metadata was inadvertently disclosed. In the vast majority of situations, the metadata may be disclosed, but the disclosure is not inadvertent.

The rule does not deal with situations in which the lawyer knows or should know that the document or "electronically stored information" was, as a comment to the rule characterizes it, "inappropriately obtained." So if Lisa Lawyer represents Cindy Client in a divorce matter and Cindy gives Lisa documents that she says she took from her husband's computer, Lisa has reason to believe that the documents may be "inappropriately obtained." Rule 4.4(b)(DE) does not apply to this scenario.

5. The Attorney-Client Privilege

If Larry Lawyer believes that an inadvertently disclosed letter is a privileged communication, he can act to protect the privilege. This usually requires requesting the court to determine whether or not the attorney-client privilege protects the letter even though Larry sent it to Lisa and even though Lisa may have read it.

In evaluating whether an inadvertently produced document retains privileged status, many modern courts apply a factor-based analysis. A court might consider the precautions Larry took to prevent an inadvertent disclosure, the precautions Larry could have taken but did not, the importance of the disclosure to the substance of the matter, the degree of the disclosure, situational factors such as the pressure of a deadline or the need to deal with a large number of documents, and the action Larry takes after the disclosure to protect the privileged character of the document. Another view is that the disclosure of the communication waives the privilege regardless of the inadvertent manner of the disclosure. A third approach is that the privilege cannot be waived inadvertently because the only the client can waive the privilege and can only do so voluntarily. *See Chapter 16 The Attorney-Client Privilege and the Work-Product Doctrine.*

Rule 502(b) of the Federal Rules of Evidence provides that an inadvertent disclosure in a federal context is not a waiver of the privilege if "the holder of the privilege or protection took reasonable steps to prevent disclosure" and the party "promptly took reasonable steps to rectify the error, including (if applicable) following Federal Rules of Civil Procedure 26(b)(5)(B)." Rule 502(e) provides that the parties can enter into an agreement about the effect of a disclosure that will bind the parties to the agreement but not third parties. *See Chapter 16 The Attorney-Client Privilege and the Work-Product Doctrine.*

6. Remedies

A court could determine that the letter Larry sent to Lisa originally was privileged because it was a confidential communication between a lawyer and a client for the purpose of rendering legal advice. *See Chapter 16 The Attorney-Client Privilege and the Work-Product Doctrine.* Using a factor-based analysis or using the approach that recognizes only voluntary waivers of the privilege, the court could then conclude that the letter retains its privileged status even though it was disclosed to Lisa.

If a court so concludes, the court will order Lisa to not rely upon the disclosed communications in any way. In rare cases courts have disqualified lawyers in Lisa's position but usually only if the receiving lawyer does not notify the opposition of the disclosure.

Related Sections of the *Restatement (Third) of the Law Governing Lawyers*

Sections 79, 103, and 106

Checkpoints

- A lawyer must not mislead any unrepresented nonclient of the lawyer's role in representing a client.
- A lawyer must make "reasonable efforts to correct" any misimpression about the lawyer's role an unrepresented nonclient might have.
- A lawyer must not give legal advice to an unrepresented person if the lawyer "knows or reasonably should know that the person's interests" have a "reasonable possibility" of conflicting with the client's interests.
- A lawyer must not use "means that have no substantial purpose other than to embarrass, delay, or burden" another person or infringes on the rights of a third party.
- A lawyer who receives a communication relating to the representation of a client and "knows or reasonably should know" the communication was mistakenly sent must "promptly notify" the sender.
- While the rules of professional conduct do not require return of an inadvertently disclosed communication, other law, such as Rule 26 of the Federal Rules of Civil Procedure, may require such action.
- An inadvertently disclosed communication may or may not retain its privileged status. Many modern courts apply a factor analysis to determine whether the communication retains the privilege.

Section IX
Practicing Law

Chapter 38

Supervision and Responsibility for Other Lawyers, Nonlawyer Employees, and Other Assistants

Roadmap

- Rule 5.1(DE)
- Rule 5.2(DE)
- Rule 5.3(DE)
- Rule 8.4(a)(DE)
- The duty of lawyers with "managerial authority" in a firm
- The duty of lawyers with "direct supervisory authority" over other lawyers or nonlawyer assistants
- The responsibility of lawyers for the acts of other lawyers or nonlawyer assistants
- The responsibility of subordinate lawyers for acts directed by a supervising lawyer

A. A Professionally Responsible Work Environment

Lawyers have a basic responsibility to provide a professionally responsible environment for their subordinates. In a traditional law firm setting, not all lawyers have the authority to set firm policies and practices. If a lawyer is a partner in a firm or has "managerial authority" similar to that of a partner, that lawyer has a duty to make the firm environment conducive to behavior by lawyers and nonlawyer assistants in accord with professional responsibility rules. This is true whether or not the nonlawyer assistants are employees of the lawyer or firm or rather simply retained by the firm or associated with the firm.

If the environment is not a traditional law firm but rather an in-house law department, a legal service organization such as legal aid, or a government entity such as a state public defender's office, the rule is the same. Rule 1.0(c)(DE) defines "firm" broadly to include these other practice settings. In any such setting lawyers with "managerial authority" have the responsibility to provide an environment for their subordinates conducive to behavior in accord with the rules of professional responsibility.

1. Subordinate Lawyers

Rule 5.1(a)(DE) states that partners in law firms and other lawyers with "managerial authority" have a duty to "make reasonable efforts to ensure that the firm has in effect measures giving reasonable assurance that all lawyers in the firm conform to the Rules of Professional Conduct." What is reasonable must be judged by the specific circumstances.

For example, if a firm of fifty lawyers, some of whom are partners and some of whom are associates, has no mechanism in place to check for conflicts of interest, the partners of the firm have violated Rule 5.1(a)(DE). Without a fairly sophisticated mechanism to check for conflicts, there is no way a firm of fifty lawyers can possibly abide by the applicable conflict of interest rules. A smaller firm may abide by Rule 5.1(a)(DE) by using a less sophisticated conflicts checking procedure, but even the smaller firm violates the rule by not having an effective conflicts checking mechanism in place. Implementing and maintaining such a mechanism is not an unreasonably burdensome task.

Rule 5.1(a)(DE) applies to even the smallest legal practice environments. For example, if Larry Lawyer has only one associate lawyer, Al, working as Larry's employee, Larry violates Rule 5.1(a)(DE) by having a practice of assigning Al so many cases that the associate cannot possibly handle all of the matters competently or diligently. Larry also violates Rule 5.1(a)(DE) by having a practice of not supervising Al and not providing guidance and direction if Al is an inexperienced associate.

2. Nonlawyer Assistants

With regard to nonlawyer employees and other nonlawyer assistants, the responsibility of a partner and other lawyers with "managerial authority" for maintaining a professionally responsible environment is virtually the same. Rule 5.3(a)(DE) states that the measures taken must give "reasonable assurance that the person's conduct is compatible with the professional obligations of the lawyer." Nonlawyers such as secretaries, paralegals, student law clerks, runners, investigators, and other assistants may not have a set of conduct rules applicable to them. Yet because they carry out the lawyer's work, the lawyer must take steps to ensure the assistants heed the professional responsibility precepts governing their employing lawyer.

For example, all assistants should be instructed at the beginning of the employment and periodically throughout the employment about the lawyer's duty of confidentiality. The lawyer can never be certain that an assistant will not breach the lawyer's duty of confidentiality. By explaining the duty to the assistants and reminding them on a regular basis, the lawyer is taking reasonable steps to ensure that the employee or other assistant will not violate the duty. A lawyer with "managerial authority" might also have procedures in place that make it less likely that nonlawyer assistants breach the duty of confidentiality. For example, a firm may have a policy that files are accessible only by employees working on the matter, not by the entire employee population of the firm. *See Chapter 15 The Duty of Confidentiality.*

B. The Duty to Supervise

1. Supervision of Subordinate Lawyers

Regardless of the "managerial authority" of a lawyer, if that lawyer has "direct supervisory authority" over another lawyer, the supervising lawyer must act to ensure that the supervised lawyer abides by the applicable rules governing lawyers. Rule 5.1(b)(DE) states that a lawyer with "direct supervisory authority over another lawyer shall make reasonable efforts to ensure that the other lawyer conforms to the Rules of Professional Conduct."

A lawyer with "managerial authority" could violate Rule 5.1(a)(DE) by having a workload assignment practice that provides, in general, no supervision of inexperienced lawyers. A lawyer with "direct supervisory authority" over an inexperienced lawyer could violate 5.1(b)(DE) by failing to supervise the inexperienced lawyer in a case. Perhaps Larry Lawyer, an experienced lawyer who has "direct supervisory authority" over Lisa Lawyer but no "managerial authority" in the firm, assigns a complicated medical malpractice matter to Lisa even though she has only recently graduated from law school and been admitted to practice. Larry then never follows up with Lisa about the progress of the case. Larry probably has violated Rule 5.1(b)(DE) even if Lisa ultimately obtains a positive result for the client.

2. Supervision of Nonlawyer Assistants

Regardless of the "managerial authority" of a lawyer, if that lawyer has "direct supervisory authority" over a nonlawyer assistant, regardless of the employment status of the assistant, the lawyer must act to ensure that the assistant abides by the professional responsibilities of the lawyer. Rule 5.3(b)(DE) states that a lawyer with "direct supervisory authority over the nonlawyer shall make reasonable efforts to ensure that the person's conduct is compatible with the professional obligations of the lawyer."

Lawyers are disciplined under this rule when they fail to adequately supervise their nonlawyer assistants. Perhaps Peter Paralegal, a paralegal who works in Larry Lawyer's office, appears in court without Larry. Larry has no knowledge of Peter's appearance. A discipline authority might well find Larry violated Rule 5.3(b)(DE) because of a lack of supervision of Peter.

C. Responsibility for the Acts of Other Lawyers and Nonlawyer Assistants

1. The Rules

A violation of Rule 5.1(a)(DE), Rule 5.1(b)(DE), Rule 5.3(a)(DE), and Rule 5.3(b)(DE) result in just that—violations of those provisions. Violations of Rule 5.1(c)(DE) and Rule 5.3(c)(DE) result in a lawyer being guilty of violating whatever rule the other lawyer has violated or whatever rule the nonlawyer would violate if the nonlawyer was a lawyer subject to the rules. The nonlawyer assistant may be an employee or otherwise associated with the lawyer or the firm. In the disciplinary context, a lawyer is responsible for the conduct of another lawyer or nonlawyer assistant in four situations:

1. if the lawyer orders the conduct of the other lawyer or nonlawyer assistant;
2. if the lawyer knows of the specific conduct of the other lawyer or nonlawyer assistant and ratifies it;
3. if the lawyer is a partner or has similar "managerial authority" in the firm in which the other lawyer or nonlawyer assistant is employed and, as stated in Rule 5.1(c)(2)(DE) and Rule 5.3(c)(2)(DE), "knows of the conduct at a time when its consequences can be avoided or mitigated but fails to take reasonable remedial action"; or

4. if the lawyer has "direct supervisory authority" over the lawyer or nonlawyer assistant and, again, quoting Rule 5.1(c)(DE) and Rule 5.3(c)(DE), "knows of the conduct at a time when its consequences can be avoided or mitigated but fails to take reasonable remedial action."

Note that a separate provision of the rules also states that a lawyer acts improperly by violating a rule through the acts of another. Rule 8.4(a)(DE) states that it is misconduct to "violate or attempt to violate the Rules of Professional Conduct, knowingly assist or induce another to do so, or do so through the acts of another." Thus, lawyers who are responsible under Rule 5.1(c)(DE) and Rule 5.3(c)(DE) for the acts of other lawyers or nonlawyers may also be in violation of Rule 8.4(a)(DE). There is no doubt that lawyers who order another lawyer or nonlawyer assistant to take prohibited action have acted contrary to Rule 8.4(a)(DE). The only question is what other conduct might be considered blameworthy under Rule 8.4(a)(DE). *See Chapter 48 General Misconduct.*

2. Applying the Rules

If Larry Lawyer orders another lawyer in his firm, Lisa, to improperly solicit a potential client in violation of Rule 7.3(DE), Larry may be disciplined for violating Rule 7.3(DE). *See Chapter 45 Communications about Lawyer Services.* If Larry orders Peter Paralegal, his assistant, to improperly solicit a potential client in violation of Rule 7.3(DE), Larry may be disciplined for violating Rule 7.3(DE) even though Peter cannot be disciplined for a violation of Rule 7.3(DE). Larry also would violate Rule 8.4(a)(DE).

If Larry finds out about the improper solicitation after it has occurred but continues to represent the client solicited, a discipline authority might succeed in claiming that Larry ratified the action of the other person. Larry could be found guilty of a violation of Rule 7.3(DE). Larry's conduct also may violate Rule 8.4(a)(DE).

Perhaps Larry is a partner in a firm or has "managerial authority" and does not order the solicitation by the other lawyer, Lisa. Larry discovers that Lisa plans to improperly solicit. If Larry does nothing to stop the solicitation, Larry can be disciplined for a violation of Rule 7.3(DE). The same would be true if Peter Paralegal or another nonlawyer assistant plans the solicitation. Larry's conduct also may violate Rule 8.4(a)(DE).

Lastly, assume that Larry has "direct supervisory authority" over Lisa, a lawyer. Larry does not order the solicitation by Lisa but he discovers that Lisa plans to improperly solicit. If Larry does nothing to stop the solicitation, he can be disciplined for a violation of Rule 7.3(DE). The same would be true if the person planning the solicitation is Peter Paralegal or another nonlawyer assistant. Larry's conduct also may violate Rule 8.4(a)(DE).

D. Civil Liability of a Lawyer for the Acts of Other Lawyers or Nonlawyer Assistants

The rules governing professional conduct do not establish standards of civil liability. The "Scope" section of the rules states: "The Rules are designed to provide guidance to lawyers and to provide a structure for regulating conduct through disciplinary agencies. They are not designed to be a basis for civil liability." The rules do not address the civil liability of a lawyer with "managerial authority" or a supervising lawyer for acts of other lawyers or nonlawyer assistants.

The parameters of such liability must be determined by principles of agency law and basic tort concepts. Recall, for example, from first-year torts class that an employer generally is liable for the negligent acts of an employee if the employee commits the acts in the scope of the employment. Acts of other lawyers and nonlawyer assistants must be measured against this and other tort and agency principles.

E. The Subordinate Lawyer

Lawyers often give other lawyers direction. Usually, a more experienced lawyer supervises and directs, to some extent, the actions of a less experienced lawyer. If two lawyers are working in an environment in which one of the lawyers supervises the other, the question arises as to the subordinate lawyer's responsibility for following the instruction of the supervising lawyer if that instruction results in a violation of a professional responsibility rule.

Suppose a supervising lawyer, Larry, directs a subordinate lawyer, Lisa, to tell the court that Cindy Client has no criminal record when Cindy does have a record. Assume that Lisa knows of Cindy's record and yet she does as Larry tells her. This action violates Rule 3.3(DE) because Lisa knowingly has made a false statement of fact to the court. *See Chapter 28 Honesty and Candor.* Rule 5.1(DE) tells us that Larry, the supervising lawyer, can be responsible for the violation of Rule 3.3(DE). Is the subordinate lawyer, Lisa, also subject to discipline for the violation of Rule 3.3(DE)?

The answer to the query is that Lisa has violated Rule 3.3(DE) and is subject to discipline. Rule 5.2(a)(DE) provides that Lisa has no refuge in the argument that she was simply following orders. Rule 5.2(b)(DE) contains a small exception. Lisa is *not* responsible if she follows Larry's direction if Larry's direction is a "reasonable resolution of an arguable question of professional duty." If there is no "arguable question," Lisa must abide by the rules and deny Larry's direction. If she gives in to the pressure of the employment relationship and acts as Larry directs, Lisa is subject to discipline. In the example, Larry tells Lisa to lie to the court. There is no doubt here; there is no "arguable question." This conduct is a clear violation of Rule 3.3(DE). Lisa can easily determine its impropriety at the time Larry tells her to so act.

Lisa can find solace in the exception to responsibility in 5.2(b)(DE) in the following set of facts. Assume that Lisa is in the midst of preparing a reply brief in a civil matter. Opposing counsel has failed to cite to the court a case that is hurtful to Lisa's case but helpful to the opposition. Lisa is unsure whether the case, which is from the supreme court of her jurisdiction, can be considered "directly adverse" to her position such that she has an obligation, under Rule 3.3(a)(2)(DE), to disclose the case to the court. *See Chapter 28 Honesty and Candor.* An argument can be made that the document is "directly adverse" and an argument can be that it is not. Lisa consults with Larry, her supervising partner on the case. Larry directs Lisa not to disclose the case to the court. Lisa does not disclose the case. Even if the failure to disclose is determined to be a violation of Rule 3.3(DE), Lisa would not be subject to discipline because she followed Larry's "reasonable resolution of an arguable question of professional duty."

Related Sections of the *Restatement (Third) of the Law Governing Lawyers*

Sections 11, 12, and 58

Checkpoints

- Partners and other lawyers with "managerial authority" must "make reasonable efforts to ensure that the firm has in effect measures giving reasonable assurance" that all lawyers in the firm and all nonlawyer assistants, regardless of employment status, act in accord with the relevant rules of professional conduct governing lawyers.

- A lawyer with "direct supervisory authority" over another lawyer or a nonlawyer assistant, regardless of employment status, must "make reasonable efforts to ensure" that the lawyer or nonlawyer assistant acts in accord with the relevant rules of professional conduct governing lawyers.
- A lawyer is responsible for the conduct of another lawyer or nonlawyer assistant, regardless of employment status, in four situations:
  1. if the lawyer orders the conduct,
  2. if the lawyer knows of the "specific conduct" of the other lawyer or nonlawyer assistant and ratifies it,
  3. if "the lawyer is a partner or has comparable managerial authority" in a firm in which the other lawyer or nonlawyer assistant is employed and "knows of the conduct at a time when its consequences can be avoided or mitigated but fails to take reasonable remedial action," or
  4. if the lawyer has "direct supervisory authority" over the lawyer or nonlawyer assistant and "knows of the conduct at a time when its consequences can be avoided or mitigated but fails to take reasonable remedial action."
- Civil liability of lawyers for the acts of other lawyers and nonlawyer assistants must be determined by application of tort and agency principles.
- A subordinate lawyer is not subject to discipline for his or her actions if he or she relies on a supervising lawyer's "reasonable resolution of an arguable question of professional duty." Otherwise, the subordinate lawyer is subject to discipline even if the subordinate lawyer acted at the direction of a supervising lawyer.

Chapter 39

Professional Independence

Roadmap

- Rule 2.1(DE)
- Rule 5.4(NE)
- Rule 1.8(f)(DE)
- Rule 7.2(b)(NE)
- The lawyer's role as advisor to the client
- Independence of a lawyer's professional judgment
- Legal fees paid by a third party
- Prohibition of sharing legal fees with nonlawyers
- Prohibition of allowing nonlawyers to be organizationally involved with the practice of law such that they might influence lawyers' professional judgment
- Referral fees

A. "Independent Professional Judgment"

A basic notion underlying the provision of legal services is that lawyers should render the best advice possible to their clients. Rendering the best possible advice requires a lawyer to be an all-purpose advisor to clients. A lawyer must be truthful and frank with a client and must exercise "independent professional judgment." Rule 2.1(DE) states that a lawyer "shall exercise independent professional judgment and render candid advice." The rule notes that fully counseling and advising a client may require a lawyer to not only rely on law but also to raise nonlegal issues that the client may need to consider to resolve the matter. Rule 2.1(DE) specifically notes that a lawyer may refer to "moral, economic, social and political factors." A lawyer should attempt to assist a client in having a complete picture of the situation so the client can choose the optimal path.

A vital component of a lawyer's role as advisor is the exercise of "independent professional judgment." Exercising "independent professional judgment" means a client receives advice untainted by bias created by other interests or parties. Lawyers should advise clients on the basis of what is best for those clients without the interference of considering what the effect of such advice might have on other clients, on the lawyer, or on other third parties. While perfectly independent judgment is elusive, many of the rules of professional conduct are designed to maximize the "independent professional judgment" of lawyers. The rules governing conflicts of interest are designed to permit representations only when a lawyer is not unduly burdened with concern about the interests of others or the lawyer's own interests. For example, Rule 1.7(DE) provides that a lawyer cannot represent a client in a matter if there is a "significant risk" that the representation of the client "will be materially limited by the lawyer's responsibilities to another client, a former client or a third person or by a personal interest of the lawyer." *See Chapter 18 Conflicts and Current Clients.*

Other rules are designed to protect "independent professional judgment" by specifically limiting situations in which a nonlawyer may be in a position to influence a particular lawyer's judgment. An example of such a rule is Rule 5.4(b), which prohibits a lawyer from being in a partnership with a nonlawyer if the partnership's activities involve the practice of law.

B. The Duty to Guard against Interference with "Independent Professional Judgment"

1. Guarding against Interference

A basic statement of the lawyer's duty to guard against interference with the exercise of the lawyer's "independent professional judgment" is in Rule 5.4(c)(NE). Rule 5.4(c)(NE) simply states that a lawyer must not allow anyone "who recommends, employs, or pays the lawyer to render legal services for another to direct or regulate the lawyer's professional judgment" in providing the services. This rule exhorts the lawyer to guard against interference from anyone, be the interferer a lawyer or a nonlawyer.

The import of Rule 5.4(c)(NE) is that Lisa Lawyer must always be both in the lawyer-client relationship and also cognitively above it. While rendering legal advice and services, Lisa always must be analyzing the situation and questioning whether her advice is truly the product of "independent professional judgment" or is rather the product of the taint of third-party influence or self-interest.

2. Interference from a Third Party Who Pays the Fee

Rule 1.8(f)(DE) supports the basic statement in Rule 5.4(c)(NE) in that Rule 1.8(f)(DE) allows a lawyer to accept payment from a third party for services rendered to a client only if the client consents, only if the lawyer honors client confidentiality, only if the arrangement does not cause "interference with the lawyer's independence of professional judgment," and only if the arrangement does not otherwise interfere with the relationship of the lawyer and the client. *See Chapter 21 Conflict of Interest Rules for Particular Situations.*

Lisa Lawyer might agree to represent Cindy Client in a divorce matter. Because Cindy has little money, Cindy's father, Fred, desires to pay for the representation. Lisa violates no rule by representing Cindy in this setting. Lisa must take care to ensure that Cindy understands and consents to the arrangement and would do well to explain to Fred the boundaries of Fred's involvement in the matter as defined by Rule 1.8(f)(DE) or as agreed to by Cindy. If Fred telephones Lisa and instructs Lisa about what Lisa must do in representing Cindy, Lisa must guard against allowing Fred to influence the advice and service Lisa renders to Cindy.

C. Sharing Legal Fees and Referrals

To prophylactically further the principle that a lawyer's professional judgment should be independent and not controlled or influenced by anyone or anything other than the ideal of the best interests of the client, the rules of professional conduct for lawyers have long prohibited sharing legal fees. Referral systems have also been prohibited by the rules on the basis of the notion that sharing legal fees creates an environment in which the interests of another may constrain a lawyer's judgment regarding a representation. Referral systems involving nonlawyers are simply a form of sharing legal fees with nonlawyers.

1. Sharing Legal Fees with a Nonlawyer

a. The Prohibition

Because of the potential adverse effect on the "independent professional judgment" of lawyers, lawyers may not share legal fees with nonlawyers. If a lawyer works in an environment that permits sharing legal fees with a nonlawyer, the nonlawyer's stake in the financial pie puts the nonlawyer in a position to influence the lawyer's professional judgment and gives the nonlawyer the incentive to influence the lawyer's professional judgment. Rule 5.4(a)(NE) contains this general prohibition.

Lisa Lawyer and Austin Accountant may work together on a matter for a client. The fee for Lisa and the fee for Austin must remain separate so that there is no possibility that Austin is sharing in the fee for legal services. Lisa also could not be employed by a corporation, render services to third parties, and allow the corporation to take any part of the fee for Lisa's services. If the corporation receives payment for Lisa's services and then pays Lisa a salary, Lisa is, in effect, sharing the legal fee with a nonlawyer, the corporation. This Lisa cannot do. In addition, some jurisdictions would hold that the corporation is engaging in the unauthorized practice of law because even though Lisa is admitted to practice, the corporation is not. *See Chapter 40 The Unauthorized Practice of Law.*

b. The Exceptions

There are several recognized exceptions to the general rule that lawyers may not share legal fees with nonlawyers. These exceptions are situations in which improper influence on lawyers' professional judgment is unlikely to occur.

1. A Payment upon a Lawyer's Death

First, a lawyer can agree with the lawyer's practice entity that the entity is to pay the lawyer's estate, or one or more persons, upon the lawyer's death, money derived from legal fees or other sources. The fees should be paid to the estate "over a reasonable period of time after the lawyer's death." Rule 5.4(a)(1)(NE) so provides. If the lawyer practices in a firm, the agreement can be with the firm entity regardless of whether the entity is a partnership, limited liability corporation, or other entity form. The agreement can be with the lawyer's partner if the entity consists of only two lawyers. The agreement can be with the lawyer's associate if the firm is comprised of the more senior lawyer and one associate. The payment must occur within a reasonable time so that the odd relationship of the firm or lawyer and the nonlawyer is not a continuing one. The exception recognizes the necessity of allowing a sharing of legal fees, but the payment should be prompt so that the nonlawyer has less opportunity to seek to influence, the lawyer or lawyers involved have less opportunity to be influenced, and there is no appearance of influence created by the short-term relationship.

If Larry Lawyer and Lisa Lawyer practice law together, they can agree that the surviving partner, upon the other partner's death, can and should pay some amount to the estate of the deceased lawyer. If the amount to be paid relates to legal fees billed by the deceased lawyer, then the payment is the sharing of fees with a nonlawyer. Yet the rule permits such a payment because the money rightfully should go to the party or entity designated by the lawyer and the danger of compromise of the professional judgment of any lawyer is minimal.

2. A Payment to Purchase a Law Practice

A lawyer may purchase the practice of a "deceased, disabled, or disappeared lawyer" from a nonlawyer representative of the "deceased, disabled or disappeared lawyer." Rule 1.17(KS) provides that a lawyer may purchase the practice or an area of a practice from a lawyer leaving the practice of law entirely, moving to another geographical region, or ceasing to practice in a particular subject area. *See Chapter 12 Sale of a Practice.* A comment Rule 1.17(KS) clarifies that the lawyer may purchase the practice of a "deceased, disabled, or disappeared lawyer" from a nonlawyer representative. Rule 5.4(a)(2)(NE) provides that purchasing the practice from a nonlawyer representative of a "deceased, disabled, or disappeared lawyer" is not contrary to the prohibition on sharing legal fees with nonlawyers. This situation is quite a distance away from the kind of fee sharing with nonlawyers at which the general prohibition is aimed.

3. Including Nonlawyers in a Compensation or Retirement Plan

Third, even though one could argue that such a framework involves the sharing of legal fees with nonlawyers, lawyers may have retirement or profit sharing plans for their practice staffs and can include both lawyers and nonlawyers in the plans. Rule 5.4(a)(3)(NE) so provides. Such an arrangement looks less like sharing legal fees with nonlawyers if the payouts received by the nonlawyers do not relate to results in any one case but relate to profitability generally.

The rule does not specifically prohibit a sharing of a fee in a single case. Some ethics opinions have interpreted the rule to not allow such a sharing of a fee. Rather, those opinions require any sharing of fees to be done on the basis of overall profits. Certainly, a sharing on the basis of overall profits deemphasizes the link between specific legal work done and decisions made in that work on the one hand and the creation of profit on the other hand. Thus, the assumption is that there is less incentive for nonlawyer interference in the rendering of legal services.

4. Sharing Court-Awarded Fees with a Non-profit Organization

Fourth, though a lawyer generally may not share legal fees with nonlawyers, lawyers may share fees awarded by a court with a non-profit organization that "employed, retained or recommended" the lawyer regarding that matter. Rule 5.4(a)(4)(NE) provides this exception. For example, perhaps Lisa Lawyer, an employee lawyer of the American Civil Liberties Union (ACLU), agrees that if a court awards fees in any case she handles for the ACLU, she will forward the court-awarded fee to the ACLU and will not keep it for herself. Several years later, Lisa leaves the employ of the ACLU but continues to handle several matters the ACLU had assigned to her. A court then awards a fee to Lisa in one of those matters. Lisa does not violate Rule 5.4(NE) if she forwards the fee to the ACLU as she has agreed.

This exception makes clear that lawyers can pay a share of the fee award for referrals from nonprofit organizations that result in court-awarded legal fees. Thus, if Lisa, a solo practitioner, receives a matter through a referral by the local nonprofit bar association referral service, and she secures a court-awarded fee, she can share that fee with the bar association referral service.

2. Referral Fees Involving Nonlawyers

Referral fees involving nonlawyers generally are not permitted because they are examples of sharing legal fees with nonlawyers. There are a few exceptions. Rule 7.2(b)(2)(NE) allows Lisa to pay the "usual" fee for referrals even if there is no court-awarded fee if the referral entity is a "legal service plan," a "not-for-profit" service or a "qualified" service. The rule states that a "qualified lawyer referral service is a legal referral service that has been approved by an appropriate regulatory authority."

In addition, Rule 7.2(b)(4)(NE) provides that a lawyer also may agree with another lawyer or with a nonlawyer professional that the lawyer will refer clients to the nonlawyer and the nonlawyer will refer clients to the lawyer. Such an arrangement cannot be exclusive and the lawyer must tell the client of the arrangement. This situation is not a sharing of a legal fee, but it may touch upon the lawyer's independence of professional judgment. Lawyers should always be wary of allowing a referral arrangement to interfere with the lawyer's professional judgment. *See Chapter 45 Communications about Lawyer Services.*

3. Lawyers Sharing Fees

Lawyers in the same firm can, of course, share fees without restrictions. All lawyers in the firm owe duties to the client. Rule 1.5(e)(NE) deals with the issue of lawyers who are not in the same firm sharing fees.

When lawyers are not in the same firm, Rule 1.5(e)(NE) allows lawyers to share fees to the extent that the split of the fee represents the share of the work each lawyer completed. If Lisa Lawyer, a generalist, evaluated a matter and determined that Cindy Client needed to be represented by a certain specialist in tax law, and if Cindy heeded Lisa's advice and obtained the services of the tax lawyer, then the fee for services could represent payment for Lisa's work and payment for the tax lawyer's work. The part of the fee for Lisa's work might be characterized as a referral fee.

Rule 1.5(e)(NE) also provides that the lawyers can split the fee in any manor if they both agree to be responsible for the work of the other. In either scenario the arrangement would be in accord with Rule 1.5(e)(NE) only if a writing confirms that Cindy agrees to the fee division and to the share each lawyer receives.

D. The Prohibition of Nonlawyer Control over a Lawyer's Provision of Legal Services

Since the overall goal is to protect the professional judgment of lawyers from interference by nonlawyers who may have an interest in the legal representation, a core concept is that nonlawyers cannot be in a position to exercise managerial control over the rendering of legal services. Nonlawyers cannot have such control as the result of job assignment or ownership of the endeavor.

Rule 5.4(b)(NE) prohibits a lawyer from forming a partnership with a nonlawyer if "any of the activities of the partnership" are the practice of law. Lisa Lawyer can certainly form a partnership with a Joe, a nonlawyer, to develop real estate, run a coffee store, or buy a boat. None of these partnerships involves the practice of law. Lisa could not form a partnership with Joe for the practice of law. Such an arrangement would put Joe in a position to interfere with Lisa's "independent professional judgment" and would provide Joe with an incentive, profit maximization, to interfere.

Likewise, Rule 5.4(d)(NE) prohibits a lawyer from practicing law for profit in any corporate or other form if a nonlawyer owns an interest in the entity, is a director or officer of the entity, has a similar position in the entity, or "has the right to direct or control the professional judgment of a lawyer." A fiduciary of a lawyer's estate may hold an interest for a "reasonable time" during the estate administration. Any of the prohibited situations would provide the nonlawyer with the means and incentive to interfere with the "independent professional judgment" of the lawyer.

Thus, Lisa Lawyer cannot form a corporation for the practice of law and raise capital by selling shares in the corporation to nonlawyer members of the public. If Lisa forms a limited liability entity for the purpose of offering legal services as well as accounting services, Lisa cannot allow Joe, a nonlawyer employee who assists with the accounting endeavor, to be a director or member of the limited liability entity because then Joe would be in a position to influence Lisa in her rendering of legal services and Joe, perhaps, would have an incentive to influence Lisa improperly.

Related Sections of the *Restatement (Third) of the Law Governing Lawyers*

Section 10

Checkpoints

- A lawyer must "render candid advice" and may consider not only legal issues but also other factors such as "moral, economic, social and political" issues.
- A lawyer must "exercise independent professional judgment" in representing clients.
- A lawyer should prevent interference with the lawyer's professional judgment even though the potential interferer recommends, employs, or pays the lawyer.
- If a third party pays the lawyer's fees for a client, the lawyer must not allow the one paying to interfere with the lawyer's professional judgment or the lawyer-client relationship.
- A lawyer must not share legal fees with nonlawyers because the sharing of fees puts the nonlawyer in a position to and gives the nonlawyer an incentive to interfere with the lawyer's rendering of legal services.
- A lawyer may
    1. pay a share of legal fees to a deceased lawyer's estate or another nonlawyer upon the death of the lawyer;
    2. pay a share of legal fees to a nonlawyer in a purchase of a law practice of a "deceased, disabled, or disappeared lawyer";
    3. "include nonlawyer employees in a compensation or retirement plan" based on fees; and
    4. "share court-awarded fees with a nonprofit organization that employed, retained or recommended" the lawyer.
- A lawyer must be vigilant and evaluate situations such as reciprocal referral arrangements with nonlawyer professionals or other lawyers and fee sharing arrangements between lawyers to avoid interference with the lawyer's "independent professional judgment."

- To prophylactically protect a lawyer's independence, a nonlawyer must not have any control over the rendering of legal services by a lawyer. A nonlawyer must not have an ownership interest that gives the nonlawyer a measure of control and the nonlawyer must not hold any office or position within the organization rendering legal services that would give the nonlawyer control.

Chapter 40

The Unauthorized Practice of Law

Roadmap

- Rule 5.5(KS)
- Defining the practice of law
- The unauthorized practice of law by a nonlawyer
- Assisting in the unauthorized practice of law
- The unauthorized practice of law by a lawyer
- Situations in which a lawyer may practice law in a jurisdiction in which the lawyer is not admitted
- Having an office or other continuous presence in a jurisdiction in which the lawyer is not admitted
- Advertising or otherwise holding the lawyer out as a lawyer admitted in a jurisdiction if such is not true

---

A. The Traditional Approach

The traditional rule for many decades was that, except for *pro se* representation, only individuals who were admitted to the bar of a jurisdiction could practice law in that jurisdiction. This notion should come as no surprise given the elaborate admissions process in place in United States jurisdictions. The admissions process was created on the theory that the practice of law requires a high level of skill and expertise and that the public should be protected from people lacking that skill and expertise. It is logical that jurisdictions would allow only those individuals certified as exhibiting the requisite level of skill and expertise to practice law. *See Chapter 2 Admission to the Bar.*

The issue of the unauthorized practice of law typically arises in two settings:

1. practice by a nonlawyer, a person not admitted to practice in any jurisdiction, and
2. practice by a lawyer admitted to practice in a jurisdiction but not admitted in the jurisdiction in which the lawyer is practicing.

The first setting is the most obvious. A person with no legal training or expertise, not admitted in any jurisdiction, engages in conduct within the definition of the practice of law. For example, Joe Schmo, a college graduate with no legal training and not admitted to practice law in Delaware, is in the business of giving estate planning advice and drafting wills in Delaware. By so acting, Joe engages in the unauthorized practice of law in Delaware. Many states make the unauthorized practice of law a crime. A court might punish Joe or issue an injunction prohibiting Joe from engaging in these activities.

In the second typical setting, Larry Lawyer is admitted in a jurisdiction such as Georgia. If Larry renders legal advice in Delaware when he visits a factory in Delaware owned by a client he serves in Georgia, Larry engages in the unauthorized practice of law under the historical view. Larry is practicing law in Delaware, a state that has not admitted Larry. Professional responsibility standards traditionally prohibited lawyers from engaging in the unauthorized practice of law so Larry's conduct would have been improper as well as possibly criminal.

Some commentators speculate that the true rationale for forbidding the practice of law by those not admitted to the bar is control of competition. Some question such restrictions in light of the inability of some members of the public to access legal assistance. These commentators argue that any constraint on the supply of legal services is improper. The rationale of protecting the public from the unskilled charlatan might justify a restraint on a person with no legal training. The rationale fails when the person not admitted in the jurisdiction is a lawyer admitted elsewhere. In light of customs and standards of legal education and bar admission requirements today, any argument that a lawyer admitted in one jurisdiction but not admitted in another jurisdiction is incapable of rendering proper competent legal assistance in that second jurisdiction is disingenuous.

But the modern practice of law often crosses state boundaries and in many situations is global. Also, any danger to the public is minimal when lawyers admitted to practice law in another jurisdiction render the legal services. In recognition of these facts, professional responsibility standards have been redrafted to modify the traditional position by permitting some conduct that would historically have constituted the unauthorized practice of law.

Rule 5.5(a)(KS) restates the traditional prohibition that a lawyer may not practice law or assist another in the practice of law if those actions are a "violation of the regulation of the legal profession in that jurisdiction." Rule 5.5(KS) also provides exceptions to the traditional rule. If a lawyer's situation fits within an exception, that lawyer may practice law in a jurisdiction in which he or she is not admitted. Under the current rule, Larry's conduct in rendering legal advice in Delaware though he is admitted only in Georgia may not be the unauthorized practice of law and thus Larry may be acting properly.

B. The Practice of Law Defined

For lawyers to know that they are practicing law unauthorizedly and thus improperly, they must know what activities are within the definition of the practice of law. What conduct constitutes the practice of law? There is no one definition shared by all states. Rather, each state, by rule, statute, or case law, has developed its own definition. In 2000, the ABA created a commission to develop a definition that could be used to provide uniformity to the states. Ultimately, however, the commission determined that a uniform definition was not possible. Most states have broad definitions that can be read to include almost any conduct. For example, in *In re Thonert*, 693 N.E.2d 559(Ind. 1998), the Indiana Supreme Court stated:

> A person who gives legal advice to clients and transacts business for them in matters connected with the law is engaged in the practice of law.... Thus, the practice of law is not defined only as the giving of legal advice or acting in a representative capacity—it also had been extended by this Court to conducting the business management of a law practice.

Id. at 563.

Joe Schmo, the nonlawyer in the earlier example, in drafting wills for others, engages in conduct within common definitions of the practice of law. Likewise, Larry, the lawyer in the second of the earlier examples, renders legal advice to another and thus engages in conduct within common definitions of the practice of law.

C. Assisting in the Unauthorized Practice of Law

Joe Schmo, a person without legal training and not admitted to the bar in any jurisdiction, engages in the unauthorized practice of law if he engages in conduct within the definition of the practice of law. Rule 5.5(KS) forbids a lawyer from assisting a person in practicing law when that person is not admitted in the jurisdiction. If Lisa Lawyer is admitted to practice in Delaware and assists Joe Schmo, a nonlawyer, in setting up his estate planning and will preparation business, Lisa has assisted Joe in the unauthorized practice of law. Lisa has violated Rule 5.5(KS).

More commonly, the issue of a lawyer assisting a nonlawyer in the unauthorized practice of law arises regarding the lawyer's employees. A lawyer cannot allow anyone working with or for the lawyer to take action within the definition of the practice of law if the person is not a lawyer, unless that activity is done under the lawyer's supervision. Often, paralegals and other law office workers develop skill and expertise. Often, lawyers allow or require these individuals to perform tasks that are within the definition of the practice of law. Lawyers who allow or require employees to so act without lawyer supervision are violating Rule 5.5(KS) unless the jurisdiction has a special rule permitting the nonlawyer's conduct. In addition, the lawyer may run afoul of Rule 5.3(DE) on the basis of lack of supervision of employees. Even though Larry Lawyer has utmost confidence in Peter Paralegal's abilities, Larry must take care to see that Peter does not, for example, render legal advice to Larry's clients. *See Chapter 38 Supervision and Responsibility for Other Lawyers, Nonlawyer Employees, and Other Assistants.*

Occasionally, a lawyer may employ an individual who was an admitted lawyer at one time but is now suspended or disbarred. The employee has certain lawyer skills and expertise and the employing lawyer may be tempted to allow the employee to, in effect, practice law. Allowing such a person to practice law would be assisting in the unauthorized practice of law and would violate Rule 5.5(KS). Larry Lawyer may have hired Denny, a disbarred lawyer, to do legal research, thinking that Denny could do great work at a bargain price. Larry must be careful not to rely on Denny to practice law. Denny must work under Larry's careful supervision. Some jurisdictions forbid disbarred lawyers from certain activities, regardless of lawyer supervision.

Finally, a lawyer cannot assist another lawyer in the practice of law in a jurisdiction in which the lawyer is not admitted if that lawyer otherwise is not granted the right to practice in that jurisdiction. So a Delaware lawyer such as Lisa cannot assist a Georgia lawyer such as Larry in practicing law in Delaware if Rule 5.5(KS) does not permit Larry to practice in Delaware.

D. A Lawyer Admitted in a Jurisdiction but Not Admitted in This Jurisdiction

1. The Problem

If Larry Lawyer is admitted in Georgia but not Delaware and renders legal advice in Delaware, the traditional analysis is that Larry engages in the unauthorized practice of law because he is practicing law in Delaware, a jurisdiction that has not admitted him.

This stance does not mesh well with the realities of the modern practice of law. Today, a client in Georgia may ask Larry, a lawyer admitted in Georgia, to go to the client's office or factory in Delaware. Larry may render legal advice while there. Such conduct would be improper under the traditional rule yet is necessary for efficient and proper representation of the client. In addition, there is little support for the argument that Larry's advice is somehow lacking simply because Larry renders that advice in Delaware.

Larry might depose a witness in Delaware who has information important to a litigation matter in Georgia. Again, it is quite a stretch of logic to say that Larry is not competent to take the deposition. Yet Larry's conduct would be improper under traditional unauthorized practice notions. Lawyers today take these sorts of actions every day in an attempt to service far-flung clients or cases with far-flung evidence.

Rule 5.5(KS) significantly modifies the traditional rule to allow several common practices if those practices occur on a temporary basis. In addition, the rule provides an exception to the traditional rule for the in-house counsel setting and an exception for practice that federal or other law permits.

2. Permitted Conduct: Legal Services on a Temporary Basis

Rule 5.5(KS) maintains the traditional ban on practicing law where not admitted but provides four specific exceptions when the practice of law occurs on a temporary basis and the lawyer is admitted to the bar of another United States jurisdiction and is in good standing—not disbarred or suspended. These temporary practice exceptions are as follows:

1. The association of admitted counsel exception.
2. The proceeding before a tribunal exception.
3. The alternative dispute resolution exception.
4. The related activities exception.

These exceptions allow a lawyer to have conferences, mediations, client meetings, depositions, and any other sort of occasion for the rendering of legal services in jurisdictions in which the lawyer is not admitted as long as the rendering of legal service is temporary. There is little guidance as to how often a lawyer could render legal service in a particular jurisdiction before the temporary exception would no longer apply. A comment to the rule notes the absence of any one test but also states that the exception conduct can be temporary even if the conduct is recurring or "for an extended period of time, as when the lawyer is representing a client in a single lengthy negotiation or litigation."

a. Association with an Admitted Lawyer

A lawyer admitted in a United States jurisdiction and in good standing but not admitted in a particular jurisdiction may practice law in that jurisdiction on a temporary basis if the lawyer associates with an admitted lawyer who "actively participates in the matter." Rule 5.5(c)(1)(KS) states this exception. Larry Lawyer, a lawyer admitted in Georgia, may find himself practicing law in Delaware by taking depositions in Delaware or giving legal advice to a client at the client's Delaware facility. If Larry engages in the practice of law in Delaware only temporarily and he associates with a Delaware lawyer who remains involved in the litigation or other representation, Larry has not engaged in the unauthorized practice of law in violation of Rule 5.5(KS).

b. Activities "Reasonably Related" to a Proceeding before a Tribunal

A lawyer admitted in a United States jurisdiction and in good standing but not admitted in a particular jurisdiction can practice law in that jurisdiction on a temporary basis if the conduct is "in or reasonably related to a pending or potential proceeding before a tribunal" if the lawyer expects to be authorized to appear in the proceeding. The tribunal need not be in the jurisdiction in which the conduct occurs. In addition, the rule recognizes that often more than one lawyer works on a matter. Rule 5.5(c)(2)(KS) provides that this tribunal exception applies even if the lawyer does not expect to be authorized to appear but the person the lawyer is assisting expects to be authorized to appear.

Larry Lawyer, admitted in Georgia, may take a deposition or interview witnesses in Delaware relating to a proceeding before a tribunal in Georgia. Larry may do so even if the proceeding does not exist yet but is only a "potential proceeding." Larry may participate in these activities in Delaware even if the matter will culminate in a proceeding before a South Carolina tribunal if Larry expects to be admitted *pro hac vice.* Larry may take the deposition even if the matter will be tried in Delaware and even if Larry does not expect to be admitted in any manner in Delaware if he is, for example, an associate preparing a case for another lawyer who does expect to be admitted *pro hac vice.*

c. *Activities "Reasonably Related" to an "Arbitration, Mediation, or Other Alternative Dispute Resolution Proceeding"*

Rule 5.5(c)(3)(KS) provides that a lawyer admitted in a United States jurisdiction and in good standing but not admitted in a particular jurisdiction may practice law in that jurisdiction on a temporary basis if the lawyer's conduct is "in or reasonably related to a pending or potential arbitration, mediation, or other alternative dispute resolution proceeding." The activity must "arise out of or ... reasonably relate[] to the lawyer's practice" in an admitted jurisdiction and the situation must be one in which the jurisdiction does not require *pro hac vice* admission. The proceeding need not be in a jurisdiction in which the lawyer is admitted as long as the activities relate to the lawyer's practice in an admitted jurisdiction.

Larry Lawyer, a Georgia lawyer, may interview witnesses in Delaware relating to an arbitration in Georgia involving his Georgia client. Larry may also interview witnesses relating to an arbitration in Delaware if the arbitration relates to the representation of one of Larry's Georgia clients.

d. *Activities "Reasonably Related" to Practice in an Admitted Jurisdiction*

Rule 5.5(c)(4)(KS) provides a huge exception to the ban on unauthorized practice. A lawyer admitted in a United States jurisdiction and in good standing but not admitted in a particular jurisdiction can practice law in that jurisdiction on a temporary basis if

1. the activities "arise out of or are reasonably related to the lawyer's practice" in an admitted jurisdiction,
2. the tribunal proceeding exception does not apply, and
3. the alternative dispute resolution exception does not apply.

Larry Lawyer, a Georgia lawyer, may render legal advice when he visits his Georgia client's facility in Delaware because that advice is "reasonably related" to Larry's representation of his client in Georgia.

3. Permitted Conduct: In-House Counsel

In-house lawyers may practice law in a jurisdiction and, thus, have "an office or other systematic and continuous presence" in a jurisdiction in which they are not admitted

1. if they render legal services only for the employer or the employer's subsidiaries or affiliates,
2. if the lawyers are admitted in another United States jurisdiction or a foreign jurisdiction and are in good standing, and
3. if the jurisdiction generally does not require *pro hac vice* admission for the activity.

This exception is stated in Rule 5.5(d)(1)(KS). This treatment of in-house lawyers is a recognition that employers of in-house lawyers sometimes require the lawyers to move, sometimes repeatedly. Admission in multiple jurisdictions becomes a chore for these lawyers with no great benefit given that the only client is the entity requiring the moves.

The in-house counsel exception is also a recognition that in-house lawyers may be working in one state but rendering advice and thus practicing law in other states. It is not uncommon for an in-house legal department for a large corporation to render legal advice to arms of the corporation located in many other states or countries. Lois Lawyer, an in-house lawyer, may work for a corporation in Georgia and may be admitted in Georgia. Yet Lois may often visit facilities of the employer in other states such as Delaware and may render legal advice in those states. Perhaps Lois is admitted in Georgia but works for a corporation in Delaware. She regularly renders legal advice to her employer in Delaware. Rule 5.5(KS) eliminates any suggestion that Lois is engaging in improper conduct.

Some jurisdictions require that the in-house lawyer register with the bar of the jurisdiction even though the state does not require full admission to the bar of that jurisdiction.

Unlike the temporary practice exceptions, which require that the lawyer be admitted in a United States jurisdiction, the in-house exception applies to lawyers admitted in a foreign jurisdiction in addition to lawyers admitted in United States jurisdictions. Yet not all countries regulate lawyers as jurisdictions in the United States do. To ensure that bestowing limited practice rights on a foreign lawyer is appropriate, Rule 5.5(e)(KS) requires that the foreign lawyer "be a member in good standing of a recognized legal profession in a foreign jurisdiction, the members of which are admitted to practice as lawyers or counselors at law or the equivalent, and are subject to effective regulation and discipline by a duly constituted professional body or public authority." Even so, when a foreign lawyer provides advice on the law of a United States jurisdiction, that lawyer may do so only if he or she bases that advice on the advice of a lawyer licensed by the jurisdiction or authorized by the jurisdiction to render such advice.

4. Permitted Conduct: Conduct Authorized by Other Law

Rule 5.5(d)(2)(KS) acknowledges that a lawyer may not be admitted in a particular jurisdiction and yet may have the right to practice in the jurisdiction by application of federal law or other specific law. This exception to the traditional ban on practice in a jurisdiction in which a lawyer is not admitted applies to lawyers admitted in other United States jurisdictions and also lawyers admitted in foreign jurisdictions. Such lawyers must be in good standing. A foreign lawyer must "be a member in good standing of a recognized legal profession in a foreign jurisdiction, the members of which are admitted to practice as lawyers or counselors at law or the equivalent, and are subject to effective regulation and discipline by a duly constituted professional body or public authority."

a. Federal Law

The federal law exception recognizes that federal courts can set rules that preempt state regulation. For example, the United States Sixth Circuit Court of Appeals in *In re Desilets,* 291 F.3d 925 (6th Cir. 2002), considered the question of whether a lawyer could practice federal bankruptcy law in a jurisdiction in which the lawyer was not admitted. The lawyer was admitted in Texas but not Michigan. He had an office in Michigan and practiced federal bankruptcy law in the Western District of Michigan. The lawyer was admitted to the bar of the Western District of Michigan. The Western District required admission to a state bar but did not require admission to the bar of Michigan. The Sixth Circuit held that the right to practice in federal court included not only the right to appear in federal court in the Western District of Michigan but also the right to engage in activities outside the courtroom, such as consulting with and advising clients. Thus, the *Desilets* court determined that the state law prohibiting the lawyer from engaging in these activities impermissibly conflicted with federal law.

b. Other Law

Jurisdictions also recognize the concept of *pro hac vice* admission. A lawyer not admitted in a jurisdiction but admitted in another United States jurisdiction or foreign jurisdiction and in good standing may request that a court admit the lawyer so that the lawyer may appear for the purpose of the matter only. *Pro hac vice* admission requirements and procedures are usually stated in general court rules.

Larry Lawyer, a lawyer admitted in Georgia, may have a client with a litigation matter in Delaware. Larry may ask the Delaware court presiding over the matter to allow him to practice law and appear in the court for that matter only. Courts routinely grant *pro hac vice* admission though a common requirement of the admission is that local counsel be associated as well.

States may have other idiosyncratic rules that allow a lawyer admitted in another jurisdiction to practice law in certain specific settings. For example, a state might have a rule allowing lawyers admitted elsewhere but not in the particular jurisdiction to appear in administrative proceedings.

5. Impermissible Conduct: Establishing "an Office or Other Systematic and Continuous Presence"

A lawyer to whom the in-house lawyer exception or the other law authorization exception cannot apply cannot have an office in a jurisdiction in which the lawyer is not admitted and cannot otherwise maintain a "systematic and continuous presence" in that jurisdiction for the purpose of practicing law, according to Rule 5.5(b)(1)(KS).

If Larry Lawyer, a lawyer practicing personal injury law, is admitted in Georgia, but not Delaware, Larry cannot have an office in Delaware. He is not an in-house lawyer and there are no federal or state laws to permit such.

6. Impermissible Conduct: Advertising or Otherwise Representing That a Lawyer Is Admitted in a Jurisdiction in Which the Lawyer Is Not Admitted

Lawyers may not present themselves to the public as admitted in a jurisdiction if the lawyers are not admitted in that jurisdiction, according to Rule 5.5(b)(2)(KS). Larry Lawyer may not advertise himself as a Delaware lawyer or as someone capable of practicing in Delaware unless Larry is in fact admitted in Delaware. Given the *Desilets* opinion, one would assume that Larry could advertise himself as a lawyer capable of practicing federal law in a jurisdiction in which he is not admitted if he is admitted to the relevant federal court.

Related Sections of the *Restatement (Third) of the Law Governing Lawyers*

Sections 3 and 4

Checkpoints

- The practice of law by one not admitted to the bar of a jurisdiction and not otherwise having permission to practice law in the jurisdiction is the unauthorized practice of law.
- A lawyer who assists another person in the unauthorized practice of law is acting improperly.
- Though admitted in another jurisdiction, a lawyer practicing law in a jurisdiction in which the lawyer is not admitted is practicing law unauthorizedly unless an exception stated in Rule 5.5(KS) applies.
- A lawyer admitted in another United States jurisdiction and in good standing may practice law temporarily in a jurisdiction in which the lawyer is not admitted if
    1. the lawyer associates admitted counsel who remains active in the matter,
    2. the lawyer engages in activities "reasonably related" to a proceeding before a tribunal in a jurisdiction in which the lawyer or the lawyer's colleague in the representation is admitted or otherwise is or will be authorized to appear,
    3. the lawyer engages in activities "reasonably related" to an alternative dispute resolution proceeding in connection with practice in a jurisdiction in which the lawyer is admitted and the proceeding does not require *pro hac vice* admission, or
    4. the lawyer engages in activities "reasonably related" to practice in a jurisdiction in which the lawyer is admitted and neither the tribunal exception nor the alternative dispute resolution exception applies.
- An in-house lawyer admitted in a United States jurisdiction or a foreign jurisdiction may practice law in jurisdictions in which the lawyer is not admitted if *pro hac vice* admission is not required and the lawyer represents only the employer.
- A lawyer admitted in a United States jurisdiction or a foreign jurisdiction may practice law in jurisdictions in which the lawyer is not admitted if federal or other law permits such conduct.
- A lawyer may not have "an office or other systematic and continuous presence" in a jurisdiction in which the lawyer is not admitted unless the in-house lawyer exception applies or other law permits it.
- A lawyer may not advertise or otherwise hold himself or herself out as a lawyer admitted in a jurisdiction in which the lawyer is not admitted.

Chapter 41

Restrictions on a Lawyer's Right to Practice Law

Roadmap

- Rule 5.6(DE)
- Restrictions on the right to practice law accompanying partnership or other similar agreements
- The exception for restrictions that relate to retirement benefits
- Restrictions on the right to practice law that accompany settlement of a client's matter

---

A. Prohibition of Restrictions

1. The Rule

In most jurisdictions, nonlawyer professionals may enter into agreements that restrict the right of those professionals to compete if the restriction is reasonable. The rule for lawyers is quite the contrary. Rule 5.6(a)(DE) prohibits a lawyer from participating in any "partnership, shareholders, operating, employment, or other similar type of agreement" that restricts a lawyer's right to practice unless the agreement deals with retirement benefits. A lawyer who is a party to such an agreement is subject to discipline.

The rationale for the rule is a mix of concern for lawyers and for clients. The concern for lawyers is that restrictive agreements limit lawyers' freedom to practice law. The concern for clients is that these agreements constrain clients' ability to have counsel of choice.

In addition to discipline exposure for the attorneys involved, courts generally do not enforce agreements restricting lawyers' right to practice because these agreements are contrary to the rules of professional responsibility for lawyers and thus contradict public policy. Courts are virtually unanimous in their disapproval when an agreement directly restricts competition. Most courts also refuse to enforce agreements that restrict competition indirectly by imposing financial disincentives or penalties for competition. For example, the Supreme Judicial Court of Massachusetts in *Eisenstein v. David G. Conlin, P.C.*, 827 N.E.2d 686 (Mass. 2005), refused to enforce a contract that required departing lawyers to pay a share of fees to the former firm if the fees related to past or current clients of the former firm.

A few courts have enforced contracts with financial disincentives to competition. These courts evaluate the restrictions on competition using a reasonableness standard, just as they do with restrictions on nonlawyers.

2. The Retirement Exception

Rule 5.6(a)(DE) generally prohibits restrictions on the lawyer's right to practice. There is an exception, however. If the restriction is part of an agreement regarding retirement benefits, the restriction is permissible. The rationale for the exception is that a retiring lawyer would not be available for clients anyway so restricting that lawyer's right to practice really has no practical effect on the lawyer or on the client populace.

The real question is how to determine whether an agreement relates to retirement benefits. *ABA Formal Opinion 06-444 (2006)* clarifies that an agreement or a provision of an agreement does not relate to retirement benefits and, thus, does not fit within the exception, unless the provision affects benefits available only to lawyers retiring from the practice of law. To be considered a provision relating to retirement benefits, the provision cannot penalize the lawyer by taking away funds already earned. Other indicators that are not independently dispositive of a retirement benefit arrangement include benefit calculation formulas, provisions for benefits to increase as years of service increase, and provisions that provide for the payment of amounts for the remaining lifetime of the lawyer.

3. Sale of a Practice

When a lawyer sells a practice pursuant to Rule 1.17(KS), that lawyer must no longer practice in the geographic area. If a lawyer sells a subject segment of a practice, that lawyer cannot continue to practice in that subject area. *See Chapter 12 Sale of a Practice.* The agreements relating to such sales may include restrictions that would otherwise violate Rule 5.6(DE) but are consistent with Rule 1.17(KS).

B. Restrictions on the Right to Practice in Connection with a Settlement

1. The Rule and Rationale

Rule 5.6(b)(DE) prohibits a lawyer from entering into, offering, or making any agreement that is part of a settlement of a client's matter if that agreement also restricts the lawyer's right to practice. The following is a typical setting. Lisa Lawyer represents Cindy Client in a product liability action against Big Corporation. Lisa does a really good job developing Cindy's case. As a result, Big Corporation would like to settle for a reasonable amount with Cindy. Big Corporation would also like to prevent Lisa from representing other plaintiffs with similar claims against it because the defendant fears Lisa could be particularly effective in handling similar claims. Big Corporation might offer a very respectable settlement amount to Cindy but the offer includes the requirement that Lisa not represent clients with similar claims against Big Corporation.

This example makes the rationale of the prohibition on these agreements more obvious. Clearly, this offer creates a conflict of interest between the lawyer, Lisa, and her client, Cindy. Lisa might be pressured to accept the restriction because Cindy wants the settlement money. An opposite kind of conflict can occur also, especially if Big Corporation includes in the offer a special monetary treat for Lisa. If Big Corporation offers Lisa a respectable amount in exchange for her promise not to represent clients with claims against it and if this arrangement is in connection with the settlement of Cindy's claim, Lisa may allow her own personal interest in the money cloud her advice to Cindy regarding the settlement. The lawyer disciplined in *In re Hager*, 812 A.2d 904 (D.C. 2002), agreed, in connection with a settlement of his clients' claims, to accept $225,000 in exchange for a promise not to represent other clients with claims against the defendant. The lawyer also agreed not to disclose any information he had gathered and agreed not to tell his clients about the arrangement between the lawyer and the defendant. These facts make the conflict of interest rationale for the rule obvious. Prohibiting these restrictions on a lawyer's right to practice is an attempt to minimize these types of conflicts.

Another rationale is that if Lisa, a lawyer who has some expertise in claims against Big Corporation, cannot represent clients with similar claims against Big, the very best of the supply of lawyers has been taken away from those potential clients. A related thought is that the expertise and knowledge Lisa has developed by way of the operation of the judicial system, perhaps a public good, is lost if she cannot use that expertise and knowledge. If such restrictions are permissible, the settling client perhaps enjoys a larger payment than the claim actually deserves since the client may be capturing part of the payment for the restriction on the lawyer.

Some have criticized Rule 5.6(b)(DE). For example, in *Feldman v. Minars*, 658 N.Y.S.2d 614 (N.Y. App. Div. 1997), the New York court was not dealing with the issue of discipline but rather faced the issue of whether to enforce an agreement entered into as part of a settlement of the claims of clients. In that agreement the lawyers representing certain plaintiffs agreed not to "assist or cooperate" in the pursuit of claims of other persons against the original defendants. Later, those lawyers did "assist or cooperate," but claimed that the agreement could not be enforced because it was contrary to the applicable rules of professional responsibility and thus against public policy. The court held that the earlier agreement precluded the later representation even though the lawyers involved with that earlier agreement might be subject to professional discipline. The *Feldman* court stated: "[W]e find persuasive the reasoning of Professor Gillers, who contends that 'Rule 5.6(b) ... is an anachronism, illogical and bad policy.'" Id. at 617 (quoting Stephen Gillers, *A Rule Without A Reason: Let the Market, Not the Bar, Regulate Settlements That Restrict Practice*, ABA Journal, Oct. 1993, at 118).

2. Types of Improper Agreements

Agreements that restrict a lawyer's right to practice by prohibiting that lawyer from representing other clients in claims against the original adverse party violate Rule 5.6(b)(DE) and are not proper. Lisa Lawyer, therefore, could not enter into such an agreement just as the lawyer in *Hager* could not enter into the arrangement the defendant offered to him.

Other more indirect restrictions on a lawyer's right and ability to practice law also are not in accord with Rule 5.6(b)(DE). For example, if Lisa Lawyer agreed, in connection with the settlement of Cindy Client's claim, that Lisa would not disclose or use information gained in the representation but not otherwise protected by the duty of confidentiality owed to Cindy, Lisa would violate Rule 5.6(b)(DE). Big Corporation might offer such a deal to Lisa so that Lisa would, in effect, be barred from representing other clients with similar claims against Big. If Lisa could not use the information she had discovered about Big, it would be impossible for Lisa to provide competent representation to any other client with a claim against Big. The ultimate effect of such an agreement would be a limitation on Lisa's ability to practice law, contrary to the rule prohibiting such limitations.

Another type of agreement that has been held to be improper and unenforceable is an agreement in connection with a settlement of a client's claim that provides for the future employment of the lawyer by the opposing party. Big Corporation might agree to settle with Cindy Client if Lisa Lawyer agrees to be retained by Big. If Lisa agrees to this arrangement, she is agreeing not to represent other clients on claims against Big. If Big retains Lisa, she cannot, in accordance with conflicts principles, represent clients with claims against Big. *See Chapter 18 Conflicts and Current Clients.* Once again, the effect of the agreement is to limit Lisa's ability to practice law. Courts and discipline authorities see through the subterfuge and find such arrangements improper and unenforceable.

Related Sections of the *Restatement (Third) of the Law Governing Lawyers*

Section 13

Checkpoints

- A lawyer may not be a party to, offer, or participate in making a partnership, employment, or other such agreement that also restricts a lawyer's right to practice law unless the restriction relates to retirement benefits.
- Determining when a restriction relates to retirement benefits is a fact-specific analysis. A retirement benefit is a benefit available to retiring lawyers only. A retirement benefit should not require a lawyer to forfeit compensation already earned.
- Indirect restrictions, such as financial disincentives to practice, are improper.
- In connection with the settlement of a client's matter, a lawyer cannot agree to, offer, or participate in the making of any agreement restricting a lawyer's right to practice law.
- Indirect restrictions, such as agreements not to disclose or use information about an opposing party or agreements to be retained in the future by the opposing party, are improper.
- Most courts find agreements with direct or indirect restrictions on a lawyer's right to practice unenforceable because they are contrary to public policy.

Chapter 42

Ancillary Services

Roadmap

- Rule 5.7(DE)
- Offering "law-related services"

A. Lawyers May Offer Ancillary Services

In recent times lawyers have sought to offer more varied services to their clients. For example, a law firm that frequently represents corporations on corporate matters might like to offer accounting services to its clients as well. The clients could obtain these services without looking elsewhere. There is little chance that the law firm accountant servicing the client will suggest that the client go elsewhere for legal services.

Rule 5.4(NE) prevents an accountant from having an ownership interest or other control over the rendering of legal services by the firm. *See Chapter 39 Professional Independence.* The reverse, however, is not true. Lawyers and law firms can operate accounting ventures. Lawyers and firms might operate lobbying entities, consulting ventures, insurance agencies, or real estate brokerages, for example, if the laws and regulations pertaining to those businesses allow the arrangement. A large firm with a substantial corporate practice might find offering lobbying services or tax consulting services very helpful to its clients. A solo practitioner might desire to sell real estate and also provide the legal services for real estate sales and purchases. Rule 5.4(NE) simply provides that no nonlawyer involved in these alternate ventures can have ownership interest in or managerial control over the rendering of legal services. Rule 5.4(NE) does not limit a lawyer's involvement in these ventures.

B. Lawyers Must Guard against Conflicts

If a lawyer chooses to become involved in a venture offering ancillary services, the lawyer always must be aware of and guard against impermissible conflicts of interest just as the lawyer must do with regard to all his or her business ventures. A lawyer providing real estate legal services and also real estate brokerage services always must be wary of the impact of the real estate business on the advice the lawyer renders to the legal services clients.

Larry Lawyer, a lawyer who also sells real estate, must always be wary that he not advise a legal services client to buy a property simply because Larry wants to handle the real estate sale. Larry's advice truly must be in the best interest of the client. Rule 1.7(DE), which deals with conflicts of interest involving current clients, applies and determines whether Larry may handle a particular legal representation that touches upon his other business ventures. *See Chapter 18 Conflicts and Current Clients.*

C. Lawyers Must Guard against Client Confusion

In addition, however, a lawyer such as Larry must be aware of the confusion clients may have about ancillary services being rendered and the obligations of the lawyer with regard to those services. Rule 5.7(b)(DE) states special requirements for a lawyer providing "law-related services." Rule 5.7(b)(DE) defines "law-related services" as services that "might reasonably be performed in conjunction with and in substance are related to the provision of legal services, and that are not prohibited as unauthorized practice of law when provided by a nonlawyer." A comment to Rule 5.7(DE) clarifies that Larry Lawyer might be providing "law-related services" if he provides "title insurance, financial planning, accounting, trust services, real estate counseling, legislative lobbying, economic analysis, social work, psychological counseling, tax preparation, and patent, medical or environmental consulting."

If a lawyer provides such services, the lawyer must abide by the applicable rules of professional conduct for lawyers if the lawyer does not make absolutely clear to the customer that the usual protections of the lawyer-client relationship do not attach. A lawyer can make this clear to a customer by providing the services in a way that is "distinct from the lawyer's provision of legal services to clients" and by "tak[ing] reasonable measures to assure" that the person utilizing the services knows that the usual protections inherent in a lawyer-client relationship are not applicable. As with any other disclosure, such disclosure is best in writing, though Rule 5.7(DE) does not mandate a written disclosure or a written explanation.

Larry Lawyer, a solo practitioner, may act as a real estate broker, but if Larry is not very careful, all the duties to clients recognized in the rules applies to his real estate customers even though he might render no legal services to those customers. Thus, Larry would owe these customers duties of confidentiality and loyalty, for example. To avoid such a situation, Larry must provide the real estate services in a manner distinct from his provision of legal services. The easiest first step would be for Larry to have separate offices for the two businesses. Of course, such may not be economically possible. Even if Larry provides the services in a "distinct" manner, Larry must take "reasonable measures" to be sure that the real estate customers understand that he is not providing legal services and that they are not clients in that sense.

Larry might be a partner in a large firm that also offers lobbying services through a subsidiary business of the law firm. The partners of the law firm might therefore control the lobbying business. In such a situation, Larry owes clients of the lobbying business the duties he would owe any legal services client unless Larry and the other members of the firm take "reasonable measures" to clarify to the lobbying clients that no legal services are being rendered and no duties inherent in the lawyer-client relationship attach as a result of the lobbying relationship.

D. Lawyers Must Abide by the Requirements Regarding Contracting with a Client

If Larry agrees to provide real estate services to a party for whom he also renders legal services, Larry must abide by Rule 1.8(a)(DE). Rule 1.8(a)(DE) provides a procedure that Larry must follow in entering into a business relationship with a client. The procedure is designed to minimize the lawyer's powers of persuasion and also is designed to provide full information to the client. *See Chapter 21 Conflict of Interest Rules for Particular Situations.* If Larry is in a large firm and refers a client to the firm's lobbying subsidiary, any contract between the client and the lobbying subsidiary must be entered into in accord with Rule 1.8(a)(DE).

Related Sections of the *Restatement (Third) of the Law Governing Lawyers*

Section 10

Checkpoints

- Lawyers may offer "law-related services."
- In any such endeavor lawyers always must guard against impermissible conflicts of interest.
- If a lawyer offers "law-related services," the lawyer must take steps to avoid any client confusion regarding the nature of the relationship.
- If the "law-related services" are not "distinct from the lawyer's provision of legal services to clients," or the lawyer does not take "reasonable measures" to clarify to customers of the "law-related services" that the usual protections of a lawyer-client relationship do not apply, all protections inherent in a lawyer-client relationship apply.
- In entering into any agreement with a customer of "law-related services," the lawyer offering the service must abide by the requirements of Rule 1.8(a)(DE) regarding contracting with clients.

Section X
Lawyers as Public Servants

Chapter 43

Pro Bono Service

Roadmap

- Rule 6.1(ID)
- Lawyers' responsibility to provide pro bono publico service

A. The Pro Bono Aspiration

Only lawyers may practice law. Some people and entities need the legal services only a lawyer can render but cannot afford the cost of the service. As a matter of professional responsibility, lawyers are encouraged but not required to render service to those who cannot afford it. This service is called pro bono publico service, which means "for the public good."

Rule 6.1(ID) encourages lawyers to render fifty hours of pro bono service each year. States may vary on the suggested number of hours. The states make pro bono service voluntary, but some states encourage compliance by requiring lawyers to report pro bono hours each year. Pro bono service generally is service rendered without any expectation of a fee. A lawyer who bills fifty hours to a client who then does not pay has not satisfied the pro bono aspirational goal because the lawyer rendered the legal service expecting standard remuneration.

B. Preferred Pro Bono Service Activity

Rule 6.1(ID) outlines a priority system for pro bono service. The top priority is service to people of "limited means"—people who need legal services but cannot afford to pay for them. Service to "charitable, religious, civic, community, governmental and educational organizations" in their service of people of "limited means" also enjoys top priority. The rule states that a "substantial majority" of the fifty hours of pro bono service a lawyer provides should be in these categories. A comment to the rule defines the category of people a lawyer should seek to serve as "those who qualify for participation in programs funded by the Legal Services Corporation and those whose incomes and financial resources are slightly above the guidelines utilized by such programs."

Larry Lawyer might provide his fifty hours of service by representing several clients of "limited means" who are being evicted from their apartments for not paying rent. Or Larry might provide his fifty hours of service by assisting a community organization that settles refugees of "limited means."

C. Secondary Pro Bono Service Activity

The second priority level of pro bono service includes three types of service. First, a lawyer may render service for no fee or for a significantly smaller than usual fee to organizations with a public focus. These organizations must be "charitable, religious, civic, community, governmental" or "educational" or must be organizations pursuing the protection of civil or public rights or liberties. If paying legal fees at the customary rate would "significantly deplete" such an organization's funding or "would be otherwise inappropriate," the rendering of legal services in matters in accord with the organization's purpose without charge or for a reduced rate would satisfy the pro bono aspiration stated in Rule 6.1(ID).

The second type of pro bono service in this second priority level is rendering legal assistance for a "substantially reduced fee" to people of "limited means." Larry Lawyer might serve as a court-appointed lawyer to represent David Defendant in a criminal matter. David has no money to pay Larry, and the court pays Larry at a rate significantly lower than Larry's standard fee rate.

The third type of pro bono service in this second priority tier is actually not rendering legal service at all. A lawyer can fulfill the pro bono requirement by participating in organizations and activities for the improvement of the "law, the legal system or the legal profession." A lawyer who works in the government or in an in-house position may not be permitted to represent private clients. Such a lawyer can satisfy his or her pro bono responsibility by serving on bar association committees and such. *See Chapter 44 Legal Services Organizations, Law Reform, and Legal Services Programs.*

D. Financial Support

Rule 6.1(ID) also states that a lawyer should financially support organizations that provide legal services to people of "limited means." Thus, lawyers should contribute to legal services organizations. The rule does not state that a financial contribution should take the place of service. A comment to the rule, however, does state that all lawyers should "provid[e] direct pro bono services or mak[e] financial contributions when pro bono service is not feasible."

Checkpoints

- As a matter of professional responsibility, lawyers are encouraged but not required to render fifty hours of pro bono service each year.
- A "substantial majority" of the fifty hours of pro bono service a lawyer provides should be service to people of "limited means" and service to "charitable, religious, civic, community, governmental and educational organizations" in their service of people of "limited means."
- As a residual matter, a lawyer may render pro bono service in any of the following three ways:
    1. With no expectation of a fee or an expectation of a "substantially reduced" fee, to organizations with a public focus or to "charitable, religious, civic, community, governmental and educational organizations" if paying legal fees at the customary rate would "significantly deplete" the organization's funding or "would be otherwise inappropriate."
    2. For a "substantially reduced fee," to people of "limited means."
    3. By participating in organizations and activities for the improvement of the "law, the legal system or the legal profession."
- A lawyer should financially support organizations that provide legal services to people of "limited means."

Chapter 44

Legal Services Organizations, Law Reform, and Legal Services Programs

Roadmap

- Rule 6.3(DE)
- Rule 6.4(DE)
- Rule 6.5(DE)
- Service with legal services organizations
- Participation in law reform activities
- Participation with limited legal services programs

A. Legal Services Organizations

In addition to providing pro bono representation to people of "limited means," lawyers are encouraged to serve their profession and communities in other ways. Even if a lawyer does not represent clients as part of a legal services organization, a lawyer can contribute by serving in another capacity with the organization. For example, a lawyer might serve as a member of the overseeing board for such an organization. A lawyer might avoid such an activity if involvement with the legal services organization creates conflicts of interest with other facets of the lawyer's practice. To remove this practical disincentive, Rule 6.3(DE) provides that a lawyer may serve as an officer, director, or member of a legal services entity even though the entity serves or represents people whose interests are adverse to a client of the lawyer. Service with the legal services entity does not create a conflict of interest for the lawyer. In such a role, the lawyer does not represent the clients of the legal services organization. Larry Lawyer may represent Property Corporation, an owner of apartment buildings often adverse to the tenant clients of the legal services organization even though Larry is a member of the governing board of the organization.

Rule 6.3(DE) places a small limitation on a lawyer serving as an officer, director, or member of a legal services organization. First, a lawyer must be cautious not to participate knowingly in any "decision or action of the organization" if participation violates Rule 1.7(DE). *See Chapter 18 Conflicts and Current Clients.*

The second limitation Rule 6.3(DE) states is that a lawyer must be cautious not to participate knowingly in any "decision or action of the organization" if the "decision or action" could affect a client of the legal services organization in a "materially adverse" manner and if the interests of a lawyer's client are adverse to the interests of the legal services organization's client. For example, Larry, as a legal services organization board member, cannot participate in a vote to strip certain organization clients of representation if those clients are involved in matters adverse to Property Corporation, Larry's client. Larry cannot participate because the vote would adversely affect the organization's clients who are adverse to Larry's client. Larry cannot participate in a vote that would assist his client at the expense of the organization's clients.

B. Law Reform Activities

Another way lawyers may serve their profession and communities is by participating in law reform organizations and activities. Who better to urge change in law and the judicial system than lawyers who work in and with the subject matter? Rule 6.4(DE) clarifies that lawyers may serve as officers, directors, or members of law reform entities. Serving as an officer, director, or member does not create a lawyer-client relationship. A law reform entity is one engaged in reform of an area of law or the administration of the law. In this context, if a lawyer knows that a decision in which the lawyer participates may materially benefit a client of the lawyer, the lawyer must disclose within the organization the fact that the client may be "materially benefited." The lawyer need not disclose the identity of the client.

If a lawyer is involved in law reform activity likely to harm a client, the lawyer must consider whether there is a "substantial risk" that the representation of the client may be "materially limited" by the lawyer's personal interest in the law reform project. If the lawyer concludes in the affirmative, the lawyer has a conflict of interest under Rule 1.7(DE) and must act accordingly. *See Chapter 18 Conflicts and Current Clients.*

Larry Lawyer may be a contributing member of a project to ease recovery for plaintiffs in medical malpractice cases. If Larry's clientele consists of plaintiffs with medical malpractice claims, Larry must disclose this fact when acting in relation to the law reform project in a way that will materially benefit his clients. This would be the usual scenario—that a lawyer pursues law reform consistent with the lawyer's client's interests.

If Larry represented doctors and hospitals, his law reform efforts might create a Rule 1.7(DE) conflict of interest for him. In any event, his clients would likely terminate the lawyer-client relationship when they learn that their lawyer is acting contrary to their interests.

C. Limited Legal Services Programs

Bar associations, law schools and other nonprofit organizations often offer programs to the public that include very limited legal advice or service. For example, a law school might have a one-day tax preparation clinic, wills fair, or general advice day for people of "limited means." A bar association might sponsor such as event as well. The general understanding of lawyers and the people being served by these programs is that a participating lawyer renders advice and service for that occasion only.

Unfortunately, the general conflict of interest rules create disincentives to lawyer participation in these desirable service offerings. A lawyer might not want to participate in a limited legal services program if the lawyer must screen for conflicts before assisting someone in the program setting. Likewise, lawyers might not participate in such a program if by doing so they create significant conflicts of interest for their primary practice. Rule 6.5(DE) minimizes these disincentives to participation.

Rule 6.5(DE) applies only if the activity in which the lawyer participates is a limited legal services program and only if a nonprofit organization or court sponsors the program. Rule 6.5(DE) applies only if there is no expectation of a continuing lawyer-client relationship. This means that the limited scope of the relationship must be explained to each client and each client must consent to the limited scope. Rule 1.2(c)(NE) requires "informed consent" to a limited representation. *See Chapter 8 Scope of the Representation and Communication with the Client.*

If Rule 6.5(DE) applies to the program, it removes some of the disincentive to participation created by the general conflict of interest rules. A lawyer participating in a qualified limited legal service program is subject to the constraints of Rule 1.7(DE), the conflict of interest rule for current clients; Rule 1.9(a)(DE), the conflict of interest rule for former clients; and Rule 1.10(NE), the rule dealing with the imputation of conflicts, *see Chapter 18 Conflicts and*

Current Clients and *Chapter 19 Conflicts and Former Clients*, only if the lawyer knows that the short-term representation creates a conflict of interest for the lawyer or for other lawyers in the lawyer's firm.

If Larry Lawyer participates in a general legal advice day sponsored by the local law school, Larry need not do a detailed conflict of interest check to ensure that he may representation a client in the clinic. Because of Rule 6.5(DE), Larry can be certain that he may advise a client as part of the advice day if he knows of no conflict on behalf of Larry or other lawyers in Larry's firm.

Rule 6.5(DE) does not change other aspects of the lawyer-client relationship. If Larry advises Clint Client at the legal advice day, Clint is Larry's client for purposes of that occasion. Larry owes Clint all other duties owed to any other client such as the duty of confidentiality. *See Chapter 15 The Duty of Confidentiality.*

Rule 6.5(DE) does not eliminate all the conflicts of interest issues. A limited representation can create conflicts of interest for the lawyer going forward. If Larry Lawyer, at the advice day, discusses a claim Clint may have against Lawnmower Corporation, Larry cannot defend Lawnmower Corporation later when Clint, represented by another lawyer, sues Lawnmower Corporation on the same claim. Rule 1.9(a)(DE), the rule governing conflicts of interest and former clients, prohibits the representation absent "informed consent, confirmed in writing" because the interests of Lawnmower Corporation and Clint would be "materially adverse" and the matter would be the "same" or "substantially related." *See Chapter 19 Conflicts and Former Clients.*

Rule 6.5(DE) does provide some relief from the conflict of interest disincentive by removing any imputation of disqualification from the lawyer's conflicts created by participation in a limited legal service program. Larry Lawyer, because of his representation of Clint at the advice day, cannot represent Lawnmower Corporation later when Clint sues Lawnmower. Lisa, Larry's partner, can represent Lawnmower. Of course, Rule 1.9(c)(DE) makes clear that any lawyer such as Larry could not use any information about Clint to Clint's disadvantage unless a rule permitted or required such a disclosure or unless the information became "generally known." The duty of confidentiality to Clint would continue as well.

Checkpoints

- A lawyer may serve as an officer, director, or member of a legal services entity even though the entity serves or represents people whose interests are adverse to a client of the lawyer.

- There are two limitations on service with a legal services organization:
    1. A lawyer must be cautious not to participate knowingly in any "decision or action of the organization" if participation violates Rule 1.7(DE).
    2. A lawyer must be cautious not to participate knowingly in any "decision or action of the organization" if the "decision or action" could affect a client of the legal services organization in a "materially adverse" manner if the interests of a client of the lawyer are adverse to the interests of the client of the legal services organization.
- Lawyers may serve as officers, directors, or members of law reform entities.
- If a lawyer knows that a decision in which the lawyer participates, relating to a law reform activity, may materially benefit a client of the lawyer, the lawyer must disclose the anticipated benefit but need not disclose the identity of the client.
- A lawyer participating in a qualified limited legal service program is subject to the constraints of Rule 1.7(DE), the conflict of interest rule for current clients, Rule 1.9(a)(DE), the conflict of interest rule for former clients, and Rule 1.10(ID), the rule dealing with the imputation of conflicts, only if the lawyer knows that the short-term representation creates a conflict of interest for the lawyer or for other lawyers in the lawyer's firm.
- Any conflict of interest for a lawyer created by participation in a limited legal service program is not imputed to other lawyers in the firm.

Section XI
Advertising and Other Communications about Legal Services

Chapter 45

Communications about Lawyer Services

Roadmap

- Rule 7.1 (DE)
- Rule 7.2 (NE)
- Rule 7.3 (DE)
- Rule 7.4 (DE)
- Rule 7.5 (DE)
- Impermissible communications about lawyer services
- In-person solicitation
- Paying for communications about a lawyer's services
- Referrals
- Communicating fields of practice and specializations
- Restrictions on firm names and other designations

A. The History

While lawyers advertised in the early years of the 1900s, by the 1930s the organized bar prohibited lawyer advertising. The motivation for the prohibition was that advertising made the practice of law appear to be less of a professional endeavor. Many practitioners believed that allowing lawyers to advertise would destroy the profession. In 1977, however, the United States Supreme Court decided *Bates v. State Bar of Arizona*, 433 U.S. 350 (1977), and forever changed the lawyer advertising landscape. In *Bates*, several lawyers advertised their legal clinic in the newspaper. The advertisement, in addition to listing the address and telephone number of the clinic, listed the routine services the lawyers offered and the prices for those services. Arizona refused to allow the advertisement, though it was truthful. The United States Supreme Court refused to uphold Arizona's broad ban on lawyer advertising, holding that the First Amendment protected such truthful communications as was at issue in *Bates.*

In *Bates* and several cases since *Bates,* the United States Supreme Court has made clear that lawyer advertising is commercial speech. Lawyers advertise as a way of ultimately making money. As such, their speech about their services enjoys First Amendment protection, though to a limited degree. To the extent that lawyer advertising might be political speech in a particular setting, it may enjoy even greater protection.

In *Shapero v. Kentucky Bar Association,* 486 U.S. 466 (1988), the Supreme Court addressed solicitation. The Court clarified that targeted mail communications are similar to general lawyer advertising and are subject to similar, but not identical, constitutional protections. In-person solicitation, however, carries with it much more danger of undue influence and can be more significantly restrained.

From these and other cases discussing constitutional principles, the following is clear. A state can regulate lawyer advertising or other communications by requiring that the communications take certain forms or contain certain statements. Such requirements must be reasonable in light of the goal of preventing false or misleading information, cannot be unduly burdensome, and cannot be unconstitutionally vague.

Supreme Court decisions have fleshed out this general concept. For example, in *Peel v. Attorney Registration & Disciplinary Commission,* 496 U.S. 91 (1990), the Supreme Court stated that Illinois could not prohibit a lawyer from noting in a communication that he was certified as a specialist by the National Board of Trial Advocacy if the lawyer was in fact so certified. Recognizing the bounds of permissible regulation in *Florida Bar v. Went For It, Inc.,* 515 U.S. 618 (1995), the Supreme Court upheld the application of a state rule requiring a thirty-day waiting period for targeted mail communications. The rule required lawyers to wait thirty days before sending any mail specifically directed to people who had been involved in accidents or disasters or to the relatives of such people. The Supreme Court upheld the restriction, noting that Florida had the right to protect its residents from lawyer intrusion at a particularly private time.

B. The Basic Rule: Nothing "False or Misleading"

The rules governing the professional responsibility of lawyers incorporate the teachings of *Bates, Shapero,* and their progeny that have spoken to the issue of the constitutional bounds of regulation of lawyer speech about lawyer services. Rule 7.1(DE) contains a general statement regarding all communications by a lawyer about the lawyer's services. The rule states that a lawyer commits misconduct by making statements about the lawyer's services that are false or statements that are misleading. The rule explains that a communication is false or misleading if the communication contains "a material misrepresentation" or if the communication omits information that would prevent the communication from being misleading.

One situation in which lawyers make misleading statements is when the statements, though true, raise unjustified expectations. A lawyer who states his or her results in past cases may lead listeners to believe that future results will be the same. The lawyer can eliminate this effect by noting that past results do not guarantee future results and that every matter is different.

Another situation in which lawyers make misleading statements is when the statements compare the lawyer's abilities and achievements in a way that leads the listener to believe that the comparison can be substantiated when, in fact, it cannot. A lawyer cannot say he or she is the best lawyer in town or the cheapest lawyer in town unless the lawyer has a verifiable basis for the statement.

C. Solicitation

The Supreme Court established in *Shapero v. Kentucky Bar Association,* 486 U.S. 466 (1988), that lawyer communications about services can be prohibited if the communications are in-person, or the equivalent of in-person communications, soliciting professional employment for compensation. The contact can be prohibited because of the danger that a lawyer's powers of persuasion might overcome the will of the target potential client. This danger is even more real if the lawyer knows the target needs the services offered.

Consistent with *Shapero,* Rule 7.3(a)(DE) prohibits "in-person, live telephone or real-time electronic contact" in which a lawyer solicits employment for legal services and a "significant motive" is compensation. A lawyer can provide a person with information about his or her services. The communication simply cannot be face-to-face or the equivalent of face-to-face. Assuming Larry Lawyer seeks to earn compensation from any resulting representation, he cannot sit in the local hospital emergency room and discuss his services with people who come into the hospital with injuries.

There are several exceptional situations in which such contact is permitted. First, in-person solicitation is permitted if the person solicited is a lawyer. The soliciting lawyer's power of persuasion is reduced when the target of the persuasion has similar ability. Second, in-person solicitation is allowed if the target is a member of the lawyer's family, if the target and the lawyer have enjoyed a "close, personal" relationship, or if the target and the lawyer have, in the past, enjoyed a "professional relationship." Lastly, in-person solicitation is allowed if the lawyer's motivation is not the desire to make money from the relationship.

According to Rule 7.3(b)(DE), a lawyer may not solicit employment regardless of the manner of the solicitation if the targeted potential client has indicated that he or she does not wish to be solicited by the lawyer. Also, no communication with a potential client is proper if it is coercive, if the result is duress, or if the communication constitutes harassment.

To prevent confusion, Rule 7.3(c)(DE) requires an additional disclosure for any solicitation a lawyer aims at a potential client the lawyer knows to be in need of the lawyer's services. Any such "written, recorded or electronic communication" must state that it is "Advertising Material." This legend should appear on the envelope of the written communication and should appear at the beginning and end of any recorded or electronic message. The only exceptions to this requirement are if the target is a lawyer, is a member of the lawyer's family, is a person with whom the lawyer has a "close personal" relationship, or is a person with whom the lawyer has had a "professional relationship." The rule is written so that any communication not sent to a person or entity known to be in need of the lawyer's services need not carry the "Advertising Material" legend. Lawyers often include the legend on everything just to be sure of abiding by the rule.

Rule 7.3(d)(DE) contains an explicit exception for in-person contact by prepaid or group legal service plans. These entities can have in-person contact with people not known to need specific legal services. This contact is not an issue for the lawyers who provide services to members of the plan if the lawyers do not own the plan and do not direct the operation of the plan.

D. Permitted Communications

If a lawyer's communications about the lawyer's legal services are not "false or misleading," and if the communications are not in-person solicitations, they generally are permitted. Rule 7.2(a)(NE) provides general recognition of the lawyer's right to advertise or otherwise communicate about the legal services offered.

Any communication must include the name and professional address of the responsible lawyer, according to Rule 7.2(c)(NE). If the communication is about a firm or other group of lawyers, the communication must contain the name and address of the firm or a lawyer responsible for the communication.

Rule 7.2(b)(NE) clarifies that a lawyer generally cannot pay for a referral. Paying for the cost of an advertisement or communication is not the same as paying for a referral and, is, of course, permitted. Likewise, a lawyer may pay for a law practice as Rule 1.17(KS) allows. *See Chapter 12 Sale of a Practice.* A lawyer may pay the "usual" fee for referrals if the referral entity is a not-for-profit service or a qualified referral service. The rule states that a "qualified lawyer referral service is a legal referral service that has been approved by an appropriate regulatory authority." Larry Lawyer can pay a fee to the local bar association referral service, a nonprofit operation, in exchange for the bar association referring a potential client to Larry. A lawyer also may participate in a legal service plan.

Finally, a lawyer may agree with another lawyer or with a nonlawyer professional that the lawyer will refer clients to the lawyer or nonlawyer and that person will refer clients to the lawyer. Such an arrangement cannot be exclusive and the lawyer must tell the client of the arrangement. All of these situations involve communications about lawyer services and are permitted. *See Chapter 39 Professional Independence.*

E. Communicating Fields of Practice and Specializations

1. Fields of Practice

Historically, states limited what a lawyer could say about what kind of law he or she practiced. Typically, lawyers could use only approved categories of practice like "property" when identifying fields of practice. The rules warned lawyers not to state that their practice "concentrated in" or was "limited to" a particular subject area. The rationale for these rules was to prevent potential clients from concluding that a lawyer who stated that he practiced "personal injury" law was an expert in that area. Unfortunately, what a lawyer could say within these rules often was not particularly helpful in conveying information to potential clients. A person who had a real-estate matter may not have realized that the matter was a property matter, for example.

In the case of *In re R.M.J.*, 455 U.S. 191 (1982), the Supreme Court addressed Missouri's version of these restrictions. The lawyer in the case had identified his field of practice using "real estate" rather than the approved term, "property." The Court found that the lawyer's communication was truthful and not deceptive. The Court held that Missouri's rules unconstitutionally restrained lawyer speech.

Rule 7.4(a)(DE) now states that a lawyer may communicate the "fields of law" in which the lawyer practices. A comment to the rule states that a lawyer may state that the lawyer accepts only matters in a certain area of the law or does not accept matters in a particular area of law. If Larry Lawyer has a personal injury practice, in order to have an effective communication of what he does, he might have a website that states: "I handle Auto Accidents, Trucking Accidents, Wrongful Death, Personal Injury, Medical Malpractice, and Hospital Negligence."

2. Patent and Admiralty Lawyers

Lawyers who want to have a practice in patent law usually are admitted to practice before the United States Patent and Trademark Office. Rule 7.4(b)(DE) provides that a lawyer who is so admitted may advertise or otherwise communicate this fact by using the phrase "Patent Attorney" or a similar statement. In addition, Rule 7.4(c)(DE) states that lawyers who have an admiralty practice may so state by using the terms "Admiralty" or "Proctor in Admiralty" or a similar term.

3. Stating or Implying Certification as a Specialist

A lawyer may state that he or she is a "specialist" if that is not a false or misleading statement. In contrast, a lawyer may not state that he or she is "certified as a specialist" in a particular subject area of law unless the certification has occurred and the state bar authority has approved the certifying entity or the ABA has accredited the entity. To communicate such a certification, the lawyer must clearly state the certifying organization.

This rule is in accord with the teachings of *Peel v. Attorney Registration & Disciplinary Commission*, 496 U.S. 91 (1990). In *Peel* the Supreme Court stated that a state could not prohibit a lawyer from noting a valid certification by a reputable entity. The lawyer in *Peel* sought to communicate certification as a specialist by the National Board of Trial Advocacy. So Larry Lawyer can indicate that he specializes in a particular subject area like personal injury work but he cannot indicate that he has been certified as a specialist unless that is true and the state bar authority has approved the certifying entity or the ABA has accredited the certifying entity.

F. Firm Names and Other Professional Designations

1. Firm Names

In an effort to give more texture to the general prohibition on false or misleading communications, Rule 7.5(DE) gives guidance on issues involving firm names and other designations. In the past, lawyers practiced using only their names or the names of other lawyers who were associated with them or had been associated with them. Lawyers need not be so conservative. A lawyer can use any firm name, letterhead, or other designation that is not false or misleading. Rule 7.5(a)(DE) clarifies that a lawyer or group of lawyers can practice using a trade name if the trade name does not imply that the entity is connected to a government agency or a "public or charitable legal services organization" and is not otherwise "false or misleading." Many traditional firm names are now trade names because the lawyers whose names are in the firm name have passed away.

A firm name might be misleading if it included the name of a lawyer who had never been associated with the lawyers using the trade name. A group of lawyers practicing as the Brandeis Law Firm might be using a misleading trade name if no one in the firm has the name of Brandeis and no lawyer named Brandeis ever associated with the firm. The public might be misled to believe that the firm had a connection with the Supreme Court Justice Louis D. Brandeis.

Another way a trade name might be misleading is if it used a geographic designation such as Chicago Legal Clinic. The name might mislead the public might to believe that the City of Chicago or some other government entity sponsors the clinic.

A third way a firm name may be misleading is if the firm name includes the name of a lawyer holding public office. Rule 7.5(c)(DE) prohibits the use of a public official's name in a firm name "during any substantial period" in which the public official does not "actively and regularly" practice with the firm. The rule also prohibits the use of the public official's name in any communications on behalf of the firm.

If Larry Lawyer practices with the firm of Larry, Harry, and Moe, and Larry becomes the Mayor of City, Harry and Moe must remove Larry's name from the firm name if Larry does not practice law while he is the Mayor. Also, Harry and Moe cannot use Larry's name in advertisements for Harry and Moe. Harry and Moe cannot advertise as "the law firm of your beloved Mayor."

2. Jurisdictional Designations

In the practice of law today, law firms are often global enterprises. Firms may have offices in multiple states in the United States as well as in other countries. Rule 7.5(b)(DE) states that lawyers may use the same firm name in multiple jurisdictions. This allows firms to capitalize on their brand.

Any list of lawyers in an office must identify the lawyers who are and are not admitted in the particular jurisdiction. This means that a law firm with offices in Indiana and Illinois may list all of its lawyers on its letterhead but must indicate where the lawyers are admitted. The Indiana office may even use a letterhead that lists only the lawyers in that office but must indicate which lawyers are admitted and which lawyers are not admitted to practice law in Indiana.

3. Form of Practice

Another way a firm name or designation can be misleading is with regard to the form of practice. Rule 7.5(d)(DE) provides that lawyers may state or imply that they practice in a certain entity form only if they in fact practice in that form. Lawyers cannot state that they practice in a partnership unless the lawyers are in fact partners. If lawyers practice in a limited liability entity rather than a partnership, they must not imply that they practice in a partnership. Of course, to imply a partnership relationship when one does not formally exist may actually create liability that partners would have for the acts of the other lawyers. *See Chapter 4 Basis of Duty: The Lawyer-Client Relationship.*

Checkpoints

- A lawyer acts improperly by making statements about his or her services that are "false or misleading."
- A lawyer may not engage in "in-person, live telephone or real-time electronic contact" in which a lawyer solicits employment for legal services if a "significant motive" is compensation. In-person solicitation is permitted if
    1. the person solicited is a lawyer,
    2. the target is a member of the lawyer's family,
    3. the target and the lawyer have enjoyed a "close personal" relationship,
    4. the target and the lawyer have, in the past, enjoyed a "professional relationship," or
    5. the lawyer is not motivated by the desire to make money.

- A lawyer may not solicit employment regardless of the manner of the solicitation if
    1. the potential client has indicated that he or she does not wish to be solicited by the lawyer, or
    2. the communication is coercive, the result is duress, or the communication constitutes harassment.
- Any "written, recorded or electronic communication" must state that it is "Advertising Material" if it is directed to someone known to need the lawyer's services.
- Prepaid or group legal service plans may have in-person contact with people not known to need specific legal services as a way to solicit memberships.
- Any communication must include the name and professional address of the responsible lawyer or law firm.
- A lawyer may pay the cost of an advertisement or other communication.
- A lawyer may pay the "usual" fee for referrals if the referral entity is a not-for-profit service or a qualified service.
- In a nonexclusive arrangement, a lawyer may agree with another lawyer or with a nonlawyer professional that the lawyer will refer clients to the lawyer or nonlawyer and that person will refer clients to the lawyer.
- A lawyer may communicate the lawyer's "fields of practice."
- A lawyer who is admitted to practice before the United States Patent and Trademark Office may communicate this fact by using the phrase "Patent Attorney" or a similar term.
- A lawyer who has an admiralty practice may state so by using the terms "Admiralty" or "Proctor in Admiralty" or a similar term.
- A lawyer may state that the lawyer is "certified as a specialist" in a particular subject area of law if the certification has occurred and the state bar authority has approved the certifying entity or the ABA has accredited the entity.
- A lawyer may use any firm name, letterhead, or other designation that is not "false or misleading."
- A firm name cannot imply that the practice entity is connected to a government agency or a "public or charitable legal services organization" or otherwise be "false or misleading."
- A firm name cannot include a lawyer's name who is a public official "during any substantial period" in which the lawyer does not "actively and regularly" practice with the firm.
- A lawyer may use the same firm name in multiple jurisdictions.
- Any list of lawyers in a firm office must identify the lawyers who are and are not admitted in the particular jurisdiction.
- A lawyer may state or imply that the lawyer practices in a certain entity form only if the lawyer practices in that form.

Chapter 46

Paying to Play: Political Contributions

Roadmap

- Rule 7.6(DE)
- Political contributions for the purpose of obtaining legal engagements or appointments

Rule 7.6(DE) prohibits the practice of paying to play. In other words, Rule 7.6(DE) prohibits a lawyer from accepting an engagement with a government entity if the lawyer or the lawyer's firm or an entity controlled by the lawyer or the lawyer's firm makes a political contribution so as to be considered for the engagement. Also, a lawyer may not accept an engagement with a government entity if the lawyer or the lawyer's firm or an entity controlled by the lawyer or the lawyer's firm solicits political contributions so as to be considered for the engagement. The engagement is a sufficient motivator if the lawyer would not make the contribution absent the wish to obtain the engagement. Larry Lawyer cannot handle legal work for City if Larry contributes to the Mayor's reelection campaign in an effort to ensure that the Mayor sends City's legal work to Larry.

The rule also prohibits the acceptance of an appointment by a judge if the lawyer or the lawyer's firm or an entity controlled by the lawyer or the lawyer's firm makes a contribution to the judge's reelection campaign or solicits a contribution for the judge's reelection campaign for the purpose of securing such an appointment. For purposes of the rule's prohibition, an appointment, as defined in the comments, is "an appointment to a position such as referee, commissioner, special master, receiver, guardian or other similar position." This kind of activity is prohibited because if it occurs, it calls into question the integrity of the process of selection of lawyers for government work and appointments.

With this rationale as a guide, the comments clarify that the prohibition does not apply when the engagement obtained or the appointment obtained is "substantially uncompensated." The prohibition also does not apply if the engagement or appointment is the result of a process that ensures that no untoward influence can have any effect on the award of the work or the appointment such as a selection process based on "experience, expertise, professional qualifications and cost following a request for proposal." Lastly, the prohibition does not apply if an engagement or appointment results from a rotational process using a list of lawyers, regardless of contributions. If Larry Lawyer is granted an appointment because his name is next on a list of all lawyers in the area, regardless of contribution history, then the contribution has no effect.

Checkpoints

- A lawyer may not accept an engagement with a government entity if the lawyer or the lawyer's firm or an entity controlled by the lawyer or the lawyer's firm made a political contribution or solicited political contributions for the purpose of being considered for an engagement.
- A lawyer may not accept an appointment by a judge if the lawyer or the lawyer's firm or an entity controlled by the lawyer or the lawyer's firm made a political contribution or solicited political contributions to the judge's campaign for the purpose of securing such an appointment.
- A lawyer may accept a government engagement or appointment regardless of contributions or solicitation of contributions if the engagement or appointment is
    1. "substantially uncompensated,"
    2. the result of a process that ensures that no untoward influence can have any effect on the award such as a selection process based on "experience, expertise, professional qualifications, and cost following a request for proposal"; or
    3. the result of a rotational process using a list of lawyers, regardless of contributions.

Section XII
General Duties

Chapter 47

Judicial Candidates and Statements about Judges

Roadmap

- Rule 8.2(DE)
- Judicial candidates' duty to abide by the applicable rules of judicial conduct
- The duty of a lawyer not to knowingly or recklessly make false statements about the "qualifications or integrity" of a judge, a judicial candidate, an adjudicatory officer, a public legal officer, or a candidate for legal office

A. Abiding by the Rules of Judicial Conduct

A lawyer who seeks judicial office, like all lawyers, is subject to the rules of professional conduct governing lawyers. Rule 8.2(b)(DE) clarifies that a lawyer seeking election or appointment to the bench must abide by the applicable rules governing judges as well. Often this set of rules is referred to as a Code of Judicial Conduct because that is the name of the ABA's model version. If Larry Lawyer is a candidate for a judgeship, he must carefully review the applicable rules of judicial conduct so that he does not step afoul of the specific rules governing judges and judicial candidates.

B. Statements about Judges

Rule 8.2(a)(DE) contains a restriction on lawyer speech when the statements relate to a judge, an adjudicatory officer, a public legal officer, or a candidate for a judgeship or legal office. A lawyer violates Rule 8.2(a)(DE) if he or she makes a false statement about a judge or any other person in the above categories if the lawyer knows that the statement is false or the lawyer is reckless with regard to the statement's truthfulness.

Lawyers are not often disciplined for violating this provision but if they are disciplined it is often as the result of statements the lawyers make in court or in briefs filed with the court. Occasionally, the statement may be in correspondence to a third party. Courts do not find speech violative of Rule 8.2(DE) to be protected by the First Amendment. A good example of the application of the rule is *Notopoulos v. Statewide Grievance Committee*, 890 A.2d 509 (Conn.), *cert. denied*, 127 S. Ct. 157 (2006). In *Notopoulos*, a lawyer was disciplined for sending a letter to members of the court's staff and others. The letter accused the judge of extorting funds from an estate and other improper conduct. The lawyer was not acting in a representational capacity regarding the matter of which he spoke in the letter. The Connecticut Supreme Court affirmed the imposition of discipline and held that the First Amendment did not protect the lawyer's speech.

Related Sections of the *Restatement (Third) of the Law Governing Lawyers*

Section 114

Checkpoints

- A lawyer seeking election or appointment to the bench must abide by the applicable conduct rules governing judges.
- A lawyer violates the rules of professional conduct if he or she makes a knowing or reckless false statement about a judge, an adjudicatory officer, a public legal officer, or a candidate for a judgeship or legal office.

Chapter 48

General Misconduct

Roadmap

- Rule 8.4(DE)
- Violating the rules of professional conduct on the basis of the acts of another person or by inducing or assisting another to engage in conduct that violates the rules of professional conduct
- Criminal acts "that reflects adversely on the lawyer's honesty, trustworthiness or fitness as a lawyer in other respects"
- Acts of dishonesty
- Activities "prejudicial to the administration of justice"
- Stating or implying an ability to exercise improper influence on a government official or agency
- Stating or implying an ability to succeed by violating the rules of professional conduct or other law
- Knowingly assisting a judge in conduct that violates law or the rules of judicial conduct

A. Violating the Rules of Professional Conduct

Rule 8.4(DE) contains a laundry list of activities that qualify as professional misconduct. As an initial matter, Rule 8.4(a)(DE) states that a lawyer commits misconduct by violating, attempting to violate, or assisting another in violating a rule of professional conduct. Larry Lawyer is guilty of misconduct if he assists Lance Lawyer in destroying evidence in violation of Rule 3.4(DE). *See Chapter 29 Fairness.*

In addition, a lawyer may violate a rule of professional conduct through the acts of another or by inducing or assisting another person in conduct that violates the rules of professional conduct. If Larry Lawyer directs Penny Paralegal to talk with the opposing party in a litigation matter and Penny does as Larry directs, then Larry is responsible and can be disciplined for Penny's actions in violation of Rule 4.2(DE). See *Chapter 36 Contact with Represented Persons* and *Chapter 38 Supervision and Responsibility for Other Lawyers, Nonlawyer Employees, and Other Assistants.*

A question that often arises is whether Larry Lawyer can be disciplined if his client, Cindy, talks with the represented opposing party. In recognition of the parties' right to talk with each other, Larry Lawyer does not violate Rule 4.2(DE) through Cindy's actions if he tells her of her right to talk with the opposing party and Cindy does so. *ABA Formal Opinion 11-461 (2011)* states that a lawyer may counsel a client about issues the client should discuss with the other party and strategies to use in the discussion. The *Opinion* cautions that a lawyer should not overreach by assisting the client in eliciting confidential information or admissions against interest.

B. Criminal Acts

Lawyers should uphold the law, not violate it. While not all violations of law are professional misconduct, it is professional misconduct, as Rule 8.4(b)(DE) states, for a lawyer to commit a criminal act that "reflects adversely on the lawyer's honesty, trustworthiness or fitness as a lawyer." The criminal act need not occur in the context of the practice of law. The rule requires the commission of a criminal act but not necessarily a conviction. If Larry Lawyer steals from a client or even a neighbor, Larry's action is a criminal act relating to honesty and thus would be professional misconduct. Often discipline authorities have held that violent criminal acts reflect poorly on a lawyer's fitness to practice law and thus commission of a violent criminal act is professional misconduct. Sometimes a repeated pattern of minor criminal offenses may be viewed as criminal acts that reflect on the lawyer's fitness to practice law because the conduct shows disrespect for or indifference to the law.

C. Dishonest Conduct

Even if the conduct does not amount to a criminal act, if the conduct involves dishonesty, it is professional misconduct, according to Rule 8.4(c)(DE). Honesty is so vital to the role of a lawyer in the justice system that any dishonesty cannot be tolerated. Once again, dishonest conduct can be professional misconduct even when the conduct does not occur in the midst of the practice of law. *In re Carpenter*, 95 P.3d 203 (Or. 2004), is a good example of the application of this rule. In *Carpenter* a lawyer heard rumors that a high school classmate who was working at the high school as a guidance counselor and coach had been involved in an extramarital affair with a student. The lawyer left a message on a website, written in the first person as the coach, boasting about the coach's wife and all the high school women whose company the coach had enjoyed. The coach discovered that someone had posed as the coach in posting these comments. He reported the matter to the Oregon State Police after his employer, the school, told him his job was in jeopardy because of the message. The police discovered the source of the message was the classmate lawyer. The lawyer was not charged with any crime, yet, the Oregon Supreme Court determined that the lawyer had committed an act of dishonesty and must be disciplined.

D. Conduct "Prejudicial to the Administration of Justice"

A lawyer commits professional misconduct if he or she engages in conduct "prejudicial to the administration of justice." Rule 8.4(d)(DE) states this prohibition. Unfortunately, exactly what constitutes such conduct is not obvious. Courts' conclusions about what sorts of lawyer conduct might be conduct "prejudicial to the administration of justice" are varied. For example, a court determined that a lawyer had engaged in such problematic conduct by repeatedly failing to take proper procedural steps in a court-appointed representation. Another court determined that a lawyer had engaged in conduct "prejudicial to the administration of justice" by telling the client that making misrepresentations to the court would be acceptable conduct.

E. Stating or Implying the "Ability to Influence Improperly a Government Agency or Official" or the Ability to Obtain Results in a Manner Contrary to Law or the Rules of Professional Conduct

A lawyer commits professional misconduct if he or she states or implies that he or she can obtain a result with improper influence, says Rule 8.4(e)(DE). A lawyer cannot state or imply that he or she can improperly influence a government agency of official. Also, a lawyer cannot state or imply that he or she can obtain results in a manner contrary to law or to the rules of professional conduct.

The lawyer's statement of ability or implication of the ability is the misconduct, regardless of whether the lawyer actually has the ability to exercise influence. The statement or implication itself damages the general confidence in the justice system and the entities involved. If the lawyer actually exercises improper influence, or actually violates law or the rules of professional conduct, then the lawyer commits further improper acts. Thus, Larry Lawyer commits professional misconduct by telling Cindy Client that he is a good friend of the judge presiding over her matter and that Larry will talk to the judge privately to obtain the result Cindy desires. Larry's statement is professional misconduct, even if he is lying to Cindy about his abilities and intentions.

F. Assisting a Judge in Conduct Violating the Rules of Judicial Conduct or Other Law

A lawyer commits professional misconduct by knowingly assisting a judge or other judicial officer in conduct violates the rules of judicial conduct or violates other law. Rule 8.4(f)(DE) contains this prohibition. Because accepting a bribe in exchange for a favorable decision is illegal and contrary to the rules of judicial conduct and Larry knows this, Larry Lawyer commits professional misconduct by participating in offering the bribe. Of course, the act of offering the judge a reward for a decision is illegal in itself and professional misconduct as well.

Related Sections of the *Restatement (Third) of the Law Governing Lawyers*

Sections 5 and 113

Checkpoints

- A lawyer commits misconduct by assisting another or inducing another to engage in conduct that violates a rule of professional conduct.
- A lawyer commits misconduct by violating a rule of professional conduct by his or her owns acts or through another person's acts.

- A lawyer commits misconduct by committing "a criminal act that reflects adversely on the lawyer's honesty, trustworthiness or fitness as a lawyer."
- A lawyer commits misconduct by committing an act of dishonesty.
- A lawyer commits misconduct by engaging in conduct "prejudicial to the administration of justice."
- A lawyer commits misconduct by stating or implying "an ability to influence improperly a government agency or official."
- A lawyer commits misconduct by stating or implying an ability to succeed by violating the rules of professional conduct or other law.
- A lawyer commits misconduct by knowingly assisting a judge in conduct that violates law or the code of judicial conduct.

Chapter 49

The Duty to Report Misconduct

Roadmap

- Rule 8.3(ID)
- A lawyer's duty to report the misconduct of other lawyers and judges

A. The Justification for a Reporting Rule

Lawyers are in the best position to know of ethical misdeeds of other lawyers and judges. Clients sometimes know of lawyer misdeeds but clients do not have the knowledge of the rules to truly determine when a lawyer or judge is behaving in a professionally inappropriate manner. Lawyers are in a position to see the conduct of other lawyers and judges and they know when conduct is inappropriate. So lawyers have a duty to report the conduct of each other and of judges. In addition, a reporting rule makes sense in light of the profession's claim to the right to regulate itself. As the Louisiana Supreme Court stated in *In re Riehlmann*, 891 So. 2d 1239 (La. 2005):

> Reporting another lawyer's misconduct to disciplinary authorities is an important duty of every lawyer.... [T]he lawyer's duty to report professional misconduct is the foundation for the claim that we can be trusted to regulate ourselves as a profession. If we fail in our duty, we forfeit that trust and have no right to enjoy the privilege of self-regulation or the confidence and respect of the public.

Id. at 1249. On a very basic level, lawyer reporting increases compliance with the rules because the chance of being caught is greater. Either the threat of being reported deters a bad actor or a bad actor is more likely to be caught.

B. The Duty to Report Other Lawyers

Rule 8.3(a)(ID) requires a lawyer who knows that another lawyer has violated the rules of professional conduct to report that lawyer if the violation "raises a substantial question as to that lawyer's honesty, trustworthiness or fitness as a lawyer." A lawyer need not report if to do so would require the lawyer to disclose confidential information protected by Rule 1.6(DE). *See Chapter 15 The Duty of Confidentiality.* Rule 8.3(c)(ID) contains this qualification.

In addition, a lawyer need not report if the lawyer learned of the violation by way of a lawyer assistance program. Lawyer assistance programs are designed to assist lawyers who have substance abuse problems or other such issues. No lawyer would attempt to get help from an assistance program if the information the lawyer conveys in the program can be used against him or her.

The reporting rule has two significant limitations on its application. First, in many situations a lawyer may not know that a lawyer has behaved improperly. Perhaps the lawyer has a *reasonable belief* that another lawyer behaved improperly but does not *know* that the lawyer behaved improperly. The duty to report arises only with knowledge.

Second, the duty to report applies not to all violations of the rules but only to violations that raise "a substantial question as to that lawyer's honesty, trustworthiness or fitness as a lawyer in other respects." This qualification narrows the situations requiring reporting but, unfortunately, does not give much guidance as to when a violation of the rules of professional conduct might qualify for reporting. Rule 1.0(l) define "substantial" as follows: "when used in reference to degree or extent denotes a material matter of clear and weighty importance."

Perhaps Cindy Client comes to Larry Lawyer for legal assistance. Cindy discloses to Larry that another lawyer has taken settlement money belonging to her and she wishes Larry's help in recovering the money. Larry investigates the matter and concludes that the evidence is clear that the lawyer violated the rules of professional conduct. In fact, the lawyer behaved dishonestly by taking a significant amount of money that belonged to his client. The lawyer violated the rules by committing an act of dishonesty and that act of dishonesty "raises a substantial question as to that lawyer's honesty." Larry asks Cindy if she will consent to him disclosing the information to the state professional discipline authority. Cindy refuses because she believes that to do so might jeopardize her ability to recover what the lawyer took from her. Larry may not report the matter to the discipline authority. If Cindy agrees to the disclosure, Larry must report the matter.

C. The Duty to Report Judges

Lawyers have a similar duty to report judges, according to Rule 8.3(b)(ID). If a lawyer knows that a judge has violated the rules of judicial conduct that "raises a substantial question as to the judge's fitness for office," the lawyer must report the judge to the judicial discipline authority.

Similar qualifications apply to the judge reporting requirement as apply to the lawyer reporting requirement. First, a lawyer has no duty to report if reporting would require the lawyer to disclose confidential information protected by Rule 1.6(DE). Second, a lawyer has no duty to report if the lawyer came upon the information about the judge's conduct through a lawyer assistance program. Third, a lawyer must *know* of the violation. Finally, a violation of the rules of judicial conduct alone does not trigger the duty to report. The violation must raise "a substantial question as to the judge's fitness for office."

D. Reporting is Difficult

Many lawyers are uncomfortable with a reporting requirement. Everyone learns in elementary school that "tattling" is frowned upon. But more important, the situations in which a lawyer must report are often very difficult. For example, in *In re Riehlmann,* 891 So. 2d 1239 (La. 2005), a Louisiana lawyer met his friend at a bar. The two lawyers both had served as prosecutors and both had become defense lawyers. The lawyer's friend disclosed that he was dying of cancer. In a bit of a confession, the dying friend told the lawyer that as a prosecutor he had suppressed exculpatory blood evidence in one case. The Louisiana professional conduct rule required a lawyer to report any unprivileged knowledge of a professional responsibility violation of any kind. The lawyer did not report his friend. After the friend died and five years had passed, the lawyer discovered that the lawyers of a man scheduled to be executed in one month had discovered an exculpatory crime lab report that had never been shared with the defense team. The lawyer then concluded that this blood report was the evidence his dead friend had mentioned to him. The lawyer notified the defense team about his conversation with his friend and reported the matter to the discipline authority. The Louisiana Supreme Court publicly remanded the lawyer for failing to abide by the mandatory reporting rule in a timely manner.

Related Sections of the *Restatement (Third) of the Law Governing Lawyers*

Section 5

Checkpoints

- A lawyer who knows that another lawyer has violated the rules of professional conduct must report that lawyer if the violation "raises a substantial question as to that lawyer's honesty, trustworthiness or fitness as a lawyer."
- A lawyer who knows that a judge has violated the rules of judicial conduct must report that judge if the violation "raises a substantial question as to the judge's fitness for office."
- A lawyer need not report if
    1. to do so would require the lawyer to disclose confidential information protected by Rule 1.6(DE), or
    2. the lawyer learned of the violation by way of a lawyer assistance program.

Mastering Professional Responsibility Master Checklist

Section I Regulation of the Legal Profession

Chapter 1 • Sources of Professional Responsibility Law

- ❑ The many standards for lawyer and judge conduct

Chapter 2 • Admission to the Bar

- ❑ The system of state regulation
- ❑ Admission requirements for a novice lawyer
- ❑ Admission requirements for a lawyer admitted in another jurisdiction
- ❑ The application process
- ❑ The requirement of honesty in the application process

Chapter 3 • The Discipline Process and Jurisdiction for Discipline

- ❑ The discipline process
- ❑ Authority of a jurisdiction to discipline a lawyer
- ❑ Reciprocal discipline
- ❑ Choice of law for discipline

Section II Basics of the Lawyer-Client Relationship

Chapter 4 • Basis of Duty: The Lawyer-Client Relationship

- ❑ Creation of a lawyer-client relationship and the lawyer-prospective client relationship

Chapter 5 • Competence and Diligence

- ❑ The duty of competence
- ❑ The duty of diligence

Chapter 6 • Malpractice and Other Civil Liability

- ❑ Elements of a malpractice action
- ❑ Liability for breach of fiduciary duty
- ❑ Liability for breach of contract
- ❑ Liability to nonclients
- ❑ Agreements to limit liability to clients

Chapter 7 • Ineffective Assistance of Counsel

- ❑ The Sixth Amendment basis of the claim of ineffective assistance
- ❑ Constitutional requirements for a claim of ineffective assistance of counsel

Chapter 8 • Scope of the Representation and Communication with the Client

- ❑ Defining the scope of the representation
- ❑ Decision-making authority within the representation
- ❑ Prohibition of lawyer involvement in criminal or fraudulent activity of the client
- ❑ Required communication with the client

Chapter 9 • Fees

- ❑ General procedural requirements for fees
- ❑ Procedural requirements for contingent fees
- ❑ The requirement of a reasonable fee
- ❑ Definition of a reasonable fee
- ❑ Situations in which a contingent fee is not allowed
- ❑ Nonrefundable fees
- ❑ Requirements for lawyers sharing fees with lawyers
- ❑ Requirement of billing honesty

Chapter 10 • Dealing with the Property of Clients and Third Parties

- ❑ Keeping the property of others safe and separate
- ❑ Recordkeeping and notice requirements
- ❑ Process when there is an ownership dispute

Chapter 11 • Refusing to Form a Lawyer-Client Relationship or Ending a Lawyer-Client Relationship

- ❑ Situations in which a lawyer must refuse or terminate a representation
- ❑ Situations in which a lawyer may end a representation
- ❑ Responsibilities upon termination of the lawyer-client relationship
- ❑ Treatment of the client's file upon termination
- ❑ Situations in which a lawyer may refuse or terminate an appointed representation

Chapter 12 • Sale of a Practice

❑ Process for selling a law practice

Section III Special Types of Clients

Chapter 13 • Organizational Clients

❑ Guidelines for representing an organization
❑ The reporting up process
❑ The reporting out option
❑ The Sarbanes–Oxley Act

Chapter 14 • Clients with Diminished Capacity

❑ The duty to protect a client with diminished mental capacity

Section IV Confidentiality

Chapter 15 • The Duty of Confidentiality

❑ The duty not to disclose information relating to a client's representation
❑ Situations in which disclosure is permitted to further a client's interests
❑ Situations in which disclosure adverse to a client's interests is permitted
❑ Situations in which disclosure is required

Chapter 16 • The Attorney-Client Privilege and the Work-Product Doctrine

❑ Definition and application of the attorney-client privilege
❑ Situations in which waiver of the privilege may occur
❑ Application of the privilege to organizational clients
❑ Definition and application of the work-product doctrine

Section V Conflicts of Interest

Chapter 17 • Introduction to Conflicts of Interest Concepts

❑ Policies and interests at issue in conflicts situations

Chapter 18 • Conflicts and Current Clients

❑ Definition of a conflict of interest regarding a current client
❑ Situations in which representation with a conflict is not permitted
❑ Situations in which representation with a conflict is permitted
❑ The imputation rule

Chapter 19 • Conflicts and Former Clients

❑ Definition of a former client conflict of interest
❑ The imputation rule

- ❑ Restrictions on the use of former client information
- ❑ Conflict of interest principles for lawyers who migrate
- ❑ The screening process

Chapter 20 • **Conflicts and Prospective Clients**

- ❑ Definition of a prospective client
- ❑ Standard regarding the use or disclosure of prospective client information
- ❑ Definition of a prospective client conflict of interest
- ❑ The imputation rule
- ❑ The screening process

Chapter 21 • **Conflict of Interest Rules for Particular Situations**

- ❑ Requirements for transactions with clients
- ❑ Standard regarding use of client information
- ❑ Permitted and prohibited gifts
- ❑ Prohibition of obtaining literary and media rights regarding a representation
- ❑ Permitted and prohibited financial assistance to a client
- ❑ Requirements for accepting payment from someone other than the client
- ❑ Requirements for participation in aggregate settlements
- ❑ Requirements for agreements limiting a lawyer's liability
- ❑ Prohibition of acquiring a proprietary interest in the cause of action or subject matter of litigation
- ❑ Prohibition of sexual relationships with clients
- ❑ The imputation rule

Chapter 22 • **Conflicts and Lawyers Who are Public Officials or Other Government Employees**

- ❑ Responsibilities of lawyers who move from public office or other government employment to private practice
- ❑ Responsibilities of lawyers who move from private practice to public office or other government employment
- ❑ General responsibilities of public officials or other government employees regarding conflicts of interest and negotiating employment

Chapter 23 • **Conflicts and Former Judges, Other Adjudicative Officers, Law Clerks, and Third-Party Neutrals**

- ❑ Identification of conflicts of interest
- ❑ Treatment of conflicts of interest
- ❑ Restrictions on negotiating future employment

Section VI When a Lawyer Is Not in an Advocate Role

Chapter 24 • Lawyer Evaluation of a Client's Matter for a Third Party

- ❑ Requirements for preparing evaluative reports for use by third parties
- ❑ Liability to third parties

Chapter 25 • A Lawyer as a Third-Party Neutral

- ❑ General responsibilities of third-party neutrals to explain and clarify the neutral role
- ❑ Identifying conflicts of interest created by service as a third-party neutral
- ❑ Restrictions on a third-party neutral seeking employment

Section VII The Lawyer as an Advocate

Chapter 26 • Frivolous Positions

- ❑ The duty to avoid frivolous positions
- ❑ A prosecutor's duty to not pursue a charge absent probable cause
- ❑ Federal Rule of Civil Procedure 11
- ❑ The tort of abuse of process
- ❑ The tort of malicious prosecution

Chapter 27 • The Duty to Expedite Litigation

- ❑ The duty to expedite litigation

Chapter 28 • Honesty and Candor

- ❑ Prohibition of false statements of fact or law
- ❑ The duty to correct false statements
- ❑ The duty to disclose legal authority
- ❑ Prohibition of offering false evidence
- ❑ The duty regarding discovering the falsity of evidence already presented
- ❑ The duty to act when a client intends to engage or engages in criminal or fraudulent conduct relating to an adjudicative proceeding
- ❑ The duty to disclose in ex parte proceedings

Chapter 29 • Fairness

- ❑ Prohibition of obstructing access to evidence or destroying evidence
- ❑ Prohibition of falsifying evidence
- ❑ Prohibition of disobeying an obligation under the rules of the tribunal
- ❑ Prohibition of referring to irrelevant or inadmissible facts

- ❑ Prohibition of stating "personal knowledge" of facts or expressing an opinion as to culpability, credibility, guilt, or justness
- ❑ Restrictions on requests not to cooperate with others

Chapter 30 • Impartiality

- ❑ Standards regarding contact with the judge, jurors, prospective jurors, or other officials
- ❑ Prohibition of conduct done with the goal of disrupting a proceeding

Chapter 31 • Publicity Relating to Trials

- ❑ Forbidden extrajudicial communications
- ❑ Permitted extrajudicial communications

Chapter 32 • The Lawyer Witness

- ❑ Prohibition of a lawyer serving as a lawyer and a witness in a trial
- ❑ Exceptions to the prohibition

Chapter 33 • The Lawyer as Prosecutor

- ❑ A prosecutor's duty to protect the basic rights of the accused
- ❑ A prosecutor's constitutional and ethical responsibility to disclose exculpatory evidence
- ❑ Restrictions on seeking subpoenas for lawyers
- ❑ Restrictions on public statements by prosecutors
- ❑ A prosecutor's post-conviction responsibilities

Chapter 34 • Duties in Nonadjudicative Proceedings

- ❑ Definition of a nonadjudicative proceeding
- ❑ Requirements for lawyers appearing in nonadjudicative proceedings

Section VIII Dealing with Nonclients

Chapter 35 • Truthfulness to Third Parties

- ❑ Prohibition of material false statements
- ❑ Requirement of disclosure of material facts to avoid assisting a client's crime or fraud

Chapter 36 • Contact with Represented Persons

- ❑ Prohibition of contact with represented persons
- ❑ Application of the prohibition to organizations

Chapter 37 • Respect for the Rights of Nonclients

- ❑ Responsibilities when dealing with an unrepresented nonclient
- ❑ Standards regarding sending and receiving inadvertent disclosures
- ❑ The effect of inadvertent disclosure on the attorney-client privilege

Section IX Practicing Law

Chapter 38 • Supervision and Responsibility for Other Lawyers, Nonlawyer Employees, and Other Assistants

- ❑ Responsibility for an ethical work environment for all
- ❑ The duty to supervise
- ❑ Responsibility for the acts of other lawyers and nonlawyer assistants
- ❑ Civil liability of a lawyer for the acts of other lawyers or nonlawyer assistants
- ❑ Responsibilities of a subordinate lawyer

Chapter 39 • Professional Independence

- ❑ Requirement of "independent professional judgment"
- ❑ Prohibition of sharing legal fees with nonlawyers
- ❑ Exceptions to the prohibition
- ❑ Standards regarding referrals
- ❑ Prohibition of nonlawyer control of provision of legal services

Chapter 40 • The Unauthorized Practice of Law

- ❑ The traditional approach to the unauthorized practice of law
- ❑ Definition of the practice of law
- ❑ Situations in which a lawyer who is admitted to a bar but not admitted in the jurisdiction may practice in the jurisdiction
- ❑ Specifically prohibited activities

Chapter 41 • Restrictions on a Lawyer's Right to Practice Law

- ❑ Prohibition of restrictions in general agreements
- ❑ The retirement benefit exception to the prohibition
- ❑ Prohibition of restrictions on the right to practice in connection with a settlement

Chapter 42 • Ancillary Services

- ❑ Rights and responsibilities of lawyers involved in ancillary businesses

Section X Lawyers as Public Servants

Chapter 43 • Pro Bono Service

- ❑ The pro bono aspiration

Chapter 44 • Legal Services Organizations, Law Reform, and Legal Services Programs

- ❑ Requirements for lawyers participating in legal services organizations, law reform activities, and limited legal services programs

Section XI Advertising and Other Communications about Legal Services

Chapter 45 • Communications about Lawyer Services

- ❑ Prohibition of "false or misleading" communications
- ❑ Permitted and prohibited solicitation
- ❑ Generally permitted communications
- ❑ Limitations on communicating fields of practice and specializations
- ❑ Standards regarding firm names and other professional designations

Chapter 46 • Paying to Play: Political Contributions

- ❑ Prohibition of political contributions made to obtain legal work

Section XII General Duties

Chapter 47 • Judicial Candidates and Statements about Judges

- ❑ Judicial candidates' duty to abide by the applicable code of judicial conduct
- ❑ Prohibition of knowingly or recklessly making false statements about judges

Chapter 48 • General Misconduct

- ❑ Prohibition of violating the applicable rules of professional conduct
- ❑ Prohibition of criminal acts
- ❑ Prohibition of dishonest conduct
- ❑ Prohibition of conduct "prejudicial to the administration of justice"
- ❑ Prohibition of stating or implying the "ability to influence improperly a government agency or official" or the ability to obtain results in a manner contrary to law or the applicable rules of professional conduct
- ❑ Prohibition of assisting a judge in conduct violative of the applicable code of judicial conduct or other law

Chapter 49 • The Duty to Report Misconduct

- ❑ The duty to report other lawyers
- ❑ The duty to report judges

Table of Cases

Table of Rules

Index